EARTH AND GODS

AN INTRODUCTION TO THE PHILOSOPHY OF MARTIN HEIDEGGER

VINCENT VYCINAS

EARTH AND GODS

AN INTRODUCTION
TO THE PHILOSOPHY OF
Martin Heidegger

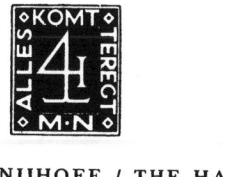

MARTINUS NIJHOFF / THE HAGUE
PHOTOMECHANICAL REPRINT 1969

ISBN-13: 978-94-010-3361-9   e-ISBN-13: 978-94-010-3359-6
DOI: 10.1007/978-94-010-3359-6

To Prof. Dr. Bernard J. Boelen, my mentor

PREFACE

Earth and Gods is an attempt to introduce the reader to Heidegger's fully developed philosophy. The title *Earth and Gods* gives an impression of not being a general study of Heidegger's philosophy. However, this is not true – the *earth* and the *gods* are fundamental ontological symbols of his fully developed philosophy, namely, his third and final phase of thought. This phase repeats the problems of both preceding phases in a fuller and more developed manner; hence, it implies them.

The two preceding phases are the phase of *Dasein* and the phase of Being. These two phases are a natural flow of fundamental problems which reach their final formation and development in the phase of earth and gods. *Dasein* (the first phase) leads to Being, and Being (the second phase) bursts into fundamental ontological powers of Being (*Seinsmächte*) which are earth and sky, gods and mortals (the third phase). Since earth is unthinkable without sky and since gods are gods in the world of mortals – of men, the title *Earth and Gods* is an abbreviation of these four fundamental powers of Being.

Hence, an investigation of earth and gods is an attempt to present Heidegger's philosophy as a whole. Such a presentation provides the reader with the background necessary for a more adequate and efficient understanding of the writings of Heidegger himself. Thus, *Earth and Gods* may rightly be considered an introduction to Heidegger's philosophy.

Earth and Gods is an attempt to elucidate the thought of Heidegger within the philosophy of Heidegger himself, instead of elucidating it within some other philosophical doctrine already established and accepted as true. By virtue of the latter approach, heretofore Heidegger's philosophy has been treated negatively, namely: as nihilism, as irrationalism, as subjectivism, as aestheticism, as atheism, etc. Such treatment can never be adequate: it fails to clarify the thought of Heidegger himself; rather it clarifies the other philosophy within which Heidegger's philosophy is treated.

Previous treatises on Heidegger are limited mainly to the Heidegger of *Sein und Zeit; Earth and Gods* is not so limited: it is an investigation of Heidegger in all his works.

The translation of quotations or of single terms in Heidegger is not a matter of equating words of various languages, but is a matter of making any language adequate to his thought. Therefore, quotations and terms in this study are often given in English not with philological or linguistic precision, but with a faithful interpretation of their meanings within the framework of Heidegger's thought. Heidegger's language cannot be bound by strict philological rules of any conventional language because it is ontologically prior to any of such rules.

Greek words used in this study are written in Latin characters, except those which appear in original Greek in the selected quotations.

Great indebtedness is expressed to Prof. Bernard J. Boelen of Duquesne University, Pittsburgh, Pennsylvania, for his positive attitude which encouraged the writer's line of thought held throughout this study. Gratitude is also expressed to collegian Albert Bautz of New Eagle, Pennsylvania, for his assistance in revising the language of this study, and to Tr. Donald R. Simpson, Jefferson School in Cottage Grove, Oregon, for his idiomatic editing and final proofing.

The Introduction gives a very compact general taste of Heidegger's highly untraditional thinking, and by reason thereof leaves an impression of confusion. Nevertheless, it is proper in the case of this study that it has an introduction which makes the reader disorientated – makes the ground give way beneath his feet. This creates a readiness to search for a foothold in the thought of Heidegger himself. Anyone who studies the thought of a great thinker, must first set aside his own prejudices, otherwise he is apt to lack the openness and readiness to receive the thought of the thinker. There can be no true philosophizing from secure grounds. Philosophy always means a venture, or it is a mere pretense.

Finally a plea is made for patience on the part of the reader until he reaches Chapter V ("Gods"). Throughout Chapters I–IV, there is a slow ascent to the gradually broadened fundamental problems of Heidegger's philosophy, and thus patience on the part of the reader is required. Commencing with Chapter V, reading becomes less difficult, and the crop of Heidegger's thought can be reaped with reward. Thereby a broad, a new, and a free view of the world in which we live can be attained.

Pittsburgh, Pa.
April 17, 1959   Dr. Vincent Vycinas

CONTENTS

THE PLACE OF EARTH AND GODS IN
HEIDEGGER'S PHILOSOPHY

The earth and the gods are strange problems for philosophical investigation. The earth seems to be too obvious, too real to become a philosophical problem; and the gods, on the other hand, are too unreal to be of any interest for philosophical consideration; they can only have a religious, mythological, or possibly a poetical importance.

Nevertheless, these problems are highly Heideggerian problems. Born in the German Black Forest, Heidegger, of peasant stock, has vigorous earthbound thinking; yet, standing with his feet set firmly on the earth, he is able to reach up high to the stars, unto the realm of the gods. Often he seems to be somewhat poetical rather than philosophical. Nevertheless, in all his problems he remains a philosopher of the world, a profound ontologician, and a thorough realist.

"Poetically dwells man on the earth" – a line from a poet who was highly respected by Heidegger – can well characterize Heidegger's thinking: his thinking is poetical, yet earthbound.

I. CHARACTER OF HEIDEGGER'S PHILOSOPHY

In contemporary philosophy Martin Heidegger possesses an outstanding place. He is usually considered to be a philosopher belonging to the circle of existentialists. Heidegger himself, however, resists such a classification and rather stands alone. None of the philosophers, so far as they are true philosophers, is identical in his thinking with that of any other philosopher. However, there is usually some similarity in problematic or philosophical attitude among philosophers so that they can be grouped or classified to a greater or lesser degree into certain families of thinkers. Heidegger does not fit into any group; he actually stands alone and somewhat apart from all the philosophers of history. Often he seems not to even be a philosopher. To Karl Löwith, Heidegger's thought seems to be "essentially religious, however not Christianly disposed thought." [1] Sometimes this thinking appears to him rather poetical, but not philosophical. "Often it is hardly possible to determine," says Karl Löwith, "whether Heidegger poetizes philosophically or thinks poetically." [2]

According to Heidegger himself, his thinking is not of the forward-looking type which aims to surpass any former philosophy, but is rather primary. Primary thinking is not primitive, but archaic. It does not presuppose anything but goes back to the beginning, the roots, the very origins of reality. It is philosophical, religious, and poetical at the same time. In no wise, however, can this thinking be deemed philosophically inadequate, for it goes back to the forgotten beginnings of Western thought which have been presupposed by traditional philosophy as self-evident and have never been reconsidered in the light of philosophical meditation. Heidegger's thinking is philosophical to a higher degree than any traditional thinking. Because of its originality and fundamentality, Heidegger's thought cannot be classified (classification presupposes differentiation). In many respects Heidegger stands outside the realm of traditional philosophy. "He has, furthermore, abandoned time-honored ways of thinking to an extent that makes it almost impossible to fit his philosophic concepts into any established categories." [3]

Contemporary language often is inadequate to express Heideggerian thought. Heidegger, therefore, frequently goes back to the archaic roots of words and arrives at the primary meanings which express his problems. Often, especially in his *Sein und Zeit*, he uses complexes of words to express a unique phenomenon. For instance, care (*Sorge*), the basic ontological structure of *Dasein*, is expressed in the following way: the being-ahead-of-oneself as already-being-in-the-world as being-with-the-within-the-world-encountered-beings. For philological reasons alone Heidegger is difficult to read even for a German reader. Karl Löwith calls Heidegger "untranslatable." [4] This is true not for one or a few, but for many of his concepts.

---

[1] Karl Löwith, *Heidegger Denker in Dürftiger Zeit* (Frankfurt a. M.: S. Fischer Verlag, 1953), p. 10.

[2] *Ibid.*, p. 11.

[3] Kurt F. Reinhardt, *The Existentialist Revolt* (Milwaukee: The Bruce Publishing Company, 1952), p. 131.

[4] Löwith, *op. cit.*, p. 15.

II. HEIDEGGER'S PROBLEM OF BEING

In spite of the great variety of Heidegger's philosophical themes, he basically holds to one and the same thought, the thought of Being.[5] All his other problems are either concerned with the same problem of Being approached differently and revealed in different aspects, or they are concerned merely with concepts leading to this basic phenomenon. This consideration is true even for his very basic concepts, such as 'existence' or *Dasein*. "In order to emphasize the reference of Being to the essence of man as well as man's essential relation to the openness (*Da*) of Being as such, in which man, as man, is standing, the word '*Dasein*' has been chosen." [6] Man is not a self-sufficient being in the sense that he can be essentially thought of without considering his relation to Being. Man *is* this relation. Relation to Being, existence, is the very heart of human essence. All the acts of man, *as* man, are only his responses to Being. Through these responses man becomes man. "Whenever a man, in his own way, discovers the sojourning beings [7] within the revelation, he merely responds to the assertion of revelation [8] itself, even where he contradicts it." [9]

Being, as thought [10] by Heidegger, has a temporal character. With the word 'sojourning' (Anwesen) he indicates Being as time itself. Sojourning expresses the dynamic character of Being. Being is never sealed into itself, but is constantly coming out of itself into revelation or openness. This coming out of Being from concealment into revelation gives birth to time; it *is* time. Being cannot be thought of as separate from time; time is Being's coming to openness. Being is its own time. Heidegger's *Sein und Zeit* results in the demonstration that time is the "horizon of Being." [11] Being is sojourning.

---

[5] In this study the word 'Being,' the basic concept in Heidegger's philosophy, will be written with a capital 'B' in order to distinguish it from the word 'being' which expresses a particular being or 'being' which is the participle of the verb 'to be.' 'Being' will correspond to the German *Sein* and 'being' to the German *Seiendes*.

[6] Martin Heidegger, *Was ist Metaphysik?* (Frankfurt a. M.: Vittorio Klostermann, 1949), p. 13.

[7] The sojourning beings (*Anwesendes*) are beings in the light of Being and not in their relation to a subject, i.e. not in their objectivity.

[8] The revelation (*Unverborgenheit*) is Being itself in its openness or in its truth.

[9] Martin Heidegger, *Vorträge und Aufsätze* (Pfullingen: Günther Neske, 1954), p. 26.

[10] In some English expression, this would be 'Being, as thought of.' However, it seems closer to the spirit of Heidegger's philosophy to say 'Being, as thought', because he is not treating being in a subject-object relationship which is implied in 'thinking *of* being.'

[11] Martin Heidegger, *Sein und Zeit* (Halle a.d.S.: Max Niemeyer Verlag, 1941), p. 438.

Since man is essentially a relation, he is constantly beyond himself in the sense that he stands out into the openness of Being; he understands and approaches himself from his beyondness; he is constantly coming to himself. The German words for 'coming-to' (*Zu-kunft*) and for 'future' (*Zukunft*) are spelled and pronounced identically. According to Heidegger, the primary meaning of 'future' is 'coming-to.' Only because man is coming to himself from his future, can he have a past which is past in the light of future, and from future and past can he be in the present. As far as things are concerned, they are not temporal but intra-temporal in the sense that they are encountered in time, whereas man is not truly immersed in time. Temporality belongs to his structure, and, in a certain sense, man is forming or making time. Man, in forming or making time, stands in the service of Being. He helps Being to break into his history.

Just as is time, so are all other fundamental concepts of Heidegger ultimately Being, having brought itself to revelation or truth. Such are *Dasein*, *physis*, *logos*, world, etc. Heidegger is a thinker of one and the same thought, the thought of Being. To maintain one and the same thought throughout the investigation of various fundamental problems is to be a great thinker.

> Every thinker thinks only one single thought. This essentially distinguishes the thinker from the scientist. Research constantly needs new discoveries and ideas; otherwise, science would lapse into stagnation and falseness. A thinker needs only one single thought; and the difficulty is for a thinker to grasp this one solitary thought, as a thought which alone is his thought, to think it as the one and the same in a proper way. However, we talk of the same in a proper way only when we say of the same constantly the same, namely, in such a way that we ourselves at the same time are taken into its demand. The limitlessness of the same for such a thinking is thus the sharpest limit.[12]

By standing in the demand of the limitless same which he is thinking, the thinker becomes what he is, i.e. he is thrown into his limits. Heidegger's thought is Being, and the limitlessness of Being is that which gives limits to man who stands under the norms of Being. A thinker does not merely speculate; he stands in history as 'befalling' [13] – stands under the superior norms and responds to them.

Heidegger is the thinker of Being. This same thought is thought by him in diverse modes. These diverse modes, however, are ultimately the same. Always there is Being which reveals itself. For revelation of

---

[12] Martin Heidegger, *Was Heisst Denken?* (Tübingen: Max Niemeyer Verlag, 1954), p. 20.
[13] History as befalling indicates that man in his history is subordinated to the guidance of Being and stands in its mission.

itself, Being takes man in demand; thus it places man into his essence (*Dasein*) and brings itself forward into the things. Just as light cannot be perceived without the things which it illuminates, Being also could not possibly be brought into appearance without the things which appear on its horizon. On the other hand, beings can only appear in the light of Being. Sojourning, the openness of Being, is presupposed by beings which sojourn in the sojourning and thus appear in their ontological weightiness. Their presence and essence is made possible by Being.

III. HEIDEGGER'S STAND IN THE HISTORY OF PHILOSOPHY

Having lost the primary understanding of Being, traditional philosophy lost the true understanding of time, the essence of man, and things. Instead of considering beings in the light of Being, traditional philosophy thinks of them in respect to their relation to a subject. In respect to a subject, things are objects. Beings as objects can only be thought of by forgetting Being itself. Such a philosophical attitude which thinks of beings as objects without considering Being itself, according to Heidegger, is subjectivism. Metaphysics, as the investigation of the objectivity of beings, is subjectivism.

Modern man is tending to the extremes of subjectivism. The meaning of human existence seems, for the modern man, to be the ruling of the world as the totality of objects. Lacking meaning in himself, he is trying to control and master the objects. On the other hand, modern man bases the meaning of objects in himself as a subject. In this highly dynamic but meaningless circling between subject and objects, modern man lives an essentially nihilistic life. Subjectivism in its basis is nihilism. By trying to restore the philosophy of Being, Heidegger is on the way toward overcoming Western nihilism.

In regarding traditional philosophy as subjectivism, Heidegger takes a rather negative stand. Heidegger is positively related only to the early Greek philosophers and to the meditating poet Hölderlin. Anaximander, Heraclitus, and Parmenides were true thinkers of Being. This beginning of Western thought in Heidegger's estimation was not something small which grew and developed into something great; on the contrary, it was the greatest phase in the history of Western philosophy. "Everything great," says Heidegger, "can only begin great."[14]

[14] Martin Heidegger, *Einführung in die Metaphysik* (Tübingen: Max Niemeyer Verlag, 1953), p. 12.

And also, according to him, "it ends great. This is the way it is with the philosophy of the Greeks – it ended great with Aristotle." [15] Thereafter there was no philosophy of Being but merely of beings. Being was thought of solely as 'beingness' of beings (the 'is' of beings) but not as sojourning of the realm in which beings sojourn and thus appear.

While he takes a negative stand towards metaphysics, Heidegger does not reject it as being fully meaningless. The forgottenness of Being, by which metaphysics is characterized, is an event of Being. With this event (*Ereignis*), forgottenness of Being, Metaphysics is nourished and founded. To follow the trend of the divergence from Being in metaphysics, Heidegger studies it profoundly. Egon Vietta gives a list of courses held by Heidegger in different years at the University of Freiburg:

1927/28   Kant, Critique of Pure Reason.
1928   Logic, Leibniz.
1929   The German Idealism.
1929/30   Basic Concepts of Metaphysics.
1930   The Human Freedom (Critique of Causality).
1930/31   Hegel, Phenomenology of Spirit.
1931   Aristotle, Metaphysics, Book IX.
1931/32   The Essence of Truth.
1932   The Beginning of Western Philosophy.
1933   The Basic Question of Philosophy (Question of Being).
1934   Logic.
1934   Course on Hölderlin.[16]

The above list shows Heidegger's wide range of acquaintance with Western thought. Of all 'metaphysicians' Heidegger was especially interested in Kant, Husserl, and Nietzsche. In addition to these, he was under the indisputable influence of the Danish thinker, Kierkegaard.

Kant's famous so-called 'Copernican reversal in philosophy' impressed Heidegger. With this reversal, Kant stressed the finiteness of human knowledge. Instead of regarding human knowledge as knowing things absolutely the way they are, Kant considered things as determined by our finite knowing power, i.e. not the way they really

---

[15] *Ibid.*
[16] Egon Vietta, *Die Seinsfrage bei Martin Heidegger* (Stuttgart: Curt E. Schwab, 1950), pp. 28–29.

are in themselves. According to Heidegger, Kant was the first philosopher in the history of metaphysics to question the nature of metaphysics itself. Kant, however, performed his analysis of metaphysics by metaphysical means, namely, on the level of subjectivity. Heidegger's questioning of the nature of metaphysics transcends metaphysics and leads the mind out of the captivity of the subject-object level into the level of Being, i.e. into a transmetaphysical level.[17]

By considering things or beings merely as objects, traditional philosophy violates them by forcing them into various systems and by not treating them the way they are in themselves. Heidegger's respectful approach to things was stimulated, at least partly, by one of his great teachers, Edmund Husserl. In his phenomenological studies, Husserl argued against the violation of things which occurred by approaching them from presupposed artificial systems. He was aiming to go back to the real and true things without any abstractions or eliminations. His method was not normative but descriptive. The descriptive method portrays phenomena the way they appear themselves without the interference of any presuppositions. That which does not appear does not belong in the phenomenological philosophy. Such was the Kantian *Ding-an-sich* and, according to Husserl, the phenomenon of Being. In this respect Heidegger diverges from the Husserlian standpoint. According to Heidegger, Being always appears and is always understood; however, we do not deal with Being as with an object faced by us as spectators; we belong to Being ourselves, and we always have its knowledge, and only because of this knowledge are we in a position to know things or phenomena. Heidegger maintains a careful and respectful approach to things throughout all his works. In his late works the ontological importance of things seems even to be increased.

With his stress on concrete reality, Heidegger resembles Nietzsche. Nietzsche's turning to concrete reality, however, was not a transcendence to Being, but merely an opposition to Platonic, ideal supernaturality. Heidegger, nevertheless, considers Nietzsche to be a Platonic philosopher, simply because an opposition to a philosophical movement remains within this movement; it does not transcend it. For instance, Kierkegaard's non-systematic opposition to Hegel's overstressed systematization appears to Heidegger a Hegelianism. By opposing the supernatural values, Nietzsche created natural values

---

[17] Heidegger distinguishes metaphysics from ontology by considering ontology as the proper study of Being and metaphysics as an investigation of beings. Since ontology has been often used as a synonym for metaphysics, he calls his own study of Being 'fundamental ontology.'

determined by the will to power (*Wille zur Macht*). The will to power is the 'beingness' of beings; everything that is, is willed by the will to power – the source of all values. The will to power itself is above all values; it is being to the utmost. Nietzsche, therefore, rather wills nothing instead of abstaining from willing at all. Here Heidegger sees the extreme subjectivism, and the importance of Nietzsche for him is that he is the last metaphysician in the history of philosophy. The next step beyond Nietzsche's philosophy is a step beyond metaphysics as well. This beyondness of metaphysics is the realm of Heideggerian thought.

In many ways Heidegger appears to resemble Kierkegaard. Both of them are, or at least seem to be, misty and gloomy. Their basic problems are strikingly alike, namely: death, dread, existence, sin or guilt, etc. In spite of all their similarity, Heidegger still does not consider Kierkegaard to be a philosopher. "Kierkegaard is no thinker," says Heidegger, "but merely a religious writer." [18] In his *Sein und Zeit* Heidegger attributed to Kierkegaard a good analysis of dread [19] and admitted that he had "grasped and penetratingly thought out" [20] the problem of existence. However, so far as the problem of Being is concerned, Kierkegaard does not offer even the "smallest relation" [21] to it, and therefore, in Heidegger's estimation, he hardly belongs to the history of philosophy.

IV. THREE PHASES OF HEIDEGGER'S THOUGHT

The first and the second phase

Heidegger's works can be divided into three basic phases, namely: the phase of *Dasein*, the phase of Being, and the phase of the earth and the gods. The transition between the first two phases is the *Essence of Truth* (*Vom Wesen der Wahrheit*), wherein Heidegger relates truth to human freedom, and wherein freedom, again, presupposes the truth of Being. The two phases, however, do not divide Heidegger's works abruptly; they are the continuous and natural flow of his thought.

In his *Sein und Zeit*, Heidegger goes into a refined analysis of *Dasein*. This analysis is guided consistently, carefully, and exhaustively toward

[18] Martin Heidegger, *Holzwege* (Frankfurt a.M.: Vittorio Klostermann, 1950), p. 230.
[19] Heidegger, *Sein und Zeit*, p. 190.
[20] *Ibid.*, p. 235.
[21] Heidegger, *Was heisst Denken?*, p. 129.

the problem of Being. The phase of *Dasein*, therefore, is not a phase of his anthropological philosophy, but rather an introduction to truly ontological philosophy. *Sein und Zeit*, Heidegger's masterpiece, was planned in two parts, each part having three major chapters. Only two of the major chapters of the first part appeared, namely: "Preparative Fundamental Analysis of *Dasein*" and *"Dasein* and Temporality." The third chapter, "Time and Being," did not appear. In the framework of the third chapter the problems of *Dasein* were supposed to be reversed – instead of approaching Being from a human standpoint, the human essence was to be considered from the standpoint of Being itself. "The chapter in question," says Heidegger himself, "had been detained because the thought failed in adequate assertion and did not come through with the help of metaphysical language." [22]

Because of the failure of the metaphysical and systematic language to clarify his problems, Heidegger, in his later works, turned more and more to primary or pre-metaphysical thinking (the way the early Greek philosophers had thought) or to a thinking analogous to Hölderlin's poetical meditation. Although Heidegger's thinking here frequently is highly poetical, in no wise does it indicate his inability to think logically or scientifically. That he can think sharply is shown in his *Sein und Zeit*, where "the carefulness of the concepts is not less strictly applied than in the work of Kant." [23]

For Karl Löwith, Heidegger's non-systematic thinking in some of his post-*Sein und Zeit* works seems to degenerate from the thinking in *Sein und Zeit* itself. According to him, Heidegger, in his later publications, had given up a systematic advancing to his problems – instead of proving he was merely hinting. "The subjects treated are not developed phenomenologically any more, but simply told and said." [24] The thinking in which Heidegger handles his problems of the later phases is the thinking which responds to the truth of Being. This primary thought is presupposed by logical or systematic thought. Although not logical, in no wise is it irrational or orderless thinking. Not determined by any objective rules, this thinking is subordinated to Being itself; it is an answer to the call of Being.

Heidegger's first phase of thought is the thought of *Dasein*, namely, of man in his ultimate essence. *Dasein* primarily is not man, but Being approaching man to reveal itself. *Sein und Zeit*, the basic work of the

[22] Martin Heidegger, *Über den Humanismus* (Frankfurt a.M.: Vittorio Klostermann, 1949), p. 17.
[23] Vietta, *op. cit.*, p. 61.
[24] Löwith, *op. cit.*, pp. 9–10.

first phase of Heidegger's philosophy, is an established bridge leading from the common man's standpoint to the road of philosophy. In this phase, therefore, the historical references are insignificant, and those which are there (early Greek philosophers, Descartes, Kant, Hegel, etc.) are used only as a secondary means for the above-said bridge to bring man from his elementary path of everydayness onto the road of philosophy; they are not there as fragments of the road of philosophy itself.

The second phase of Heidegger's thought, namely, the phase of Being, is abundant with historical references. In various ways, Heidegger brings the road of philosophy from the early Greeks up to his own time. This road of philosophy, basically, is the road of the drifting away from thinking of Being. Here, Heidegger treats various milestones on this road. Freely choosing one or another of these milestones – one or another philosopher of history – he constantly brings the road of thought itself into view and constantly reveals it more and more at each turn. These turns are various stages of the drifting away from thinking of Being.

Heidegger has done this with his 'destructive' method. Such a method means going into one or another historical philosophy and trying to find its ultimate principles, that is, by trying to reach the foundations on which it had been built. After having thus disclosed these foundations, Heidegger goes into them with the intention of discovering what made them possible. Since Being is that which holds and carries the foundations of all philosophies, the distance between these foundations and Being indicates how far one or another philosopher has lost his way from the thinking of Being itself, i.e. how deep is his forgottenness of Being. In such a way the fixed series of degrees of 'being-lost-from-Being' of various philosophers represent a consequent way or a path of increased drifting away from Being – represent the road of philosophy.

Since the various thinkers in the history of philosophy often were not in personal contact with their predecessors and often were not even acquainted with their thought, presumably then their philosophies were somehow under a certain necessity and not totally in their own control. In other words, their thought was under a guidance. This guidance was nothing but Being itself, away from which these thinkers were drifting. Being, even though fallen into forgottenness, held the thinker on the road of philosophy. Being sends the thinker away from itself onto the road of philosophy, sends man into his history as 'befalling.' [25] Commissioned by Being, man as a secondary hand builds the road of philosophy. For instance, "Nietzsche, as well as any other philosopher," according to Heidegger, "neither has made nor has chosen his way. He has been sent on his way." [26]

Even the early Greek philosophers, for whom Being began to shine, initiated Western philosophy somehow by letting Being fall into the margin of thought – thus they paved the way for forgottenness of Being. The forgottenness of Being is originated by omission of the difference between Being and beings, i.e. by thinking Being as a being. That which throws beings into beingness, itself comes to be considered as a being. "The omission [of the difference between Being and beings] even warrants to Greek thought the character of beginning: the light of Being of beings becomes veiled as light." [27]

Since Being has not been thought [28] and all throughout history has kept itself in forgottenness, it is the problem of the future; a problem which is yet to be thought. Modern science which can be characterized by an increased interest in things as objects of investigation, now in the last decades, is faced by the disintegration of these objects, too. According to Heidegger, "we ourselves live, if we look carefully, in a world where there are no objects anymore." [29] Under precisely instrumented scientific sight, objects are dissolved and become mere complexes of atomic particles. Modern art also indicates that objects are disintegrating. "That art in such an era becomes objectless, shows its historical legitimateness." [30]

According to Heidegger, metaphysics and science are signified by the forgottenness of Being. Taken to extremes (the modern spirit is heading that way), the forgottenness of Being becomes nihilism. Here, not only Being is lost from sight, but also beings become deprived of their 'beingness.' When they disintegrate as beings, "in the phase of completed nihilism, it seems as though there is no *Being of* beings." [31] The knowledge that Being is lacking is much closer to knowledge of Being than mere ignorance of it, in the sense of indifference to it. The knowledge of Being as lacking is a mode of knowledge of Being.

---

[25] Cf. footnote 13, page 4.
[26] Heidegger, *Was heisst Denken?*, p. 61.
[27] Heidegger, *Vorträge*, pp. 240–241.
[28] Cf. footnote 10, p. 3.
[29] Martin Heidegger, *Der Satz vom Grund* (Pfullingen: Günther Neske, 1957), p. 65.
[30] *Ibid.*, p. 66.
[31] Martin Heidegger, *Zur Seinsfrage* (Frankfurt a.M.: Vittorio Klostermann, 1956), p. 34.

The third phase

The third phase of Heidegger's thought can be characterized as an attempt to think Being [32] as the problem of future. Here, Heidegger in a certain sense ties together the very early problems and the problems of the future. He thus brings the history of Western thought to completion. Gods and the earth are the basic problems of this phase just as they were for the early Greeks.

The third phase is not separated from the second one in time, as the second one was from the first, but is interlaced with it. Some comparatively early works of Heidegger (for instance *Erläuterungen zu Hölderlins Dichtung*) belong to this phase, and the very last works (for instance *Der Satz vom Grund*) belong to the second phase. Some of his works (*Holzwege, Vorträge und Aufsätze*) contain essays of the second phase along with the essays of the third phase.

Heidegger deals with the problems of the earth and the gods in comparatively very few places, and in none of these places is either earth or gods his direct theme. Nevertheless these problems are the most typical for his thought in its most developed stage. Heidegger *is* the philosopher of the earth and the gods.

The first place where Heidegger deals with the earth in a rather extensive way is the first essay in his *Holzwege*. In this essay (*"Der Ursprung des Kunstwerkes"*) Heidegger attempts to determine the essence of an artwork. Since an artwork is always a thing, he starts his investigation with the consideration of the 'thingness' of a thing as the problem leading to the understanding of the essence of an artwork. Such an attempt to investigate the 'thingness' of a thing, Heidegger justifies by showing the insufficiency of the traditional theories of 'thing.' Instead of placing a thing into the framework of any of these theories, Heidegger tries to approach the 'thingness' of a thing by a phenomenological method, namely, by letting things rest in themselves, i.e. appear the way they are in the light of Being.

Such a letting of things to rest in themselves is not easy, because a thing "withdraws itself from thinking." [33] A phenomenological description shows things not as faced by an onlooker but the way they appear in use or in being handled by man. In a phenomenological description, the thinker sustains himself from any *a priori* interpretation of the described thing and lets the thing appear as not placed in one or another theory. In this way Heidegger investigates a pair

---

[32] Cf. footnote 10, p. 3.
[33] Heidegger, *Holzwege*, p. 21.

of peasant's shoes and later, in the same essay (*Der Ursprung des Kunstwerkes*), a Greek temple.

By considering a painting of Van Gogh as his guide, he finds that the essence of the peasant's shoes is expressed by their servility (*Dienlichkeit*). The servility is ultimately grounded in dependability (*Verlässlichkeit*). These features, however, are essentialy features of an implement; they are not the 'thingness' of the thing.

Thus, by the frustrated attempt to determine the 'thingness' of a thing, Heidegger nevertheless makes an important and interesting discovery: the essence of an artwork cannot be disclosed through an implement, but, on the contrary, the implementality of an implement can be disclosed through a work of art. An artwork is not an implement with some aesthetic values added, and a thing is not an implement detached from its servility and dependability. "The way to determine the thing-like reality of an artwork is not from the thing to the work, but from work to the thing." [34]

An artwork is an artwork when it stands within its own world. Whenever a world into which an artwork belongs is gone, the artwork then is not an artwork in the proper sense any longer. The cathedral of Bamberg (Germany) towers high into the sky and is well preserved in its place. It can be touched and looked upon; nevertheless, ontologically it no longer *is*. It is there merely as something which *had been*. When the world is gone, things are not what they were. The cathedral of Bamberg, even though still standing, actually is denatured by being torn out from its world and is no longer the cathedral it was.

By his description of a Greek temple in the same essay Heidegger shows that the world is inter-related with the phenomenon of the earth. The Greek temple reveals the world of the Greeks in which they lived their lives and made their historical decisions, suffered their pains, won their victories, enjoyed the fruits of the earth, and the blessings of their gods.

The world brought forward by this temple was necessarily related to the earth. The white massive temple disclosed the darkness and the strength of the rock beneath, the height and the blueness of the sky, the power of the storm, and the vastness of the sea. Trees and grass, eagle and cricket – everything arose in the world which was disclosed by the temple. All which arises in its totality into the world of the Greeks as disclosed by this temple, is the earth. "The temple standing

[34] *Ibid.*, p. 28.

there opens up a world and sets it, at the same time, back on the earth which thus itself appears as the native ground." [35]

An artwork is not like an implement: it does not consume materials and does not let them disappear unnoticed by being overshadowed by the usefulness of the implement; but, on the contrary, it shows them in their materiality (for instance, marble is really marble only in the structure of the temple); an artwork brings materials to blossom in the world. "Artwork projects the earth itself into the openness of a world and holds it within it. Artwork allows the earth to be the earth." [36]

Although the earth appears in diverse forms, colors, and tones, it never appears as the earth in its full revelation; rather it appears as that which keeps itself veiled while it unveils all the forms, colors, and tones. The earth comes up into the world as that which shuts itself off in itself. "The shutting-itself-off of the earth, however, is no uniform, rigid remaining-veiled, but it unfolds itself in an inexhaustible fullness of the simple modes and shapes." [37]

The work of art thus shows a world which is essentially openness, and the earth which is essentially concealment. These two opposites necessarily refer to each other and belong together. They stand in a strife which is the truth of Being. An artwork is that which brings up the truth of Being by letting the world and the earth appear in their strife. We men, by standing out in the strife opened up by an artwork – by standing in the truth of Being – become true, i.e. free towards the things the way they are assembled in our world on our earth.

In addition to his essay on artwork (the first essay of his *Holzwege*), Heidegger deals with the problems of the earth and the gods in two other essays of great importance in his *Vorträge und Aufsätze*. One of these two essays is *Bauen-Wohnen-Denken* (Building-Dwelling-Thinking) and the other one *Das Ding* (The Thing).

In the essay on Building-Dwelling-Thinking, Heidegger does not go into any ethical problems in the traditional sense; also he does not try to establish any rules for dwelling or building. He merely attempts to go into the ontological roots of these phenomena.

Building and dwelling are not two separate modes of the human way of being. "Building, namely, is not merely a means and a way for dwelling; building is in itself already dwelling." [38] In the Old

[35] *Ibid.*, p. 32.
[36] *Ibid.*, p. 35.
[37] *Ibid.*, p. 36.
[38] Heidegger, *Vorträge*, p. 146.

High German, according to Heidegger, 'building' had meant 'dwelling,' and, again, both of these words had been related to 'being.' Dwelling or building is "the manner by which we men are on the earth." [39]

In Gothic, Heidegger also finds that the word 'dwelling' has the character of 'sparing' (*schonnen*), which means the tolerance of something in its own essence, letting something be the way it is in itself. Such a letting-be is sharply or diametrically contrasted to the modern domination of things. Not by ruling or controlling, but by respectful sparing, can we let the earth appear in its gifts. The attitude of a peasant is marked by such a sparing character, and the German word for 'cultivating' and for 'building' is one and the same, *bauen*. Hence, building and dwelling ultimately have a sparing character such as cultivating has.

According to Heidegger, dwelling, as "abiding of the mortals [men] on the earth," [40] is at the same time their wandering under the sky, sojourning in the proximity of divinities, and their belonging in to-getherness.[41] These four – earth, sky, gods, and mortals – belong together in an original unity.

Sky is characterized by the sun, moon, stars, seasons of the year, days, nights, winds, and clouds. Gods are "the hinting messengers of the divine." [42] A god appears from out of the sway held by the divine (Being). The mortals are characterized as those who have the capacity for death as death.[43]

Each of these four refers necessarily to the others. To name one of them is *eo ipso* to think the other three. Heidegger calls them *Geviert*. *Vier* is 'four,' and *Geviert* is 'that-which-is-foured' or 'foursome.'

To dwell is to spare the earth, receive the sky, expect the gods, and have a capacity for death. The sparing of the earth and receiving of the sky means letting all the things on the earth and in the sky be the way they are in themselves by not subjugating them forcefully to our subjective order. Earth and sky themselves represent an order which holds sway over the things. Awaiting the gods is being open to the signs of the gods in our vital surroundings or also being aware of their absence. The capacity for death stresses man in his completion.

To dwell ultimately means to spare or to preserve the foursome. Such sparing or preservation can only take place by man's sojourning

[39] *Ibid.*, p. 147.
[40] *Ibid.*, p. 149.
[41] *Ibid.*
[42] *Ibid.*, p. 150.
[43] *Ibid.*

among the things and sparing the things. One of such modes of dwelling, as sparing the foursome by sparing the things, is building.

A bridge built across a river 'assembles' the banks and the countries lying on both sides of the river; it also 'assembles' the stream and the stormy and peaceful sky; it guides mortals on their daily errands, on their ways of suffering or being blessed by the gods, and, finally, on their last journey into the beyond.

Thus a thing, by 'assembling' the foursome, essentially is an assembler. Interestingly, according to Heidegger, the Old German word for thing had been *thing*, meaning 'assembler.' [44]

A bridge is a thing not only by its 'assembling' of the foursome, but also by its 'assembling' of the places. A bridge throws a variety of places into certain distances in respect to itself, and thus they become places. Such an 'assembling' of places actually is breaking into the space or spacing-in (*Einräumen*) of space. This spacing-in renders space possible, and ultimately it is the letting or admission of foursome into space – granting home to it or lodging it. Such lodging is achieved not only by building a temple or a home but also by building any other thing – such as a bridge.

By assembling the foursome, a building receives from the foursome the references or standards for organization or mutual interrelation of places. By doing this, the building guards the foursome. To build thus means to guard or to spare – to dwell.

One of the examples of a building given in the essay is the example of a typical peasant home in the Black Forest built about two centuries ago.[45] Such a home assembles the foursome; and men, by having built it or by having dwelt in it, spared the foursome. Such a home is well suited to the terrain of the Black Forest; it is well prepared against the storms of winter and the heat of summer. It has a built-in corner for praying, a place for the cradle, and also a place for the coffin. Knowing how to dwell enables us to know how to build. Dwelling is the basic mode of being man, as man, on the earth.

In his essay on thing, contained in *Vorträge und Aufsätze*, Heidegger takes into consideration a simple thing, a ewer.

A ewer is a container which has a bottom and sides. It can become an object of consideration when faced by us. Even when it is not faced by us, it stands there at our disposition. Although a ewer is not an object in the sense of standing-in-front-of-us for our representation, it

---

[44] *Ibid.*, p. 153.
[45] *Ibid.*, p. 161.

is an object which is made for us and is placed in front of us for our use. Objectivity, the standing-in-front-of-us for our representation as well as the being-placed-in-front-of-us for our use, is in no wise the 'thingness' of a thing. The production of a ewer merely releases it into its proper essence, but it does not make this essence; it merely uses this essence as a guide for the production of the ewer.

A scientific consideration never reveals a thing the way it is in itself because "science always encounters only that which by its way of representation was permitted, in advance, as its possible object." [46] In its late phase, science does not even deal with objects anymore but only with dissolved objectivities faced by a scientific subject.

What a ewer is in its essence can be revealed by approaching it without any presuppositions, by trying to describe it phenomenologically. A ewer takes and holds; it pours and retains. "The ewer-ness of a ewer 'essentiates' in the outpouring of the gush." [47] The essence of an empty ewer still is the pouring because only a ewer can fail to pour, and not a hammer or a scythe.

In the spring-water, which is contained by a ewer, linger the stones and dark caves of the earth and the rains and dews of the sky. The mortals quench their thirst by the gush of the ewer. Out of a ewer the sacrifices to the gods are made on feast days. In the word 'gush' (Guss) Heidegger indicates the remnants of the word 'sacrifice.' [48]

In the gush of the ewer linger earth, sky, gods, and mortals as belonging necessarily together. The gush brings the foursome to the light. To be truly a man, to be involved in the foursome, means to approach things in a respectful manner. By letting them be the way they are, man lets them then be the assemblers of the foursome. By assembling the foursome, a ewer assembles itself to ewer-ness; it becomes a *thing*.

The foursome is never four separate beings. "Each of the four reflects in its own way the others." [49] Heidegger compares such a reflection to a play wherein each player lets the others be what they are and, by doing so, brings to being his part in the playing. A player is, in a certain sense, the other players.

The play of foursome is the 'worlding' of the world (*das Welten der Welt*). By assembling the foursome, a thing assembles or 'things' (*dingt*) the world. Man, by thinking a thing in a proper way, becomes determined by it and thus he abandons his indeterminateness, his

[46] *Ibid.*, p. 168.
[47] *Ibid.*, p. 170.
[48] *Ibid.*, p. 171.
[49] *Ibid.*, p. 178.

isolation in his subjectivity, and becomes the guardian of world and things.[50]

Things are ultimately not made by man; however, they are not without the sparing attitude of man. Sparing indicates having an eye for the thing the way it 'essentiates' in the world, instead of blindly subjugating it to one's subjective aims. Only with a sparing attitude or openness can we attain the world, and only in the world is a thing a thing.

These three rather short essays are the only places where the problems of the earth and the gods are treated extensively. In the other essays or works of Heidegger, there are scattered passages which deal with these problems. Most of these passages refer to *physis*, and only very few to gods.

Even these three essays, in spite of their very profound treatment of the ultimate problems, do not seem to take adequate space to present them more comprehensively and thus to make them accessible for an average philosophical reader. They seem to be treated on a high level without much attention or effort to help the reader to reach the height of the problems in a gradual ascent.

The summary of these three important essays is given here, in the introduction, to allow a preliminary feel of Heidegger's late thought and, at the same time, to show the obscurity of his problems. The obscurity is mainly caused by the too condensed and too profound manner of treatment of these problems as regards the comprehending capacity of the average reader. Another reason for such obscurity, of course, is the strangeness of the problems themselves and the highly untraditional way of approaching them. It follows that a supplementary investigation and additional sources are needed to make these problems, to a certain extent, clearer and more convincing.

The problems of the third phase of Heidegger's thinking, roughly speaking, can hardly be considered as philosophical in terms of traditional or classical philosophy. Neither the earth nor the gods were previously thought of in philosophical treatises, except in early Greek philosophy where not so much the gods as the earth, understood as *physis*, was the pre-eminent, or even the only, problem.

Throughout all traditional philosophy, however, the problem of matter can be pursued. For Aristotle, and many philosophers influenced by him, matter belongs to the structure of material things as their potential principle. Matter as the potential principle is exposed

[50] *Ibid.*, p. 179.

to the active, formative principle, the form. It never is the source, in the sense of *physis* of the early Greeks, from which anything whatsoever can rise as an existing thing. *Physis* for the early Greeks was not a passive principle as opposed to the active or spiritual principle. *Physis* comprised everything whatsoever without exclusion of that which later was considered under the concepts of life and spirituality, as distinct and opposed to mere matter.

The Aristotelian prime matter does not exist. What exists is a unique mass, the sum of all the secondary matters – the matters which are formed to a certain extent and thus made actual. These secondary matters can be used and formed and actualized again to something else. *Physis* for the early Greeks was a dynamic phenomenon; it was dynamism itself. *Physis* was that which constantly brings itself forward in diverse forms, and everything whatsoever starts and ends in it. Heidegger's problem of the earth has nothing to do with matter because it is thought of much more primarily than a potential principle; it is thought of on the same level as the early Greek *physis*.

The modern physical and chemical sciences in their understanding of the physical world also cannot contribute anything to Heidegger's problem of the earth, since these sciences investigate objects, or rather certain groups of objects, which necessarily presuppose the earth in the Heideggerian sense. Heidegger's problem of the earth strictly transcends the level of beings or objects and belongs to the level of Being, just like *Dasein* or world.

The early Greek phenomenon of *physis* is the only point in philosophy to which Heidegger's problem of earth can be related historically. Beside the philosophies of the early Greeks, there is another, however non-philosophical, source which has formed and highly influenced Heidegger's problem of the earth. This is the poetry of Hölderlin.

The phenomenon of nature in Hölderlin's poetry is strangely and profoundly approached as holiness, the realm of gods. From here, the necessary relation of Heidegger's earth and gods can be clarified or illustrated.

Alongside of the early Greek philosophies and the poetry of Hölderlin, the importance of the Greek religion cannot be overlooked. Hölderlin's phenomenon of holiness appears to be analogous to the Chthonian power Mother Earth, and his gods – to Olympian deities. Therefore, the Greek religion is to be considered as the ultimate source for the understanding and clarification of Heidegger's, as well as Hölderlin's, problems of earth and gods.

V. DETOUR FROM GODS TO EARTH

In spite of the strangeness by which Heidegger's problem of the earth, as being related to the gods, is marked, nevertheless, it is not constructive in the sense that it would be speculatively constructed and thus leaving or forsaking concrete reality and tending to higher spiritual spheres. On the contrary, his thought in the third phase turns more radically to the things of everyday life with a highly respectful attitude towards them and with a genuine and profound disclosure of their essences. In fact, the investigation of the earth and the gods brings forward the serenity which backs things and which shows that dwelling as sojourning on the earth among the things is a highly sacred mode of being – being in the neighborhood of gods.

To be in the neighborhood of gods means to be back home or to make oneself at home in that which is nearest to oneself. However, "the path leading to that which is nearest to us men is always the most distant and therefore the most difficult." [51]

In one of Hölderlin's hymns, investigated by Heidegger, the poet is shown as the one who is returning home to the "place of proximity to the primeval source." [52] The poet comes home from the Alps, and he is the one who tells about home to his countrymen. These people who have been at home have had to be told about the essence of home by one who is coming from abroad, from beyond the *Bodensee* (a lake in the Alps), from snowy high and serene mountains where gods dwell. A homecomer, one who comes to proximity, can only be the one who has been in the distance. Only he can tell the secrets of dwelling at home as dwelling near gods.

Dwelling here undoubtedly means 'ec-sisting,' the standing in the light of Being or of holiness, which is brought to one who 'ec-sists' by the gods, the messengers of holiness. Such standing is understanding: it enables us to be near things the way they are in the light of Being. By being near the true things, we dwell authentically, i.e. we are at home, which means abiding in the neighborhood of gods.

A rock is what it is and man is not what he is because he 'ec-sists,' i.e. he comes home to himself from the distance of not himself, from

---

[51] Heidegger, *Satz*, p. 16.
[52] Martin Heidegger, *Erläuterungen zu Hölderlins Dichtung* (Frankfurt a.M.: Vittorio Klostermann, 1944), p. 21.

Being. The way home, to that which is nearest to us, is only possible by a detour abroad through Being, through that which is the most distant from us.

Dwelling is not the highly spiritual mode of living of an educated man or the way of life of a philosopher. To dwell means to live a concrete life, namely: to make a home on the earth, acquire food for the family, handle and use, build and cultivate things. For such a very concrete way of living or dwelling, the understanding of the interplay of earth and sky, gods and mortals is already presupposed. This again shows that to dwell is to be near things and the earth (be in the proximity) and at the same time to be near the gods (be in the distance).

To reflect this idea of detour from the gods to the earth, in the present study four chapters (Chapters III–VI) will consist in treating the problem of the world (the realm of gods) as our detour into distance, and the last two chapters (Chapters VII–VIII) will deal with the things and dwelling (the realm of earth), as our coming back home from the distance of the world.

The understanding of Heidegger's problem of the world requires more or less the knowledge of Heidegger's philosophy as a whole. The problem of world cannot be separated from the rest of Heidegger's problems and presented briefly by pinning it down with a few definitions. Heidegger is a philosopher of the world. His thought is the constant investigation of the problem of the world. Therefore, the detour into the distance of the world has to be preceded by a summary review of Heidegger's philosophy in general. Consequently, the first chapter of this study will attempt to give the early thought of Heidegger, the thought of *Dasein*. The second chapter will deal with the second phase of Heidegger's thought, the thought of Being. The remaining six chapters can be considered as the presentation of Heidegger's late thought, the thought of the earth and the gods.

Generally in all treatises by various philosophers or interpreters of Heidegger, the investigation of his philosophy consists almost exclusively in the investigation of *Sein und Zeit*. Indeed, *Sein und Zeit* is a great work indicating a turn in Western thought. It is the masterpiece of Heidegger's philosophy due to its extensive, constructive, systematic, and detailed elaboration of fundamental philosophical problems. Nevertheless, *Sein und Zeit* is only a grand prelude to the philosophy of the world, never thought of since the time of the early Greeks or even before – since the time of *mythos*.

The crest of Heidegger's thought is the thought of the world. Foursome stands for a fully developed philosophy of the world. The most significant, most original, and most interesting wordly realities are the earth and the gods.

The detour into the realm of the gods is not a tour beyond the world; gods belong to the world and can be experienced. In Heidegger's philosophy we do not start with experience with the intention to leave it behind us and proceed merely speculatively in the higher realms of reality. Already Husserl maintained that man cannot leap beyond experience: he remains within it. According to E. Parl Welsh, "Husserl agreed with Kant that all knowledge begins with experience but, in addition to redefining experience, he further affirmed that it endures and ends in experience." [53] 'To experience' here is 'to see,' and philosophy is making-see instead of granting a ladder of speculative proofs which one can climb blindly, mechanically – without really seeing himself.

The problems of the earth and the gods are not provable, but they can be seen because they are real. To investigate them means to attempt to see that which we already know and always did know – that which has merely been dulled by our over-subjectivized attitude.

The problems of the earth and the gods are of the utmost importance in Heidegger's philosophy. They can be considered as the blossoms of his thought. The first phase of Heidegger's thought was the building of a bridge guiding us onto the road of philosophy; the second has brought forward into our sight the whole road of philosophy from its early beginning up to our times; and the third phase is the crest of this road as the outline of future thought guiding us into the freedom of Being from imprisonment in our subjectivity.

[53] E. Parl Welsh, *The Philosophy of Edmund Husserl* (N. York: Columbia University Press, 1940), p. 235.

CHAPTER I

DASEIN

In his *Sein und Zeit*, Heidegger gradually and systematically builds up the problem of *Dasein*. Therefore, here in this chapter, the review of Heidegger's thought will follow the format of *Sein und Zeit* itself – not in all its detailed steps, however, but rather in its most characteristic points by trying to reveal these points and thus to give the feeling of Heideggerian thought, which is so distinct from the traditional mode of thinking.

Emphasizing Being as the basic aim of his investigation, Heidegger in his *Sein und Zeit* begins with the pre-ontological knowledge of Being in which he finds hints which point out the direction for attaining an ontological knowledge of Being. Man, as the only being essentially having the understanding of Being, is the medium to approach Being itself for Heidegger. Man, as *Dasein*, is not an empirical subject but the understander of Being, in the sense that he is essentially related to Being. Man, as *Dasein*, *is* this relation to Being.

Dasein, as an understanding being, is characterized by openness or to-be-in-the-world, which Heidegger analyzes in three aspects – as to-be-in, as world, and as openness itself, the *Da* of *Dasein*. In *Da* he finds three ways of disclosure of *Dasein*: (1) moodness, disclosing *Dasein* as thrown; (2) understanding, disclosing it in its projection; and (3) parlance, disclosing it in its decline. After thus exhibiting *Dasein* as care, i.e. declining thrown projection, Heidegger proceeds to show the structure of *Dasein* in its wholeness. This he achieves by considering the phenomenon of death in *Dasein* as running forward toward death (the possibility of the impossibility of *Dasein*), and the phenomenon of conscience in *Dasein*'s readiness for the call of conscience (its resoluteness). Both these phenomena together, as the resolute-running-forward to death of *Dasein*, reveal *Dasein* in its wholeness – reveal it as temporal. In its temporality *Dasein* discovers itself from its future and finds thus its past which together with its future sets *Dasein* in the present. The thinking in *Sein und Zeit* concludes that temporality or time is the basis or horizon for understanding Being.

The first section of this chapter is a general approach to the problem of *Dasein* which, in the broadened sense, is to-be-in-the-world. General understanding of the to-be-in-the-world will constitute the theme of the second section of the chapter. The great importance of the phenomenon of to-be-in-the-world renders it necessary to go into its components separately; hence, the third section of this chapter will consider the to-be-in, and the fourth section, the world. Since world implies space, in the fifth section of the chapter the problem of space will be treated. The to-be-in-the-world is always the to-be-together with others, which will be shown in the sixth section. The basic character of the to-be-in-the-world, openness, is best expressed by the German *Da* as the fundamental part of the phenomenon *Dasein*. *Da* thus will be the topic of the seventh section of the chapter. The openness of *Dasein* is basically experienced in the mood of dread, a phenomenon which will be considered in the eighth section of the chapter. The mood of dread indicates the authentic *Dasein*. Death as the total disclosure of *Dasein* will be the problem of the ninth section. The authentic *Dasein* is increasingly shown in Heidegger's investigation of the phenomenon of conscience as *Dasein*'s readiness for the call of the to-be-in-the-world. Conscience will be the theme of the tenth section of the chapter. Death and conscience in their combination represent *Dasein*'s temporization, which is fundamentally the eruption of Being in time and in the history of man. Temporality is the topic of the last section of the chapter.

I. APPROACH TO THE PROBLEM OF *DASEIN*

Meaning of the word 'Dasein'

Sein und Zeit is a profound analysis of *Dasein*. In direct or literal translation into English, this word means 'to-be-there.' Such a literal translation does not adequately express the meaning of the word which it has in the German language or in which it is used in Heidegger's philosophy. *Dasein* is hardly translatable into English. Instead of trying to translate it, it seems better to retain it in its German form after an interpretation of its meaning. In German, *Dasein* means 'existence,' 'life,' and 'presence.' Generally it expresses the concreteness of here and now. In Heidegger's philosophy the word '*Dasein*' retains all these shades of meaning in contemporary German but in a deepened and unified way. Primarily, *Dasein* for Heidegger is the presence of Being [1] in concrete life and situations. Man is the only being who has an understanding of Being, therefore, only for man can Being be present. Man is the place of the presence of Being; he is this presence. Man is *Dasein*. *Dasein* is not identical with empirical man, but is rather his essence.

Question of Being

Man is a questioning being; he can question the meaning of 'to be' in everything that is. He can even question his own being, take a standpoint toward it. Heidegger's intention is not to give an account of the nature of man, but rather, through a detailed analysis of *Dasein*, to reveal Being itself ontologically. In order to be able to question Being, man has to have some understanding of Being beforehand, otherwise he could not question. A question always presupposes a certain knowledge of that which is being questioned. Questioning is pointing, hinting toward the answer. Man always has an understanding of Being; this understanding, however, is not explicit, not ontological, but merely practical understanding which Heidegger calls ontic understanding. Ontic understanding is a challenge to man – it calls for exploration and hints the direction in which man has to go for an explicit answer of Being.

According to Heidegger, the long tradition of philosophy has not answered the question of Being, it has merely covered up this question by attracting attention toward the particular problems of beings and by leaving the question of Being unasked. For traditional philosophy there is no need to even ask the question of Being, because Being is self-evident and clear. Everybody knows what being is. On the other hand, Being is undefinable; and as such it cannot be clearly formulated. "The indefinability of Being," says Heidegger, opposing the attitude of traditional philosophy, "does not dispense from questioning its meaning, but rather it demands it." [2] Throughout all his works Heidegger is constantly striving after Being, constantly asking the question of Being.

Starting from the ontic (pre-ontological) knowledge of Being, i.e. from Being itself, he determines the essence of man, *Dasein*. With *Dasein* he reveals Being itself. By doing this, Heidegger seems to be proceeding in a circle. However, according to Heidegger, the essence

[1] Cf. footnote 5, p. 3.
[2] Heidegger, *Sein und Zeit*, p. 4.

of man can be determined from an ontic understanding of Being, i.e.
without an explicit knowledge of Being. After an explicit understanding of *Dasein* is attained, Being itself can be approached and
explicated. Such a procedure is in no wise a meaningless, illogical
circling; it has a guidance. This guidance is the guidance of Being
itself. By starting from our ontic knowledge of Being, we start from
Being itself, because ontic knowledge is not of our making, but is given
to us by our being open to Being. Ontic knowledge points to the
answer; in a way it determines the answer. Without it we could neither
ask nor answer the question of Being. Our ontological revelation of
Being is led by Being itself. Being reveals itself in us through us. Heidegger's philosophy of *Dasein* is ontocentric, whereas traditional
philosophy has been mainly anthropocentric.

Nature of man

Throughout his *Sein und Zeit* Heidegger temporalily suspends himself from dealing directly with Being. He goes into precise and careful
investigation of *Dasein*.[3] By doing this, however, he constantly guides
this investigation of *Dasein* in such a way that the structure of Being
itself is revealed. The first characterization of man, given in *Sein und
Zeit*, is as a being which exists in such a way that this way of existence
itself is his problem.[4]

The essence of man cannot be expressed as his 'whatness' but rather
as his attitude toward his own way of being. Man is not determined
as an objective thing; he, in a sense, determines himself. He can take
a stand as regards his own being. His 'is' is not determined but potential.
Man is a being who can be or not be himself. This possibility or potentiality to be himself or not to be himself, Heidegger calls existence.
An existing being is distinguished by its understanding of Being.
"Understanding of Being is one of the determinations of *Dasein*." [5]
To be an understanding being or to know that which is, means to
stand in the openness of Being. In this openness we can encounter
beings and have attitudes toward them.

Man is always in an openness, in a certain 'existentiel' surrounding
which he himself did not create but into which he was either born,
entered by chance, or which he chose. In any case, as long as a man *is*,
he is always in a certain 'existentiel' environment with different

---

[3] Investigation of *Dasein* ultimately, however, *is* the investigation of Being.
[4] Heidegger, *Sein und Zeit*, p. 12.
[5] *Ibid.*

possibilities. In dealing with these possibilities, seizing them, rejecting them, developing them, etc., man understands himself. Understanding himself in this way is 'existentiel' understanding. 'Existentiel' or ontic understanding is an understanding of things which is achieved by standing in the world and handling these things. Therefore this understanding of things is *eo ipso* an understanding of man himself. Although 'existentiel' understanding is attained by handling things, it is not. practical as opposed to theoretical understanding. Both practical and theoretical understanding investigate things without their reference to the world. 'Existentiel' understanding is more fundamental than these because it sees things as related to or as founded in the world, i.e. it sees them fundamentally. With such an understanding not only things but also man is seen as standing in the world, existing. 'Existentiel' understanding is a fundamental awareness of things made possible by being aware of the world in which we stand. We are aware of the world by being in the world. To-be-in-the-world is *Dasein*. Awareness of the world is awareness of *Dasein*'s own being. Such fundamental awareness renders cognition, be it practical or theoretical, possible.

'Existentiel' understanding differs from existential understanding. Existential understanding reveals the structure of *Dasein*, which is also the structure of the world; whereas 'existentiel' understanding stresses *Dasein*'s awareness of its own being in its surroundings as engaged with the things of these surroundings. It stresses *Dasein* in its existence. Existential understanding exposes *Dasein* structurally; whereas 'existentiel' understanding exposes *Dasein* as the foundation of things in ontic environment. *Dasein* grants meanings to the things by which things become things. Such meaning-granting activity essentially belongs to *Dasein*; *Dasein* is essentially related to things. Without things, *Dasein* can never be revealed as the giver of meanings; and without *Dasein*, things are void of meaning.

The 'existentiel' understanding is not existential, i.e. ontological, understanding, but rather ontic. An ontological understanding of existence is that which reveals its structure. These ontologically revealed structural elements of existence Heidegger calls existentials. The unity of all existentials is existentiality. Ontological understanding revealing *Dasein* in its structure is existential understanding.

The existentials are specific characteristics of the human essence which are analogous to the categories, the essential characteristics of non-human beings or objects. In traditional philosophy, man was considered under the norms and measurements of objects, therefore, his essence or the structure of his very self was never revealed. An adequate understanding of human essence or *Dasein* is needed to approach the meaning of Being itself. Man is not a being that can be analyzed in isolation; isolated in himself man is not man, but rather a human thing. Man in his very essence is not a substance but a relation.[6] Only as a being standing in the openness of Being, understanding and encountering things in the totality (the world) – is man man. This totality, the world, is the openness of Being, and not the sum of all possible objects. To-be-in-the-world, to stand in the openness of Being, to be related to Being, constitute the very structure of human essence, the *Dasein*. The worldliness of man (existential of *Dasein*) is ontologically prior to all the categories. An object and its categorical structure can only be revealed in a world which is presupposed by any objectivity or 'thingness.' Without a worldly being, i.e. a being which is marked by an understanding of Being, no object can ever be revealed categorically or in any other way. It is just because man is worldly that he can come upon things. "This distinguished being," says Heidegger, quoting St. Thomas Aquinas, "the *ens, quod natum est convenire cum omni ente*, is spirit (*anima*)." [7] Spirit corresponds here to Heideggerian *Dasein*.

Phenomenology as ontology

Since traditional philosophy constantly dealt solely with things, their essences, or their categorical determinations, but never with the problem of the world as world,[8] it cannot be called primary ontology. To reach solid ontological foundations, an existentialistic ontology is needed. An ontology which is consolidated through the analysis of *Dasein* – which Heidegger calls fundamental-ontology – is more primarily ontological than is traditional ontology.

According to Heidegger, traditional philosophy rests on presuppositions which are not verified, and is frequently entangled in artificial constructions, which instead of revealing the true picture of Being, cover it up and violate it by fitting it into distorting and subjective viewpoints. Trying to approach beings the way they truly are, Heidegger uses the phenomenological method. "The title 'phenomenology' expresses a maxim, which can also be formulated 'to the things them-

---

[6] Relation here in no wise is a categorical but an existential relation.
[7] Heidegger, *Sein und Zeit*, p. 19.
[8] World for traditional philosophy is simply the totality of objects.

selves' against all non-founded constructions, against accidental findings, against the overtaking of merely seemingly proven concepts, against semblance questions, which often expand themselves throughout generations as 'problems.' " [9] The phenomenological attitude is a respectful stand in face of reality which allows this reality to appear in its own way, undistorted by 'approaches.' In one of his latest works, Heidegger states that modern man has lost this ability to face things as they are. He takes the example of a blossoming tree, which we, modern men, no longer face the way it is in itself, but in fully distorted form. Modern man feels that standing on the earth and facing such a blossoming tree is fully clear and presents no problems. Yet Heidegger warns that such thinking is hasty. "Because," says Heidegger, "unintentionally we give everything up as soon as the sciences of physics, physiology and psychology together with scientific philosophy explain, with the entire display of their verifications and proofs, that we nevertheless do not truly observe a tree, but actually observe an emptiness with randomly interspersed, tiny electric charges which fly about with great speed." [10] Yet, a scientific approach does not see reality the way it is. As far as science is concerned, to stand in front of a tree is an event which occurs in our head rather than in reality, or, to be more exact, in our brain rather than in reality. This brain-event can be measured by specific instruments and expressed in numbers or diagrams. By trying to 'explain' the blossoming tree strictly scientifically, we end up with brain circuits. "Where is the blossoming tree in these recordings of the brain-streams?" asks Heidegger.[11] Truly we do not deal with the tree anymore, but merely with scientific, logical constructions which distort the true picture of reality. Scientific approaches are meaningful and useful in their own way; through them we can use or control reality but we can in no wise reveal scientifically the essence of reality and things in their ontological foundation. Trying to find true reality, Heidegger, unburdened by presuppositions, goes into its phenomena and views them in their primary genuineness. A phenomenological approach to reality is determined by the reality itself; we do not dictate reality, reality dictates us.

Since a phenomenon is an appearance (*phainomenon*), it may appear the way it is and also it may appear the way it is not and only seemingly is. Therefore, the approach to phenomena is not easy and simple, but

[9] Heidegger, *Sein und Zeit*, p. 28.
[10] Heidegger, *Was heisst Denken?*, p. 18.
[11] *Ibid.*, p. 17.

rather tricky. It must be careful and cautious because usually phenomena are masked or concealed and are not the way they appear to be. Most of the time reality shows itself in its concealments; these concealments themselves, however, are hints toward disclosure or truth. According to Heidegger, disclosure (*aletheia*) is the primary meaning of truth. Throughout all of his works he retains this concept of truth. Disclosure implies in itself concealment, for there cannot be any disclosure without previous concealment. Truth and untruth belong together.

For Edmund Husserl, phenomenology is plainly a philosophy revealing the essences in reality; about Being, it has nothing to say, for Being does not appear. On this very important point Heidegger breaks away from Husserl. Since phenomenology aims to disclose phenomena, according to Heidegger, the theme of phenomenology is truly *the* outstanding phenomenon, i.e. that phenomenon "which primarily and mainly does not display itself, and which, when compared to that which primarily and mainly does display itself, remains *concealed* and nevertheless essentially belongs to that which primarily and mainly displays itself. It belongs to it in the sense that it constitutes its meaning, founds it." [12] This outstanding phenomenon is Being, and phenomenology basically is ontology.

II. TO-BE-IN-THE-WORLD

Existence

The consideration of human being in Heidegger's philosophy is on an entirely different level from that of objects, which he calls disposables (*Vorhandenheiten*). Disposables are things which we face in their full finiteness and stability; they are static objects. The essence of man is dynamic; Heidegger calls this essence existence. "The 'essence' of *Dasein* lies in its existence." [13] In Heidegger's philosophy existence cannot be identified with the *existentia* of scholastic philosophy, where *existentia* is opposed to *essentia*. An existing being lacks a stable substance by which the disposables are characterized. Stone is stone, a chair is a chair, a tower is a tower, etc.; things do not transcend their realm. They are balanced and centralized in themselves. Man is eccentric; he is not stable but dynamic He

---

[12] Heidegger, *Sein und Zeit*, p. 35.
[13] *Ibid.*, p. 42.

is a possibility of himself which he can realize, develop, neglect, reject, forget, etc. In a certain sense we are what we make of ourselves. Our being is our unsolved problem; to be existing is to be constantly solving this problem. We have a great interest in our being. *Dasein* has a character of 'my-ness' (*Jemeinigheit*), of profoundly personal interest in *Dasein*'s own being.

Since *Dasein* is existent, i.e. related to its own being as its very personal possibility (or potentiality); it has an understanding of its own being. From our existence, i.e. from our relation to our own being, we can disclose the structure of our being. Although most of the time we do not apprehend our existence in its true structure but exist inauthentically, nevertheless, in our everyday inauthentic way of existence, its basic structure is retained. It is hidden there or concealed. Even in complete forgottenness of our own self, we still are related to it and determined by it in an inauthentic way. Our inauthentic life, if severed from the foundation of existence on which it rests, would be dissolved into complete nothingness. Forgottenness of our self is yet an event which holds us in unity in our everydayness and forms us into a somethingness.

Character of existence

Turning to our everydayness, without the interference of any presuppositons, Heidegger reveals the first outline of our structure which is the to-be-in-the-world. To-be-in-the-world is a unique phenomenon which tradition has dissolved and thus obscured. *Dasein*, the to-be-in-the-world, is not a thing in a thing like an apple in a basket. On the other hand, *Dasein* does not extract and establish the world out of itself. To-be-in-the-world is a way of 'to be' of a being which differs from disposables (*Vorhandenheiten*). An existing being does not face the world as an object, but *is* worldly – belongs to the worldliness of the world. On the other hand, it can also be said that the world belongs to our structure. There can be no world without man, just as no man can be without the world. "The subjective man of present times does not know that he primarily stands within the world; he merely makes a picture of the world for himself. He puts the world forward and places it in front of himself. He is not in a unity with the world, but torn out from it. He is an isolated, worldless 'I.' " [14] Man can never be understood adequately without the world, and the world is meaningless without man.

[14] Vietta, *op. cit.*, p. 41.

III. TO-BE-IN

Dwelling

The one and the same phenomenon of to-be-in-the-world is treated by Heidegger in three aspects, namely: (1) as to-be-in (*Insein*), (2) as world, and (3) as being which is in the world, the *Dasein* itself.

The to-be-in means our being accustomed to or belonging to our environment. We are interested in the beings of our surroundings; we handle them and take care of them. To-be-in expresses our close entanglement with the things of our environment. In his later works Heidegger refers to to-be-in as dwelling (*Wohnen*) which is described by him as the "sojourn of man on the earth." [15] This sojourning on the earth expresses the concreteness of to-be-in or dwelling. On the other hand, however, Heidegger relates dwelling to poetics, which does not mean a profession of making verses, but rather a way of to-be-in or to dwell. Poetics is not an unrestrained fancy, but rather a response of man to the parlance of Being. A poet subordinates himself to Being from which he takes his norm (*Mass-nahme*) to measure out dimensions for his dwelling; hence, poetics is "the true measuring of the dimension for dwelling." [16] For a real and concretely human way of being, knowledge of Being is presupposed. This concrete, non-theoretical knowledge expresses itself in the form of knowing the basic standards by which we can approach things, or be approached by things. To-be-in is made possible by the nearness of Being. In the neighborhood of Being man can come near the things. We are able to encounter things, deal with them, handle them, worry about them and take care of them, only because we stand in the world (to-stand is to-be-in) whose dimension we measure by the norms received from Being. The world is discovered prior to the discovery of things. The wordliness of man puts him in a position to encounter things; their physical nearness does not. "Two beings, which are disposed within the world but which are worldless in themselves, never 'touch' one another." [17]

Care-taking

Heidegger enumerates many different ways in which the to-be-in of *Dasein* comes to be. These ways are as follows: "having something

---

[15] Heidegger, *Vorträge*, p. 192.
[16] *Ibid.*, p. 202.
[17] Heidegger, *Sein und Zeit*, p. 55.

to do with something; producing something; consuming something; abandoning something or letting it get lost; undertaking, accomplishing, inquiring, questioning, considering, talking over, determining . . ." [18] All these activities show man's interest in things, his anxiety about things, and his concern for them. Expressed in one word all these activities can be called care-taking (*Besorgnis*). To-be-in is to-be-careful in the sense of to-take-care-of. Care-taking is not an occasional feature of man but a feature essentially belonging to him. Even when *Dasein* stops doing things, abandons them, misses them, or is careless about them, even then these activities are only possible because *Dasein* is essentially a careful or care-taking being.

Care-taking is the basis of man's relation to the world, and in no wise is this basis the reference of man as a subject to the world as an object. In the world man can encounter things. Man is a caretaker because he is worldly. Cognition is also one of the ways of care-taking. When *Dasein* abstains from direct dealings with things and merely stands facing them as a spectator, only then is it in a cognitive care-taking mode. In cognitive care-taking, *Dasein* encounters things simply by means of their looks. These looks, again, are more or less determined by the directions of our viewpoints. In his later works Heidegger frequently comes upon these problems while considering the nature of metaphysics. The first move to consider things 'optically' had been made by Plato with his ideas. 'The 'idea' is a look granting a view into beings." [19] With Plato, Western thought turned into subjectivism.

Understanding beings as objects, and man as a subject, modified the concept of truth. For the early Greek philosophers, truth was the disclosure of reality, and in the era of subjectivism (or metaphysics), truth was considered to be an agreement between the subject and the object. According to Heidegger, we do not carry the images of things around in our consciousness to compare them occasionally with the things outside of our consciousness, but when we apprehend, talk, or merely think of things, we are with the things themselves outside of us. On the other hand, all 'outside' is 'inside' in respect to *Dasein* or to-be-in-the-world. Therefore the place of the truth is not consciousness or a sentence but reality itself.

---

[18] *Ibid.*, pp. 56–57.
[19] Martin Heidegger, *Platons Lehre von der Wahrheit* (Bern: Francke Verlag, 1954), p. 34.

IV. WORLD

Surroundings

Traditional philosophy does not come upon the problem of the world because it does not think primarily enough. Dealing with the beings as disposables, it can never encounter the world itself, which is prior to beings and is always presupposed by them. Things are always within the world; without the world they cannot be encountered. Since the world, on the other hand, is always in the form of to-be-in-the-world (there is no world without a wordly being), beings or things by presupposing world presuppose *Dasein*. "World is a characteristic of *Dasein* itself." [20]

In everyday life we exist inauthentically. Therefore to-be-in-the-world is rather to-be-in-the-surroundings (*Umwelt*), because the inauthentic world is surroundings. The inauthentic world (surroundings), nevertheless, is a mode of the world. Just as everydayness retains the structure of *Dasein*, so surroundings retain the structure of the world. In order to approach and reveal the phenomenon of the world, Heidegger proceeds to investigate the surroundings and the beings within the surroundings.

In his everyday life man is constantly dealing with things by using, making or handling them. In all these dealings man is not guided by a theoretic, but rather by an 'existentiel' knowledge. For Heidegger, this 'existentiel' knowledge is not opposed to theoretical knowledge simply as non-theoretical, and it is not an inferior knowledge. This knowledge is prior to theoretical as well as practical knowledge as both are conventionally understood.[21] The everyday dealings with things, Heidegger calls commerce (*Umgang*). "The manipulating commerce is not blind; it has its own way of seeing, which guides manipulations and grants to them a specific 'thingness.'" [22]

Implement

The primary encounter with things is not subjective; therefore, these things cannot be treated as objects. Objects are the things or beings in theoretical, visualized relation to a subject. They have

[20] Heidegger, *Sein und Zeit*, p. 64.
[21] Cf. p. 27.
[22] Heidegger, *Sein und Zeit*, p. 69.

clear-cut contours and are definable; they belong to a certain system
or order into which they are statically fitted. The beings or things, as
encountered by the inauthentic *Dasein*, i.e. by the to-be-in-the-
surroundings, are not objects. Things of the surroundings Heidegger
calls implements (*Zeug*). Implements are not visualized or known
objectively, but they are used in our everyday commerce and known
circumspectly (*umsichtlich*). Things, in the sense of objects, Heidegger
calls disposables (*Vorhandenheiten*); they are there disposed to our
practical or theoretical consideration. They are faced by our passive,
merely viewing attitude and lie ready for our use or disposition, but
actually they are not used. Implements are always determined by
usage. Even if they are not used immediately, still they are sometimes
used, or can be used, or were used. Implements belong to care-taking
commerce.

An implement never has a meaning in itself; it is always related to
a totality. Its basic feature is in its 'for' (a pencil is *for* writing; a
hatchet is *for* chopping; a car is *for* riding). The 'for' refers to the
totality, and from this totality it receives its meaning. A bolt has no
meaning in itself. In reference to the bridge where this bolt is holding
the steel framework, it becomes meaningful and is what it is – a bolt.
However, the bridge is not the totality, but rather the modern traffic
system to which this bridge refers is the totality. The bridge with all
its parts, the sections of town and country, the vehicles, roadhouses,
and maps – all belong or refer to this totality. Even the traffic system
itself is not the totality because it refers to our living surroundings.
These living surroundings are the totality. Fundamentally *they* give
meaning to the traffic system, bridge and bolt.

This reference ('for'), the basic feature of an implement, is not only
a reference to the totality (the surroundings) but also to other implements: beams, piers, roads, roadsigns, traffic lights, stores, motels,
picnic grounds, etc. Circumspection, the 'existentiel' cognition, in
knowing all these implements, already presupposes the knowledge of
living surroundings. Our circumspection never starts with a detail (a
bolt), but approaches all the details from the totality (surroundings).
Before an implement is discovered, "the implement-totality is always
prediscovered." [23] Most of the time, however, the everyday *Dasein* does
not have a clearly apprehended concept or idea of this totality or even
of the implements.

The more an implement is fitted for its purpose, the more primarily

[23] *Ibid.*

36   DASEIN

the user is related to it, the less this implement appears as a thing of
objective consideration, i.e. as an object. The way of being of an implement Heidegger calls handiness (*Zuhandenheit*). Handiness cannot be
theoretically discovered, but can only be disclosed in circumspect
commerce. Circumspection is the cognition where the knower subordinates himself to the reference complexity of the 'fors' (*Um-zu*).
Only by using a hammer, but not by objectively considering it, can we
discover its handiness. Just as the 'commercial' way of discovering
handiness is not blind, but has its own way of seeing, (circumspection founded in care-taking), so objective or cognitive discovery is
a mode of care-taking circumspection.

Disintegration of implements

The implements, the beings of our surroundings discovered by our
care-taking *Dasein*, are known circumspectly (i.e., by their handiness),
but not objectively. When do they become known objectively, i.e.
when do they become disposables rather than implements? According
to Heidegger, when an implement is not suitable for the work for which
it is used, when it is not fitted properly into the implement-totality to
which it refers, as well as to each implement in that totality, when it
tends to fall out of this totality by its unsuitability to it, then it becomes striking (*auffallend*). We start to see it as taken by itself, as
lying before us, as a 'disposable' which is not fitted to our disposition.
A driver on a smooth road does not notice or does not comprehend the
road objectively. He is merely using it as an implement, and is handy
with it. Only when he hits rough pavement, does the road strike him as
a road. Only then it becomes an object of somewhat objective consideration, namely: the road is then exposed to the driver as unsuitable
and not the way it should be. Then, and not until then, does the driver
know the way a good road should be: he comes to know it objectively.[24]

Besides 'strikingness' (*Auffallenheit*), Heidegger considers two other
ways which announce the objectivity of an implement. One of them is
the missing of an implement at work. When a worker, occupied with
some sort of work, needs a certain tool which is not at hand, he looks
for it as something taken out of the totality of the work, as something
for itself. This tool *quasi* falls out of the wholeness and becomes dis-
coverable as isolated and overlookable, i.e. objective. Heidegger refers
to this way of a thing becoming disposable as salience (*Aufdringlich-*

[24] Perhaps it should be noticed that nowadays rather the opposite is true: a smooth road
is noticeable or striking, whereas a bumpy road is very 'usual.'

keit). When an implement or tool of care-taking commerce is left un-completed and lies around calling for completion, it becomes striking in this specific way: it resists being fitted into surroundings by not being ready for them. By its non-readiness, this implement directs attention toward itself as isolated and standing out from the whole of the work. Such a way of announcing the objectivity of an imple-ment, Heidegger calls obstinacy *(Aufsässigkeit).*

These three modes of eliminating or individualizing implements from their natural whole: 'strikingness,' salience and obstinacy, are not the characteristics of objectivity as such, but rather the ways of losing the handiness of implements. By losing its handiness an imple-ment tends toward objectivity. These three modes of the loss of handiness cause a demolition of the wholeness of the work. They in-vade the framework of the 'for-ness' *(Um-zu)* [25] of the implements. In this demolition of the system of natural organization of the implements of the surroundings, not only singular implements become exposed, but also the totality itself. The whole 'workshop,' the surroundings, become visible. Indirectly "through this wholeness the world an-nounces itself," says Heidegger.[26] In this connection Arland Ussher remarks: "The 'world as world' is only revealed to me when things go wrong." [27]

Dasein *and the world*

Heidegger's investigation of things in their surroundings show how closely things are related to the world, and that the world is not a thing, nor the sum of things, but rather the totality toward which the implements are pointing by their structure – their 'fors.' *Dasein* always has the knowledge, although not always theoretical knowledge, of this reference-totality *(Verweisungsganzheit)* of the 'fors.' It is entrusted with it because *Dasein* essentially is to-be-in-the-world. Due to this worldliness, *Dasein* can use and discover implements in its care-taking commerce. The 'fors' *(Um-zu)* of the implements refer to *Dasein. Da-sein* is the basis of all implemental relations. Knowing world, and all references of implements to it, circumspectly, *Dasein* reveals itself as an understanding being. "To the being of *Dasein* belongs the under-

[25] To the structure of an implement belongs a 'for' (cf. p. 35) pointing toward the totality and toward the other implements. For example, a key is *for* opening another implement, namely a door; and both, key and door, are *for* the totality, namely the household.

[26] Heidegger, *Sein und Zeit*, p. 75.

[27] Arland Ussher, *Journey Through Dread* (New York: The Devin-Adair Company, 1955), p. 80.

standing of Being." [28] The everyday understanding of *Dasein* is
expressed in its ability to reveal the meanings and orders of its living
surroundings (the inauthentic world, which is nevertheless a mode of
the world), i.e. the openness of *Dasein* to Being. In *Dasein*'s openness
to Being "word and language are founded." [29] A talking being is a
worldly being.

The Heideggerian problem of world is not characterized by 'what,'
by substantiality (only disposables are substantial), but by 'how,' i.e.
by the way the world appears. Such a 'how'-structure Heidegger sees
in the Greek problem of cosmos. "κόσμος does not mean this or that
being which presses itself forward and oppresses us, nor does it mean
all of the beings taken together, but it signifies the 'state,' i.e. the 'how'
in which being is in its *wholeness*." [30] This 'how' of being in its
wholeness, namely the world, belongs to the structure of *Dasein*, the
to-be-in-the-world. Only in *Dasein* is the world (the 'how' in the whole)
revealed. "Consequently the world belongs directly to the human
Dasein, even though the world comprises all the beings and also the
Dasein with these beings in the whole." [31] In his post-*Sein und Zeit*
works, where Heidegger deals with Being itself rather directly, he
interprets the world as "the openness of Being." [32]

The world is not a thing, nor is it a framework for all things, but the
world *is* in a more primary way than *are* things. "In the moment that
the world opens itself, all the things obtain their leisure and haste,
their remoteness and proximity, their broadness and narrowness." [33]
The world opens itself only with man, the being who has the knowledge
of Being. The world is the realm wherein our history occurs, wherein
we encounter things and encounter ourselves. A stone or an animal is
a worldless being because it lacks openness (it is statically enclosed in
itself). Only a being which stands open to the openness of Being, has
a world. "The *Dasein* is a point where the world flashes up." [34]

[28] Heidegger, *Sein und Zeit*, p. 85.
[29] *Ibid.*, p. 87.
[30] Martin Heidegger, *Vom Wesen des Grundes* (Frankfurt a.M.: Vittorio Klostermann,
1949), p. 22.
[31] *Ibid.*
[32] Heidegger, *Humanismus*, p. 35.
[33] Heidegger, *Holzwege*, p. 34.
[34] Vietta, *op. cit.*, p. 58.

V. SPACE

Spatiality of implements

The structure of an implement is its reference (the 'for') toward the implement-totality. An implement belongs to the whole and refers to the other implements in a spatial way; it is near the whole and near the other things. An implement is characterized by nearness. The way of being of an implement (its handiness, at-handedness) shows this characteristic of nearness. The nearness of an implement is not identical with mathematically expressed nearness. For an astronomer, a star several light years away may be nearer than the glasses on his nose. The nearness of the implements is determined by *Dasein*'s circumspect handling and usage.

In human everyday commerce and dealings with the implements, they are always placed, not in respect to general mathematical space, but in respect to the other implements and their inter-relation. Things are always somewhere up on a shelf, down under a bench, outside near a tree, etc. "All 'wheres' are discovered and circumspectly elucidated by the affairs of everyday commerce, and are not determined and recorded by a surveying measurement of space." [35] Place does not appear simply as a place for itself, but as that which organically belongs to the implements. Places are not indifferent. Implements have their own place, where they belong, or they have places belonging to them. Things are 'placey.' Even if they are lying about, out of their proper places, still the place-character remains with them. For an implement not to be where it belongs means that it is essentially characterized by spatiality (placeness). The here or there, up above or down below, inside or outside, etc., have not just the character of nearness, but also of direction.

Just as an implement is not an object of theoretical consideration, so the circumspectial space of implements is not an object of a theoretical consideration. Place becomes striking and noticeable as a place only when an implement, which belongs in that place, is not there. The place stands out and becomes objectively noticeable.

Spatiality of Dasein

Space is based in the world as the context of all the meanings of the

[35] Heidegger, *Sein und Zeit*, p. 103.

implements.[36] In this characteristic of the world (context of meanings), the unity of space is based; in no wise is it based in the unity of mathematical space. Mathematical space is less primary: it builds itself up through the neutralization of the implemental places when they cease to belong circumspeçtly to the implements themselves. Such places are indifferent, and they are considered to be isolated and objectivized. They are not places anymore, but merely dimensions.

Just as all meaning-contexts (all 'fors' of the world) are pointing toward *Dasein*, so the spatiality of the implements is based on the care-taking (the to-be-in) of *Dasein*. "Encountering the handy things in the space of their surroundings is ontically possible only because the *Dasein* itself, in respect to its to-be-in-the-world is 'spatial.' " [37] The spatiality of *Dasein* is not identical with the spatiality of things. *Dasein*'s spatiality is a function of its commerce with the implements. *Dasein* places things. It places them by approximation and by direction.

The German word for 'distance' is '*Ferne*' or '*Entfernung*'; *Ferne* indicates remoteness and *Entfernung* – the distance between two points. Heidegger, however, treats the word *Entfernung* in a modified sense, namely, as *Ent-fernung*. *Ent-* stands for removal. Therefore, *Entfernung* for Heidegger is "a removal of remoteness",[38] i.e. a placing of the thing in the nearness of *Dasein*, in the realm of its surroundings.[39] Approximation is accomplished by approximating the implement from a distance, i.e. from a certain direction. Therefore, *Dasein* not only approximates, but also directs the implements. By approximating and directing the implements, *Dasein* organizes its ways and goings in its concrete world (surroundings). It develops the play-world (*Spielwelt*). In the play-world of *Dasein* the things (implements) have their places. Things are spatial because we, in a more primary way, are spatial.

VI. TOGETHERNESS

Dasein *as* co-Dasein

Dasein, the to-be-in-the-world, does not have a direct understanding of itself. Only by handling the implements, or dealing with the things

---

[36] An implement becomes meaningful by its reference (through its 'for' structure) to the world as the coherency of all these references.

[37] Heidegger, *Sein und Zeit*, p. 104.

[38] *Ibid.*, p. 105.

[39] Heidegger's coined words are not really 'coined'; they usually are the archaic forms in which the conventional words originated.

of its surroundings, does it reveal itself to itself as caretaker and as being in the world. It never reveals itself in isolation, however, but rather in togetherness with others. *Dasein* is always taking care of things, and in this care or at its work it meets other *Daseins* – not as things, but as to-be-together-in-the-world, i.e. as co-*Daseins*. We are together by doing things together; we are together in the same world. "The world of *Dasein* is the co-world. The to-be-in is the to-be-with-the-others." [40]

Togetherness with others belongs to our existential structure as one of our existentials, just as care-taking, worldliness, spatiality, etc. Our very existence has the character of togetherness, and only because of this character can we reveal the others and have their understanding. If our way of existing would not be existing-together, we would always be alone without knowing that we were alone; and never would we encounter the other *Daseins*. Since we are in the way of being together, even if we are away from physical togetherness with the others, we are still in the mode of togetherness. To be indifferent or even to hate the others is still a mode of togetherness.

Our to-be-in, besides being in the mode of taking care of the things of our surroundings, also is concerned with the care of other *Daseins*. This concern is guided by respect, as a way of knowing or under-standing others, just as the care-taking of implements is guided by circumspection, the understanding of the implemental beings of our surroundings. In respectful concern (*rücksichtige Fürsorge*), we reveal our being in togetherness with others. Concern is not a moral but an existential (ontological) attitude; it is a way of being. The unconcern for others, or recklessness in relation to them, is yet a mode of concern.

We understand each other, not by objective means or statements, but through the very way of our existence. We are (we exist) in the way of togetherness with others; therefore, we understand others. The understanding of others (just as of ourselves) is never a direct one. By taking care of the implements encountered in our surroundings, we understand ourselves in togetherness with others, i.e. we under-stand them too.

Inauthentic Dasein

In everyday life *Dasein* exists inauthentically. The inauthentic way of to-be-together is to-be-together in the sense of being identical with common man (*das Man*). "The common man, who is positively nobody

[40] Heidegger, *Sein und Zeit*, p. 118.

and yet everybody, though not as the sum of all men, prescribes the way of being for the everydayness." [41] *Dasein* as the common man is not its own self, but the self of another. It is not a self-reliant being. The common man goes to work at his appointed hour. After work he looks for some sort of entertainment or relaxation; in his proper time he takes a vacation. He reads what one is supposed to read and avoids things to be avoided. Sometimes he avoids crowds and seeks inner development. The common man, the nobody and everybody at the same time, dictates our culture. "Everybody is another and nobody is himself." [42] The domination of the common man tends to uniformity (everyone is an average person equal to others; everyone is selfless), and to publicity (all the ways of the common man are clearly marked out and publicly prescribed so that he does not need his own self to guide his ways). In his life there are no problems because these problems are solved by the common man. One must take it easy and live comfortably following the rules of the common man. Under the rules of the common man it is easier to live because "one depends on another; one is secured in another, and finally nobody is responsible. The common man unburdens the *Dasein* thus from its being itself by concealing its real self." [43]

Although the picture of the common man is drawn in negative colors in Heidegger's philosophy, nevertheless, the common man is not something strange to *Dasein* or something into which *Dasein* occasionally falls. The common man belongs to the structure of *Dasein*. "The common man is an existential and belongs as a primary phenomenon to the positive composition of *Dasein*." [44] Even if we return to our true self and live authentically, still we have only modified the common man in us. A man always discovers himself not as himself, but as the common man in himself. Living a life not his own (being inauthentically in his everyday world), he can reach and reveal his own self. This revelation is accomplished "as a removal of concealments and obscurities, as a smashing of the barriers with which *Dasein* bars itself from itself." [45] The inauthentic way of existence is needed to provide the grounds on which the authentic mode of being can be built. Authenticity is nothing but a modified inauthenticity. [46]

[41] *Ibid.*, p. 127.
[42] *Ibid.*, p. 128.
[43] Vietta, *op. cit.*, p. 51.
[44] Heidegger, *Sein und Zeit*, p. 129.
[45] *Ibid.*
[46] It is interesting to remark that Heidegger understands his own philosophy as an attempt to remove all the concealments imposed by traditional philosophy which concealed the primary, authentic thought of the early Greek thinkers.

VII. *DA* AS OPENNESS

Heidegger's thought is in no wise advanced thought, but rather archaic thought. This again is not primitive, but primary: it goes back to the very profound beginning of reality. In his thought he transcends all differentiations. The to-be-in-the-world is for him a unique phenomenon, where things, world, and man himself are revealed primarily. "The *Dasein* is its disclosure," says Heidegger, and immediately adds the interpretation of this remark: "the way of 'to be' of this being which is interested in its own being is the way of 'to be' its own *Da*." [47] The *Da* [48] for Heidegger is the openness or disclosure of *Dasein*. Disclosure belongs essentially to *Dasein* as its *Da* which it must be. *Da* is more basic and more primary than the concreteness. "The 'here' and 'there' are only possible in a '*Da*,' i.e. in the spatiality disclosed by a being which is the being of the *Da*." [49]

Mood

Disclosure of *Dasein* is primarily not theoretical, but rather mood-like. This mood in Heidegger's German terminology is called '*Befind-lichkeit*,' which implies moodness as well as the finding of oneself by oneself. We find ourselves in the world always in one or another mood. We do not start our existence, but we find ourselves as already existing, as already started. We find ourselves as thrown into the world not knowing from where, but as already disclosed, as being. We do not find ourselves as 'coldly' being-there: we undergo our being-there in one or another mood. To-be-in-the-world is never colorless: it is deeply penetrated by a color of one or another ontological mood; we always *are* in a mood-like way.

Moodness reveals *Dasein* as 'thrown' and not as "of its own making," [50] and yet moodness reveals it as a being which must be responsible for itself as though it were of its own making. *Dasein* has to overtake its 'thrownness' and be fully responsible for it. Our mood-like disclosure of ourselves is not a theoretical cognition of our 'whatness,' nevertheless it is in our mood that we disclose our *Da*. "In each

---

[47] Heidegger, *Sein und Zeit*, p. 133.
[48] The German word '*da*' implies spatiality as well as temporality and expresses concreteness. In English this word is usually translated by 'there' inadequately.
[49] Heidegger, *Sein und Zeit*, p. 132.
[50] Reinhardt, *op. cit.*, p. 136.

mood in which we feel ourselves in one or another way, our *Dasein* is
disclosed for us. We understand Being and yet we lack a concept." [51]
Our 'thrownness' is a burden given to us. We take it over as a way of
'to be' which we must be, and for which we are responsible. Egon
Vietta compares the disclosure of *Dasein* in mood, which discloses us
to ourselves as already existing, with a light which is suddenly turned
on in a dark room. This light "makes the description of the previously
dark room possible without a need to know who switched on the
light." [52]

In our revealing mood we are not revealed as isolated subjects, but
rather as the whole to-be-in-the-world. Along with our existence, the
existence of the other *Daseins*, the world, and the within-the-world-
beings are revealed. It is interesting that in finding ourselves in our
'thrownness,' most of the time we find ourselves as turned away from
ourselves, or better, as turning away from our 'thrownness' and
existing in an inauthentic way – not in the way in which we were
thrown. We find ourselves not as objects but as a way of 'to be,' and
this way of 'to be' is a way of withdrawing ourselves from our 'thrownness.' We exist dynamically.

Understanding

Understanding is another mode of *Dasein*'s disclosure. For Heidegger
this phenomenon does not coincide with the traditional concept of
understanding. Whereas the traditional concept of understanding
always refers to the intellectual or rational understanding, the Heideggerian understanding emphasizes the mode in which we live our over-
taken 'thrownness.' 'Understanding' (*Verstehen*) implies the 'stand'
found in the word itself. We have to be able to 'stand' our 'thrownness,'
in the sense that we have to carry it out by actively developing it (not
bringing it into a higher stage, but keeping it up in its primary heights).
Most of the time, however, we are falling away from 'thrownness' into
the inauthentic way of carrying it.

Understanding, as well as moodness, is an existential, – i.e. one of
the structural elements which constitutes the make-up of *Dasein* –
one of the basic ways in which *Dasein is* its *Da*. Moodness and understanding are not two different or separate ways of disclosing the
Dasein; they overlap each other. "Moodness has always its under-

---

51 Martin Heidegger, *Kant und das Problem der Metaphysik* (Frankfurt a.M.: Vittorio
Klostermann, 1951), p. 205.
52 Vietta, *op. cit.*, p. 40.

standing ... Understanding is always mood-like." [53] Just as moodness discloses the whole to-be-in-the-world, so, too, understanding discloses the whole to-be-in-the-world. By revealing the meanings of the implements (the primary things), understanding reveals the world and *Dasein* itself.

Basically understanding is ability. This ability is not an attribute of *Dasein* but is a mode of being. "*Dasein* is always that which it can *be*, and how it can *be* its own potential." [54] The potentials or possibilities of *Dasein* are those of taking care of things, of concern for others, and mainly the ability of *Dasein* to be for its own sake. These potentials or possibilities are not logical possibilities, nor categories of disposables, nor potentialities as opposed to actualities. The possibility of a disposable is that which is not yet actual, or that which is not indispensable. The existential possibility is not potentiality to some act but the very actuality of *Dasein*. *Dasein* essentially is its own possibility or possibilities; it is not the way *to something* but the way itself. Existential possibility is of more primary origin than categorical possibility; it is the basis from which categorical possibilities arise. *Dasein* is that in which all the 'fors' (meanings) of the implements are based; and from these implements the disposables originate. Therefore, *Dasein*, the existential possibility, is the most basic foundation of any kind of possibility or potentiality. Only on the basis of the existential possibility (the *Da*), can any categorical possibility be discovered or disclosed.

Moodness opens to *Dasein* certain possibilities which were not created by *Dasein* but into which it was thrown (*geworfen*). *Dasein* either positively seizes these possibilities or misses them, rejects them, or simply lets them pass away. *Dasein* is thrown into the world not as a factual being, but as an open possibility which may or may not be the way it is thrown. *Dasein* is a thrown possibility, a free being in its 'thrownness.' "*Dasein* is a possibility to be free for its very own way of being." [55]

Dasein does not passively undergo or subordinate itself to its 'thrownness,' but actively overtakes it or participates in it, i.e. it projects its own 'thrownness' (as though it were helping the thrower in throwing itself). "As thrown, *Dasein* is thrown into a projecting way of being." [56] *Dasein* is thrown so that it can project itself upon its thrown

[53] Heidegger, *Sein und Zeit*, p. 142.
[54] *Ibid.*, p. 143.
[55] *Ibid.*, p. 144.
[56] *Ibid.*, p. 145.

possibilities and thereby be an understanding being. "All projection and
consequently all 'creative' activities of man also are thrown." [57] Egon
Vietta compares projection (*Entwurf*), the possibility given to us in
our 'thrownness,' with an ability to swim which man must have in
order to survive in the sea of life.[58]

Understanding, the thrown projection, does not mean that man
explicitly understands all the possibilities into which he is thrown. If
he would do so, these possibilities would cease to be possibilities. In
understanding, possibility remains a possibility. "Understanding is,
as projection, the way of being of *Dasein* in which it *is* its possibilities
as possibilities." [59] In the thrown projection, as in mood-like understanding, *Dasein* sees in a mood-like fashion its own possibilities, and
on the quivering ground of these possibilities, exists.

With his problem of 'thrownness,' Heidegger accentuates the
finiteness of the human way of being. In his *Kant und das Problem der
Metaphysik*, Heidegger considers Kant's problems from the viewpoint
of *Sein und Zeit*. His intention is to show the finiteness of human
cognition. According to Heidegger's interpretation, Kant's cognition
is basically perception (*Anschauung*). "For any understanding of the
critique of pure reason, it is necessary to keep in mind: cognition
primarily is perception." [60] Kant deals with two kinds of cognition:
divine and human. Divine cognition originates that which is perceived
in perception, whereas human cognition presupposes it. "Divine
cognition is that act which first of all creates being as such perceived
in perception." [61] Human cognition, as "finite cognition, is non-
creative perception." [62] The basic feature of man is his finiteness;
human cognition, as well as sensuality and thinking, presuppose beings
not of human making, and thus, the finiteness of man. In thinking,
man directs himself to already existing beings and does not create
them. "Thinking as such, accordingly, is already the seal of finiteness." [63]

Although thinking presupposes beings, it has some spontaneity in
respect to the 'how' of the beings. This 'how' depends on the stand of
man, on his cognitive power. Heidegger does not consider divine
cognition, nor is he interested in the *Ding-an-sich*; because there

[57] Heidegger, *Kant*, p. 212.
[58] Vietta, *op. cit.*, p. 55.
[59] Heidegger, *Sein und Zeit*, p. 145.
[60] Heidegger, *Kant*, p. 29.
[61] *Ibid.*, p. 31.
[62] *Ibid.*
[63] *Ibid.*

cannot be anything said, positively or negatively, about what human *Dasein* cannot attain. Heidegger is only interested in Kant's problem of the finiteness of human cognition which, even though finite, is active by determining the 'how' of the beings known. Kant's cognition, as presupposing things not of human making, corresponds to Heidegger's problem of the 'thrownness' of *Dasein*. The activity of human cognition in respect to the 'how' of things in Kant, corresponds to projection [64] in Heidegger.

We are flung into a world with given possibilities which we either take over or reject (just another mode of taking over), develop or leave alone, take responsibility for or remain indifferent to. In any case, we are free and projecting, but our freedom as well as our projection is finite, i.e. always related to our thrown possibilities. The human *Dasein* is thrown into its own *Da*, "whereby the '*Da*' is supposed to indicate the fully determined place in which *Dasein* always finds itself placed. The fact that man could not choose the place for himself, according to his wishes or inclinations, but that he simply found it and thereby, from the very beginning, has been constrained and burdened – this fact thus is supposed to be expressed in the concept of 'thrownness.' " [65] Man did not bring himself into his *Da*; nevertheless, this *Da* belongs to him as his own. By taking the full responsibility for this *Da* or by rejecting it, the human *Dasein*, in either case, founds his own way of being. And yet, since he is dependant in his 'thrownness' (even his projecting possibility is given to him in his 'thrownness'), "understanding is not an attitude which man possesses as his feature; but, on the contrary, understanding is that event in whose possession man is." [66]

Parlance

Understanding is interpreting. All interpretation is done against the background of the world. *Dasein* approaches and encounters the things of its natural surroundings (implements) in the understanding

---

[64] Projection does not properly substitute the German *Entwurf*. Projection tends to a fully indetermined outline of some creative work. It does not even truly imply the character of possibility. German *Entwurf* indicates realization of the *Geworfenheit* (thrownness), the possibilities given in 'thrownness.' *Entwurf* means the throwing of oneself back along the path of 'thrownness' along which we primordially were thrown. *Entwurf* is re-jection in the properly philological sense of the prefix 're-,' namely, re-jection in the sense of throwing back, throwing again, re-throwing along the path given in 'thrownness.' Such a 're-jection' is analogous to 're-making,' where making holds the path of former making.

[65] Otto Friedrich Bollnow, *Existenzphilosophie* (Stuttgart: W. Kohlhammer Verlag, n.d.), p. 350.

[66] Heidegger, *Einführung*, p. 108.

of the world. The world gives meaning or significance to implements. Through the understanding of the world the meanings of implements are revealed. *Dasein* is in a position to apply (*bewenden*) them with regard to their meanings or significances. This application can be characterized through its structure, namely 'something as something.' With this structure of 'existentiel' [67] interpretation of implements, *Dasein* adopts its understandings. Interpretation, as the adoption of these understandings, is the knowing that an implement is a 'something for.' [68] In order to know what application a thing has, the knowledge of the world, the context of all applications, is needed. Such a knowledge Heidegger calls pre-possession (*Vorhabe*). All interpretation is based on this pre-possession. The course of interpretation is guided by the respect in which the implement is interpreted. Such a respect, in accordance with which the implement is interpreted, Heidegger calls pre-sight (*Vorsicht*). Through the pre-possession and the pre-sight the understandable thing becomes apprehendable; it tends to a certain conceptuality. This intention towards a conceptuality is called pre-grasp (*Vorgriff*).

Approaching the implements with pre-possession, pre-sight, and pre-grasp, *Dasein* makes them understandable by giving them meanings. The meanings of things are based in *Dasein*. A meaning is never primarily located in a judgment, but in *Dasein*. Since judgment is based on interpretation (as an existential, a way of being of *Dasein*), it has a meaning in a secondary sense. As the originator of all meanings of things, *Dasein*, however, is not totally unrestrained with respect to rendering these meanings. *Dasein* is not a subject, but a to-be-in-the-world. The structures of things are based and rooted in *Dasein* as in the to-be-in-the-world. The world is the context of all meanings. On the other hand, world is the openness of Being; and man is the only being who partakes openly in the world. Therefore interpretation, as granting meanings to things, can only happen in human *Dasein*.

The existential in which the phenomenon of interpretation is based, Heidegger calls parlance (*Rede*). Along with moodness and understanding, parlance is the basic structural element constructing the phenomenon *Da*. Just as moodness is understanding and understanding is mood-like, so moodness as well as understanding is interpreted and articulated. As the mood-like "articulation of the understanding," [69]

---

[67] Cf. p. 27.
[68] Cf. p. 35.
[69] Heidegger, *Sein und Zeit*, p. 161.

parlance is not language but the foundation of language. The meanings of implements are bases for words. "First there is a uniqueness of meaning. Later it is expressed by a word." [70] The *Da* as the revelation or disclosure reveals itself by moodness, understanding, and parlance. Since all of these structural elements of *Dasein* actually are one unique phenomenon, it is more adequate to say that "the mood-like understanding of the to-be-in-the-world utters itself as parlance." [71]

Just as togetherness with others belongs to to-be-in-the-world, so the disclosed *Da* is a *Da* of togetherness (the co-*Da*), mood is co-mood, understanding is co-understanding, and parlance is a heard parlance. Hearing is "existential openness of *Dasein* as co-being [72] with the others." [73] We understand and hear others because we are in the same world with them, handling implements together.

We hear because we understand. We never hear just plain noises. We hear a storm in the trees, a crackling fire, a tapping woodpecker, etc. Even if we hear a language we don't understand, still we hear an unfamiliar language – not simply noises. We are always with things; we are dealing with their meanings; we participate in parlance; therefore, we can talk and have a language. A language always presupposes a certain interpretability of *Dasein*'s understanding which is parlance. In his late works Heidegger goes deeper into the problem of language and clearly states that parlance is the language of Being and that existentially interpreted meanings primarily belong to Being. Our understanding as well as our language is a response to the parlance of Being.

In the everyday usage of language, the speaker and the listener are not oriented to the parlance, but they merely stick to the spoken words and their combinations separated from their ontological basis (parlance). Thus, the *dictum* replaces reality and becomes the location of truth. Such an eradicated parlance, Heidegger calls chatter (*Gerede*). Just as parlance means the disclosure (openness and also truth) of *Dasein*, so chatting means the opposite, namely, the concealment (untruth) of *Dasein*.

The *Da*, the revealed to-be-in, is an illumination of *Dasein*. An illumination makes seeing possible. When in the everydayness chatting veils the illumination of *Dasein*, sight is replaced by curiosity (*Neugier*). Curiosity is a sight but not a sight of understanding; it does not see to

---

[70] Vietta, *op. cit.*, p. 71.
[71] Heidegger, *Sein und Zeit*, p. 161.
[72] 'Being' is used here as the participle of the verb 'to be.'
[73] Heidegger, *Sein und Zeit*, p. 163.

understand but merely to see. In curiosity, *Dasein* is going after the
new and the sensational. It hops continuously from one sensation to
another, and therefore is characterized by lack of sojourning (*Unver-
weilen*). The lack of sojourning of curiosity expresses the eradication
(*Entwurzelung*) of the everydayness of *Dasein*.

In everyday *Dasein*, chatting and curiosity make everything appear
clear and understandable although nothing is actually understood.
This ambiguity (*Zweideutigkeit*) is the third phenomenon of everyday
Dasein.

Chatting, curiosity, and ambiguity, the three forms of eradicated
Dasein, express the inauthentic level of being of the common man.
Such inauthentic existence is called by Heidegger the decline (*Ver-
fallenheit*) of *Dasein*. In decline, as a way of being, *Dasein* is cut off
from itself, estranged from itself, living without decisions – a safe,
fully determined life in the realm of the common man. Decline is not
a falling out of *Dasein*: it still is *Dasein*, although inauthentic. Inauthentic existence is not separated from the authentic way of being,
but the authentic way of being is merely a modification of the inauthentic, declining way of to be. Decline even belongs to the disclosure
of *Da* (there cannot be any disclosure without previous concealment,
no truth without untruth, no upcoming without decline). In decline
Dasein is disclosed, however inauthentically, i.e. as a common
man but not as *Dasein* in its own self. Even in decline *Dasein* is interested in self – however, not its own self, but the self of the common
man – worrying about it, and taking care of it. The inauthentic understanding of Being in decline is still a mode of an understanding of
Being. "Being may be uncomprehended, but it never is fully un-
understood." [74]

Truth

Dasein exists as disclosure. This disclosure (*Da*) is presupposed in
order that any beings be revealed; even Being itself announces itself
only in the *Dasein*.

Indeed, only as long as a *Dasein* is, i.e., only as long as there is an ontic
possibility of understanding of Being, does Being 'give itself.' If *Dasein* does not
exist, then there 'is' no 'independence' and there 'is' no 'in itself.' Such phenomena are neither understandable nor ununderstandable. Furthermore, if
Dasein does not exist, then the within-the-world-being is neither disclosable
nor can it lie in concealment, and also if *Dasein* does not exist *then* it can neither
be said that a being is nor that it is not. However, as long as there is an under-

[74] *Ibid.*, p. 183.

standing of Being – and therefore an understanding of disposability [75] – it can *now* be said that being will yet abide.[76]

Disclosure, for Heidegger, is a problem of utmost importance. The essence of truth, according to him, is *aletheia*, disclosure. Since *Dasein* discloses, it is the basic truth in which all the truths of beings are rooted. The truth of the within-the-world-things is less truth than the truth of *Dasein*, because *Dasein* as disclosure is a way of being which makes possible any disclosability or truth. The truth of *Dasein* is a to-be-disclosing, and the truth of within-the-world-things is a to-be-disclosed.

In its everydayness, *Dasein* discloses (or unconceals) itself out of its inauthentic interpretation which ontologically is concealment. In everyday *Dasein* the phenomena are concealed; however, they are not fully concealed, but rather distorted, i.e. disclosed as not what they really are. They reveal themselves in the mode of seemingness. Concealment as distortion belongs to the disclosure of *Dasein*. Whatever is disclosed falls back again into concealment; *Dasein* is always in the untrue. "The full existential-ontological meaning of the sentence '*Dasein* is true' says simultaneously '*Dasein* is untrue.' " [77] Consequently, a disclosure can never be accomplished once and for all. The truth has to be continuously re-uncovered and gained by fighting against seemingness.

The disclosure of *Dasein* formulates itself in the parlance. The parlance is not a language; although, without the parlance no language is possible. Since *Dasein* understands the parlance, language and verbal statements are possible. Gradually our statements leave their primary context within the parlance and become disposable beings. Parlance itself falls into forgottenness and becomes replaced by a language as the sum of words disposed to our usage. The to-be-disclosing (as an understanding of the parlance) as well as the to-be-disclosed (as the truth of beings) become disposable beings. The relation between the to-be-disclosing and the to-be-disclosed becomes a relation between a disposable language in one's mind and the disposable object named or labeled by the term of language – a relation between the intellect and the object. The truth then is an agreement, *adequatio intellectus et rei*. According to Heidegger, a sentence is not the place of truth, but the *Dasein* is the place of sentence, i.e. the ontological condition of the

[75] Objectivity.
[76] Heidegger, *Sein und Zeit*, p. 212.
[77] *Ibid.*, p. 222.

truthfulness or falseness of the sentence or judgment. Since all the truths of beings are rooted in the primary truth of *Dasein*, there cannot be any eternal truths unless *Dasein* is eternally existing. This applies to the untruth as well. Truth as well as untruth is "relative in respect to the being of *Dasein*." [78]

VIII. DREAD

'Thrownness' reveals *Dasein* as not created by itself but as given to itself, and not as starting at a certain point but as already there (*da*). Most of the time *Dasein* is revealed not in its authentic self but as declining from itself. This declining *Dasein* is revealed in 'thrownness' as clinging to the self of the common man, but not to its own self. This fleeing, of course, does not disclose the self; nevertheless, it points to it as to that from which the declining *Dasein* is fleeing. "Only because *Dasein* ontologically is brought before itself through disclosure which essentially belongs to it, can it flee from itself." [79]

In its 'thrownness' *Dasein* is brought before itself, not in an indifferent manner, but in a mood-like manner. The most apt mood to reveal the self of the *Dasein*, according to Heidegger, is dread. Phenomenologically he describes dread as distinguished from fear. Fear is always a fear of a within-the-world-being which approaches *Dasein* from a certain direction and raises fear in it. The flight of the everyday *Dasein* from its own self is not a flight from a within-the-world-being because the everyday *Dasein* is frankly turned toward the within-the-world-beings and is not fleeing from them. Dread approaches from nowhere, i.e. from no direction; and it is there so close "that it constrains one and takes his breath away." [80] Dread does not come from any direction; that which raises dread is nowhere. However, according to Heidegger, this 'nowhere' is prior to any 'where'; it is that in which all the 'wheres' are rooted; it is the world itself. 'From no direction' means 'from the world.'

In dread, all the within-the-world-beings appear to be meaningless. Only in the complete meaninglessness of the within-the-world-beings can the world as such and the to-be-in-the-world as such appear. Dread as fleeing away from the to-be-in-the-world reveals this to-be-in-the-

[78] *Ibid.*, p. 227.
[79] *Ibid.*, pp. 184–185.
[80] *Ibid.*, p. 186.

world. On the other hand, that for whose sake *Dasein* is in dread is its own self, the to-be-in-the-world. Revealing our self (even though not thematically), dread frees us to our authentic way of being. In dread, the familiarity of the realm of the common man disintegrates, and *Dasein* is thrown into its own self (from the common man's self). This to-be-self is gloomy and uneasy. In his German terminology, Heidegger expresses this uneasiness with the word '*Unheimlichkeit*,' which in addition to uneasiness, implies homelessness. In the realm of the common man, *Dasein* is in a secure home. Dread throws it out of this security and forces it be itself. Fleeing from its own self in its everydayness, *Dasein* flees the uneasiness of homelessness.

Dread is not a psychological factor, but is truly ontological and of profound importance. Dread is not the only mood of this kind. However, any other existential mood basically is dread. "Boredom, depression, desperation become of existential importance thereby repeating, in corresponding forms, the performance of dread, i.e. recalling man out of the everydayness of his *Dasein* into the authenticity of his existence. These moods basically are only shadings at the final end of the same basic mood." [81] Eugen Fink sees this basic mood as enthusiasm or the lack of Being by which the essence of man is signified. The degree of the lack of Being indicates man's ontological intensity. "The greatness or pettiness of man is determined by the power of his enthusiasm. From the most wanting soul the ladder of the order of precedence descends to the trouble of having-no-troubles which [82] is implied in the dull, impious self-satisfaction, where no star shines in the sky of man and all desire of the soul is extinguished." [83] Fink's enthusiasm is ontologically the same phenomenon as Heidegger's dread. In it he sees that which frees man to his very self. The objections to Heidegger as a pessimistic philosopher, on the basis of his investigation of the phenomenon of dread, show only a failure to grasp the true meaning of this investigation. Through dread Heidegger points out man's essential reference to Being. Whether this reference is revealed by dread or by enthusiasm is not of any substantial importance.

Dread reveals man as a being who not only *is*, but who *is related to* his own way of being. In dread, *Dasein* comes upon itself from its authentic self; in understanding it is related to itself as its own possibility – it is ahead of itself; and in decline it falls away from its au-

[81] Bollnow, *op. cit.*, p. 372.
[82] The security of the inauthentic everydayness is 'the trouble of having-no-troubles.'
[83] Eugen Fink, *Vom Wesen des Enthusiasmus* (Freiburg i.Br.: Verlag Dr. Hans V. Chamier, 1947), p. 13.

thentic self. In all these basic existentials *Dasein* is out-of-itself. To exist, to-be-in-the-world, is the to-be-out-of-itself of *Dasein. Dasein* can only be ahead of itself because it is already there (*da*); it is thrown. Also, *Dasein* is always in the factual world, always deals with things and lives an everyday life, is always declining. The full ontological structure of *Dasein*, Heidegger expresses as "to-be-ahead-of-oneself as already to-be-in-the-world by being with the within-the-world encountered beings." [84] In one word 'care' (*Sorge*), Heidegger expresses this whole complex structure of *Dasein*. Care is the basic existential-ontological phenomenon. It includes in itself care-taking (respect for the things), concern (respect for the others), and self-concern (care for *Dasein*'s own self).

IX. DEATH

Death and wholeness of Dasein

Dasein exists dynamically. It is the possibility of development, essentially a relation, a way. *Dasein* is signified by non-termination. A terminated *Dasein* is not *Dasein* any longer. "As long as *Dasein* is a being it has never attained its wholeness. If it attains it, then this gain becomes a loss of the to-be-in-the-world all together" [85]; this gain is death. Since *Dasein* essentially is un-whole, the achievement of wholeness is its death. Death in this existential sense is different from mere biological death, called by Heidegger cessation (*Verenden*). Cessation is the going out of the world of a being which merely lives, whereas death is *Dasein*'s going out of the world.

In its togetherness with others, *Dasein* frequently can be substituted by others; however, each *Dasein* must die itself. "In death everyone is alone with himself." [86] Death is *Dasein*'s very own and inevitable possibility of the impossibility of *Dasein*. The impossibility of *Dasein* is not something separated from *Dasein*. "*Dasein* always exists in such a way that to it belongs its 'not-as-yet.' " [87] Therefore death belongs to the structure of *Dasein*. Heidegger stresses that death is not an ending in the sense that *Dasein* diminishes and finally disappears, but rather a way of 'to be' which constantly faces death. According to

---

[84] Heidegger, *Sein und Zeit*, p. 192.
[85] *Ibid.*, p. 236.
[86] Vietta, *op. cit.*, p. 108.
[87] Heidegger, *Sein und Zeit*, p. 243.

Egon Vietta, death is the "co-fashioner of life." [88] Death is interspersed into our life and gives to it a specific mark. It belongs to life. "Death in the widest sense is a phenomenon of life." [89]

Although *Dasein* is constantly its 'not-as-yet,' this does not mean that its 'not-as-yet' is already there. If it were there, it would cease to be a 'not-as-yet.' Death, this 'not-as-yet' of *Dasein*, remains a 'not-as-yet' as long as *Dasein* exists. *Dasein* is constantly facing its death, the possibility of the impossibility of its *Dasein*. This constant facing of death throws *Dasein* back into its very own existence, its very own self (just as *Dasein* dies itself, so in facing death *Dasein* exists itself, exists authentically). Everydayness discloses our inauthentic self, and ever-present death reveals our authentic self. Death is just like a wall which, after having been hit by man, "throws man back into his authentic existence ... without this wall, without this repulsion, the authentic self of *Dasein* would not be visible to *Dasein*." [90] Reflected from death, light illuminates *Dasein* in its wholeness. Death is that which makes *Dasein* really *Dasein*, just as night makes day to stand out as day. Without night, day would never be perceived as day; it would lack its somethingness. According to Karl Lehmann, death is "the power which holds *Dasein* together." [91]

In Heidegger's problem of death, Karl Lehmann sees traces of the poet Rainer Maria Rilke, the novelist Leo Tolstoi and the philosopher George Simmel. Rilke saw life and death in a deep unity. According to him, modern people do not know authentic death just as they do not know authentic life. "Previously," Lehmann quotes Rilke, "they used to know (or may be they had a presentiment) that they had death in themselves like a seed in fruit." [92] Tolstoi also thought that death "dwells" [93] in us. In the same context Lehmann brings up a thought of Simmel which has a somewhat Heideggerian character. "Death," he quotes Simmel, "limits, i.e., forms our life not merely in the hours of death, but it remains a formal moment of our life which affects all its contents. The limiting of the whole of life by death acts upon each instant of life." [94] Lehmann illustrates Simmel's though by comparing death to the peel of fruit. "Just as fruit is held togethe

---

[88] Vietta, *op. cit.*, p. 111.
[89] Heidegger, *Sein und Zeit*, p. 246.
[90] Vietta, *op. cit.*, p. 113.
[91] Karl Lehmann, *Der Tod bei Heidegger und Jaspers* (Heidelberg: Evangelische Verl: J. Comtesse, 1938), p. 75.
[92] *Ibid.*, p. 70.
[93] *Ibid.*, p. 71.
[94] *Ibid.*

by its limiting peel," he says, "so human life, only by its limiting and forming death, is preserved from elapsing into substancelessness and formlessness." [95] Also O. F. Bollnow in his *Existenzphilosophie* indicates that the Heideggerian problem of death does not consider the moment of dying, but "the meaning that this event has today, this very day, for this my momental life and the transforming power exercised on life by the knowing of death." [96] Death is so much involved in existence itself that without it existence is not adequately grasped. "To exist means to stand face to face with death." [97]

Death and dread

The phenomenon of death is closely related to the phenomenon of dread. Dread is the basic mood which brings *Dasein* from its being lost in its everyday life back into its authentic way of being. Since facing death is the authentic way of existing, so dread is that which brings *Dasein* to face its death. To be in dread, to exist authentically, or to die – in all these cases, ontologically one and the same event is considered. "The being-to-death is essentially dread." [98]

Dread is not the fear of death as cessation but rather the anguish of the authentic way of existing. The everyday *Dasein* flees death because to die is uneasy. Since *Dasein* is constantly dying, "it is constant uneasiness itself." [99] Uneasiness as *Unheimlichkeit* is not just uneasiness but also homelessness. To die, as to be authentic, is at the same time to be outside of the secure realm of the common man – to be homeless. The realm of the common man takes away uneasiness and bestows tranquillity. In everyday life everyone knows that one has to die someday, but since this 'one' is 'no one,' so death, too, does not belong explicitly to anyone. The inauthentic *Dasein* lives a life where death does not implicitly belong, where it is not permitted, and where it can only invade. *Dasein* in everyday life avoids death, closes its eyes to it, lives deathlessly. Even this avoidance of death shows that existence is marked by death.

Death and truth

Death discloses *Dasein* in its truth. Since everyday *Dasein* is a selfless or deathless way of existing, it is in concealment – in untruth.

[95] *Ibid.*, pp. 71–72.
[96] Bollnow, *op. cit.*, p. 376.
[97] *Ibid.*, p. 403.
[98] Heidegger, *Sein und Zeit*, p. 266.
[99] Heidegger, *Einführung*, p. 121.

Untruth – here best described as existence without facing death – is a mode of truth or is an attitude in respect to death. The flight from death is not just negative: it gives a specific mark to *Dasein*. Death is always, even in the inauthentic way of existence, a possibility of *Dasein*. This possibility is not a potentiality which can be actualized in an event. This would simply mean suicide. Death can be a forming factor of our existence when it remains a possibility. "In our being to death ... possibility must be understood as possibility in its full strength, must be developed as possibility and must be preserved as a possibility in our relation to it." [100] When death is preserved as death (as the possibility of impossibility of our *Dasein*) it reveals our *Dasein* authentically. This authentic way of existence which preserves death as a possibility and thus discloses *Dasein* in its truth, Heidegger calls forward-running (*Vorlaufen*). Running forward into the possibility of impossibility of our existence is the *Dasein*'s way of being. We *are*, due to our running forward to death, to our openness to death. Here is the point where death throws *Dasein* into existence. In death, in this extreme possibility, *Dasein* is disclosed in its wholeness; it is in its truth. Death strikes *Dasein* in its very self and shows it in its funda-mental truth. Here everything that was of importance, everything that was taken care of, and everything that was of deep concern – all this is drifting away in the sense that it is losing its reputation as the ultimate ontological ground. Everything that seemed to be of utmost importance, that seemed to give foundation to our life, disintegrates and falls apart. Only our very own ontologically denuded self remains. The being-to-death throws light on the inauthenticity of everydayness and shows to *Dasein* where it is standing and thus frees it to an au-thentic way of being.

X. CONSCIENCE

Conscience as call of self

Self is not a thing and not an I-thing, but a way to be, a way to exist. *Dasein* in everyday existence is not a self, but a oneself (the self of the common man). The authentic self, again, is not something fully separated from the oneself, but is rather its modification. As decline, everydayness is an existential and necessarily belongs to the structure of *Dasein*. The modification of everyday existence is accomplished by

100 Heidegger, *Sein und Zeit*, p. 261.

choosing a way of being based on the very self of *Dasein* instead of on the oneself. In this choice the phenomenon of conscience is involved.

The phenomenon of conscience is usually characterized as that which brings something forth for understanding, i.e. as that which discloses something. Consequently, it belongs to the disclosure of *Dasein*. That which brings forth something for understanding, or simply that which calls, is our own self. In conscience, our self calls us back from having been lost in the selfless realm of the common man; it calls from the common self back into our own self. The call of conscience does not narrate anything concerning the beings or things. It does not come from a certain direction, but rather from nowhere (just as dread approaches from nowhere). And that which this call says is rather nothing, because it has nothing to do with the points of interest of everyday life. "The call does not declare anything, does not give any information concerning world-events, narrates nothing. Not at all does it strive to open a soliloquy with the appealed self. There is 'nothing' to be said to the appealed self; it merely is *called onto* itself, i.e. to its authentic way of being." [101] Although the call of conscience is a call of my self, nevertheless, it is not a call planned by me or accomplished by the efforts of my will. This call is completely strange to me in respect to my everyday self; it is uneasy and thus dreadful. Following this call, I exist authentically; refusing to follow it or fleeing from it, I am declining, i.e. I exist inauthentically.

Guilt

Since conscience is always related to guilt, Heidegger also, along with the consideration of conscience, deals with the phenomenon of guilt. Guilt for Heidegger is not a moral but rather an ontological phenomenon. Guilt is not brought about or caused by an act of guilt; on the contrary, we can commit an act of guilt because we are guilty in our existence.

Heidegger sees the basis for guilt in the lacking character which essentially belongs to the structure of *Dasein*. This lacking character Heidegger calls nullity (*Nichtigkeit*). He sees it in the fact that *Dasein* was thrown into its *Da*; it did not bring itself into it; *Dasein* did not start itself, but found itself already there (*da*). *Dasein* did not lay down its own ontological foundations; they were given to it in its 'thrownness.' And yet *Dasein* must be its own foundation by projecting itself upon possibilities given to it in its 'thrownness.' 'Thrownness' is not

101 *Ibid.*, p. 273.

an event which happened once and for all in the past; we are constantly projecting ourselves on the possibilities given us in our 'thrownness.' We can never go beyond our 'thrownness' and start ourselves without a given basis; yet we ourselves *are* the given basis. "Being-self, *Dasein* is a thrown being as self. It is released not through its self but upon its self – from the basis which it must be." [102] The very self of *Dasein* is given to *Dasein*. 'Thrownness' is the mark of *Dasein*'s nullity – mark of its guilt.

The nullity of *Dasein* is revealed not only in the 'thrownness' but also in projection. While projecting itself on certain possibilities of its 'thrownness,' *Dasein* necessarily has to reject the other possibilities. Egon Vietta illustrates the nullity of projecting with an example of a light in the forest. "The light can only be caught by those trees confronting the light. Though each tree is touched by the same light, nevertheless each singular tree is the 'cause' for its not being the *whole* light. Each tree is 'guilty,' because by being only *a* possibility of catching the light it never is master of the dawned light." [103]

Dasein's inauthentic way of being in its decline (selfless existence) is also featured by nullity. The whole structure of *Dasein*, expressed by care, as the declining–thrown projection, in each of its basic structural moments, is marked by nullity. "The *Dasein* as such is guilty." [104] This ontological understanding of guilt in Heidegger's philosophy is more primary than the understanding of guilt in respect to traditionally understood morality. The traditional *bonum* (and *malum* as *privatio boni*) is not based on existential but on categorical ontology, and therefore it is ontologically inferior (less primary).

Belonging essentially to *Dasein*, guilt remains concealed in its inauthentic way of existence. The call of conscience calls *Dasein* from its guiltless everydayness into the guilt of authenticity. Conscience calls us back to our forgotten guilt, calls us back to our 'thrownness,' as the null-basis of our null-freedom (we are free in projecting ourselves upon our thrown possibilities). The call of conscience is soundless because it calls directly our self-being and skips the care-taken implements and needs of everyday importance. By hearing the call of conscience, *Dasein* chooses itself and thus becomes free.

---

[102] *Ibid.*, p. 284.
[103] Vietta, *op. cit.*, p. 116.
[104] Heidegger, *Sein und Zeit*, p. 285.

Resoluteness

According to Heidegger, we do not choose conscience or the call of
conscience, but, on the contrary, conscience chooses us by calling us.
We choose ourselves merely as being open for the call of conscience.
This openness is readiness for the authentic way of existence. By being
ready for an authentic way of existence, we understand our self in its
guilt, i.e. we disclose our self as guilty. Secondly, in its readiness for
the call of conscience, *Dasein* discloses itself in the uneasiness of its
isolation in its own self. Since the call of conscience is not coming from
the realm of the common man, it rather comes from the authentic self,
which is in uneasy homelessness. Therefore the readiness for the call
of conscience is a readiness for dread. Thirdly, the readiness of *Dasein*
for the call of conscience is silence. By keeping silent, *Dasein* is ready
for the call of conscience. "The parlance of conscience never comes to
divulgence. Conscience calls only soundlessly, i.e. the call comes from
the silence of uneasiness and calls the summoned *Dasein* as hushed
back into the silence of itself." [105]

The readiness of *Dasein* to the call of conscience is thus expressed
in each of the three basic ways of *Dasein*'s disclosure, namely: in
understanding (as understanding of authentic *Dasein* in its guilt), in
moodness (as dreadful uneasiness of self), and in parlance (as the
silence of authentic *Dasein* which is diametrically different from the
noisiness of inauthentic everydayness). The disclosure of *Dasein* by
its readiness to the call of conscience, Heidegger terms resoluteness
(*Entschlossenheit*). This German word as used by Heidegger has two
aspects: it implies resoluteness as well as disclosure. He formulates it
as "the silent, ready-for-dread projection upon the authentic being-
guilty." [106] Resoluteness here does not aim toward some objective
end or thing but to the very self. According to Otto F. Bollnow,
resoluteness is really disclosing: it discloses the self of the *Dasein*.[107]
In his later works Heidegger emphasizes that resoluteness, this authentic disclosure, is *Dasein*'s openness to Being. "Resoluteness as
thought in *Sein und Zeit*," he says, "is not a resolute action of a subject, but the disclosure of *Dasein* from its imprisonment in beings to
the openness of Being." [108]

In resoluteness, *Dasein* does not turn away from taking care of the
things of its surroundings nor from concern for the other *Daseins*, but

105 *Ibid.*, p. 296.
106 *Ibid.*, p. 297.
107 Bollnow, *op. cit.*, p. 408.
108 Heidegger, *Holzwege*, p. 55.

merely considers them from its authentic self and not from the self of the common man. "Resoluteness leads the self precisely into an actual being with the implements in a care-taking mode and pushes it into being together with the others in a concerning mode." [109] Resoluteness brings *Dasein* back into true and unfalsified (by inauthentic considerations or 'general' viewpoints) concrete reality or situations. For Heidegger, a situation is only attainable in an authentic, namely, in a resolute way of being. "On the contrary to this, the situation is essentially blocked off for the common man." [110] The authentic or resolute 'relation to things does not violate them by forcing them into a subjective framework but discloses them in their truth (disclosedness). *Dasein* accomplishes this by disclosing or revealing itself in its authentic truth (disclosingness). Resoluteness is an attitude of *Dasein* which is presupposed by the things in their truth. As an answer to the call of conscience, resoluteness has a character of passivity: it does not primarily disclose the truths of things but rather reveals itself for the action of Being. "The essence of resoluteness lies in the exposure of human *Dasein* to the light of Being and in no case in the power resources of acting." [111] By being the torch-bearer of Being, *Dasein*, however, lets things, too, appear in the light of Being – instead of in the light of common man viewpoints – and thus it is the bearing grounds of their truths.

XI. TEMPORALITY

Temporality and forward-running resoluteness

Heidegger brings together these two profound phenomena in the problem of temporality. These phenomena are: 1) running-forward into death, as the understanding openness of *Dasein* in its totality, and 2) resoluteness, as *Dasein*'s openness to the call of conscience which reveals the guilt of *Dasein*. Running forward to death is more of a primary phenomenon: it brings forth the deepest trend of the mode of being of *Dasein*. Running forward (to death) and resoluteness are authentic ways of existing. When *Dasein* projects itself upon the running forward to death, this utmost primary way of being, it is resolute at the same time. Resoluteness takes *Dasein* over as guilty. *Dasein* is guilty as the null-projection upon its 'null-thrownness' and

---

[109] Heidegger, *Sein und Zeit*, p. 298.
[110] *Ibid.*, p. 300.
[111] Heidegger, *Einführung*, p. 16.

as falling into its null-decline. Death, too, as the possibility of the
impossibility of existence, is the nullity of *Dasein*. The nullity of *Dasein* reveals itself in its being resolute toward death. The question of
the wholeness of *Dasein* is not a theoretical question but an 'existentiel'
question: it can only be answered by resolute openness to death. In
doing this, *Dasein* exists as self; it is not lost in the inauthentic self of
the common man. *Dasein* is self in its forward-running-resoluteness.

In its forward-running-resoluteness, *Dasein* comes upon itself in its
authentic possibility. The possibility (potentiality) of *Dasein* to come
upon itself is the future (the German word for 'coming upon' is '*Zu-
kunft*' and for 'future' is '*Zukunft*'). The existential of future for Heidegger is not a 'now' which did not as yet occur and which is coming,
"but the coming by which *Dasein* comes upon itself in its authentic
way of being." [112] Running forward makes *Dasein* a future-making
being. Taking a positive standpoint toward Heidegger's relating of
death to time, Arland Ussher says: "In a universe without death (if
such a thing can be imagined) we would be mere solipsists; we would
never really believe in a 'world outside.' Time has been called many
things, but it is foremost of all a flight from our own graves." [113]

Dasein, in its forward-running-resoluteness (in its future-making-
ness), understands itself as guilty, as thrown. Taking itself over in its
'thrownness,' *Dasein* exists in its past. The coming-to-itself (future)
of *Dasein* is simultaneously its coming-back (past). By advancing
from its future to meet itself in its past, *Dasein* discloses the situation
(the authentic, concrete to-be-in-the-world) which is its own *Da* with
all its care-taking implements and with its concerning togetherness
with others. Implements and others here are considered in relation to
our authentic self, and not as objects viewed from an absolute, logical
standpoint of universal no-one,[114] and also not as things of the inauthentic everyday *Dasein* – things of the common-man's self. This way
of being of *Dasein*, which discloses the situation out of its future and
past by encountering the sojourning beings [115] of our surroundings,
is the present.

[112] Heidegger, *Sein und Zeit*, p. 325.
[113] Ussher, *op. cit.*, p. 85.
[114] 'Universal no-one' here is a strictly scientific, fully abstract subject. It is nobody (no-
one) really; nevertheless, in the modern times it is increasingly becoming the almighty principle which determines the life and aims of individuals as well as nations, and even the
widely spread civilizations. It is becoming the fundamental principle of humanity as such.
[115] The sojourning beings (*Anwesendes*) are beings appearing the way they are in themselves without having been forced into the distorting viewpoints of a subject. Beings appearing the way they are, appear in the light of Being or in the light of *Dasein* which is not
a subject, but the place where the light of Being breaks into concreteness.

Temporality and intra-temporality

The future as revealing the past and disclosing the situation in the present is, according to Heidegger, a unique phenomenon, temporality (*Zeitlichkeit*). The structure of care [116] represents this temporality of *Dasein*. Care is the being-ahead of oneself (future) as being-already-in-the-world (past) and as being with the within-the-world-beings (present). A disposable (*Vorhandenes*) thing neither has a future, a past, nor, therefore, a present. It can only be a disposable for a temporal (not a temporary!) being, the *Dasein*. A disposable thing cannot be a thing of the past but only a bygone thing. Similarly, it is not a thing of the future but merely a thing not originated as yet. It cannot, also, be present in a situation; it merely can be found or encountered in it by a temporal being.

Dasein always implies its future and past, not as the dimensions of universal, mathematical time, but as the ways of being or existentials. The time of the concrete surroundings is not this universal, mathematical time either. Heidegger calls it intra-temporality (*Innerzeitlichkeit*). Intra-temporality, as the time of the implements, is based on the temporality, the time of *Dasein*, just as the spatiality of implements is based on the spatiality of *Dasein*. The time of the implements is always 'time-to' (time to go to work, time to go to bed, time to retire, time to start a trip, etc.). The everyday *Dasein* understands itself and guides itself in its everyday doings by this inauthentic time, intra-temporality.

In the Greek era the concept of being had a temporal character. Beings for Greeks were sojourning beings (τα ἐοντα). Beings as sojourning beings were not related to a subject but to Being itself. By coming into the open realm of Being – which can be compared to an illuminated region surrounded by darkness – sojourning there (*verweilend*), and leaving it again, the sojourning beings *are*. This temporal sojourning of beings in the realm of revelation is dynamic. The being "sojourns by coming forth and by going away. Sojourning is the passage from coming to going." [117] When a being in its sojourning is taken from its two absences (where it comes from and where it goes to) it loses its dynamic character and becomes a static and timeless being, a disposable (*Vorhandenes*), and *eo ipso* it is no longer a sojourning being. The Heraclitian beings, arising from the fire of Being, sojourning in its light and returning to it, are the sojourning beings.

[116] Cf. p. 54.
[117] Heidegger, *Holzwege*, p. 323.

The sojourning beings are beings in the truth of Being. They presuppose time or light, "the horizon of Being." [118]

Time and history

Existing temporally, *Dasein* exists between birth and death. "As care, *Dasein* is the 'between.' " [119] In its 'between' *Dasein* is dynamic; it never rolls as a ball between birth and death, but in its 'between' it is constantly being born and dying – it is dynamically befallen (*geschehend*). History is founded in befalling. Befalling, on the other hand, is rooted in time as temporality. *Dasein* is not temporal because it is in history; but, on the contrary, it is befallen and is in history, because it exists temporally.

History is subjective. Man here faces his environment as his object and has it or tries to get it under his control. Man here is free or is freeing himself from destiny. That which is called 'blows of destiny' is something accidental; it is evitable and gradually can be eliminated. Befalling, unlike history, in no wise is anthropocentric; it is necessarily related to the nullity of *Dasein*. Running forward to death *Dasein* discloses itself in its resolute readiness for the call of conscience which is its readiness for its destiny. Such a readiness for one's destiny is openness to befalling. Only a befallen man may become anthropocentrically historical by ignoring or 'freeing' himself from his destiny.

The things are never befallen, never historical; however, they are called historical because they belong to the historical world wherein *Dasein* is relinquished to itself. "If there is no *Dasein*, the world is not *da* either." [120] Therefore *Dasein* is historical in the primary sense – in the sense of befalling – whereas the within-the-world-things are historical in a secondary sense – in the sense of belonging in the world of the befallen *Dasein*.

Lost in the diverse possibilities of its inauthentic way of being, *Dasein* can, only by its running forward unto death, distinguish and eliminate its inauthentic possibilities and free itself to its authentic way of being. Only freed to its authentic way of being, can *Dasein* rise up from the multiple ways of existing of its everydayness into its true destiny (*Schicksal*). By being in correspondence with its destiny, *Dasein* is befallen. History as befalling is not the unrestrained activities of man, but is his response to his destiny. "The *Dasein* can be struck

[118] Heidegger, *Sein und Zeit*, p. 438.
[119] *Ibid.*, p. 374.
[120] *Ibid.*, p. 365.

by the blows of destiny only because it *is*, in the very foundation of its being, destiny." [121] Being its destiny, *Dasein* is freed to its own self. Destiny is never the destiny of an individual in his isolation, but the co-destiny with others. The history of a nation or a tribe is based on the destiny of *Dasein*.[122]

The future, past, and present are three ecstasies of time. Ecstasy is the way of being-out-of-oneself.[123] Only a being which is out of itself can come upon itself: it can exist temporally and thus be befallen and be historical. Understanding, as the projection upon *Dasein*'s own possibilities, primarily is the ecstasy of the future; moodness, as the mood-like disclosure of *Dasein*'s own 'thrownness,' primarily belongs to the ecstasy of the past; and decline, as the flight of *Dasein* from its authentic way of being, primarily is rooted in the ecstasy of the present. All three ecstasies of temporality belong together; they are in a unity. This unity is the *Da* of *Dasein*. Without the *Da* of *Dasein* there cannot be time or history. "In every *time*, man was and is and will be because time temporizes itself only as long as man *is*. There is no time in which man is not there. This does not mean that man exists from eternity to eternity, but only means that time is not eternity, and that time only temporizes with human historical *Dasein*." [124]

Temporality expresses the total structure of *Dasein*. *Dasein* is temporal because it stands in the openness of Being. The philosophical analysis of *Dasein* in *Sein und Zeit* results in "time as the possible horizon of the understanding of Being" [125] and prepares thus the grounds for seizing the problem of Being itself.

---

[121] *Ibid.*, p. 384.
[122] Destiny does not indicate fatalism. Fatalism occurs when a being is determined by another being, whereas destiny means man's being-determined by Being.
[123] Ecstasy etymologically indicates this being-out-of-oneself: *ex* (out), *histanai* (to stand).
[124] Heidegger, *Einführung*, p. 64.
[125] Heidegger, *Was ist Metaphysik?*, p. 17.

CHAPTER II

BEING

The phase of Being, to which practically all post-*Sein und Zeit* works of Heidegger belong, is not worked out systematically or gradually, but rather consists of many excursions or invasions into the problem of Being; yet, beyond all the variety of these approaches and the diversity of these problems, the great unique whole of Being can be felt. In order to illuminate and to reveal this basic problem of Heidegger's post-*Sein und Zeit* works, the second chapter of this study will consider several characteristic phenomena leading to the problem of Being. By revealing several of the most characteristic features of Heideggerian thinking and by selecting and stressing a few of the most important problems of his philosophy, the disclosure of the problem of Being itself in its diverse aspects will be accomplished.

This chapter on Being starts with the general characterization of Heidegger's post-*Sein und Zeit* works. Modified understanding of *Dasein*, as openness of Being, in the second phase of Heidegger's thought makes it necessary to return to the problem of *Dasein* in the second section of the chapter. *Dasein*, as the openness of Being, is disclosure which is the fundamental truth for Heidegger. Truth thus is the theme of the third section of the chapter. Since truth is related to thinking, the following (fourth) section will consider thinking. Fundamental thinking is indicated by the Greek *logos* which also constitutes the foundation of language. The investigation of the problem of language will be attempted in the fifth section of the chapter. In thinking and language, which primarily belong in the hands of Being, the fundamental history (befalling) of man is founded. The problem of history thus will be the topic of the sixth section of the chapter. Since the history of Western thought is marked by subjectivism, subjectivism will be the point of interest of the seventh section. That subjectivism is fundamentally nihilism will be clarified in the eighth section. Thought of Being for Heidegger is a way leading man out of his subjectivistic, nihilistic entanglements. Consequently, man in his awareness of Being will conclude the chapter.

I. HEIDEGGER'S POST-*SEIN UND ZEIT* WORKS

Sein und Zeit was a systematic and gradual pursuit, whereas the post-*Sein und Zeit* works, whose theme is Being, are merely a multitude of scattered, small, but profound approaches revealing Being in diverse contexts and aspects. Most of these approaches are historical: they deal with a particular philosopher, or better, with a limited problem of one of the philosophers (Heraclitus' *logos*, Hegel's concept of experience, Plato's truth, etc.). All these approaches of Heidegger are very condensed (average *circa* 30 pages) but profound. He had, of course, some lengthy publications after his *Sein und Zeit* (e.g. his *Holzwege* or *Vorträge und Aufsätze*); nevertheless, they are merely collections of essays with little more coherency than among the separately published essays. Heidegger published a couple of works of average book size dealing with a homogeneous problem. These were *Was Heisst Denken?*, dealing with the problem of thinking, and *Die Einführung in die Metaphysik*, dealing with the problem of metaphysics. All Heidegger's articles, essays or approaches have one and the same basic character – the striving to reveal Being in its profound meaning.

The originality of Heidegger's philosophy frustrates even beginning a comparison of his philosophy with any other philosophy, except possibly with the philosophy of the early Greeks. On the other hand, since Heidegger transcends all the classic divisions of philosophy into its disciplines (ethics, logic, cosmology, etc.), it is impossible to clarify his standpoint by applying such a classification. Dealing with the very primary consideration of Being, Heidegger in a certain sense is a logician, cosmologician, epistemologician, etc. – all at one and the same time in his profound way. This primary Being of the Heideggerian philosophy is near to everybody. We are always in the understanding of Being by existing and living in it. On the other hand, however, this problem is the most difficult and distant for an explicit or ontological knowledge.

The layers of the interpretation of Being which were laid down over the centuries, are, according to Heidegger, rather its concealment. Therefore, the biggest part of Heideggerian thinking in his post-*Sein und Zeit* works is a removal of these concealing layers of traditional thought. These concealments are important insofar as they are hints

toward that which they are not, just as an image of a thing in the
mirror is not what it appears to be, and yet it is an orientation point
hinting toward the real thing. By removing these concealments, Heidegger reaches the truth of Being. The truth for him is disclosure
(*aletheia*). Almost every essay of Heidegger's post-*Sein und Zeit* works
is an invasion into Being through the deadening interpretations of the
centuries. With these invasions he tries to bring out the primary
radiance of Being, its revelation.

II. *DASEIN*

Man and Being

Heidegger does not go into a fine and profound analysis of *Dasein*
for anthropological purposes. *Dasein* is not man, but rather that in
which the essence of man is rooted. Also in *Dasein* are assembled the
important phenomena, such as world, space, time – in their fundamental sense never investigated by previous philosophy. By going
into these entanglements, Heidegger aims to experience Being itself.
"The display of the composition of *Dasein* remains but *a way*. The *aim*
is the elaboration of the question of Being as such." [1]

Being, the ultimate aim of philosophical investigation, is already
known, however implicitly, and pre-discovered in *Dasein*'s everyday
enterprises. Therefore *Dasein* was chosen by Heidegger as a way
leading to Being. By reason of *Dasein*'s essential relationship to Being,
by its standing out into the world, *Dasein* can understand the singu-
lars and bring them into appearance. "That which is ...," says Heidegger, "in no way could be revealed without its *opportunity* of getting
into a world." [2] It can only have such an opportunity through *Dasein*,
for without a *Dasein* there cannot be any world. Only in the world does
a being become meaningful (as well as meaningless), because world is
the consolidation of all meanings of beings. Further, world can be the
cohesion of all meanings because *Dasein* exists for its own sake, is
interested and takes care of its own being. "To the self-ness belongs
world; this is always *Dasein*-related." [3] Since everything that is can
be revealed only in the world and since world is incorporated into the
structure of *Dasein*, *Dasein* is the place of the understanding of Being,
is the place where Being reveals itself. "Man 'essentiates' [4] in such a

---

[1] Heidegger, *Sein und Zeit*, p. 436.
[2] Heidegger, *Vom Wesen des Grundes*, p. 36.
[3] *Ibid*, p. 35.
[4] Heidegger uses the word 'essence' (*Wesen*) as a verb. By 'man essentiates' he signifies
man in his basic way of being which makes man man.

way that he is the *Da*, i.e. the manifestation of Being." [5] Primarily *Dasein* does not express the essence of man, but this bringing into the light of Being, the revelation of Being. The *Da* in *Dasein* is Being itself revealed or brought out of concealment into disclosure. Since disclosure in Heideggerian thinking is truth, *Dasein* is the truth of Being. "By the word '*Dasein*' is signified that which must be experienced and then accordingly thought of as a location, namely, as the place of the truth of Being." [6] *Dasein* is Being fixed in a certain place. This place, however, is not a spatial place but man, and yet not empirical man, but man as man, i.e. man as 'ec-sisting' (standing-out into the openness of Being). "Being truly is bound to human *Da*; Being is placed in man alone and there is no other place attainable for us where Being would occur for itself." [7] For the revelation of Being man is necessary, just as the moon is necessary to reveal the light of the sun in the night. *Dasein* and Being can never be considered as two separate beings. Being is not a statically unchangeable whole: it constantly brings itself forward into openness (just as Heraclitian fire), into the *Da* of Being. And man is not a closed-in-itself being: he stands out in the openness of Being and is the carrier of this openness – he 'ec-sists.'

Dasein *and Being*

The stress on Being in Heidegger's post-*Sein und Zeit* works, replacing the stress on *Dasein* in *Sein und Zeit*, is interpreted by Karl Löwith as an essential variation of standpoint in Heideggerian thinking. With the most profound phenomena of *Sein und Zeit*, conscience and death, Heidegger accentuates *Dasein* in its authentic self. But in his later works Heidegger deals with "the disclosure of *Dasein* out of the captivity of beings into the openness of Being" [8] and not any longer merely to its own self. "It would be difficult," says Karl Löwith, "in this openness to the totally different dimension of Being to still recognize the earlier resoluteness to man's own self." [9] In such statements Karl Löwith seems to misunderstand the relation between Being and *Dasein*. Being is not "the totally different dimension" with respect to *Dasein*. *Dasein* is Being in its openness. *Sein und Zeit* concluded with temporality, the being-out-of-itself of *Dasein*.

---

[5] Heidegger, *Humanismus*, p. 15.
[6] Heidegger, *Was ist Metaphysik?*, p. 13.
[7] Vietta, *op. cit.*, p. 34.
[8] Löwith, *op. cit.*, p. 16.
[9] *Ibid.*

This ecstasy [10] (being-out-of-itself) of *Dasein* is at the same time the revealed structure of Being. Being is ecstatic: it constantly appears, comes into time – into *Da*. The *Da* of Being is *Dasein* ('*Sein*' is the German word for 'Being'). The problems of the post-*Sein und Zeit* works are not the problems of a new standpoint but of a further development of the same.

Exactly the same thing has to be said of the problem of the world, which for Karl Löwith seems to be essentially changed in Heidegger's later works. According to him, "the 'world' now is not, as in *Sein und Zeit*, the existential structure of our to-be-in-the-world, but the manifestation or openness of Being itself." [11] Karl Löwith does not seem to see that world remains the structural element of our to-be-in-the-world even though it is the openness of Being itself. Being, brought to openness, is that which constitutes our existential structure. We are what we are by standing in the openness of Being, in the world – by being our to-be-in-the-world.

For Karl Löwith some assertions of Heidegger seem to be pure contradiction. "In his work on humanism," he says, "Heidegger interprets the sentence of *Sein und Zeit:* 'only as long as *Dasein* is, there is (*es gibt*) Being' in that way that 'there is' becomes 'it gives.' [12] Accordingly the sentence of *Sein und Zeit* turns into the completely opposite assertion: only as long as Being gives itself, is there *Dasein.*" [13] Purely logically, by sticking to mere terms, there may be a contradiction. However, there does not seem to be any contradiction in Heidegger's thought itself. Heidegger is not experimenting with the mechanics of logic, but he is thinking Being.[14] To apprehend this thought is of more importance than to consider if or in what degree his sayings correspond to the iron rules of logic. Being can only be revealed in *Dasein*. Therefore, as long as there is a *Dasein*-kind of being (man), Being can be revealed. On the other hand, man is man because Being breaks into openness which is the essence of man (*Dasein*). Without the sun, the moon is not the moon, in the sense that it cannot be illuminated, and without the illuminated, and thus revealed, moon, the sun is not revealed in the night. Without *Dasein* Being is not Being

---

[10] Cf. p. 65.
[11] Löwith, *op. cit.*, p. 54.
[12] The German *es gibt* normally is translated into 'there is'; literally it means 'it gives.' Heidegger, just as in most of his philosophical terms, here probably implies both aspects of the expression. Being is in a peculiar way: in its being it gives itself into the openness, it is *Dasein*.
[13] Löwith, *op. cit.*, p. 26.
[14] Cf. footnote 10, p. 3.

in the sense that it is not revealed; it does not come out of concealment
into revelation, which means there cannot be any truth of Being.
Furthermore, there cannot then be any untruth of Being either, because only for *Dasein* can Being be concealed. Therefore, without
Dasein, Being can neither be said to appear, nor not to appear; nothing
can be said whatsoever. Only as long as *Dasein* is, does Being give
itself.

Understanding of Being and concreteness

Man never can be hidden in his "relation to the illumination" [15] of
Being, because he "is nothing other than this illumination itself". [16]
This does not mean, however, that man is something before his illumination by Being (like the moon is something before it has been struck
by the light of the sun). Man is "in the illumination not only illuminated but also given to himself in this light." [17] Thanks to this light
giving him to himself, man himself can be illuminating "and thus he
can guard the illumination" [18] of Being. Man does not possess his
being; he does not build his own foundation for himself; but he receives it from Being in his 'thrownness' and needs to be this *Da* of
Being as his own self. To be the illumination of Being and guard this
illumination is for man to be his very own self. To the truth of Being
belongs the coming into the light or appearing. Appearing can only
be appearing if received in the sense of being understood (*Vernehmen*).
There is no Being without the understanding of Being. "Being holds
sway, and because it holds sway and inasmuch as it holds sway and
appears, *with* the appearance occurs necessarily the understanding,
too." [19] Understanding belongs primarily to Being as *Dasein*, but not
to man as a subject. Man as *Dasein* is involved in Being; he is the
guardian of the appearance of Being. He never stands in front of
Being by facing it as an object.

The close relation of *Dasein* to Being does not mean man's remotion
from concrete life. Not at all! The *Da* of Being is that in which all
concreteness is rooted, or that which is presupposed by concreteness.
Considering the Greek word *polis* not as a state or a city-state but as
"*Da* wherein and what the *Dasein* historically is," [20] Heidegger main-

[15] Heidegger, *Vorträge*, p. 278.
[16] *Ibid.*
[17] *Ibid.*
[18] *Ibid.*
[19] Heidegger, *Einführung*, p. 106.
[20] *Ibid.*, p. 117.

tains that the *Da* as *polis* is the center to which all the meanings of the
ways and doings of concrete human life are related. To *Da*, "to this
abode of historicity belong gods, temples, priests, feasts, plays, poets,
thinkers, rulers, councils of seniors, national assemblies, forces, and
vessels." [21] Only here, in *Da*, poet is poet, priest is priest, ruler is ruler,
thinker is thinker; and all their doings and the things they deal with
– words, prayers, orders, thoughts, duties, soldiers, vessels, etc. – are
meaningful elements in the all-meaning-granting whole, the *Da* of
Being.

'Ec-sistence'

Dasein exists. In *Sein und Zeit*, existence, essentially belonging to
man, meant to be ahead of one's self and, from this ahead-being, to be
related to one's self with the interest and care of one's own being,
including disregard, negligence, or misunderstanding of this self.
Understanding itself, *Dasein* understands the things of its *Da* (things
partaking in the openness of *Da*). "Man is a being who is in the midst
of beings in such a way that therewith to him are ever revealed beings –
the beings that he is not and the being that he is. This way of being of
man we call existence. Existence is possible only on the basis of understanding of Being." [22] Man's understanding of Being is his openness
to Being. Immediately after having published his *Sein und Zeit*, Heidegger emphasizes existence as openness to Being. This change is not
a shift of his standpoint but merely a new phase of his thought. The
phase of preparing to think Being is now replaced by the phase of
actual thinking of Being. Two years after having published his *Sein
und Zeit*, he says in his *Was ist Metaphysik?* that existence "names a
way of being, and namely a way of being of that being which stands
open for the openness of Being; it stands in this openness by penetrating it." [23]

Accentuating the existence as a relation to Being instead of to one's
own being, Heidegger modifies the way of writing this word. Instead
of 'existence' he has now 'ec-sistence' to signify standing out into the
openness of Being. "The standing in the glade of Being, I call the
'ec-sistence' of man," [24] says Heidegger. By standing out into the
glade of Being, man is more than what he is as a natural man in the
sense of 'in-sistence,' i.e. not 'ec-sistence.' To 'ec-sist' means not only

21 *Ibid.*
22 Heidegger, *Kant*, p. 205.
23 Heidegger, *Was ist Metaphysik?*, p. 14.
24 Heidegger, *Humanismus*, p. 13.

be what one is but also *be* the possibility of standing out into one's
beyondness. To be this possibility is not an occasional off-and-on
event for man but the very basic feature of him as man. "It is a distinguishing peculiarity of man that his essence as nature and his
essence as highest possibility do not coincide as with other beings –
with stone and with God." [25] Man's being out of himself, his eccentric
or ecstatic standing out in more than what he is, is his specific human
way to be his own self. Man exists eccentrically. Even in his inauthentic
way of being man is never concentrated in himself like a stone lying
on the ground in its full weight or an animal living a biologically well-
balanced life. In his inauthentic existence falling away from himself,
man is restlessly leaping from one object to another without sojourning
long anywhere. According to Jean Wahl, Heidegger in his lectures on
Leibniz compares the eccentric out-of-himself man with a man who
stands at the doorless and windowless monads from which he is shut
out and left "in the street, so to speak. Individuals are not 'at home,'
because there are no homes for them." [26] Man is essentially thrown
out of himself, he is an eccentric being.

III. TRUTH

Correctness

Truth, as the agreement between cognition and the thing known, is ,
according to Heidegger, not sufficiently primary thought. For a thing
to agree or disagree with cognition, this thing must appear, reveal
itself, come out of concealment. The thing in its disclosure is in a more
primary sense true than in its agreement with the mind. The truth as
agreement Heidegger calls correctness (*Richtigkeit*), hence – not really
truth. Correctness is not located in reality like the truth as disclosure,
but in sentences. "The truth of the sentence is ever and ever merely
the correctness." [27] Correctness states something concerning a thing
but never reveals its essence. "Only where such a revealing takes place,
does truth occur." [28]

The truth as correctness began with Plato. Since for him that which
is basically, is an *idea*, the 'outlook'; the correct looking or seeing is for

[25] Fink, *op. cit.*, p. 27.
[26] Jean Wahl, *A Short History of Existentialism* (New York: Philosophical Library, 1949),
p. 16.
[27] Heidegger, *Holzwege*, p. 40.
[28] Heidegger, *Vorträge*, p. 15.

him of more importance than the disclosure, *aletheia*, as such. "In this
change of the essence of the truth is also accomplished a variation of
the place of the truth. As disclosure it is still the basic feature of Being
itself; as correct 'looking' it becomes a distinction of the human attitude toward being." [29]

Man as source of truth

The truth as correctness presupposes truth as disclosure. Disclosure,
again, is rooted in *Dasein* which as such is openness. Disclosure implies
the appearing being and the attitude which gives meaning to the
'how' of this appearance. Disclosure can only be disclosure in the openness
of *Dasein*. It is beyond the split of subject and object and thus beyond
their agreement. A correct statement as "a leaf is green," according to
Egon Vietta, does not merely imply greenness of the leaf, but goes into
the opened world where alone the 'leaf' and the 'greenness' can be
meaningful concepts or phenomena. World can only be disclosed by
the to-be-in-the-world, i.e. by a being openly existing in the openness
of the world. "Since man is the source of the truth, the truth has to
be disclosed by man understood as *Dasein*." [30] Man as *Dasein* is not
just the source of the truth but rather the truth itself. Being comes
into light in *Dasein*. *Dasein* is the truth of Being.

That man is the source of truth, does not mean that man creates or
throws out from himself all different truths. Man does not create the
truths just as he does not create the things; but, by allowing things
to appear the way they are, man, by his revealing attitude, allows them
to be true. His attitude is not ruling but respectful. Man as *Dasein*, the
openness, constantly exists in a world which, like a glade in the forest,
is the necessary horizon for things to become visible, to be revealed,
to be true. Not in his isolation is man the source of truth, but in his
openness to Being, in his guarding its light. Only as *Dasein*, the truth
of Being, is man the source of truth and correctness.

Truth as freedom

In his openness to Being, man subordinates himself to the truth of
Being. This subordination makes man become his true self, gives him
his freedom. "The openness of attitude, as the innermost possible
rendering of correctness, is based in freedom. The essence of truth is

---

[29] Heidegger, *Platons Lehre von der Wahrheit*, p. 42.
[30] Vietta, *op. cit.*, p. 90.

freedom." [31] The essence of man is *Dasein*, the disclosure. As the disclosure, man is in accordance with his essence, i.e. he is free to his own self-being (*Selbst-Sein*). The need of 'to-be-disclosing' for man is the need of 'to-be-free.' Thus, freedom is never merely a property of man; rather the opposite is true: "freedom, the 'ec-sisting,' disclosing *Dasein* possesses man." [32] Therefore, truth is never a result of logical play with terms, but is an event of Being which, by coming to be, by erupting itself into time, carries man as 'ec-sistence.' Only because Being comes to be, can man stand in its openness, 'ec-sist,' be man.

The Heideggerian understanding of truth is not just another, different way of approaching the truth, but actually it follows traditional philosophy. However, the difference is that instead of following it by merely going ahead, Heidegger goes back to the very profound basis of the truth. Heidegger's understanding of truth is a deepened understanding of truth: it penetrates the most basic layers of truth, on which the traditional truth, as correctness, rests. Correctness presupposes the truth of Being on which it is based. "Only the revelation of Being renders possible the disclosure of beings." [33] The truth of Being for Heidegger is ontological truth; he refers to correctness as ontic truth. Scientific truth is a mode of ontic truth.

Truth is located not in things and not in man but in *Dasein*, the openness of Being, itself. Man can be the source of truth only because Being holds sway over him. Disclosure is not an act of man but of Being; man merely participates in this disclosure or in the truth of Being. He takes over the truth of Being and inherits it as his true self. By being his true self man is free, and freedom is truth. Since freedom, and thus truth, is not a property of man, it escapes man's control. On the contrary, it itself befalls man and applies him for itself. 'The 'befalling' [34] of disclosure constantly penetrates man thoroughly. This however, is never a fatality of a control. Because man actually becomes free by belonging to the realm of befalling and thus becomes a hearer [35] but never a slave." [36] Truth thus is not located primarily in a philosophical system established by one or another philosopher in history. Foremostly it befalls man and places him thereby in history. Truth does not belong to a philosophical system; on the contrary,

[31] Martin Heidegger, *Vom Wesen der Wahrheit* (Frankfurt a.M.: Vittorio Klostermann 1943), p. 13.
[32] *Ibid.*, p. 17.
[33] Heidegger, *Vom Wesen des Grundes*, p. 13.
[34] Cf. pp. 64–65.
[35] Hearer of the voice of Being.
[36] Heidegger, *Vorträge*, p. 32.

philosophical system belongs to truth. Standing in the openness of Being and guarding it, man is the guardian of the truth of Being. As one of the ways of guarding truth, a philosopher guards it in his philosophical system. To be a guardian of the truth of Being and to be free are one and the same.

Truth and untruth

Although man is essentially related to the truth of Being, he is not steady in the truth. Freedom allows a being to be such and such a being. On the other hand, freedom, because it is freedom, may allow being to be something it is not rather than something it is. Since freedom is not the unruly actions of man but his subordination to Being, therefore untruth as well as truth primarily is rooted in Being. "Because the 'ec-sistent' freedom, as the essence of truth, is not a property of man, but man merely 'ec-sists' as the property of this freedom and thus becomes capable of history, therefore the 'non-essentiation' of truth also cannot originate simply as a subsequence of the impotency and negligence of man. The untruth rather must derive from the essence of truth." [37] Truth as freedom is disclosing, which is only possible due to the concealment. Since truth is an event of Being, as its coming from concealment into disclosure, it can only happen thanks to the disclosure (truth) as well as to the concealment (untruth). Truth expresses Being as dynamic, as becoming (Heraclitian fire), as time.

Heidegger does not pretend to be the only one in the history of philosophy who was dealing with the truth of Being rather than with the truth of beings. The early Greek philosophers were truly the philosophers of Being. On the other hand, all those philosophers for whom Being remained concealed were standing in the concealment and thus in the untruth of Being. Since untruth as well as truth is an event of Being (not originated merely in man), those philosophers also belong significantly to the history of Western thought.

IV. THINKING

Thinking and logic

According to Heidegger, true thinking is primary thinking. Such thinking does not stand in man's disposition and is never his instru-

[37] Heidegger, *Vom Wesen der Wahrheit*, p. 18.

ment. It is a response of man to Being rather than his direct saying. Primary thinking occurs as an echo "to the word of the soundless voice of Being." [38] It is "a thinking belonging [39] to Being." [40] Human thought is not simply 'human': it does not fully belong to man, but is primarily bound to Being itself.

So-called logical thought no longer responds to Being. It is thinking which has lost the true element of thought, Being. Such thinking is 'de-ontologized' thinking, and as such it ceases to be authentic thinking. Without its natural element (Being), thinking cannot remain fundamental thinking. An attempt to judge thinking with sole regard to its correlation to logical rules is an attempt to measure it by the wrong criterion. "Such a judging resembles a procedure which tries to estimate the essence and capacities of a fish merely with regard to its ability to live on dry land. Already long, far too long, thought has been on dry land. Can now a striving to once again bring thought back into its element be called 'irrationalism'?" [41] With these words Heidegger tries to show that primary thinking in no way is irrational thinking and that true thinking necessarily is ontological thinking, the thinking of Being. Such thought transcends logic. By transcending logic, it also transcends irrationalism, because rationalism as well as irrationalism belongs on one and the same level of thinking. Primary thinking goes beyond this level into the realm of Being. "To think against 'logic' does not mean to break a lance for the illogical, but it merely means to think *logos* and its essence which appear in the dawn of thought." [42]

Heidegger's devotion to primary thought does not imply his inability to think logically. His main work, *Sein und Zeit*, demonstrates clearly how sequentially, systematically, and logically Heidegger can think. Often, dealing with the thoughts of earlier philosophers, Heidegger shows how profoundly he can grasp the basic elements of their thoughts, analyze them, and reveal them in the sharp light of his logic. "Nobody can deny," says Karl Löwith, "that Heidegger, more than any other contemporary interpreter, is clear-sighted and possesses skill in the art of reading and explaining when he carefully takes apart and reassembles the structures of sayings in thought or poetry." [43] And yet Heidegger knows very well that logical clear-sightedness

[38] Heidegger, *Was ist Metaphysik?*, pp. 44-45.
[39] The German word '*höriges*' means 'hearing' or 'listening' as well as 'belonging.'
[40] Heidegger, *Was ist Metaphysik?*, p. 12.
[41] Heidegger, *Humanismus*, p. 6.
[42] *Ibid.*, p. 34.
[43] Löwith, *op. cit.*, pp. 84-85.

alone is meaningless. He opposes logic in the sense that he opposes a mechanism of thinking, enclosed in itself and cut off from Being. According to Egon Vietta, in one of his letters Heidegger says: "My combat is directed against the *ratio* turned to groundlessness, which in its senselessness merely drives a play of ingenuity." [44] Skillful ingenuity alone leads neither to an understanding of the human essence nor of Being.

Logos

Generally speaking, traditional philosophy anxiously tended to be logical, and yet it never investigated the essence of logic; it never raised the question of what *logos* is. According to Heidegger, logic, just as all the other disciplines of philosophy, is an ontological offspring. Parmenides understood Being as the sojourn of sojourning beings. Sojourn (*Anwesen*), in the word itself, implies presence or temporality and essence in the sense of 'essentiation.' Sojourning is "the illuminating-concealing assemblage which is what the λόγος is thought to be, and so named." [45] The sojourning beings are always related to the illuminating horizon of Being, which comprises them and in which they sojourn. Everything that sojourns, "gods and men, temple and towns, sea and land, eagle and snake, tree and bush, wind and light, stone and sand, day and night," [46] is assembled by the sojourning itself. Being is assembling; the assemblage is *logos*. Being is the most primary thought.

'Ec-sisting' is standing in the openness of Being – in sojourning, in assemblage, in the *logos*. By 'ec-sisting' we respond to the assemblage of *logos* by letting it be the way it is in itself. Permitting it to be the way it is in itself is its preservation. By preserving the thought of Being, man is a guardian of this thought and as such he is the trustee of Being. A trustee is true; he preserves the truth. We respond to Being as assemblage (*logos*) by letting that which is assembled by *logos* (by Being) be the way it is – by preserving it. Preserving is watching; watching occurs in our sayings. "Saying and speaking 'essentiate' the letting-lie-together of all that sojourns as laid in the disclosure." [47] Our thinking and language are rooted in Being. Primarily they belong to Being rather than to us. We think and talk merely as listening to

---

[44] Vietta, *op. cit.*, p. 28.
[45] Heidegger, *Holzwege*, p. 325.
[46] *Ibid.*, p. 326.
[47] Heidegger, *Vorträge*, p. 212.

the sayings laid in Being. "Thought speaks the dictation of the truth of Being." [48]

As merely a response, human thinking, nevertheless, is not just a passive attitude of man. A response requires effort and strain. The hearing of the sayings of Being is the "assembling of oneself which concentrates upon the demand and exhortation" [49] of Being. The German words 'zuhören' (listen) and 'zugehören' (belong) sound alike and in some forms are identical. Heidegger uses these words in both aspects to express man's subordination to Being in his thinking. By listening to Being we belong to it. By belonging to it we are what we are. By responding to Being we are led to our self. This means activity. Thinking is not a passive going-on of the thoughts of Being, but is a profound creative act in which we ourselves create in the sense of bringing to light, revealing – we 'ec-sist.'

Thinking of truth and untruth

Logos as "illuminating-concealing assemblage" not only reveals the truth but also it veils it. Veiling belongs necessarily to revealing since without veiling there cannot be any revealing. "The revealing requires the veiling." [50] By thinking we preserve or guard the truth (revelation or disclosure) of Being in our thoughts or words. Therefore, and only in this way, can our thoughts or words be true. Likewise, since disclosure is essentially related to concealment, by preserving the truth or by letting the assembled beings appear the way they are, we also preserve the untruth by letting the things appear not the way they are but the way they seem to be. Being as *logos* (assemblage) assembles sojourning beings in their truth as well as in their untruth, and our thinking reveals as well as veils them by responding to *logos*, the illuminating-concealing assemblage.[51]

The primary understanding of Being as *logos* fell into forgottenness,[52] and interestingly, according to Heidegger, the beginning of this for-

---

[48] Heidegger, *Holzwege*, p. 303.

[49] Heidegger, *Vorträge*, p. 214.

[50] *Ibid.*, p. 220.

[51] Heidegger considers the philosophy of past centuries rather as a veiling of the truth instead of a revelation of it. Since veiling as well as revealing is rooted in Being, his attitude toward traditional thought is rather respectful instead of simply a rejection.

[52] Forgottenness here is not a psychological factor, but Being in its concealment. Being, however concealed, i.e. forgotten, yet remains an important event forming the history of thought. The importance of the forgottenness of Being lies in the fact that Being had been known (only that which had been known can be forgotten), had been unconcealed or revealed at the beginning of history. Forgottenness of Being, as had-been-known Being, is an event which as a subterranean stream carries human history.

gottenness is the beginning of the history of Occidental thought. History is the deeper and deeper regression of Being as such in which man concentrates only on beings which have been taken out of their sojourn and turned to objects. This forgottenness of Being, based in Being itself, expresses the dynamic character of Being. Being talks to us, and our response is our thinking. Talking to us, Being reveals itself in its truth; it turns toward us. In its veiling or concealment, in its untruth, as well, Being is talking to us. In this talking, Being withdraws from us. The responses to the withdrawing Being, to its untruth, are the concealments of Being by our sayings or thoughts. Traditional philosophy, by concealing Being in its thinking, was creating the history of Western thought. "Withdrawal is not a nothing," says Heidegger, "but rather an event." [53] This event is of enormous importance. In the withdrawal of Being we move along with it. In this process of moving along with it, we *are* (or we become). We are in the way of being-moved-along; our essence lies in our relation to Being. "To be on the move toward that which withdraws itself means to be indicating that which withdraws itself." [54] We do not exist 'incentrically': we are not concentrated in ourselves but we 'ecsist' eccentrically, ecstatically, by pointing to Being. By pointing to Being, we permit Being to hold sway over us, and thus we are held together in our essence. Being holds us in our self. Even in its withdrawal, Being makes us possible, enables us to be. Forgottenness or ignorance of Being is still the fundamental force or might which unifies man unto his essence in the times of his 'in-sistence,' his being-closed-off from awareness of Being. Being gives (as well as withholds) its thoughts (*logos*) to us making us respond to them, allowing the possibility of self. Therefore, it is right to say that we do not possess a potentiality to think, but that we *are* this potentiality.

Thinking as guarding

Our ability to think is, in fact, our ability to respond to the *logos* of Being. We can respond to Being, because Being is turning toward us (or withdrawing from us); it cares (*mag*) for us. The German word '*Vermögen*' stands for 'ability,' 'capacity.' Another word, '*mögen*' indicates 'to care for,' 'to be interested,' 'to like.' We have the ability to think because Being cares for us (by turning toward us or withdrawing from us). "By this turning toward us, our essence is de-

53 Heidegger, *Was heisst Denken?*, p. 5.
54 *Ibid.*, p. 6.

manded. The turning toward us is exhortation. The exhortation takes
us into our essence, calls us up onto our essence and thus holds us to
it. Holding is actually guarding. That which holds us in our essence,
holds us, however, only as long as we ourselves on our part are holding
that which holds us."[55] In our thoughts and sayings we guard Being and
thus we testify by these thoughts and sayings to Being as guarding us.

Listening to *logos* we guard Being. This guarding of Being is a
response to Being which calls us into our essence. By our response we
render ourselves possible; we, in a way, create ourselves. The call of
Being does not determine us but frees us to our very self. By thinking
we free ourselves to our self.[56] In one of his works Heidegger illustrates
the phenomenon of thinking by an example.[57] According to him,
whenever a joiner's apprentice learns his trade, he does not learn it
merely by being handy with the tools alone, but basically he gets into
his trade and becomes a joiner through his acquaintance with diverse
kinds of wood and all their potentialities to give such and such forms,
since each kind of wood is suitable only to certain forms. These hidden
forms in the qualities of the wood represent the talk of Being, and the
joiner's apprentice, who brings these forms to actuality, is responding
to Being. By this response he becomes what he is, a joiner. By following the call of Being, we become ourselves.

Thinking and thanking

Logos, the assemblage, assembles the sojourning beings in the openness of Being. By responding to this assemblage in our thinking, we
call these sojourning beings into our words; we name them. "The
called being stands thus in the call of the word. The called being appears as the sojourning being; and as such it is secured, commanded,
bidden in the calling word." [58] Naming the things, we receive them
from the hands of Being. We ourselves, as well as everything sojourning,
primarily originate in Being, and since we come to ourselves, and
everything comes to us in our thinking, our thinking thus is simultaneously giving thanks for what is. "For what we owe thanks, we do
not receive from ourselves. It is given to us. We receive many and
different kinds of gifts. The highest gift entrusted to us remains, however, our essence, with which we are endowed in such a way that we,

[55] Heidegger, *Vorträge*, p. 129.
[56] This call-response phenomenon in thinking seems to be a variation of the thrownness-
projection phenomenon of the *Sein und Zeit* phase.
[57] Heidegger, *Was heisst Denken?*, pp. 49–50.
[58] *Ibid.*, p. 85.

on the basis of this gift only, are what we are." [59] Our thanks to Being is our thinking, and our thanklessness is our thoughtlessness.

Thinking as thanking suggests a religious character in Heidegger's philosophy. In many other places Heidegger's thought seems to be poetical. And yet a reading of any one of Heidegger's works reveals his profoundly sharp and carefully guided thinking. His thought aims to experience Being in its wholeness beyond all distinctions which, as such, instead of revealing Being, veil it. For Heidegger "philosophy is not a conceptual, intellectual occupation of the subject-man with that which is called the world of objects, but an experience of the totality by which the whole man is moved." [60]

Thinking as a way

Since science is dealing with beings but not with Being, "science on its part does not think and cannot think" [61] at all, according to Heidegger. Scientific thinking, as an instrument in man's hand, is not the true thinking which is primarily in the hands of Being as *logos* and to which we are subordinate. True thinking does not result in firm conclusions on which, as on a solid foundation, the subsequent series of thoughts can be built without having to return again to the beginnings. True thinking constantly starts over and over again. This constant beginning is not an occasional character of thinking; it essentially belongs to it. We cannot stop thinking, as though we had arrived to a certain point where thinking is no longer needed. Just as Being is constantly turning toward us (or withdrawing from us), so we are constantly responding to this turning toward us (or withdrawal), i.e. we are constantly thinking, constantly pointing toward Being and thus retaining ourselves in our essence. Thinking does not arrive at a certain place but always remains on the way. "Thinking [62] itself is a way. We correspond to this way by being on the way." [63] This way primarily belongs to Being, but it becomes really a road with us on it as travellers. "Thought builds its way primarily by an interrogating pace." [64] By going this road we, in a certain sense, create this road and ourselves as travellers thereon.

True thinking, by not resulting in univocal, universal conclusions

[59] *Ibid.*, p. 94.
[60] Vietta, *op. cit.*, p. 7.
[61] Heidegger, *Was heisst Denken?*, p. 4.
[62] Here 'thinking' is *logos*, as the thinking primarily belonging to Being.
[63] Heidegger, *Was heisst Denken?*, p. 164.
[64] *Ibid.*, pp. 164–165.

and by not coming to a determined end, remains uncertain and mani-
fold. In this diversity of not having arrived at a definite end, with
many possibilities still around him, man remains open to Being in his
essence as a traveller, the *homo viator*. Heidegger says:

> The diversity is rather the element in which thought has to wander to be
> strict thought. Let us talk in an image. For a fish the depth and extension of
> water, its streaming and calmness, its warm and cold layers are the elements of
> its manifold movements. As soon as a fish is robbed of the fullness of its element
> and is dragged onto dry land, it can only jerk and move convulsively and
> expire. Therefore, we must seek out thinking and its thoughts always in the
> element of diversity, otherwise everything will be closed off from us.[65]

V. LANGUAGE

Language and world

The problem of language is of deep ontological importance for Heidegger. In his *Sein und Zeit* he reserved a significant place for his
problem of language as parlance. As an essential constitutive element
of *Da*, the openness of *Dasein*, parlance is basically not the empirical
sound-language, but is the articulation and meaningful ordering of
Dasein as the to-be-in-the-world. By being in the world we have a
mood-like understanding of our to-be-in-the-world. Our to-be-in-the-
world, the openness of Being, is revealed to us in our 'thrownness.' It
is not chaotic but comes to us in meaningful structures. These structures – already lying in our 'thrownness' – we bring up through our
projection in our words where we preserve them. Parlance, as the
articulation of these meaningful structures of that which *is*, primarily
is the language of Being, and not of human speech. By listening to
parlance, we speak.

In his later works Heidegger frequently comes upon the problem of
language. The basic starting point for the problem of language, just as
for the problem of thinking, is *logos*, the assemblage. This assemblage
assembles the openness of Being and us, as responding to this openness. This primary conversation organizes a discourse-sphere in which
a place is given to everything that sojourns in it – things, human
works, events, etc. "Only where language is, is there a world, which
means the constantly changing circumference of decision and work,
of deed and responsibility, and also of caprice and noise, decline and
confusion. Only where world holds sway is there a history." [66]

Logos, as the articulated openness within which everything is
assembled, is world. Heraclitus' ontological symbol of war can be

[65] *Ibid.*, p. 68.
[66] Heidegger, *Erläuterungen*, p. 39.

considered as *logos*-world. "War is both," says Heraclitus, "king of all and father of all, and it has revealed some as gods, others as men; some it has made slaves, others free." [67] War, the *logos*, is the assembler, which assembles sojourning beings upon themselves and brings itself to light in the world.

Things and words

Legein is often translated as 'saying.' According to Heidegger this 'saying' has to be understood in a much more primary meaning than the sound-language. Heidegger accentuates that *legein* is primarily 'lay,' in the sense of 'letting lie in a realm.' In our 'ec-sistence,' in our standing out in the openness of Being, we do not stand in a confusion, but we find that that-which-*is* lies in orderly articulation. By letting it lie the way it is, we bring it into appearance. This letting lie does not leave us standing there in a fully passive attitude. We can only let something lie before us by saying it. By saying, we say it the way it is and thus we let it appear the way it is. "To say means to bring into appearance." [68] Lying is not opposed here to standing; it merely stresses that that which appears comes up itself. Our saying does not create it in an absolute sense but only helps it to appear the way it is. The man-made things are not fully productions of man. They originate from thrown possibilities through our responding projection. The sea, the land, the forest, the town, the house, etc. are lying before us. Just a little part of that which lies before us is made by us, and even that part was made with the help of that which is lying before us as not man-made. "The wall-stones of a house originate in the grown rock." [69]

Man-made things, as well as natural things, primarily originate in our responding *legein* to that which is laid or assembled by *logos*. Man-made things, too, can be perverted, distorted, misrepresented, and not allowed to lie the way they are, just as the so-called natural things can be. The phenomenon of home, for example, used to be an overwhelming, inexchangeable something to which we were subordinate and from which our way of life was oriented and directed even if we had left our home years before. Home nowadays is a distorted and perverted phenomenon. It is identical to a house; it can be anywhere.

[67] Heraclitus, Fragment 53 in Kathleen Freeman (ed), *Ancilla to the Pre-Socratic Philosophers* (Oxford: Basil Blackwell, 1952).
[68] Heidegger, *Vorträge*, p. 244.
[69] Heidegger, *Was heisst Denken?*, p. 122.

It is subordinate to us, easily measurable and expressable in numbers of money-value. It can be exchanged like a pair of shoes.

Distorted things accompany perverted words. Things are not prior to words, and words are not the lables added to already existing things. Our response to the *logos* of Being brings beings into appearance. Words are related to Being, and they are not given to our unrestrained disposition; we are for the disposition of the words of Being. "Words and language are not hulls into which we pack things for purposes of speech or correspondence. It is in word and in language that things become and are things." [70]

Since we know *logos*, the voiceless words of Being, we can talk and we can encounter things. "Even if we had a thousand eyes and a thousand ears, and a thousand hands and many other senses and organs, and if our essence were not the standing under the might of language – then still all beings, i.e. beings that we are no less than beings that we are not, would remain closed off from us." [71]

Words and terms

Heidegger distinguishes words (*Worte*) from terms (*Wörter*). In an assertion of a philosopher terms are the sounds or written words as empirically disposable. Words, however, are those elements of saying which primarily belong to Being itself (to *logos*) and come into appearance through terms. Heidegger, instead of sticking to the disposable terms of past philosophy and considering them with the exactness of philological and linguistic rules, goes beyond them into the silent language of Being. Thus for Karl Löwith his interpretations of the past philosophers seem to be violating interpretations. "Nobody can deny," says Karl Löwith, "that Heidegger, unlike any other contemporary interpreter, is clear-sighted and knows his way in the art of reading and explaining, when he carefully takes apart and reassembles the structures of assertions in thought and poetry. Also nobody will fail to recognize the violence of his interpretations." [72] A word is always more than a term. Scrupulously sticking to the terms instead of words, the so-called 'scientific diagnosticians' of the thoughts of former philosophers are actually far removed from the sayings of these philosophers, from the words of Being in them. One who uses words just as disposable instruments, i.e. as terms, never can bring the

[70] Heidegger, *Einführung*, p. 11.
[71] *Ibid.*, p. 63.
[72] Löwith, *op. cit.*, pp. 84–85.

language of Being into the human language. According to Heidegger, terms can be compared to the buckets with which we scoop the words of Being. "The words are wells after which the saying digs, wells which constantly are to be found and dug. They obstruct easily; however, once in a while they gush up. Without a constantly renewed going-to-the-well, the buckets and kegs get empty or their contents grow flat." [73] Sayings or thinkings never can fully scoop out the wells of Being; the words of Being cannot be said or thought once and forever. Saying and thinking remain a way, which is a way and leads to Being only if used. If not used it is not a way and leads nowhere. Therefore many 'thinkers' with an all-sided, detailed, scientific knowledge of the terms of past philosophy who do not transcend to the words of these philosophies, merely know everything but Being and its *logos*.

Language and chatter

Language implies words as well as terms, parlance as well as chatter.

This again rests in the mystery [also in the homeness] of language: It admits both – on the one hand, that it is degraded by everyone to a uniformly-used mere system of signs which are carried out as binding; on the other hand, that the language in a grand instant says only once and in only one way that which remains inexhaustable because it is always at the beginning and therefore unattainable for any kind of uniformity. Both possibilities of language lie so far apart from each other that their strangeness towards each other could not even be measured by trying to signify them as extreme opposites.[74]

Opposites can only be opposites on a presupposed openness of Being. Just as untruth belongs to the truth, so the chatter belongs to language. The true words can only burst forth through layers of dead terms to their full power and might, just as the brightness of morning is truly bright after the darkness of night.

Language and Being

The authentic language of man is needed to bring the silent words of Being into human sayings. "Thinking brings merely the unvocalized words of Being to language." [75] Man can bring these words to language because they are already on the way toward being-vocalized. "Being comes, illuminating itself, to the language. It is constantly on the way toward it." [76] Although coming itself into language, Being still needs man to spell out its words in human sayings. By doing this man brings

[73] Heidegger, *Was heisst Denken?*, p. 89.
[74] *Ibid.*, pp. 168–169.
[75] Heidegger, *Humanismus*, p. 45.
[76] *Ibid.*

Being into his sayings as in its openness. Being dwells in the openness of human sayings. "Language is the house of Being." [77] The thinkers and poets are those whose mission it is to constantly guard Being in the midst of our everyday *Dasein*.

When language is understood as a means of expressing the disposable things or the psychic events within a man, this interpretation is correct logically or psychologically but is in no wise true ontologically.[78] Words primarily are not like camera pictures of previously existing things. In words things are brought from their concealment; they begin to be. Words give birth to the things into the openness of disclosure. "Language brings a being as being foremost into openness. Where no language 'essentiates,' as in the mode of being of a stone, plant, or animal, there is also no openness of being and consequently no openness of non-being and of emptiness. While language foremostly names the being, this naming brings the being to word and to appearance. Such a naming names the being into its being ..." [79] Only insofar as we 'ec-sist' (stand in the openness of Being) and hear the articulated words of Being, can we speak. Speaking is the projecting of a world in such a way that things can be reached by the light of Being and thus be revealed. Projection is not an unrestricted human act; it is just "the release of a throw." [80] Man is thrown into *logos*, the orderly articulated language of Being. With his sayings he projects, and thus builds, his living language. Such projection is a response to the voiceless accosting of Being. *Legein* makes *logos logos*, which means that human sayings are applied and needed for the *logos* of Being just as a traveller is needed for a road to be a road.

We can talk because we always have a pre-ontological understanding of Being. We live in its language as in "the house of Being." [81] According to Heidegger, when we go through the forest, we go through the word 'forest,' even though we do not pronounce this word or think about anything linguistic.[82] Without the words of Being which are

[77] *Ibid.*, p. 5. The statement that 'language is the house of Being' does not stress the subordination of Being to man. It cannot be so because language exceeds man. Man is man by being aware of or by standing within the *logos*, the language of Being. Such standing is standing-in-the-world or to-be-in-the-world. Man is applied by Being for the establishing of a house for being – for establishing the language.
[78] Psychological or logical correctness concerns only terms but not words. Words as words are unattainable through logic. Only existential ontology can reveal the essence of language and words.
[79] Heidegger, *Holzwege*, pp. 60–61.
[80] *Ibid.*, p. 61.
[81] *Ibid.*, p. 286.
[82] *Ibid.*

constantly turned toward us, as a call demanding our answer, we would be as speechless as a rock. A language primarily belongs to Being and not to us. "Man behaves as though *he* were the modeler and master of language, while truly *it* stands as the lord of man." [83] According to Egon Vietta, Heidegger re-established the dignity of language in this "epoch of disintegration of language, of depletion of language and of the schematization of vocabulary." [84]

VI. BEFALLING AND HISTORY

Destiny

Throughout all his works Heidegger comes upon the problem of history. For him, however, this problem is not simply a problem of the raw events in the life of nations. Neither is it the succession of the different philosophies of the centuries. Nevertheless it is not without any relation to these modes of historicity. Here in the problem of history, as everywhere, Heidegger tries to get to the roots of the problem. In his *Sein und Zeit* he already showed the interwovenness of the problem of history with the most profound phenomena of *Dasein*. In resoluteness, *Dasein* is fully disclosed by its running forward into its basic possibility, the possibility of impossibility of *Dasein* – death. *Dasein* brings itself from its unessential possibilities, such as comfort, ease, tranquillity, social position, income, pleasures, etc., and brings itself into its own self, i.e. into its destiny. In its destiny *Dasein* takes itself fully into its own hands and becomes free. Destiny is man's freedom – freedom to his own self. Out of its authentic future (out of its resolute existing toward death) *Dasein* faces its past (given to it in its 'thrownness') authentically and exists in its present as in its authentic historical situation. In the midst of his situation, in his authentic *Da*, man lives historically.

History, as commonly understood, Heidegger directly calls history (*Historie*). For authentic history, the primarily understood phenomenon of history, he has another word, befalling (*Geschichte*).[85] "Chronological intervals and causal sequences belong however to history and not to befalling." [86] Befalling indicates that Being befalls man and

---

[83] Heidegger, *Vorträge*, p. 146.

[84] Vietta, *op. cit.*, p. 72.

[85] In common German usage, the word *Geschichte* coincides with the word *Historie*. Heidegger distinguishes these two words and reserves *Geschichte* for indication of the ontological essence of history, which may be expressed as 'being on the mission of Being.'

[86] Heidegger, *Holzwege*, p. 311.

sends him thus into his destiny; by undergoing this befallen destiny, man lives historically in the very fundamental sense of befalling. Befalling in itself implies destiny, which by overwhelming us (subordinating us to Being) frees us to ourselves. Befalling is a mission entrusted to us by Being; this mission is our freedom. In his later works Heidegger emphasizes Being as that which throws us into our destiny, makes us fall into our befalling. "Being is the basic event in which alone the befallen *Dasein* can 'essentiate' in the midst of the opened beings in their totality." [87]

Befalling and Being

Thinking and language belong primarily to Being as *logos*. Only responding to *logos* do we think or speak primarily. "Thinking as respondence stands in the service of language." [88] Respondence to the language of Being is not a thoughtless imitation. In his respondence to Being, man actively brings Being into openness and guards it in his sayings. "Man is the shepherd of Being." [89] As the shepherd of Being, man stands in the service of Being; he is in its mission. Being sends man into his destiny; makes him fall into befalling.

We are missionaries of Being. This mission of freedom (of destiny) may succeed or fail. It may succeed or fail because we do not make history in the sense of befalling. It is not up to our unrestrained will, according to Heidegger, as to whether and how God or gods appear in history, or how nature appears in it, and even things. We do not make history or all that appears in history. The mission or destiny of man is to let history be by letting gods, nature, and things be the way they are in the befalling of Being. By responding to Being, we take part in befalling.

Befalling would not be befalling without the approach of Being to which we respond in our befalling. Without our responses to Being, there would be neither gods, nor nature, nor things in the openness. Only by letting them appear the way they are, or the way they are not, do we guard them in the openness of Being, and they belong in the befalling. Responding in no wise is a making. The true and basic ground of everything that is, is Being. Being is the true maker of history. "But for man the question remains whether he finds the suitability of his essence to correspond to his destiny because, in accordance with this, he must guard the truth of Being."

[87] Heidegger, *Einführung*, pp. 153–154.
[88] Martin Heidegger, *Was ist das – die Philosophie* (Pfullingen: Günther Neske, 1956), p. 44.
[89] Heidegger, *Humanismus*, p. 19.

Those men making the turns of history stand under the demands of Being. They may succeed or fail. Success or failure is in the befalling – in the destiny of Being. Whenever a statesman subordinates himself to a definite value, clear and uniformly understandable principles or cleverly calculated aims, such a statesman may be within history, but he is outside befalling. He can have neither success nor failure in the ultimate sense because he is outside the realm of befalling.

Question of Being and befalling

The basic response of man to the approach of Being in the history of metaphysics is the question of being – why is there something rather than nothing? What does it mean to be? By asking the question of Being, man places himself into befalling. "Only there where Being reveals itself in the question, does befalling occur." [90] This question is not merely a human act. Nobody can ever ask the question of Being without already having a certain pre-knowledge of Being – without an approach of Being toward him. The one who asks the question of Being is the one to whom Being has already spoken, so that this question is merely an answer. This question is overtopping us; we are subordinate to it. Egon Vietta compares the openness of Being to the playgrounds which are placed in man.[91] Man is the place of revelation of Being: in man occur truth, freedom, and befalling (history). The true actor in the drama of truth, of freedom, of befalling (history) is Being; man is merely a stage.

By asking the question of Being, we disclose history.[92] The question of Being is "a hidden base of our historical *Dasein*." [93] The Greeks were the first to raise the question of Being. Being as such, and not simply beings or the totality of beings, attracted the attention of the early Greeks. The approach of Being, however, is always twofold. In befalling, Being reveals itself by letting beings appear; these can only appear in the light of Being. Being is always the 'beingness' of beings. In other words, Being cannot appear without beings which appear; the appearing beings reveal Being. However, Being in its revelation does not appear itself as beings do. It remains hidden or it appears in

[90] Heidegger, *Einführung*, p. 109.
[91] Vietta, *op. cit.*, p. 118.
[92] That which for the common understanding is the succession of different philosophies in time, is for Heidegger the befalling, the destiny of Being – in the sense that here each philosophy participates in the event of Being which, however, is the event of forgottenness of the question of Being. In the context following above 'befalling' will be replaced by 'history' where these two concepts merge together.
[93] Heidegger, *Einführung*, p. 71.

its concealment. The truth of Being in befalling is twofold. The re-velation of Being in history is, at the same time, its concealment. Being as such does not appear in history. "Being withdraws itself by disclosing itself in the 'beingness.' " [94] The truth of Being is simul-taneously its untruth. The raised question of Being is immediately the process of the forgottenness of the question of Being: it becomes replaced by the question of being. Nevertheless, the question of being is founded and carried by the question of Being which falls into for-gottenness. It is a mode of forgottenness of the question of Being. Since the question of being stands at the very beginning of the history of metaphysics and since the question of being is a mode of forgotten-ness of the question of Being – therefore, for Heidegger, the forgotten-ness of Being introduces history. Forgottenness of Being thus does not indicate an empty space in history, but rather the basic element which constitutes history. "The history of Being begins, and even necessarily begins, *with the forgottenness of Being.*" [95]

Being, as that which creates the field for beings to appear and which assembles beings upon themselves, gradually fell into forgottenness during the post-Socratic period of philosophy and for the centuries to come. This event of the forgottenness of Being was the forming principle which held the history of philosophy in meaningful unity from its very beginning. "The history of Western thought does not begin by thinking that which is most worthwhile to be thought, but by letting it fall into forgottenness." [96] The history of philosophy is a process of a deeper and deeper forgottenness of Being. In this process the event of the forgottenness of Being holds sway over the history of Western thought and carries it throughout the centuries. For philoso-phy to be philosophy the forgottenness of Being is needed. The early Greek philosophers, according to Heidegger, were not philosophers yet because they were the thinkers of Being.[97]

The meaning of the word 'philosopher'

The word 'philosopher' translated literally means 'the lover of wisdom.' For Heraclitus, a philosopher is ὅς φιλεῖ τὸ σοφόν, i.e., the one who loves σοφόν. For Heraclitus φιλεῖν, to love means "ὁμολογεῖν, to speak as the λογος speaks, i.e., to respond to λογος ... That a being reciprocally accomodates to another, that both primarily join one

[94] Heidegger, *Holzwege*, p. 311.
[95] *Ibid.*, p. 243.
[96] Heidegger, *Was heisst Denken?*, p. 98.
[97] Heidegger, *Philosophie*, p. 24.

another because they are ordained to each other – this ἀρμονία is that
which distinguishes the Heraclitian thought of φιλεῖν, of loving." [98]
The word *sophon* Heidegger interprets as Being which assembles beings
upon their being. Being is this assemblage, the *logos*. Hence, a philosopher, for Heraclitus, is the one who responds to *logos*. 'Philosopher' in
this sense does not coincide with the traditional post-Socratic meaning
of this word.

The Sophists had lost the astonishment with regard to the fact that
beings *are* and that they are assembled upon their being. The Sophists
claimed to be able to prove everything to everyone, and thus they did
not leave any room for astonishment, for the mystery of Being. Men
with a deeper insight tried to overcome this shallowness by striving
toward *en panta*, the all inclusive Being. They were the lovers of Being
(for Heidegger *sophon* is not wisdom but Being as *logos* which nevertheless is wisdom in the very fundamental ontological sense). Love in
their sense was not respondence or accordance but striving-after. In
the attention of the pre-Socratics stood *logos* which, as the assemblage,
'assembles' beings in such a way that they are beings. The interests of
the post-Socratics were directed towards beings insofar as they *are* –
the 'beingness' of beings; they did not consider Being which comes to
light of *logos* and thus *is* in its own way. According to Heidegger,
"philosophy investigates that which *is* insofar as it is." [99] The post-
Socratics saw that beings are, whereas the pre-Socratics were aware
that Being is. Therefore only the post-Socratics are philosophers.
"Heraclitus and Parmenides were not yet 'philosophers.' Why not?
Because they were the greater thinkers. 'Greater' here means not a
calculation of performance, but indicates another dimension of
thinking. Heraclitus and Parmenides were 'greater' in the sense that
they still stood in accordance with the λόγος, i.e. the εν πάντα." [100] The
'philosophers' are all the thinkers up to Nietzsche, who, in Heidegger's
consideration, is the last of the metaphysicians. Consequently, Heidegger himself is not a philosopher but a thinker of Being – a thinker
of the kind the early Greeks were.

The importance of the Greeks for Western philosophy is not simply
that of a historic nation; they are important as the originators of
Western thought. Being does not just stand at the beginning of
Western thought but also is its way throughout the centuries and still

[98] *Ibid.*, p. 21.
[99] *Ibid.*, p. 25.
[100] *Ibid.*, p. 24.

stands before us as the problem of our future. All the history of Western thought is determined by Being having shined in the early Greek *Dasein*. "We are, inasmuch as we exist historically, neither a great nor a small distance from the Greeks. We are, however, astray from them." [101] The history of philosophy is an orderly series of modes of divergence from the thinking of Being.

Thought of future

All the problems of philosophy from beginning to end are "ἐποχή of Being." [102] By 'epoch' Heidegger understands the establishment of the revelation of being in which Being itself remains concealed, holds onto itself. Epoch belongs to history; without it there cannot be any history. It is the backbone of history.

We stand at the end of the epoch of Being (i.e., of the concealment of Being) which began with the Greeks. This being at the end and not as yet being aware of this being-at-the-end in its full extent and already having forgotten the beginning gives us, contemporary people, a specific state of being lost or disoriented. "The befalling of man in modern times, so much mechanized to history, is signified by two deficiencies. He has no future because nothing comes upon him Therefore he improvises his future in utopias. He also has no tradition. Therefore he constantly breaks the ties of tradition by revolts." [103] Apparently contemporary man stands between philosophy, the epochal thought of concealment of Being, and the upcoming of a greater thought, the thought of Being, which fulfills epochal thought by bringing it back to the awarenness of Being.

The thinking of the future is not a philosophy anymore because it thinks more primarily than metaphysics which is just a different name for philosophy. The thinking of the future likewise cannot, as Hegel expected, put away the name of 'love of wisdom' and become wisdom itself in the form of an absolute knowledge. Thinking is tending to descend into the poverty of its finite essence. Thinking assembles the language into a simple saying. Language is the language of Being as the clouds are the clouds of the sky. Thinking lays with its sayings the insignificant-looking furrows in the language. They are more insignificant-looking than the ones a countryman draws following the plough with his tardy paces.[104]

The Hegelian absolute knowledge is replaced in Heidegger by human finite knowledge. Instead of the brilliancy of man with his

[101] Heidegger, *Holzwege*, p. 311.
[102] *Ibid.*
[103] Vietta, *op. cit.*, p. 143.
[104] Heidegger, *Humanismus*, p. 47.

absolute wisdom, Heidegger shows the simplicity of a countryman who insignificantly responds to the fields of Being with his drawn furrows. These furrows of thought are supported and carried by the diversely articulated terrains of Being; moreover, these furrows of thought are there only to help the assemblages of terrain (Being) to come up into light the way they are laid and assembled in the fields of Being. Furrows are used by Being-nature just as clouds and winds, streams and lakes, rocks and sand, trees and bushes, weeds and flowers – are used to bring its mighty presence into the world of being.

Since Heidegger's thinking is not a philosophy any longer, it seems to be "myth-like." [105] Man is not the true author of his thought any longer, but only a missionary carrying out the words of Being in his thought-responses. Not the thinker himself but Being determines the way of thinking of a philosopher. In one of his works Heidegger says: "Nietzsche, just as any other thinker, neither made his way nor chose it. He had been sent on his way." [106] Being sends man on the way of his thinking and like a subterranean stream carries him throughout history. This stream corresponds to *mythos*. In his profound little work *Vom Wesen des Enthusiasmus*, Eugen Fink sees in *mythos* the pro-revelation of Being in which man stands out or 'ec-sists' in three ways, namely: the religious, the artistic, and the philosophic ways of transcendence or enthusiasm as the ways of being-out-of-himself – three ways of 'ec-sistence.' Man can 'ec-sist' because he has given to him a field for his standing-out. This field is the pro-revelation of Being, the *mythos*. "Under the waves of historical changes flows a quiet stream of *mythos* throughout the times, and the nations find therein their mission preserved, their hold in the universe and in times of disintegration the strength of a turn," [107]

VII. SUBJECTIVISM AND METAPHYSICS

World of subjectivism

Heidegger's unconcern for rigorous logic, on the one hand, and a common misunderstanding that *Sein und Zeit* deals with anthropological problems, on the other hand, originated an opinion that Heidegger's philosophy is subjectivistic. However not being subjective,

[105] Wahl, *History*, p. 23.
[106] Heidegger, *Was heisst Denken?*, p. 61.
[107] Fink, *op. cit.*, p. 17.

Heidegger's philosophy neither is objective. It is beyond all subjectivisms as well as objectivisms. Both, subjectivism as well as objectivism, belong to the same level of thinking. An object can only be an object for a subject, and a subject is always opposed by objects. Therefore Heidegger considers subjectivism and objectivism under one and the same name, 'subjectivism.'

Along with subjectivism goes the consideration of the world as faced by man-subject. Such an understanding of world is an anthropological understanding. "The more the world is embraced, namely, the more penetratingly the conquered world is exposed, i.e. the more objective an object appears – by so much more is the world subjective, i.e. by so much more does the *subiectum* raise itself up prominently, and by so much more the consideration of the world, and its theory, inevitably changes to a theory of man, to anthropology." [108] Man as a subject is representation in the sense of putting things forward. Representation (*Vorstellen*) means "the placing of something in front of oneself and toward oneself." [109] In representative consideration, whatever is considered is considered as standing-in-front-of-us (*Gegenstand*); world, too, becomes that which is standing in front of us, as that which we face – it becomes a picture.

The original concept 'subject' did not signify man alone. It meant a substantial being having a number of accidents based in it, Whenever man became the only true subject, everything else was considered in respect to the human being, was considered anthropologically; and therefore everything else became objects. According to Heidegger, that which distinguishes man as man is not the relation of things as objects to man as subject, but the consideration of man as a being 'ec-sisting' in the openness of Being, i.e. as *Dasein*. Man is not a man as a subject before his standing-out in the world. This standing-out is what makes man man. It is essential to him. The phenomenon of the world or of *Dasein* as to-be-in-the-world is prior to the phenomena of subject and object. World is presupposed by subject and object and their interrelation.

Subjectivistic character of metaphysics

According to Heidegger, metaphysics is marked by subjectivism throughout its whole history. "Concern for man and man's position in the midst of beings dominates metaphysics." [110] Therefore

---

[108] Heidegger, *Holzwege*, pp. 85–86.
[109] *Ibid.*, p. 85.
[110] Heidegger, *Platons Lehre von der Wahrheit*, p. 49.

metaphysics rightly can be called humanistic (anthropocentric) in all
its different forms. The turn toward subjectivism and thus to metaphysics began with Plato, for whom being began to be considered as
looked-at, as that which stands in the aspect of the viewpoints. "The
views of that which things themselves are, the εἶδη (ideas), constitute
the essence in the light of which each particular being appears as this
or that." [111] However, things for Plato, and generally for the Greeks,
not only appear through out-looks, through viewpoints to them, but
also they appear as things in their truth by entering the range of these
viewpoints. Their being-seen (or their being-looked-at) belongs to
their sojourn in revelation. Such being-seen of things is still a perception of them the way they are in themselves, and not a forcing of
them into the certain ways of seeing, into determining viewpoint
imposed upon them. The Greeks still understood beings more ontologically than anthropologically. A being is a being not by the fact
that it is a being in the light of human seeing but by the fact that it is
a being in the light of Being.[112]

The modern attitude toward things has a character of seizing. Things
are comprehended by attacking them and capturing them in concepts
which express them as objects faced by a subject. Thing or being is
no longer a sojourning being, but a representative being, i.e. a being as
set forward in front of a subject and fitted to his sight. According to Egon
Vietta, a sharp turn toward subjectivism began with Descartes. "Since
then man and nature face themselves not as two kinds of creatures of the
same God (Middle Ages!) but as the exploiter (individual) faces the
exploited (nature, forces of earth, animal, plant, minerals)." [113] He
illustrates this with a scheme:.

God-Creator

↙   ↘

Homo sapiens   Natura

which is replaced in the modern times by:

Man-subject ↔ Nature-object.[114]

Descartes (and most of the traditional philosophers) understood
man as a being with a specific differentiation, rationality; he understood man categorically instead of understanding him properly –
existentially. Therefore, the definition of man as *animal rationale*
persisted. Man, for Descartes, puts forward the *res cogitata* as related

[111] *Ibid.*, p. 29.
[112] Max Müller, *Crise de la Métaphysique* (Paris: Desclee de Brouwer, 1953), p. 61.
[113] Vietta, *op. cit.*, p. 16.
[114] *Ibid.*, p. 17.

to himself, the *res cogitans*. Representation is certification. For Descartes the certitude *eo ipso* is truth and being (what is certain, that is true and that *is*). For a subject to know is for a subject to be (*me cogitare – me esse*). A subject is the place where all the knowledge of the objects (*scientia*) is in its togetherness (*con-scientia*). Here originates the concept of consciousness as "the convergence of the represented objectivities with man, the representative, in the middle of this circle of his secured representations." [115]

With Kant this subjectivity was modified by discovering that the objects are relative in respect to the cognitive powers of the subject. However, the basic metaphysical attitude remained: a being is always an object of a subject. Since certitude is truth (Cartesian standpoint) and since certitude is relative (Kantian standpoint), truth is relative too. The *Ding-an-sich*, the absolute certitude, and thus the absolute truth, is unattainable. "Essence is that which is essential. Since the total vision of being is impossible, nothing can be essential in itself but only essential for man, important and necessary for him. The absolute essence is thus replaced by the relative essence." [116] While the Platonic ideas are eternal and absolute essences (or objects), the Kantian essences are relative. According to Max Müller, Plato's philosophy is the metaphysics of subjectivism, and Kant's is the metaphysics of finite subjectivism.[117] Kant deals with finitude as such. In his case a subject not only views objects but also views the subject-viewing-objects. Kant is not simply a metaphysician but a metaphysician of metaphysics.

From Plato to Descartes the essences of things, even though objects of divine knowledge, were also attainable for human understanding. Kant's *Ding-an-sich* (the object of divine understanding) is no longer knowable for the human mind. In Nietzsche's philosophy man occupies the divine place, and thus a finite subject determines everything as though he were God Himself. Nietzsche's man "seeks himself as the executor of the will to power." [118] For Nietzsche the absolute values are collapsing and they are being replaced by the values of a new mankind which wants for itself the will to power.[119]

Kantian subjectivism is increased subjectivism as compared with

---

[115] Heidegger, *Holzwege*, p. 102.
[116] Müller, *op. cit.*, p. 18.
[117] *Ibid.*, p. 19.
[118] Heidegger, *Holzwege*, p. 231.
[119] Will to power is a finite subject originating all the values; it is the very 'beingness' of beings.

the Cartesian subjectivism, and Nietzsche's subjectivism is increased subjectivism as compared with the Kantian subjectivism. For Kant *Ding-an-sich* and God as supporting *Ding-an-sich*, even though unattainable for human knowledge, are not questioned in their existence; whereas for Nietzsche *Ding-an-sich*, just as all absolute ideas and supernatural values, is void of meaning. 'God is dead' proclaims Nietzsche and thus assures for man, even though a finite being, the throne of God. This is an extreme subjectivism.

Heidegger tries to show that the history of Western thought consequently and gradually tended toward extreme subjectivism. According to him, Nietzsche's 'God is dead' in no way is an expression of his personal atheistic attitude, but merely is a revelation of the fall of the supernatural values in the lives of modern men. Modern man of the eve of the 20th century (Nietzsche's time), naked in his subjectivistic freedom, began to be decreasingly determined by the supernatural values which had been usual in human life until then. By opposing idealistic, Platonic supernaturalism, Nietzsche thought he was overcoming metaphysics as such. According to Heidegger, however, "the reversal of Platonism, the reversal by which then for Nietzsche the sensible becomes the true world and the supersensible the untrue, remains thoroughly within metaphysics." [120] Nietzsche's investigation of values indicates that Nietzsche remained a metaphysician. Values can only be values in respect to a subject. "All evaluation, even positive evaluation, is subjectivization. It does not permit a being to *be* but permits the being to *be valid* merely as an object of performance." [121] The one who truly overcomes metaphysics is not a contra-metaphysician but a thinker of Being who thinks beyond metaphysics, beyond the level of subject-object.

Modern subjectivism

Man, at the height of modern science, faces the world as a field for his activities, his hunting grounds. Everything in the world is considered as related to man. Forests are resources of building materials or they may be picnic grounds. Mountains may be rich in coal, uranium, or gold. They may provide a scenic drive for vacationers. Rivers are ways of transportation or a supply ot water for the irrigation of the fields. They are also places for boat rides or sometimes for fishing. Everything is considered in relation to man as a subject – a builder,

[120] Heidegger, *Vorträge*, p. 79.
[121] Heidegger, *Humanismus*, p. 35.

an engineer, a manufacturer, a vacationer, etc., but is not considered as it is in itself. Never does earth appear as earth to the modern man but always as the object, or the multitude of objects, for exploitation. Earth as earth can only appear for *Dasein*, for a to-be-in-the-world, but not for a subject. Approaching us in the diversity of ways of revelation (not the ways forced by our subjective viewpoints), earth constantly retreats beyond our access and remains mysteriously in a concealment which puzzles and astonishes one who is still free for its approach. Earth assembles all things upon themselves – unto their 'somethingnesses' – but never reveals itself as a something. Totality as such is ignored by the modern man. For him a whole is a sum or the total of that which is faced by him, but never that which over-whelms him, involves him in its whirlpool, overtops him and makes him an eccentric being – a being whose meaning is placed beyond himself – rather than a concentric, isolated island in this totality. Being for the modern man is placed forward and related to him ob-jectively; " '*esse – percipi*' [122] being is being-represented. Being is by virtue of representation. This being is identical with thinking insofar as the objectivity of objects is joined and construed in the representing consciousness – in the 'I think something.' " [123]

Modern man sees the meaning of his life in complete domination or ruling of the world. The world is for man's use and exploitation, and this exploitation is the meaning of human life. The meaning of the world is derived from man, and the meaning of man is placed in the conquering of the world. This reciprocal relation of world and man is a meaningless circle. Heidegger says:

This Europe in its godless dazzling, constantly leaping to stab itself, is situated today between the great tongs of Russia on the one side and America on the other. Russia and America are both metaphysically equal in the same desperate madness of unchained techniques and bottomless organization of the normal men. Whenever the most distant corner of the globe will be conquered and exploited technically, whenever any event, at any place and at any time, in any speed becomes attainable, whenever an attempt on the life of a king of France and a symphony concert in Tokyo simultaneously can be 'experienced,' whenever time is only speed, instantness, and simultaneity, and time as be-falling is gone out of the *Dasein* of all nations, whenever a boxer is considered the great man of a nation, whenever a meeting numbering a million is a triumph – then, yes then the question remains as spectre over all this phantom – what for, where to, and what then? [124]

Modern man is speeding toward the extremes of his subjectivity to hold the world completely in his hands. He believes he will then be

[122] Here Heidegger uses the words of Berkeley.
[123] Heidegger, *Vorträge*, p. 235.
[124] Heidegger, *Einführung*, pp. 28–29.

fully man. However, at exactly that time the complete emptiness of modern man will be revealed. If man is not seizing the world any longer (world is conquered), who is he? What is his meaning?

The emptiness of modern man expresses itself in the rating of man's worth by regarding his exterior, e.g. dressing. Everyone is equal to everyone else as a man. One emptiness can only be distinguished from another emptiness by something external added to it. This addition which makes men distinguishable one from another becomes the essential feature of him. This addition is his uniform which represents his function in society. "A man without a uniform today gives an impression of the unreal, of something which does not belong there."[125] Such a minimization of an individual and accentuation of a group (a union, a nation, a social organization, a team, etc.) does not mean a refutation of subjectivism as such. Subjectivism is still subjectivism even though 'we' or a group of 'I's' replaces 'I.'

Overcoming of metaphysics

Metaphysics as subjectivism is a process of the forgottenness of Being. Dealing with the beings or 'beingness,' metaphysics does not consider Being itself. Being "is like a light which illuminates everything and which renders possible all investigation, but which is never examined itself." [126] Even though metaphysics ignores Being, Heidegger does not suggest its rejection. The forgottenness of Being is a characterization and not a devaluation of metaphysics. It is not a nothing, but is an event which "conceals the unlifted treasures." [127] These treasures lie in the roots of metaphysics, presupposed by it. In these presuppositions Heidegger sees a guiding trend which leads to the forgotten Being. The metaphysical thought of the past centuries proceeded "in the sign of the disclosure of the sojourning beings. This disclosure rests in the concealment of sojourning," [128] which is the truth of Being.

Heidegger is a philosopher who tries to think Being instead of the 'beingness' of beings. In order to think Being, metaphysics has to be overcome. Overcoming, however, is not the creation of a super-philosophy, but a return to "the proximity of the most near." [129] In this proximity of Being, man is not a subject, and his importance is not

[125] Heidegger, *Vorträge*, p. 97.
[126] Müller, *op. cit.*, p. 17.
[127] Heidegger, *Seinsfrage*, p. 35.
[128] *Ibid.*
[129] Heidegger, *Humanismus*, p. 37.

placed in his 'I-ness' (*Ichheit*), but in his self-ness, i.e. in him as in the place of the revelation of Being. "Man does not have to be determined as *mens*, as measure, which lies in the basis of all things (*subiectum*), but as *Dasein*," [130] the place of revelation of Being. Instead of *animal rationale* or *animal metaphysicum* man must become the shepherd or guardian of Being.

The overcoming of metaphysics is achieved not by its rejection, but by the knowledge of its nature, its theme, and its field. This cannot be known within the framework of metaphysics, just as nature of logic cannot be known within the framework of logic. "The question of the essence of Being perishes if it does not abandon the language of metaphysics, because metaphysical representation forbids us to think the question concerning the essence of Being." [131] In his *Was ist Metaphysik?*, Heidegger compares metaphysics to the roots of a tree, which represents philosophy itself. A tree has its roots firmly in the ground, which represents Being. Ground or soil enables the tree to grow and thus leave the ground. Metaphysics, as these roots, penetrates the soil of Being, the element of its 'essentiation.' Roots, although in the ground, belong to the tree, and what they perform is for the tree but not for the ground. Roots give no account of the ground. Ground falls into forgottenness for the sake of the tree. "Metaphysics does not think Being. It only represents the 'beingness'-of beings and not Being itself. Philosophy does not assemble itself on its own ground. It forsakes it constantly, and that by metaphysics. Nevertheless, it never escapes its ground." [132]

Heidegger's thinking is a return to Being, to that which metaphysics constantly forsakes and ignores. By its answers metaphysics leads our attention away from Being, cuts us off from it. On the other hand, metaphysics is a helpful means to approach or to get near Being by following it to its primary presupposition – just as by following the roots of the tree down to where they are lost in the ground, the ground itself can be discovered. By not taking metaphysical principles for granted, but by trying to think them, metaphysics can be transcended. Such a procedure tending to go backwards more deeply than traditional philosophy ever went, is called 'destruction' by Heidegger. "Destruction does not mean destroying, but dissembling, carrying away, and setting aside, namely, of the historical statements of the

[130] Vietta, *op. cit.*, p. 134.
[131] Heidegger, *Seinsfrage*, p. 26.
[132] Heidegger, *Was ist Metaphysik?*, p. 8.

befalling of philosophy. Destruction means opening our ear, making it free for that which imparts to us the Being of 'beingness' in tradition. By hearing this imparting we attain to the response." [133] With his 'destructive' analysis of the history of philosophy, Heidegger leads the basic problems of past philosophers back beyond their starting points into the realm of Being itself.

One of the most hardened presuppositions of traditional philosophy is the consideration as self-evident, that Being is opposed to appearing. Yet, the appearances of things belong to things themselves. Thing itself appears in its appearance as the stars appear by their twinklings. "Being means appearing. This does not say something supplemental, which befalls Being occasionally. Being 'essentiates' as appearing." [134] Appearing is not opposed to Being, but it belongs to it. The early Greek problem of *physis* is thought of as the appearing Being. Being is not something which is before appearance. Being is appearing – appearing constantly and essentially. In its appearing, Being appears as veiled, however. *Physis* does not appear directly as a being or a thing does, but it appears as that which is presupposed by all things. Heidegger's problem of earth is based on the Greek *physis*. Earth reveals all things in their forms and colors, and thus reveals itself, but as constantly veiled. Concealment-disclosure is truth. "Truth in the sense of disclosure, as well as appearance in the sense of a certain mode of upcoming self-manifestation, belongs necessarily to Being." [135]

Since Being is in no way *a* being, but is rather not-a-being, it can only take place as nothingness in the reality. Kant's *Ding-an-sich* is not a being, because it does not appear in appearance and never can become an object of understanding. However, even though not a being, *Ding-an-sich* is something (*etwas*). Analogically Heidegger's Being is not a being, nevertheless it is real; it 'essentiates' (*es west*) and appears in its concealment. Since man knows what *is*, he knows also what-*is not*. He "holds an open place for the totally opposite than that which is in order that in its openness, sojourning (Being) may be." [136] Being and nothingness belong together; "Being and nothingness are not outside of one another." [137]

---

[133] Heidegger, *Philosophie*, pp. 33–34.
[134] Heidegger, *Einführung*, p. 77.
[135] *Ibid.*, p. 83.
[136] Heidegger, *Seinsfrage*, p. 38.
[137] *Ibid.*

VIII. NOTHINGNESS AND NIHILISM

Nothingness and negation

Just as death is that which gives life (in the sense of existence) its fullness and makes it stand out as an organized whole, so nothingness is presupposed to give Being its framework and graspability. *Dasein* is related to death just as Being is to nothingness. Death and nothingness help to reveal *Dasein* and Being. Egon Vietta compares nothingness to a gap, which, as totally opposite to being, cuts being off and makes it outstanding and united in its whole self. "Without a gap we never would have an insight into that which is. Only where the rocks move apart, does an abyss open. If there were not something (the gap), which contrasts beings in their totality, but only being, if there were no outlet into the totally opposite, being as being could not appear or 'sojourn' for us." [138]

Nothingness is never just a negated something. "Nothingness is prior to the 'no' and the negation." [139] Negation presupposes nothingness. Nothingness *is* not, but nevertheless it is real and belongs to the event of Being. Nothingness 'noughts' (*nichtet*). Since the 'is' usually is the way of being of the disposable things or beings, Heidegger, in dealing with the phenomena of non-disposable character, uses different 'is-es,' namely: *Dasein* exists, time temporizes, Being 'essentiates,' and nothingness 'noughts.' Nothingness is not simply the not-being-there of a disposable thing (as after bread has been eaten, it is no longer there). Nothingness has the character of totality. It negates the totality of being. "The totality of being must be given beforehand so as to succumb as such to the negation from which nothingness is then bound to emerge." [140]

Nothingness and dread

Since nothingness is beyond any negation, it is also beyond logic. It cannot be proven logically. Nevertheless it can be experienced existentially. *Dasein* is revealed to itself in its 'thrownness' by the mood of dread. In everydayness we deal only with the beings, which presuppose the world and *Dasein*, but neither world nor *Dasein* is

---

[138] Vietta, *op. cit.*, p. 84.
[139] Heidegger, *Was ist Metaphysik?*, p. 26.
[140] *Ibid.*, p. 27.

experienced in everydayness. Only in dread, when everything of merely-being-character is drifting away as meaningless, do we face our true self as the to-be-in-the-world, which as the *Da* of Being is nothingness, because it is not of a being-character. It is not a being, not a thing, nothing, and yet – it is real. Our self is never graspable or measurable with the rulers of everydayness. In dread, our self, as nothingness, is revealed and real, even though it is not understood or comprehended logically or rationally. Only from our self can we encounter beings in their totality. Being can only be approached in togetherness with nothingness. The basic metaphysical question presupposes Being as well as nothingness. This question, according to Heidegger, is: "Why there is being at all, and not rather a nothing?"[141] Nothingness never appears as separated from the totality of the drifting-away-beings in the mood of dread. "On the contrary, nothingness manifests itself truly with and by the beings as drifting away in their totality." [142]

Dread is not the only mood which reveals nothingness to us as underlying the presuppositions of the basic metaphysical question of why there is being at all, and not rather a nothing. Heidegger says:

In great desperation, for instance, when all weight tends to disappear from the things and any meaning at all is obscured, then this question arises, be it only by a single stroke like a dull bell-sound which resounds into the *Dasein* and slowly dies away again. In a heart-felt joy this question is there, because here all the things are transformed and stand around us as newly born in such a way that they may almost be conceived as not being rather than as being, or moreover – as being the way they are. This question is present in boredom in which we are equally removed from desperation as well as from joy, in which the hardened ordinariness spreads a desolation, in which we are indifferent to whether the being is or is not, and thus again the peculiar question begins to sound: why there is being at all and not rather a nothing? [143]

Nothingness and Being

In the mood of dread, nothingness is revealed as repelling. We are withdrawing. Our withdrawal points to the totality of being which is drifting away. This pointing gives solidification to this totality and emphasizes is as that which is, and also as that which is different from nothingness and from nought. 'Noughting' is the repelling relegation to being in its totality. Because nothingness 'noughts,' being *is*. Nothingness never is, and being never 'noughts.' To be a being is to be

[141] Heidegger, *Einführung*, p. 1.
[142] Heidegger, *Was ist Metaphysik?*, p. 31.
[143] Heidegger, *Einführung*, p. 1.

not a nothing. This 'not a nothing' "beforehand makes possible the disclosure of being as such. The essence of the primarily 'noughting' nothingsness lies in the fact that it alone brings *Dasein* face to face with being as such." [144] The beforehand experience of nothingness in dread enables *Dasein* to encounter beings, to reveal them, and to help them to be beings. For knowledge of that which is, the knowledge of nothingness is presupposed. Since *Dasein* is constantly dealing with the things, it is always in an existential knowledge of nothingness. "*Dasein* means to be held-in-nothingness." [145] The being-held-in-nothingness at the same time means not to be fully submerged in being, but to be standing out from it, to transcend it. Without this transcendence *Dasein* would never have any understanding or experience of being, it would not possess its own self and would not be free. "Without the primary revelation of nothingness there is no being-self or freedom." [146]

The question of Being, of that which is by the 'is' of everything presupposed, leads into the midst of nothingness. Nothingness is never simply the opposite of Being, but belongs primarily to Being. Since nothingness is that which grants the 'is-character' to being, it can never be just the negation of that which is. When nothingness 'noughts,' being is. 'Noughting' belongs to Being. "The act of 'noughting' in Being is the 'essentiation' of that which I call nothingness," says Heidegger.[147] Nothingness is that "which gives the custody of 'to be' to each being. It is the Being itself." [148]

In order to think Being properly, or better, to think it at all, metaphysics, and thus the consideration of Being as a being or as the 'beingness,' has to be overcome. Just as Being is not opposed to appearance or to becoming, neither is it opposed to nothingness. "Nothingness is never a nothing, nevertheless it is not a something in the sense of an object. It is the Being itself, whose truth only then will be committed to man, when he will have overcome himself as a subject, i.e. when he will not represent the being as an object any-longer." [149] Since traditional philosophy did not think Being as such, but thought it as the 'beingness' of beings, it thought of being as opposed to nothing. Heidegger 's investigation of Being has shown

[144] Heidegger, *Was ist Metaphysik?*, p. 31.
[145] *Ibid.*, p. 32.
[146] *Ibid.*
[147] Heidegger, *Humanismus*, p. 44.
[148] Heidegger, *Was ist Metaphysik?*, p. 41.
[149] Heidegger, *Holzwege*, p. 104.

that to be opposed to beings, or to the 'beingness' of beings, is not *eo ipso* to be nothing in the sense of *nihil*. Reality in its profound basis (such is the early Greek *physis*) 'is' not the way things 'are,' and yet it is not a nothing, but it is that which makes whatever-is-real to be real. To signify Being as not-a-being and as not opposed to nothingness, in one of his late works, *Zur Seinsfrage*, Heidegger writes ~~Being~~ with crossmarks. Crossmarks indicate that Being does not exclude nothingness; it implies it in itself. Being is not a thing; it is not identical to the 'beingness' of the beings. Nevertheless it is not without the things or beings and their 'beingness.' By 'noughting,' ~~Being~~ solidifies being, grants the being-character to beings and thus enables them to acquire their 'is-es.' ~~Being~~ hinders any treatment of Being as something isolated and statically existing for itself.

The essence of man is 'ec-sistence' into the openness of Being. Since Being is ~~Being~~ (implying nothingness), this 'ec–sistence' of man is "being held-in-nothingness." [150] Inasmuch as man is the place of the Being's coming into openness, he is the place of the 'noughting' of nothingness. The relation of man to nothingness is not merely a relation in which man thinks nothingness; as being-held-in-nothingness, he 'ec-sists' in the midst of it. He is the tenant of ~~Being~~ ; hence – of nothingness as well.

Nihilism

Lost in his everyday securities, man lives the self-less life of the common man, in which Being as well as nothingness is concealed. Only in rare moments of dread, or of other existential moods, does he get into his own self and thus face Being as well as nothingness. "Dread is necessary to startle man out of the uniformity of his everyday, thoughtless living on." [151] Dread is not destructive. It may only appear destructive to a man of 'common sense' who is well informed about everyday ways and doings and for whom only beings or things are what count. For such a problemless and secure living on, dread is merely a destructive invader which marks such a living as meaningless. However, as a mood leading man into his own self, dread is of enormous ontological importance. Dread throws man back into the place where he belongs, into nothingness, which "nevertheless 'essentiates' even as the 'homeness' [152] of Being itself," [153] and thus it (dread) turns

---

[150] Heidegger, *Was ist Metaphysik?*, p. 32.
[151] Bollnow, *op. cit.*, p. 370.
[152] '*Geheimnis*' for Heidegger is not as much 'mystery' as rather 'homeness' (*Heim* – home).
[153] Heidegger, *Vorträge*, p. 177.

man to Being but not to a nihilism. Only a dreadless life – life without facing nothingness and hence, without facing Being – is nihilistic. "In the forgottenness of Being, by only being occupied with the beings, lies nihilism." [154]

The sharp turn toward the beings and the unconcern for Being of the modern man can better be called nihilism than Heidegger's devoted work to revive the understanding of Being lost since the time of the early Greeks. "Nihilism, however, never holds sway where Being is made visible or where the supporting basis of *Dasein* is brought into presentiment, but where this basis is lost – in our subjective civilization." [155] In dominating the earth and the wide ranges of beings by scientific and technical means, modern man cannot disclose this reality, i.e. cannot disclose the truth of Being. On the contrary, he closes himself off from true reality. He is a nihilist. In the whirlpool of beings, he measures everything by the measure of beings – by the subjective measure; and everything which does not fit into this scale, he considers as not being, as nothing. Therefore in Heidegger's philosophy, according to Max Müller, "Being is expressed as nothingness in reference to being of the everyday reality and its demands which are based on the pattern of beings." [156]

Since beings as beings can never reveal their own foundations, therefore, for their ontological investigation, interpretation, and justification, a reach is needed which transcends being. In his reach into the foundations of beings, Heidegger comes up with Being which is not a being or the 'beingness' of beings, but completely 'opposite' in respect to beings. It is nothingness. Heidegger's profound reach into nothingness in no wise denies Being. On the contrary, it is a great pursuit of an affirmation of Being. All his basic problems aim at the one and final problem, Being. "Freedom as conjunction, factual relation to Being; nothingness as the original coming into power of Being in *Dasein*, in human existence; dread as the fundamental accord of human being with his potential experience or realization of Being and with his, freedom for Being – all this is not 'nihilism,' but a 'thought of Being.' " [157]

---

[154] Heidegger, *Einführung*, p. 155.
[155] Vietta, *op. cit.*, p. 38.
[156] Müller, *op. cit.*, p. 55.
[157] *Ibid.*, pp. 55–56.

Overcoming of nihilism

Man's persistent interest in the particular beings or things and his
unconcern for Being is that which Heidegger understands to be the
true nihilism. In its extremes this nihilism tends to become a nihilism
which no longer sees a meaning even in being of beings. "In the phase
of completed nihilism it seems as though there is no *being of* beings," [158]
says Heidegger; and he stresses the words 'being of' which indicate
the meaninglessness of beings in their 'beingness,' i.e. their drifting
away in their totality. With such a drifting away of beings in their
totality, the nothingness 'noughts.' The experience of nothingness
always occurs in the neighborhood of Being itself. In the phase of
completed nihilism, man, as lacking a meaning of being, already
advances the concealment of Being. "In a strange way ~~Being~~ fails to
appear. It conceals itself." [159] This concealment is twofold: by man's
turning to the beings, Being is concealed, and by his denying the
meaning of beings in their 'beingness,' this 'beingness' is concealed.
In this double concealment Being as ~~Being~~ is concealed. "It holds
itself in a concealment which conceals itself." [160] Complete nihilism
is a concealment of the concealment of Being. This concealment is the
first step toward the truth of Being.[161] This step toward the truth of
Being can be realized, not simply by a rejection of nihilism, but by an
attempt to reach and penetrate its essence. The road leading to the
essence of nihilism, not only helps to overcome nihilism, but also
brings us back to Being.

With Plato, the philosophy of Being had been transformed into
metaphysics, the philosophy of being. Metaphysics as subjectivism is
essentially nihilistic – it ignores Being. "Metaphysics, as the history
of the truth of being as such, in its essence is nihilism," [162] Heidegger
says. In its extremes, nihilism runs into a dead-end alley, where the
question of Being – although two ways concealed – comes back into
the focus of philosophy. After having gone through the fire of nihilism,
philosophy emerges from metaphysics and becomes, with Heidegger,
a philosophy of Being again.

The philosophy of Being is not simply opposed to traditional philosophy or metaphysics. In the extremes of metaphysics, Being begins

[158] Heidegger, *Seinsfrage*, p. 34.
[159] *Ibid.*
[160] *Ibid.*
[161] The concealment of Being is untruth. Untruth essentially belongs to the truth as
aletheia.
[162] Heidegger, *Holzwege*, p. 244.

to radiate as that which is lacked, just as in the beginning of metaphysics Being had radiated before merging into forgottenness. Being never shines like the sun in a clear sky. It reveals itself in the twilight of sunset, in its withdrawal from us, and in the twilight of sunrise, in its approach toward us. The forgottenness of Being necessarily belongs to the radiance of Being (Being shines only in its approach or withdrawal); without it, Being does not shine. Being is just like Heraclitus' fire: it never 'essentiates' statically, but only dynamically, by coming and going. Being can only appear in history, and history begins with its forgottenness. Therefore, in Heidegger's thought metaphysics is not expelled or removed from the body of Western thought as a diseased part, but is retained in a highly respected and fully justified place. Without metaphysics there cannot be any philosophy of Being just as without untruth there is no truth, without everydayness – no freedom as being-self, without death – no life.

IX. BEING AND MAN

Dasein *as Being in man*

Heidegger thinks Being. Being cannot be thought logically. In its primary phase logic was a thinking-interpretation of the experience of Being; but from the time of Aristotle, logic degenerated into an instrument which is no longer related to Being, but "binds itself to the calculation of beings only and exclusively serves them alone." [163] Heidegger transcends logic in its traditional sense, because he thinks Being and not of beings.[164]

He does not think of a being, even if this being is of enormous importance, e.g. man. The theme of *Sein und Zeit* is *Dasein*, the essence of man. Man is man only "on the basis of *Dasein* in him." [165] *Dasein* is prior to man; it is more than man; it is the place of Being (*das Da des Seins*). Therefore the consideration of *Dasein* is not anthropology but ontology. Considering a sentence "pronounced by Sartre: *précisément nous sommes sur un plan où il y a seulement des hommes,*" [166] Heidegger confronts Sartre with his own attitude, expressing it: "*précisément nous sommes sur un plan où il y a principalement l'Être.*[167]

---

[163] Heidegger, *Was ist Metaphysik?*, p. 43.
[164] Cf. footnote 10, p. 3.
[165] Heidegger, *Kant*, p. 207.
[166] Precisely we are on a level where there are only men.
[167] Precisely we are on a level where there is principally Being.

Where does it come from and what is *le plan*? *L'Être et le plan* are the
same." [168] In the same immediate context Heidegger remarks that the
French '*il y a l'Être*' does not translate the German '*es gibt das Sein*'
adequately. This '*es gibt das Sein*' philologically means 'there is Being,'
but Heidegger means it archaically, which is more literal – 'it gives
Being,' where 'it' and 'Being' are the same. Being gives itself; it brings
itself into openness. Being, as bringing itself into openness, is disclosure, the truth, the *Da*. To guard the truth of Being, to let this truth
abide in him, i.e. to be the *Da* of Being, is the mission of man which
makes man man.

Being as sojourning

Heideggerian thinking, just as the thinking of the early Greeks, is
prior to all the differentiations of philosophy into philosophical disciplines: logic, ethics, cosmology, etc. Beyond all these specializations
there is not chaos but the structure of Being itself. Accordingly, the
Parmenidian sphere is not an object, not a mental fiction, but an
ontological symbol expressing the unity of everything that is. The
Greek word for Being, *eon*, means that which lasts, approaches,
appears; it is sojourning (*Anwesen*). It implies in itself the *en*, the
unifying One. The unifying One of all appearances is presupposed by
these appearances which sojourn in it as sojourning beings (*Anwesendes*). Sojourning secures in its realm all that which-sojourns – lasts, appears, approaches. "The well-rounded sphere, as the Being of beings, has
to be thought of in the sense of revealing, shining unification. Thus, this
unification, as the total unification, gives an occasion to name it as the
shining shell of a sphere, which, as revealing, directly does not comprise
everything, but, itself shining, admits everything into sojourning." [169]
The Parmenidian sphere is the revealing sojourn of Being itself.

Any unification implies a distinction or a split. Split signifies another
important Parmenidian concept, the *moira*. *Moira* expresses fate,
mission, destiny. It distributes destinies to everything. By such a
distribution of destinies, everything is sent to the befalling in which
it appears. *Moira*, the source of destinies, even though itself concealed,
is the disclosing power of Being. *Moira* sends everything away (things,
men, gods) into everyone's destiny; nevertheless it does not let it loose
there, but holds it onto its binding, unifying power. "In the befalling
of this duality, only sojourning begins to radiate, whereas the

[168] Heidegger, *Humanismus*, p. 22.
[169] Heidegger, *Holzwege*, p. 278.

sojourning beings begin to appear." [170] Therefore history, which is
rooted in the befalling of Being, is also twofold: it always deals with
Being as concealing and as revealing the sojourning beings in their
sojourn. The concealing-disclosure of beings can only occur on the
basis of Being which itself is always either approaching or withdrawing.
The duality of concealing disclosure settles in the factual history of
Western philosophy as the duality of Being and beings. Beings appear
and in their appearance the radiating source, which renders such
appearance possible, withholds itself – remains concealed. Parmenidian thought of Being, as a unifying sphere as well as destinies-
distributing *moira*, introduced the metaphysical, so-called 'ontological,
difference' of being and beings and thus initiated the forgottenness of
Being – the history of Western thought.

In dread, Being reveals itself as moving away, and in joy – as turned
toward us. "The prime essence of joy is the becoming-at-home in
nearness to the primordial source," [171] which is Being. Since Being is
dynamic, i.e. it conceals and reveals, approaches and withdraws, it
requires an enthusiastic openness or overtness to correspond to it.
Therefore the mission of man to be the shepherd of Being is difficult
to perform. Man is an erring being, and history is a series of man's
going astray. The road of man cannot be traveled lightly: care is
needed to face the problems and to respect the problems of past
thought. Taking them for granted or for 'solved' or being addicted to
the opinions of the day, severs man from Being. "We know too
much," says Heidegger, "and we believe too fast to become at home
in a properly experienced question." [172] By superficially regarding
the thoughts of the past philosophy, especially those of the early
Greeks, we close ourselves off from them. With his original and deep
reconstruction of the thought of past philosophies, Heidegger tries to
return to the prime meanings of the problems of these philosophies.

Being as assemblage

The Heraclitian *logos* is Being as assemblage which assembles by
concealing and revealing. The common man (the man of everydayness)
is turned away from this assemblage and turned to the business and
matters of common life. In his familiarity with the needs and doings
of his everyday life, he feels secure and at-home; but, verily, he is

[170] Heidegger, *Vorträge*, p. 252.
[171] Heidegger, *Erläuterungen*, p. 23.
[172] Heidegger, *Vorträge*, p. 259.

strange and homeless there (his home is in the neighborhood of Being). "Everyday opinion looks for the truth in the diversity of the constantly new which is spread out in front of it. It does not see the calm glow (gold) of 'homeness' which incessantly shines in the simplicity of lighting. Heraclitus says (Fragment 9),... 'Donkeys prefer chaff to gold!' " [173] The gold of Being reveals itself by shining, and, significantly, this radiance for Heraclitus as well as for Heidegger is that which conceals Being. The radiance of Being reveals and conceals Being at the same time. "The radiance of lighting as such is, at the same time, self-concealment and, in this sense, the most obscure." [174]

In the radiant and concealing assemblage of *logos* everything sojourning finds its place and meaning. In his little and rather poetic work *Der Feldweg*, Heidegger pictures Being as a country road which assembles everything in its neighborhood and thus assembles everything which sojourns in this neighborhood upon itself (upon the sojourning Being itself). "On its path [175] the storm of winter and the day of harvest meet each other; the agile thrill of springtime and the calm demise of fall encounter each other; the play of the youth and the wisdom of the aged behold each other." [176] In a very similar manner Heraclitus indicates *logos*, the assemblage, by his ontological symbol of war: "War is both king of all and father of all, and it has revealed some as gods, others as men; some it has made slaves, others free." [177]

Being as a road

Man thinks by responding to *logos*. The voice (*Stimme*) tunes (*stimmt*) man to thinking; it befalls the essence of man "in such a way that he would learn to experience Being in nothingness" [178] and thus he would guard the disclosed Being in his sayings and works. Being needs man to bring its silent speech into human words. In one of his latest works, *Zur Seinsfrage*, Heidegger, considering Being as turned toward us, emphasizes that Being cannot be understood as something in itself which also turns toward us, but as this turning-toward-us itself. Without man, Being is not turning-toward and therefore it is not Being. "Being, in its need to 'essentiate' itself in man, is thereupon

---

[173] *Ibid.*, p. 281.
[174] *Ibid.*, pp. 281–282.
[175] On the path of the country road.
[176] Martin Heidegger, *Der Feldweg* (Frankfurt a.M.: Vittorio Klostermann, 1956), pp. 5 6.
[177] Heraclitus, Fragment 53 in Freeman, *op. cit.*
[178] Heidegger, *Was ist Metaphysik?*, p. 42.

designated to abolish the seemingness of the being-for-itself, wherefore it is of a different essence than that which the representation of a principle, which comprises the subject-object relation, would be inclined to maintain." [179] Being and man are in no wise two separate beings (they are not one being either), because they are not beings: neither Being nor man as *Dasein* is a being. Man belongs to the openness of Being essentially, and Being 'essentiates' itself by sojourning toward human essence.[180]

Through the ontological symbol of the country road, Heidegger visualizes this belonging together of Being and man. Interestingly, Heidegger does not choose for this symbol merely a way or a road, but specifically a country road or a forest-trail. A mere road or street is usually a public street or road – road of the common man, whereas the country road or forest-trail is a way which is taken at one's own risk; it is a way of self-responsibility. On a public highway Being can never be experienced. The only places where Being is accessible are country roads or forest-trails. "It is said about these that they are overgrown because they are rarely trodden, and that they end suddenly in tracklessness. Man can get lost on them. They themselves get lost, however in one and the same forest of one and the same Being." [181] Whereas the highway travellers are always lost from the forest of Being without knowing that they are lost; they take this being-lost as the true security. In the face of completed nihilism these 'highway men' may despair about the ways of their life and they may turn toward the forests of Being.

The country road is not a road of crowds, but of rare travellers. It is not a man-made highway, but primarily belongs to Being. "Yet the call of the country road calls only as long as there are men who are born in its air and able to hear it. They are the hearers of the call, but not the servants of fabrication." [182] On a country road or a forest-trail man is a true traveller, because with his own foot and not with a man-made apparatus (a motor vehicle) he strikes the ground, the true natural earth (not a man-made, comfortable pavement). On the country road or forest-trail man himself responds to the call of Being; he does not respond through the medium of the common-man self. A way is a way to be travelled, and a call is a call as long as it is heard. Only in their togetherness is call a call and hearing hearing.

[179] Heidegger, *Seinsfrage*, pp. 30–31.
[180] *Ibid.*, p. 27.
[181] Löwith, *op. cit.*, p. 18.
[182] Heidegger, *Feldweg*, p. 4.

Man as the responder to the call of Being is not the empirical man or the subject, but man in his deep essence or in the rare instances of his authentic being-self. Man as a subject is not the answerer to the call of Being; but *Dasein*, Being itself *qua* man, is the answerer. "We are nothing; what we seek is all." [183] Only by responding to the 'all' do we form ourselves into something, into responders. The 'all' gives us to ourselves as responders to its call. 'All' is more in our responses than we ourselves are. "Coginition accordingly means, that man phrases the understanding of Being into an expressive announcement. This does not mean that the 'intellect,' but the Being, holding sway over man, brings itself into understanding." [184] In another place in his book (*Die Seinsfrage bei Martin Heidegger*) Egon Vietta figuratively compares thinking in Being with an earthquake and thinking in us with the seismographic instrument "which registers the quake." [185] This registering is that which constitutes the somethingness of our essence, without which we would subside into nothing. The call of Being forms us into our somethingness so that we become what we are. The title of his book *Was Heisst Denken?* Heidegger interprets not as 'what does thinking mean?,' but "what is that which refers us to thinking in the sense that it directs us into thinking, and thus accredits to us our own essence as such, which 'essentiates' insofar as it thinks?" [186]

Man is a shepherd of Being. His mission is to guard the truth of Being. The care of his very essence is for him the care for Being. His self belongs more to Being than it does to himself. Inquiry into Being is the mission of man – the mission of its shepherd. What is Being? It is the constant coming into openness, the constant breaking into the world. Inquiry into Being is inquiry into the world.

[183] Hölderlin, *Feldauswahl* (Stuttgart: Cotta Verlag, 1943), p. 76.
[184] Vietta, *op. cit.*, p. 89.
[185] *Ibid.*, p. 128.
[186] Heidegger, *Was heisst Denken?*, p. 152.

CHAPTER III

WORLD

Man is a wordly being. His essence is the to-be-in-the-world. In the second phase of his thought Heidegger shows man as an 'ec-sisting' being,[1] namely a being who stands out into the openness of Being which is the world.[2] In the third phase of his thought Heidegger deals with the same problem as dwelling. Dwelling is disclosed there as the preservation of the foursome, as letting earth and sky, mortals and gods bring up the structural world in which things can become what they are and in which man can live his life as placed in his history in the sense of befalling.[3] Dwelling is a specifically human way of being. An animal does not dwell but merely lives biologically. To dwell means to be in the world as world. All three modes of man's being, to-be-in-the-world, 'ec-sistence,' and dwelling, imply world.

As shown in the introduction, earth and sky together with gods and mortals are the phenomena whose play bestirs a world, or rather whose play *is* world.[4] Therefore, in order to properly approach these basic problems of Heidegger's third phase of thought, the problems of earth and gods, it is necessary to look into the problem of 'world' and see its development in all three phases. Before doing so, it will be necessary to briefly consider the phenomenon of 'world' in traditional or classical philosophy.

I. PROBLEM OF WORLD IN TRADITIONAL PHILOSOPHY

The traditional philosophies could be called philosophies of substances because they were oriented to the beings and their structures. World for these philosophies was not a primary problem; it was merely an abstraction deducted from the diversity of beings.

---

[1] Cf. pp. 72–73.
[2] Heidegger, *Humanismus*, p. 35.
[3] Cf. pp. 64–65; also pp. 88–89.
[4] Cf. p. 17.

World was either the sum of all the beings, or it was a region to which a certain group of beings belonged. This latter case considered a diversity of worlds, such as the world of mathematics, world of business, and world of hoodlums.

Beings, or that which-is, and not the world itself, captured the attention of traditional philosophies. World for them was a secondary problem deduced from the intra-worldly (*innerweltlich*) or within-the-world beings. When these philosophers investigated these beings, they believed they were investigating the world also. "Even if we should successfully and completely describe the different species of within-the-world beings," says Walter Biemel, "we would never reach the knowledge of the world as such this way, but merely would know that which is *in* the world." [5]

According to Heidegger, it is impossible to deduce world from beings; world has to be known some way directly. The only being who knows the world is man. Man's knowledge of the world is not theoretical knowledge. Neither is it practical knowledge. In both cases, theoretically and practically, we know beings but not the world. The knowledge of the world is ontologically prior to theoretical, as well as to practical, knowledge. It is prior to the knowledge of a being as such; it makes the knowledge of a being possible.[6]

Knowledge of the world is understanding, in the sense of *standing* in the world. This standing in the world is not the standing of one being in another being. The world is not a being and neither is man. To know man as a being, a substance, a pure *ego*, means not to know him in his full ontological extent as the to-be-in-the-world, and without such a knowledge the access to the phenomenon of the world is blocked.

For Aristotle, as well as for St. Thomas, man is a substance marked by the essential feature of intellection. Intellection means man's ability to possess all beings (if not actually, at least potentially) in an immaterial way. Knowing here is an act of transcendence from subject to objects; accordingly truth is the conformity between the intellect and thing. Neither knowledge nor truth ever involves the phenomenon of the world; they are understood in the realm of substances (the objects, as well as the subjects, are substances).

For Descartes the world is *res extensa*. Its basic character is persistence, namely, substantiality. Even though Descartes gives a

---

⁵ Walter Biemel, *Le Concept de Monde chez Heidegger* (Louvain: E. Nauwelaerts & Paris: J. Vrin, 1940), p. 16.
⁶ Cf. p. 27.

distinct place to man, as a being who opposes the whole *res extensa*; nevertheless, he thinks of man, too, as a substance. "The being of *Dasein*, to whose fundamental structure belongs the to-be-in-the-world, Descartes conceives in the same way as *res extensa*, as substance." [7] For Descartes, just as for St. Thomas, man's knowledge is understood as the transcendence from one substance (*res cogitans*) to another (*res extensa*).

For Kant, the world is an idea, and ideas for Kant are regulative principles according to which appearances are organized. Since ideas are subjective intellectual *a priori* forms, they belong to a human substance. Therefore, the knowing of things or beings is also an act of transcendence from a subject towards an object.

In Heidegger's understanding, the essence of man must be sought in deeper layers of reality than merely in substantiality. The essence [8] of man ultimately cannot be expressed in terms of substantiality or subjectivity. However, if we apply the term 'subject' to indicate *Dasein* in a way acceptable to Heidegger, the meaning of the term has to be greatly altered, and also the traditional formula of knowledge (subject's transcendence towards an object) has to be fundamentally modified.

If one chooses the title 'subject' to indicate the being which we ourselves are and which we understand as *Dasein*, then it is right to say that transcendence indicates the essence of the subject and is the fundamental structure of subjectivity. The subject never exists mainly as a 'subject' so that it can also transcend toward objects, especially if they are there at the disposal of the subject, but being-a-subject means: to be the being in the transcendence and as the transcendence.[9]

Heidegger is saying here that man, taken ultimately and ontologically, is not a substance and that transcendence for him is not transcendence to an object. "But towards what then can transcendance proceed if we exclude beings? Heidegger answers: toward *the world. Dasein* goes beyond beings towards the world." [10]

Transcendence for Heidegger is passing-over to the world, and the world is not a being. That which is not a being for traditional philosophy, and especially for the sciences, is considered a nothing. In Hei-

[7] Heidegger, *Sein und Zeit*, p. 98.

[8] For Heidegger 'essence' has a verbal (gram.) character and always indicates primariness. Primariness means the relatedness to Being. To think the essence of anything whatsoever means to go down to the ground which is Being in its openness, the world.

[9] Heidegger, *Vom Wesen des Grundes*, pp. 17–18.

[10] Biemel, *op. cit.*, p. 154.

degger's *Was ist Metaphysik?*, world is indicated as nothingness in the sense of 'no-being' or 'no-thing.'

Since *Dasein* is the to-be-in-the-world and transcendence is the passing over to the world, then "to-be-in-the-world and transcendence are one and the same." [11] Truth for Heidegger is not conformity between the subject and the object, but is transcendence, namely, the to-be-in-the-world itself. In his *Vom Wesen der Wahrheit*, Heidegger shows that the traditional formula of truth ultimately is based on man's openness (*Offenständigkeit*) which is nothing but the to-be-in-the-world. The to-be-in-the-world or freedom is more ultimately truth than is conformity, the agreement between a subject and an object.

World is nothingness and man as standing out into the world ('ec-sisting') is "being-held-in-nothingness" [12] (*Hineingehaltenheit im Nichts*). Since world and the essence of man are phenomena which are beyond substantiality, they were never investigated by the traditional philosophies, the philosophies of substances.

It being the case that traditional philosophy does not give any basis for the problem of world, the investigation of this problem must be limited to Heidegger himself. In all three phases of his thinking, this problem receives a slightly different approach and treatment. In each of these approaches, the world is never a something for itself, but it always involves things. In the first phase, the world is the referential totality (*Verweisungsganzheit*) of the things as implements; in the second phase, the world is the openness of Being in which things sojourn; and in the third phase, the world is the interplay of the foursome as assembled by a thing.

II. WORLD IN THE FIRST PHASE

In his *Sein und Zeit* Heidegger deals with the problem of world in two stages, namely: inauthentic world and authentic world. The inauthentic world is called surroundings (*Umwelt*), and it is approached from the inauthentic *Dasein*'s commerce with implements. The authentic world is called nothingness, and it is approached from the mood of dread.

Surroundings can be disclosed through the within-the-surroundings beings, the implements. They are ontologically prior to the objective

[11] *Ibid.*, p. 157.
[12] Heidegger, *Was ist Metaphysik?*, p. 32.

beings. "The disposable beings are not primarily given; they can only manifest themselves through implementality." [13] The implements and their structures cannot be known theoretically or objectively, but in the knowledge of handling or usage, i.e. in circumspection (*Umsicht*).[14] Circumspection presupposes the knowledge of the whole, the totality, within which these implements are what they are. The knowledge of the implemental totality is necessary for the discovery of the implements.[15] This totality is surroundings, the inauthentic world. "The world is that which renders possible all the within-the-world beings; it is presupposed everywhere." [16]

In our everyday pursuits we are constantly in commerce with the things and are handy with them without considering them as objects related to us as subjects. We know them 'commercially' (*umgänglich*) or circumspectly (*umsichtig*). Such a knowledge approaches or encounters things, the implements, from a whole. Thus implements belong to a whole or totality. The implementality, the essence of an implement, is the 'for' (*um-zu*), for instance: a hammer is *for* pounding nails, a shovel is *for* digging dirt, a plough is *for* ploughing fields; the meaning of the 'for' is something 'for' something. An implement can never be considered in its isolation. When isolated, it is no longer an implement. Implementality is reference: something is suitable, or unsuitable, 'for' something. Concerning the example, hammer, Biemel says: "The fact of being-related-to is not a secondary or accidental characteristic; it is the essence itself of the hammer, and also of all the implements." [17]

Even though a hammer refers to nails, primarily it refers to a whole and only secondarily to all that which takes place within this whole, such as nails, lumber, blueprints, real estate offices, buyer of the house, etc. In Heidegger's example, an automobile has a red arrow to indicate the direction in which the driver intends to turn. This arrow does not simply indicate a direction. It indicates a world which involves pedestrians crossing the streets, traffic rules, public security, business enterprises, etc. It is a something within the world of a society, and this world, or rather surroundings, is indicated, prior to the direction of the turn, by the turn signal.[18]

Each implement has its 'for,' and all the 'fors' ultimately end up in

[13] Biemel, *op. cit.*, p. 47.
[14] Cf. p. 35.
[15] Heidegger, *Sein und Zeit*, p. 69.
[16] Biemel, *op. cit.*, p. 32.
[17] *Ibid.*, p. 47.
[18] Heidegger, *Sein und Zeit*, p. 79.

the 'for the sake of' (*Worumwillen*).[19] In the above example this 'for the sake of' is for the sake of the society – its *Dasein* or its world. *Dasein* is the crosspoint of all the 'fors' of the implements. By their reference to this point, they become what they are or they take a place within this order as established by this point. Man by his very essence belongs to this order; he is standing in it; he is the to-be-in-the-world. To be in the world is to constantly possess the understanding of the world. Understanding of the world enables man to understand and to discover the implements within his world. "In order that the implemental being be possible, it is necessary that the world be pre-discovered." [20]

The world of everydayness is the inauthentic world or surroundings (*Umwelt*). It can be referred to as the world because surroundings are a mode of the world. However, world is more adequately approached authentically. In the inauthentic *Dasein* – in man's inauthentic way of being in the world and his being fully turned toward things – world's 'no-thingness' is not emphasized. Only the authentic *Dasein* brings forward this character of world.

In the ontological mood (*Befindlichkeit*) [21] *Dasein* discloses itself as the to-be-in-the-world. There are diverse moods which can disclose the to-be-in-the-world, and thus world,[22] but Heidegger chooses only one of them in his *Sein und Zeit* and elaborates the phenomenon of the world upon it. This mood is the mood of dread. Dread is not fear. Fear means fearing of something, of a within-the-world being, whereas in dread, instead of being in fear of something within the world, one dreads the to-be-in-the-world itself. Heidegger stresses that dread comes from nowhere [23] which indicates that it does not arise from *something* but rather from 'no-thing.' That for the sake of which one is in dread, according to Heidegger, also is 'no-thing." "Nothingness discloses itself in dread, however, not as something which-is." [24] The nothingness here is the to-be-in-the-world or world itself. Nothingness is dreadful, and that for the sake of which we are in dread is, too, nothingness.

The nothingness, or world in which we are placed, even though it is not 'something which-is,' nevertheless, is real. In his *Einführung in die*

19 *Ibid.*, p. 84.
20 Biemel, *op. cit.*, pp. 38–39.
21 Cf. pp. 43–44.
22 *Sein und Zeit* does not deal with the world directly, but merely with *Dasein* as to-be-in-the-world. World necessarily implies man and can only be revealed as the to-be-in-the-world.
23 Heidegger, *Sein und Zeit*, p. 186.
24 Heidegger, *Was ist Metaphysik?*, p. 30.

Metaphysik [25] Heidegger refers to one of Knut Hamsun's personages who had often been at sea and who spent his last days high up in the mountains. Here, this man could listen to true emptiness. The sea could be calm, yet here or there was always something which could be heard; but up on the mountains he heard the soundlessness itself. It was real. This total nothingness was real.

The world, even though not a being, is real. Yet, it has no reality without the beings. Nothingness necessarily refers to things or beings as receding, as falling or drifting away. "Nothingness manifests itself with and upon beings as drifting away in their totality." [26] The empty realm left behind the receding beings could not be grasped as an empty realm if there were no receding beings. On the other hand, nothingness of the world is the foundation supporting any being in its 'beingness.' By taking a place within a world, beings become beings; or by referring to the world as the referential totality, they are implements. The 'thingness' of a thing or the implementality of an implement is rooted in the 'worldness' of the world. World, this nothingness, is the foundation on which rests the ontological weight of any being. World is most intensely being and yet nothingness – the ground and the abyss. [27]

Man in the mood of dread exists in the world authentically, whereas man in his commerce with the things of everydayness, the implements, exists in the world inauthentically. When facing nothingness in dread, man is in the midst of this nothingness, and thus he *is* authentically his own self as being-held-in-nothingness. This being-held-in-nothingness is the being-held-in-the-world which is authentic to-be-in-the-world, authentic *Dasein*.

III. WORLD IN THE SECOND PHASE

With the authentic *Dasein*, – with the experience of the world in dread, and not merely its experience from the implementality of the implements as referring to the world as the referential context – the problem of the world is gradually placed on the level of the second phase of Heidegger's thought. Here world is shown as the openness of Being. In *Sein und Zeit* the phenomenon of the world is approached

---

[25] Heidegger, *Einführung*, pp. 20–21.
[26] Heidegger, *Was ist Metaphysik?*, p. 31.
[27] Heidegger, *Satz*, p. 185.

from the essence of man; world is a structural element of human essence, of to-be-in-the-world. In the post-*Sein und Zeit* works, on the contrary, human essence is approached from the world, the openness of Being: 'ec-sistence' is the standing out in the openness of Being – the world.

In his *Le Concept de Monde chez Heidegger*, Walter Biemel had exhaustively shown world as the referential context, i.e. world as approached from the ontological structures of the implements; but he did not show the world as not-a-being or nothingness, i.e. world as that to which man transcends in his authentic mode of being. Having come upon the phenomenon of dread, Biemel merely emphasized it as that which brings forward the unity of the existentials,[28] the structural elements of *Dasein*, i.e. he showed it as the manifestation of the authentic *Dasein* in its true self; but he did not emphasize that here *eo ipso* the phenomenon of the world was properly disclosed. In dread, world is not merely the referential context of implemental structures, not merely surroundings (*Umwelt*), but nothingness which, faced by us, holds us in our authentic self, our being-held-in-nothingness.

Being and world are not two different things. There is not Being as in itself, as a certain substance, which then, off and on, can come into world. Being is always its revelation, the world. To say 'Being' is to say 'openness of Being' which again is to say 'world.'

Historically only the early Greek philosophers can be of any help in the problem of the world as the openness of Being. For Thales water was not one of the beings alongside of the others. It was rather the source from which all the beings received their start and from which they drew the strength of their being. Water itself was not a being, yet for any being to be or to live, water was necessary. Water made the life or the being of a being possible. For something to start and to end, to be or to live, water had to be there beforehand as that which neither starts nor ends In this sense, water was divine. "It is significant," says Werner Jaeger, "that ancient tradition has already ascribed to Thales the statement that the Divine is 'that which has neither beginning nor end.' " [29]

Similarly Anaximenes' air was not a being which causes the other beings, but rather it was the background which is necessary for any

---

[28] Biemel, *op. cit.*, p. 113.
[29] Werner Jaeger, *The Theology of the Early Greek* Philosopher (Oxford: The Clarendon Press, 1948), p. 29.

being to be being. "Even when Anaximenes equated psyche with air," says Jaeger, "he did not identify it with any corporeal substance of the world of experience. Air for him is the originative source of all coming-to-be and passing-away, active both within and behind these processes as their divine ground." [30]

Also Anaximander, of whose philosophy there is only one fragment preserved, indicates the 'no-thingness' of that which renders any 'thingness' possible.

> So the thing with which the world begins can only be something that is identical with none of the given substances, and yet is capable of giving rise to the vast immensity of them all. The distinguishing property of this something must therefore be the fact that it is itself unbounded; and so Anaximander calls it by this very name – *apeiron*. The best ancient expositors follow Aristotle to denote the endless, inexhaustible reservoir or stock from which all Becoming draws its nourishment, not that which is qualitatively undetermined, as certain modern writers have described it.[31]

Even though in the above quotation Jaeger refers to *apeiron* as to a thing, he however indicates it as 'the thing with which the world begins' and thus relates it to the world.

According to Heidegger, the early Greeks in all the above problems were thinking Being; and since Being can only be meaningfully referred to as revealed Being, they were thinking the openness of Being, the world. "Thales and Anaximander," Eugen Fink said in his *Grundfragen der Antiken Philosophie* – the course held in the 1947–1948 fall semester at the University of Freiburg – "did not think the 'thingness' of the thing, but the worldliness of the world."

In one of his passages on the early Greeks, Heidegger indicates that traditional philosophy generally deals with the philosophy of the early Greeks as pre-Aristotelian philosophy. This means that their philosophy has not been treated as something for itself but merely as a preparative and illuminative stage of a philosophy which reached full maturity with Aristotle.

In the framework of Aristotelian philosophy, the early Greek problems are placed in the compartment concerning the philosophy of nature. Since the early Greeks did not know anything about the scheme of systematization of Aristotle, their philosophy as looked at from this viewpoint seems to be confused. However, when properly understood it is never confused. "Where the boundaries of division are not apparent, the boundlessness of indetermination and ambiguity

---

[30] *Ibid.*, p. 84.
[31] *Ibid.*, p. 24.

does not necessarily dominate. On the contrary, the very structure of a purely thought thing, free from any division, can come to language." [32]

The early Greeks thought Being as the revelation, i.e. as revealed. Such revealing or disclosure went right along with the concealment of Being. "Being withdraws itself by revealing itself in beings." [33] Light, by bringing the illuminated objects into illumination, keeps itself in concealment. Nevertheless, even in the mode of concealment, light reveals itself as that which is concealed. The illuminated objects are visible, and the light itself is invisible; however, in the visibility of the objects, light reveals itself as invisible, and as such it holds all revelation in unity and is its ground. Being, when revealing itself in its recession (concealment), leaves room for us, for our history. By responding to Being in its concealment, we live our history as befalling.[34] Thus Being sends us into our history and holds us there in the unity. "Every time that Being holds onto itself in its forward-coming, world takes place suddenly and unnoticeably." [35]

Already the attention of the early Greeks was turned to that which was disclosed instead of following that which kept itself in concealment. Nevertheless, in their way of seeing and treating the things as disclosed, this source of revelation was constantly experienced and felt. It was the base upon which everything disclosed was resting. Things were not what they were merely in their relation to a human subject, but in their relation to the light of concealed Being itself. The Greeks are important for us not merely as a nation in history, but as the very beginning of our epoch. Epoch (*epoche*) Heidegger understands as Being which holds itself in concealment and thus is the ultimate source of our history and of our world.[36]

According to Heidegger's interpretation, Anaximander's fragment explains to us the coming forward and departure of everything whatsoever in the realm of openness. The coming forward (*genesis*) has to be understood as "the breaking away which lets everything originate – break away from concealment by breaking into revelation. Even though we can translate φθορά as passing away, we must think of the passing away as a going which again steps away from revelation and

---

[32] Heidegger, *Holzwege*, p. 305.
[33] *Ibid.*, p. 311.
[34] Cf. pp. 64–65; also pp. 88–89.
[35] Heidegger, *Holzwege*, p. 311.
[36] *Ibid.*

goes away and departs into concealment." [37] That from which every-thing escapes, namely from Being itself, is precisely that which enables everything to appear in revelation. At the same time Being is also that which takes everything back into concealment or allows it to escape the revelation. By coming forward in the world or receding from it, any being lets Being, which constantly remains in con-cealment, appear.

Man is the being who sees everything in its arrival and departure, i.e. sees everything as assembled within the realm of Being. As such, man is wise because he is the guardian of Being in its truth – in its revelation.[38] A wise man is the opposite of a man who sees everything not as in the realm of Being, not as in the world, but as related to him, a worldless subject, in his representation (*Vorgestelltheit*). For such a man things are not beings sojourning in the light of Being but are objects faced by him. "Sight," here Heidegger refers to true seeing, "does not determine itself from the eye but from the light of Being." [39]

A thing as in the light of Being is the one which "sojourns in the arrival and departure. Sojourning is the transition from coming to going." [40] A sojourning being is always arranged between two absences: from one of these absences it is coming forward, and into the other one it is departing. By being in such a way, a being is in a bind (*Fug*) in the sense that it is thus held in a unity, assembled onto itself. For the presence of a thing in its full unity, both absences are necessary. From one of these absences a thing arises and into the other it departs. Both absences between which a being is joined are related to the light of Being (into which a being comes and from which it recedes); this light is reflected by the upcoming and the recession. By being in a bind, a being reflects the world which unifies it.

A being can get out of a bind, out of joint (*Un-fug*). Here a being is not seen as coming forward and departing, i.e. not as a sojourning being any longer, but as a being which adheres to itself and thus falls out of the totality of the world and becomes isolated in itself. While clinging to itself, it tends to become merely an object for a subjective repre-sentation and does not truly belong in the order of the world.

Being is not a chaos in the sense of confusion and disorder. It has its orderliness. By handing a sojourning being out into its sojourn –

---

[37] *Ibid.*, p. 315.
[38] The German word for truth, *Wahrheit*, reflects 'guarding,' *wahren, verwahren.*
[39] Heidegger, *Holzwege*, p. 322.
[40] *Ibid.*, p. 323.

i.e. by placing it into its upcoming into the world and its departure
from it – Being places it in its binds. "The binds of sojourning 'de-fine'
[throw into limits] and bind the sojourning beings as such. The
sojourning beings, τά ἐόντα, 'essentiate' in the boundaries (πέρας)." [41]
The world which gives boundaries to everything is itself boundless, *to
apeiron*. By handing everything out into its limits, Being exposes
everything to the danger of adhering to itself or hardening onto itself.[42]
Truth always risks untruth.

When the early Greek philosophers regarded *physis* as that which
hands everything out into its limits and assembles it onto its
'somethingness,' they were not just thinking of material things as
assembled by *physis* but of everything whatsoever including man and
even gods as assembled by it. Being as bounding was also known to
Parmenides under the name of *moira*, meaning "the bestowal of
share" [43] – the share of being-something. "Gods and men are subordinated to *Moira*." [44] By setting everything into its boundaries,
Being throws everything into its light and thus brings itself to revelation or to the world.

In one of his latest works, Heidegger shows that Being is the ground
of everything since it throws all beings into their limits, bounds them.
Yet by being the ground of everything, "Being itself remains
groundless. Ground as that which grounds cannot be applied to Being.
Being is an abyss." [45]

Even though world has been considered and can be considered as
nothingness in the sense that it is not-a-thing, nevertheless world, in
bestowing boundaries to everything and thus granting to everything
its 'to be,' itself is more intensively being or real than anything whatsoever. "World 'worlds' ['essentiates' itself] and is more intensively
being than that which is seizable and perceivable – than that in which
we believe to be at home." [46]

Chaos primarily did not mean confused orderlessness but Being
itself as an abyss. "The very idea of chaos," says Jaeger, "obviously
implies that that yawning empty space at the beginning of things lay
in nocturnal darkness." [47] Since chaos stands at the beginning, it is

[41] *Ibid.*, p. 339.
[42] *Ibid.*, pp. 339–340.
[43] *Ibid.*, p. 340.
[44] *Ibid.*
[45] Heidegger, *Satz*, p. 185.
[46] Heidegger, *Holzwege*, p. 33.
[47] Jaeger, *op. cit.*, p. 63.

the oldest and at the same time it is the best. "The old order is best," says Hesiod.[48]

Whether Hesiod is talking about chaos by saying that 'the old order is best,' cannot be decided from just that one fragment; however, in one of the poems of Hölderlin, according to Heidegger, he (Hölderlin) indicates the sameness of chaos and *nomos* (law, order).

(χάος) foremostly means the yawning, the gaping abyss, the primarily-disclosing-itself opening in which everything is gulped down. The abyss refuses any hold for anything distinct and grounded and, therefore, chaos seems to be mere confusion for all experience. The 'chaotic' in this sense, however, is mere perversion of what 'chaos' really means. As approached from 'nature' (φύσις) chaos means the gap from which the openness opens itself so that all the bounded assignments of everything distinct would be guarded in their truth, and therefore Hölderlin calls 'chaos' and 'confusion' 'holy.' Chaos is holiness itself.[49]

According to Greek mythology, chaos is the beginning of everything. *Mythos*, the *logos* of gods, itself arises from the sacred abyss of chaos. Since *mythos* is for the Greeks the source of their laws, chaos is more so the primordial law and order. Antigone followed the unwritten law of chaos when she refused to follow the law of the ruler forbidding her to bury her dead brother because he fought against his home city.[50]

Nietzsche's destructive attitude ultimately lies in the striving to disobey all laws for the sake of the primeval chaos, the birth bed of any law whatsoever. When man is not living ultimately,[51] he needs the laws as crutches to support his steps. "Where life grows stiff – a law towers up," says Nietzsche.[52] To be man as man ultimately means to-be-held-in-nothingness, i.e. to stand in the abyss in which everything whatsoever rests.

Being, understood by the Greeks as *physis*, has a dual character – it conceals and reveals. These two seemingly contrasting elements necessarily belong together and refer to each other. A painter in order to show a strong light in his picture must use deep colors beside light ones to emphasize the lightness of light. Chaos can be understood as *physis*, the fundamental revelation which holds the dark and the light, the true and the untrue in a diametrical tension. It can also be

---

[48] Hesiod, *The Poems and Fragments* (Oxford: Clarendon Press, 1908) (Translation and introduction by A. W. Mair, M.A.), p. 101.

[49] Heidegger, *Hölderlins Hymne* (Halle a.d.S.: Max Niemeyer Verlag, [n.d.]), p. 17.

[50] Sophocles, *Antigone* in *The Complete Greek Drama* (New York: Random House, 1938), Vol. I, p. 434.

[51] 'To live ultimately' means to be determined by the ultimate which is Being. Being as viewed from that-which-is (from a being) is nothingness, abyss, chaos.

[52] Oehler, *Nietzsche-Register* (Stuttgart: Alfred Kröner Verlag, 1943), p. 146.

misunderstood as the confusion wherein dark and light, true and untrue are mixed disorderly together.

In the second phase of his thinking Heidegger maintains the phenomenon of the world as the openness of Being. Being is its revelation. In its revelation Being reveals itself as concealed – it withholds itself. Such a withholding of itself in its revelation in no wise is a shortcoming or deficiency. Concealment necessarily belongs to revelation. World as openness of Being is *eo ipso* its concealment. World is the ground (*Grund*) and the abyss (*Abgrund*).

IV. WORLD IN THE THIRD PHASE

The early Greeks were the thinkers of Being. They considered it through the phenomena of water, of air, of *apeiron*, or of fire. They are generally referred to as the thinkers of *physis*. *Physis* is the coming-forward as bringing-itself to appearance. "Withdrawal reigns simultaneously in the coming-forward-from-itself, in *physis*. It reigns so decisively that without it the coming-forward cannot reign." [53] *Physis* as coming-forward and withdrawal, as concealment and revelation, as ground and abyss is world. *Physis* and world are one and the same problem. To see this more adequately, it is necessary to go into the problem of Heidegger's third phase of thought.

In the first essay of his *Holzwege* ("*Der Ursprung des Kunstwerkes*") concerning artwork, Heidegger touches upon the problem of world. He shows there that an artwork establishes or erects (*aufstellen*) a world. Such establishing is not a causing but a bringing forward to sight. To clarify this with an example, it will be necessary to imagine a totally empty space which is crossed by light. In totally empty space light is not revealed as light. There would be mere darkness. Only if some object (artwork) is raised into this empty space, is the light arrested upon it and thus brought forward or revealed. World (in this example light represents the world) is established or erected by an artwork. A similar character is ascribed to the implements in the *Sein und Zeit* phase where they refer to the world by their structure and, in a certain sense, reveal it.

The erecting of a world takes place simultaneously with the bringing forward of the earth. The material for making an implement disappears or gets lost in the suitability of an implement for its usage,

[53] Heidegger, *Satz*, p. 113.

whereas in an artwork such materials stand out and are really brought forward into the world. Marble is not revealed as marble in native rock; it becomes marble in the full sense of the word when placed in a wall or pillar of a Greek temple. Gold is truly gold in the spear of Athene, but the iron in a hatchet is not truly iron: it is overshadowed by the usefulness of the hatchet. A Greek temple, unlike an implement, does not stand out obtrusively and clearly itself; rather it allows the materials to stand out forward in the full light of the world, while it itself recedes into the background. "That into which an artwork recedes and which is brought forward in the recession of the artwork, we call earth," says Heidegger.[54]

The earth is not the materials of an artwork, yet by letting them come forward the earth reveals itself as what constantly remains in concealment or reservation. An attempt to reveal the earth ends necessarily in failure. The earth "only shows itself when it remains undisclosed and unexplained. Earth shatters any attempt made to invade it." [55] When science believes that it gradually penetrates and possesses earth, it deceives itself and ignores earth as earth. What science deals with are merely scientific mechanisms which are being *quasi* forced upon the earth, and the answers obtained that way are only answers previously placed into it by the sciences themselves, i.e. answers which have more to do with the sciences than with the earth. Answers gained from the earth by mathematical approaches can only be mathematical answers. Only an artwork is adequate for revealing the earth because, instead of penetrating the earth, it shows it the way it is. "To bring earth forward means to bring it into openness as concealed-in-itself." [56] Earth can be brought forward in a diversity of modes: in stone by a sculptor, in color by a painter, in word by a poet.

A work of art causes neither world nor earth but captures them in its repose. This repose, however, is the peak of dynamism: it is the strife between the world and the earth. This strife is not a struggle aiming to destroy the other side. "In an essential strife, however, the strivers raise one another into the self-affirmation of their essences." [57] World can only be erected on the earth, and the earth brings its gifts and comes forward only in the world. Such a strife is not a strife between two beings or two substances. Only in the openness gained by

[54] Heidegger, *Holzwege*, p. 35.
[55] *Ibid.*, p. 36.
[56] *Ibid.*
[57] *Ibid.*, p. 38.

such a strife can any being whatsoever find its place. "Through the world a being becomes a being." [58]

The strife between the world and the earth is the extreme moment of truth as disclosure. It is the extreme moment of truth because in the realm of such a truth the disclosure or truth of any being is made possible. The strife of the world and the earth is the truth of Being, and the disclosure of any being as made possible by the strife of the world and the earth is the truth of being.[59] In the above sense, according to Heidegger, fragment 53 [60] of Heraclitus has to be understood: "War is both king of all and father of all, and it has revealed some as gods, others as men, some it has made slaves, others free."

In the openness bestirred or gained by the strife between the world and the earth, man founds his dwelling and lives his history with his victories and defeats, with his decisions and failures. The earth is never just a mass of matter and it never can be thought of astronomically but it must be thought of in its relation to the world and thus to man. When the strife which is brought forward by an artwork dies, there is no more world or earth. "Where struggle ceases, even though that which-is [being] does not disappear, the world turns away." [61] Without the man-surpassing reality, world, things and men are 'out of joint' in the sense of being disintegrated from a superior order. Even though thrown from the superior order (the order of world, of *physis*), man still can be disposed to an inferior order (the subjective or worldless order).

In his second phase of thinking, Heidegger shows world as the openness of Being. This openness in the first phase is thought of as *Dasein*, the to-be-in-the-world. The openness of Being, as not being-like and not being, is shown as nothingness. Yet by stressing world, the nothingness, as that which enables any being to become being, Heidegger stresses it as being in a higher degree of 'beingness.' World thus is shown as the ground of everything whatsoever and *eo ipso* an abyss.

In the third phase of his thought, Heidegger attempts to look into this abyss and to discover its structure. The first step in this

---

[58] Heidegger, *Einführung*, p. 47.

[59] Here there is still some ambiguity as far as world is concerned: world as openness or truth of Being and world as strife of world and earth are the same. This ambiguity will become clarified in the next chapter when dealing with the problem of truth.

[60] Freeman, *op. cit.*

[61] Heidegger, *Einführung*, p. 48.

direction is world as in strife with the earth. The earth is not something totally new brought in from somewhere and placed alongside of the world. The earth belongs to the structure of the world.[62] The earth is implicitly known in both previous phases. Heidegger shows world there as experienced in the concrete, living situation of handling things and implements or as referred to by various sojourning beings in the realm of the world. The world for Heidegger always is an earthly world. In the third phase of his thought, Heidegger merely shows explicitly this earthliness of the world. In the essay on artwork, Heidegger shows that the world is not merely a quiet steady light, but that it stands in strife with the darkness of the earth, and that this darkness of the earth belongs necessarily to the lightness of the world.

Heidegger's problem of the foursome is another attempt to gain insight into the worldliness of the world. Instead of an artwork which assembles the earth and the world in their strife, Heidegger investigates the thing here and shows that the 'thingness' of a thing consists in the assemblage of earth and sky, mortals and gods. Earth and sky, mortals and gods are not four beings but rather the structural elements of the world. They stand in a strife here which is referred to as the round-dance. The round-dance of the foursome rounds up or bestirs the world. The round-dance is the 'worlding' of the world.[63]

This rather strangely put problem, or complex of problems, may lose its strangeness after a careful investigation of the members of the foursome. In such an investigation the guiding thought will have to be that here, just as in both previous phases, Heidegger aims to give an insight into bringing-itself-into-openness Being, an insight into the world.

In his *Zur Seinsfrage*, Heidegger introduces a strange way of writing the word 'Being,' namely ~~Being~~ With that he indicates that Being is not something which opposes nothingness. It is nothingness just as it is being; it is darkness just as it is light; it is untruth just as it is truth. Besides, with such a way of writing ~~Being~~, Heidegger denotes that Being is not something for itself which then can reach and be in touch with man as *Dasein* (as mortal), with earth, sky and gods. Earth, sky, gods, and mortals belong to the round-dance of the world. "The mark of the cross, of course, cannot be only a negative mark of deletion. It rather indicates the four directions of the foursome and their as-

---

[62] Cf. footnote 59, p. 130.
[63] Heidegger, *Vorträge*, p. 179.

semblage at the place of crossing." [64] ~~Being~~ thus becomes a symbol of
fully developed phenomenon of the world, the abyss on which everything whatsoever rests, the floor of the round-dance of the ultimate
realities – earth, sky, gods, and mortals.

[64] Heidegger, *Seinsfrage*, p. 31.

CHAPTER IV

EARTH

Previous to Heidegger there was no problem of the earth in philosophy. However, the early Greek philosophers did have the problem of *physis* which Heidegger considers akin to his problem of the earth.[1] The Greeks did not explicitly work out their problem of the world and its implication in the problem of *physis*; therefore, for them *physis* was the problem of the world as well as the problem of the earth. For Heidegger also, the earth and the world are not two separate problems when taken ultimately. The openness of Being is the world, when considered with the emphasis on revealing, and is the earth, with the emphasis on concealing. Consequently, Being can be treated as the earth as well as the world, and ultimately the earth and the world, if not explicitly, at least implicitly, involve each other. Hence, the Greek *physis* can be considered as Heidegger's earth although they are not wholly identical.

Physis for the Greeks was *eo ipso logos*, i.e. the ground where truth, language, and thinking were rooted. *Logos* basically shows or brings to appearance that which is orderly laid and articulated in *physis*. Therefore, *logos* can be considered as the bringing to light or to the revelation of *physis*. Disclosure, *aletheia*, is truth. *Logos* then is truth of *physis*, the world. *Logos*, again, is language or parlance. Since *logos* is rooted in *physis*, *physis* is the foundation of language.

Another source, or rather analogy, of Heidegger's problem of the earth is Hölderlin's problem of nature. Hölderlin considers nature as the "all-living" and "all-present." [2] Nature for him is above everything. It is not only above men, but also above gods. Gods are gods in the realm of nature. Nature for Hölderlin is *das Heilige* – best translated as holiness.

To respect these implications of the problem of the earth, this chapter will have to be divided into five sections. The first one will

---

[1] Heidegger, *Holzwege*, p. 31.
[2] Hölderlin (*Feldauswahl*) (Stuttgart: Cotta Verlag, 1943), p. 8.

deal with the problem of *physis*; the second with the implications of
physis and *logos*; the third will indicate the 'earthliness' of language;
the fourth will reflect the interconnection of *physis-logos* with earth-
world; and the fifth section will consider Hölderlin's problem of
nature.

I. *PHYSIS*

The Greek word '*physis*' is translated by 'nature.' The modern
conception of nature reflects merely a small aspect of what was understood by the Greek phenomenon of *physis*. According to Heidegger,
the concept of nature in modern physics means "the closed-in-itself
context of movements of spatio-temporally related mass-particu-
lars." [3] This nature is three-dimensional space interspersed with
various complexes of masses which endure in time. Each point in
space and time is mathematically homogeneous to any other, and has
no preference over the others. There are, however, unities in these
complexes of masses and in the forces by which they act upon one
another.

Such a nature is seen by a scientific, impersonal eye. This eye, by
calculating the intercorrelations of these masses and the laws which
govern them, itself (the eye) becomes a factor of utmost importance.
It tends to become the center of all the unities out there in the physical world. This it does by constantly dissolving the elements or
unities of nature, and by gaining more and more control over them.
The result of such a scientific attitude is a highly controllable objectless
nature. "If we look closely we will see that we already live in a world
in which there are no longer any 'ob-jects.' " [4]

By dissolving the unities of the objects, science increases its control
over them, i.e. in a certain sense it takes the place of these unities. The
ultimate aim seems to be total control of nature, wherein the impersonal scientific man will have the whole of such nature at his disposal as his instrument.

Here the question arises whether totally controlled nature *eo ipso*
is totally revealed and understood nature; whether man, by controlling
nature, is truly and ultimately man. In the Heideggerian spirit of
thinking, both of these questions have to be answered negatively.

[3] Heidegger, *Holzwege*, p. 72.
[4] Heidegger, *Satz*, p. 65.

The essence of nature cannot be disclosed by force and control, but by letting it be the way it is laid (assembled) in itself. Man is man not by controlling nature, but by guarding it in its truth, i.e. by letting nature be the way it is laid and articulated in itself. "Man is the shepherd of Being." [5] Only a guarding hand can feel nature the way it is; whereas a controlling or seizing hand is ultimately an empty hand because nature escapes it by refusing to reveal its essence to it. To guard Being means to dwell – to be on the earth as man.[6]

Physis is not nature in the sense of the modern physical sciences. It is rather nature as left to be the way it is in itself and not the way it is when faced by an impersonal, scientific subject. Instead of treating *physis* as nature in the modern sense it is necessary to see it the way the Greeks have seen it in order to understand it and thus to understand Heidegger's earth. "Because of the long habit of looking at Greekhood through a modern humanistic exposition, we fail to think Being, which disclosed itself to the ancient Greeks; and we fail to think it in such a way that we would preserve its very own and strange character." [7] We look at it as the primitive stage of our highly cultivated world, and we consider their understanding of nature as lacking the exactness and sobriety by which our approach to it is marked. "Accordingly, the Greeks become in principle just a better class of Hottentots, and our modern science as compared to theirs is infinitely far more advanced." [8]

In the Heideggerian mode of thinking, that which starts small and thinks itself great actually never becomes great because "everything great can only start greatly. Its beginning is actually the greatest." [9] The decline of the great is the beginning of the small which stays small even though it may 'progress.'

In Latin translation *physis* is *natura* meaning 'being born' or 'birth.' "With such a Latin translation the primary content of the Greek word φύσις is violated, the true philosophical strength of the Greek word destroyed." [10]

As an all-embracing mode of being, *physis* is not opposed to the physical, biological, or spiritual modes of being. It implies the laws

---

[5] Heidegger, *Humanismus*, p. 29.
[6] To show man as dwelling on the earth is the aim of this study, since the earth and the gods can properly be approached in relation to dwelling. Therefore, the phenomena of 'letting-be,' of 'guarding,' and of 'dwelling' will become clear in the course of the study.
[7] Heidegger, *Holzwege*, p. 95.
[8] Heidegger, *Einführung*, p. 12.
[9] *Ibid.*
[10] *Ibid.*, p. 10.

governing not only physical being but also those under which man moves in his social or private life. Consequently, *physis* implies *nomos* (custom) and *ethos* (morals). *Physis* also is not opposed to *techne*, knowledge of how to do things, founded in knowledge in general. *Techne*, too, is the letting come forward of that which already lies there in the *physis*. Finally, the history of man is not the record of human activity, but is ultimately the sway of *physis*.

Physis in general means the rising or breaking through, unravelling, opening, and developing. Thus *physis* appears and comes forward and sojourns in this appearance; it *is* this appearance.

It is wrong to think of *physis* as a certain substance which besides being has the property of breaking through and coming forward into appearance. The breaking through and coming forward *is* Being, *is* *physis*. It is never a property of a being but is Being itself. In breaking through, *physis* holds an order or a realm open within which it dominates all appearances. Such an order of dominating *physis* gives unity and articulation and, as a result, the strength of being to everything. Anything whatsoever would not be thinkable, would disintegrate into nothing, if it were not for the power of *physis* which throws everything into its boundaries – waters, lands, animals, men, nations, and even gods.

Walter F. Otto sees in the word *physis* the connotations of procreation and birth and also of the structure of the being-born as incorporated within a being which is born. *Physis* gives all things to themselves. It itself is in them and at the same time not in them. "Birth always revives the old and yet at the same time creates that which never was." [11] *Physis* constantly brings everything forward and, accordingly, it is the source of everything. "O earth!" exclaims Hölderlin, "You peaceful cradle!" [12] Source is brought forward in the things themselves; by reflecting their source things maintain their ontological strength, their 'somethingness.' On the other hand, source never is these things. This not-being makes the things fragile and causes their falling apart and their going back down into their source. The earth is the cradle and the bed of death.

J. J. Bachofen describes the myth of the twin sisters Auxesia and Damia as found in Herodotus: "While Auxesia sends up life, Damia takes it back into her womb. In the former, the bright side of nature

---

[11] Walter F. Otto, *Der Europäische Geist und die Weisheit des Ostens* (Frankfurt a.M.: Vittorio Klostermann, 1931), p. 23.

[12] Hölderlin, *op. cit.*, p. 53.

is exemplified, and in the latter – the dark side." [13] According to Bachofen, these two sisters are often represented in Greek mythology by one, Lamia who gives birth and death to her children.

An analogy between nature and mother is nothing accidental in this myth. Hesiod calls the earth "the mother of all things," [14] and Aeschylus often refers to the earth in exactly the same words.[15] Bachofen, a man of deep and extensive knowledge of the Greek and Roman myths, gives many examples of the earth understood as mother which in mythical understanding is not only the source of births and origin of life, but also the basis of perishing and death. "The taking back of that which is born belongs to motherhood no less than birth itself." [16]

In Heidegger's understanding, *physis* is the constant breaking-forward. In this breaking-forward, *physis* erupts as that which holds to itself and thereby remains concealed. The coming-forward is *eo ipso* withdrawal. "Φύσις is the breaking-forward going-back-into-itself." [17] In its concealed revelation *physis* creates an openness in which everything can arrive and depart, i.e. be born and die. "The by-itself-coming-forward φύσις is the bringing-forward, is ποίησις." [18] In any upcoming or recession, in birth or death, a glimpse of *physis* itself is obtained. *Physis* resembles the mythically understood nature as mother – giving birth and destroying. In his course of *Grundfragen der Antiken Philosophie* [19] Eugen Fink has said: "*Physis* is that which sends forth the many and takes them back again. *Physis* is the ground and mother of all constantly changeable things – ground and mother of this changeability. *Physis* is that which lies in the ground of all changeability." Heraclitus' phenomenon of fire obviously includes this idea. Hölderlin, too, calls earth "a mighty fire." [20]

According to Heidegger, fragment 30 indicates that Heraclitus' fire is the constant coming forward in which everything whatsoever can become present, can sojourn or *be*. Fire is that "which was brought forward neither by any of the gods nor by men,' but rather that which already stands fast in itself prior to gods and men and to what fire is

[13] J. J. Bachofen, *Der Mythus von Orient und Occident* (München: C. H. Beck'sche Verlagsbuchhandlung, MCMLVI), p. 183.

[14] Hesiod, *Poems*, p. 21.

[15] Aeschylus, *The Choephori, Greek Dramas*, Vol. I, p. 234.

[16] Bachofen, *op. cit.*, p. 177.

[17] Heidegger, *Hymne*, p. 11.

[18] Heidegger, *Vorträge*, p. 19.

[19] This course was held in the fall semester 1947–48 at the University of Freiburg (Germany).

[20] Hölderlin, *op. cit.*, p. 52.

for them. Fire rests in itself as φύσις, it remains in itself and guards all 'up-coming.' " [21] Here Heidegger adds that that which guards, that which holds everything in unity and in appearance or truth, is world.

World always indicates the realm of light within which beings can sojourn. The sojourning beings rise up from *physis* and sojourn in its light, in the light of the world. According to Heidegger, the Greek word for fire,

> πῦρ designates sacrifice-fire, hearth-fire, watch-fire and also the shine of the torch, the shimmer of the stars. That which is dominant in 'fire' is lightness, the glow, the blaze, the mild glittering – that which widens an area in light. In 'fire' sway is also held by destructiveness, the collapsing, closing-up, extinguishing. When Heraclitus speaks of fire, he is thinking primarily of the sway held by light, the reference [*weisen*] which gives measure and withdraws.[22]

The German word 'scheinen' (to shine) is related to *er-scheinen* which means 'to appear' as 'to be something by being illuminated.' *Physis* or fire, as that which illuminates things into something, i.e. lets them appear, appears itself. Fire shines (*scheint*), therefore things appear (*erscheinen*). *Scheinen* is the higher mode of *Erscheinen*. Hence, Being, *physis*, not only allows things to appear but itself appears – it appears in a higher mode of appearing. "Being opens itself up for the Greeks as φύσις. The sway of coming-forward and sojourning as such is at the same time the shining appearance. The word stems φυ- and φα- name the same. Φύειν, the in-itself-reposing coming-forward, is φαίνεσθαι, the flashing up, showing itself, appearing." [23]

Even though we cannot totally identify Being with appearing, we cannot ignore their necessary belonging together. This belonging together should not be thought of as the belonging together of two entities. Being and appearing are not two entities but one and the same phenomenon. Appearing and shining belong to the structure of Being. Fire as illumination best indicates the belonging together of Being and appearance. "Being 'essentiates' in appearance" [24] and cannot be thought as severed from appearing just as fire which does not illuminate is unthinkable. In one of his latest works Heidegger says: "Being is φύσις – is that which announces itself. This means that revelation of itself is the principal characteristic of Being." [25] It is its

[21] Heidegger, *Vorträge*, p. 275.
[22] *Ibid.*
[23] Heidegger, *Einführung*, pp. 76–77.
[24] *Ibid.*, p. 77.
[25] Heidegger, *Satz*, p. 120.

property. However, property here cannot be thought as a certain property belonging to a certain substance. The German word for 'property,' *'Eigenschaft'* has a connotation of selfness (*Eigen*); and Heidegger when indicating that revelation and appearance are properties of Being, means that the revelation and appearance are the very self of Being, its heart.

When properly thought of, things as sojourning beings cannot be thought of in their isolation. That which appears in the light or disappears when the light is extinguished, ultimately is that which brings forward or indicates the light itself. In Heidegger's *Sein und Zeit* the elaborated structure of the implements illustrates this well. A hammer is for pounding nails. Here hammer not only indicates nails, but also, and even more primarily, the whole or the totality within which a hammer is thinkable as a hammer. Or, again, the turn signal on an automobile, indicating the direction which the driver intends to take, primarily indicates the world within which men find their ways, deal with various practical problems, handle things of their surroundings, and live their lives.

Just as *scheinen* (to shine), etymologically as well as ontologically, is related to *erscheinen* (to appear), so is it also related to *schön* (beautiful). According to Heidegger, things can be and are beautiful, because *physis* is revealing itself and appearing. *Physis scheint* (shines) – *erscheint* (appears); it is *schön* (beautiful). *Physis* is primarily beautiful because it is the appearance or the coming-forward itself. "Beauty is the highest mode of being, the pure coming-forward and appearance."[26] Beauty ultimately is not a property (in the conventional sense) of *physis* but is rather *physis* itself. "The beauty of the earth is the earth in its beauty," Jean Wahl says in his commentaries on Hölderlin.[27]

Truth, when ultimately and properly thought, is rooted in *physis* as the revelation or appearance. Truth for the Greeks was *aletheia*, disclosure. A thing is true because it is disclosed: it stands in the light of *physis*. The truth of a thing presupposes the appearance of the *physis*, the revelation itself. Consequently, *physis* is the ultimate and basic truth. "The Greek essence of truth is only possible as one with the Greek essence of Being as φύσις." [28]

That which appears in the light may appear the way it is in itself or also may appear not the way it is: it may appear different than what

---

[26] *Ibid.*, p. 102.

[27] Jean Wahl, *La Pensée de Heidegger et la Poésie de Hölderlin* (Sorbonne: Tournier & Constans, 1952), p. 92.

[28] Heidegger, *Einführung*, p. 78.

it really is. Just as the appearance of any sojourning being is primarily made possible by the radiance of Being or *physis*, so also the distortion of the appearance of a being ultimately is founded in *physis*. Without a light 'mis-appearance' would not be possible. "The truth, in the sense of disclosure, as well as the appearance, in the sense of showing itself, necessarily belongs to Being." [29] Since *physis* reveals itself as concealed, it is truth, as well as untruth. Untruth for the early Greeks was not rooted in the finitude of man but in *physis* itself. *Physis*, the ground of everything the way it really is and of everything the way it may appear without really being such, is also the ground of being and appearing and the ground of the difference between being and appearing.

In commenting on one of the Hölderlinian poems, Heidegger says that "φύσις is the arising of the lucidity of the light and thus it is the hearth and the place of the light." [30] Thus he refers to *physis* not only as the source of light but also as the source of heat. Fire not only brings everything to light but also grants heat to everything and makes everything fiery. Making fiery indicates here the granting of ontological weight or 'somethingness.' By making things fiery, fire is present in them. "The φύσις is that which is present in everything. Should then 'nature,' if it is φύσις, as 'all-present,' at the same time not be all-glowing? Therefore, Hölderlin calls 'nature' in this poem [31] also the 'all-creating' and 'all-living.' " [32]

Since *physis* is that which grants life or being to everything, it itself is that in which all such life or being is based. It is as though it were a care-taking hand which places everything in its order and stands behind such order and backs it up. To indicate Being or *physis* as care-taking, Heidegger, when investigating Anaximander's fragment uses the word '*Brauch*' in its ancient German form, which has the meaning of 'sparing.' He says:

> The *Brauch* [sparing] which by granting the bind [bounding things into their boundaries], 'de-fines' the sojourning beings and hands out the boundaries; therefore *Brauch*, as τό χρεών, at the same time is τὸ ἄπειρον or that which is without boundaries insofar as it 'essentiates' itself by granting the boundaries of sojourn to the sojourning beings.[33]

Physis, by throwing everything into its boundaries, by 'defining,' is itself *apeiron* – indefinite.

[29] *Ibid.*, p. 83.
[30] Heidegger, *Hymne*, p. 11.
[31] "*Wie wenn am Feiertage* ..." in Heidegger's *Hymne*, pp. 2–4.
[32] *Ibid.*, p. 11.
[33] Heidegger, *Holzwege*, p. 339.

That which is boundless or indefinite (*apeiron*) can never be encountered. It can be experienced only as that which holds everything in limits ('de-fines'). The assertion of Heraclitus, "nature likes to hide" [34] indicates this strange mode of coming-forward of *physis*, coming-forward as concealed. That which enables everything to appear, itself appears merely as the source of all that which appears, and therefore appears as that which constantly remains in concealment. "Since Being means the coming-forward appearance, the stepping-out from concealment, therefore concealment and arrival from concealment essentially belong to Being." [35]

Since *physis*, as constant coming-forward, is constantly in concealment, it is in the mode of becoming. That which is becoming is always not-as-yet-there and not-as-yet-what it has to be; nevertheless, it is not a nothing. Such an unsteadiness of *physis* can be compared to a blinking light which can, and often does, distort the view and deceive us. The problem of becoming and appearing is based in such deceptiveness of Being. Becoming or appearing is not truly being; in a certain sense, it is opposed to being. *Physis* indicates that in another, more fundamental sense, becoming is not something opposed to Being, but necessarily belongs to it. *Physis* 'essentiates' in becoming. "Just as becoming is the radiance of Being, so the radiance, as appearing, is the becoming of Being." [36]

According to Heidegger,[37] Heraclitus' *panta rei* 'everything is in flow' does not indicate that everything flows chaotically as though there were only inconsistency and nothing but that, but it indicates that all the changes are held in the unity of the stream itself. The stream is *physis* which holds sway or rules everything which is in the stream. Everything comes and goes, and the stream itself is always there. "Heraclitus thinks the never perishing." [38]

'The never perishing' is that which is constantly coming forward; it comes forward from hiddenness. The coming-forward and the hiddenness belong together.

Thus φύσις [the coming-forward] and κρύπτεσθαι [the hiding] are not separated from each other, but are reciprocally inclined to each other. They are the same, and in their inclination they grant one another their very essence. This favoring, reciprocal in itself, is the essence of φιλεῖν and φιλία. The essence-

---

[34] Fragment 123, Freeman, *op. cit.*
[35] Heidegger, *Einführung*, p. 87.
[36] *Ibid.*, p. 88.
[37] *Ibid.*, p. 102.
[38] Heidegger, *Vorträge*, p. 269.

fullness of φύσις is rooted in this inclination which inclines into each other the coming-forward and self-withdrawal.[39]

The strife of revelation and concealment which constitutes the dynamic essence of *physis* is not a strife of arrogance, but a strife of inclination. In this strife of inclination the very essence of love (*philia*) is rooted. Heidegger indicates on various occasions that concealment belongs necessarily to openness, just as obscurity and shadows belong to illumination itself. Revelation or the coming-forward does not remove or destroy the concealment or withdrawal. On the contrary, it depends on it and is in need of it to be the revelation and the coming-forward. Total darkness as well as total light does not reveal anything. The picture of the world consists in the inter-play of light and shadows. This inter-play is the ground of struggle and of all diversities which take place in the world by separating and dividing everything within it, and at the very same time it is the ground of love which brings everything near one another and holds everything in the unifying harmony of love. This interplay itself is the fundamental strife and the fundamental love.

The Greeks as thinkers of *physis* were thinkers of the world and not of the beyondness of the world. The realm beyond the world is not attainable for the human, natural enterprise of philosophy. Therefore, philosophy does not say anything about this beyondness. Even though 'worldly,' the thinking of the Greeks was not non-spiritual. *Physis* is not opposed to spirit. The distinction between the spiritual and the natural was made after the early Greek philosophers' era. "Nature 'essentiates' in human works, in the history of nations, in the stars and in the gods, also in the stones, growths, animals, and in the streams and in the weather." [40] Nature is present in all this by assembling them in unities and by supporting them by being their utmost base and foundation. *Logos*, conventionally translated as reason, is *physis* as assembling everything upon itself.

Physis, that in which everything begins and ends, is the most primeval and, therefore, the oldest. On the other hand, it is the youngest of anything whatsoever, because it is constantly coming forward, constantly being born – is even too young to be born. *Physis* is the oldest and the youngest at the same time because it is time itself. According to Heidegger, traditional philosophy did not think time properly. It did not think time as world. Time for the traditional

[39] *Ibid.*, p. 271.
[40] Heidegger, *Hymne*, p. 6.

philosophy has always been a within-the-world time. Time, as *physis* itself, is also different from the Christian phenomenon of eternity. Eternity is beyondness of time, whereas *physis* is time itself.

As constant coming-forward *physis* is constant presence. Yet, it never is constantly present in itself, but it is present by the coming-forward and the recession of any being. Coming forward in the light of *physis*, sojourning there, and retiring from there, the sojourning beings give a glimpse of *physis* as time. Time presents the presence of *physis*.

II. *PHYSIS* AND *LOGOS*

The move which determined the course of Western thought and gave the first grounds for the rising, developing, and growth of sciences was made by Plato. There truth as *physis* was replaced by truth as idea.

Previous to Plato, truth had been thought as *aletheia*, the disclosure. Since *physis* was thought as the constant coming-forward or revelation, it itself was truth. *Physis* as constant coming-forward and appearing has a mode of view, visage or aspect. *Physis* as constant breaking-forward is 'aspective.' 'Aspectivity' belongs to *physis* and is subordinate to it. *Physis* is that which most fundamentally *is*. The *is* of the aspect or the idea is rendered possible by the *is* of revelation or breaking forward *physis*. Jean Wahl indicates that "φύσις is the origin of ideas, however, not the ideas understood in the sense of Plato, but ideas understood before Plato, namely, as the universal presence which is the presence of nature." [41] Ideas for the early Greeks were *physis* in its appearance, in its presence (time itself), in its disclosure, the *aletheia*. *Aletheia*, or rather *physis* itself, was that which was ultimately being. Everything else could only be as founded in *aletheia*. Also the 'aspectivity' or idea was founded in the *aletheia*. Idea was merely the façade of *physis*. However, this façade for the early Greeks was highly important: it was *physis* itself in its presence, in its truth. *Physis* was holding itself in its own light, in its truth. Truth of *physis*, *aletheia*, was the carrier of ideas; these were the modes of presence of *physis*, modes of *aletheia*. For Plato, on the contrary, ideas were more fundamentally being than revelation, than *physis*; they were that which discloses. In Plato's philosophy, disclosure takes place by

41 Wahl, *Hölderlin*, p. 49.

physis' participation in the power of ideas. Visage or aspect reveals nature; "ἀλήθεια gets under the yoke of ἰδέα. Plato, by referring to ἰδέα as the lord which enables disclosure, implies that henceforth the essence of truth does not unravel itself from its own essence-fullness, as essence of disclosure does, but shifts itself to the essence of ἰδέα." [42]

That which was the ultimate ground of any being by granting 'beingness' to it, becomes now dependent on the idea. "The being as ἰδέα now becomes heightened to that which truly is, and the Being itself which previously held sway sinks down to that which is named μή ὄν by Plato – that which truly should not *be* and also truly *is* not." [43]

Idea, which for the early Greeks had been the periphery of the truth as disclosure or which was the façade of *physis* (the approaching *physis* in its appearing has shown its face or façade and has been present) – becomes with Plato that which truly *is*. *Physis* is then something insofar as the idea reveals it by permitting it to participate in the idea. *Physis* becomes matter which only when formed and molded by the idea becomes being; whereas in itself it is not being, but is a mere nothing. "The appearing appearance is not φύσις anymore, not the coming-forward sway, and not the self-showing of the visage, but appearance is merely the emerging of the image." [44] An image or copy is not really being. It is only disposed to what really is, the idea. By not reflecting the idea properly, an image simply is the semblance or pretense, a sheer illusion, a nothing. A copy is not organically one with the idea; it just copies it. The rise of Plato's idea in philosophy meant a split in that which ultimately belongs together – a split in appearance and being.

When *physis* is no longer breaking forward, governing, and holding everything in its order, it becomes the field of matter which can be formed and exploited; it becomes a potential principle exposed to the invasion of the active, spiritual principle, the idea. The distinction of spirit and matter has pushed the understanding of *physis* aside into forgottenness. The later philosophers referred to the early Greek thought of *physis* only as undeveloped understanding and as a primitive concept of matter.

In all of Heidegger's investigations or interpretations of the earlier thought, he tends to go down to the ultimate, forgotten bases of reality. He attempts to revive the early Greek thought, however, not

---

[42] Heidegger, *Platons Lehre von der Wahrheit*, p. 41.
[43] Heidegger, *Einführung*, p. 140.
[44] *Ibid.*, p. 141.

as a thought of historical importance, but as thought which belongs to our future. Heidegger sees indications that the early Greek problems inevitably will have to be faced by us in the late history of Western thought.

Heidegger, the thinker of Being, thinks Being the way the early Greeks thought *physis*. *Physis* was the constant coming and breaking forward, the appearing. This appearing was thought by the early Greeks as "assembling of itself into an assemblage, bringing of itself to a stand and thus standing." [45] Concomitant with such an understanding of appearance as assemblage, there was another – more superficial, and ontologically inferior (posterior). Here 'to appear' was understood "as to hold out a surface, a periphery, a visage as an offer for an onlooking while already-standing-there." [46] This latter inferior mode of truth was made a superior by Plato. In the first mode of understanding, appearance is in the midst of Being; it is Being. In the second mode of understanding, appearance is that which is outside of being and which attains a greater or lesser degree of reality only through its accordance or discordance with being. Appearance here stands apart from being and is not being.

In the first mode, the appearance is *physis* itself which by coming forward erects an open realm in which it primarily establishes itself. In the second mode, the appearance is merely a reflection of the idea in an already established open realm. The first mode of appearance is that of the truth as disclosure of *physis*; it is the *aletheia* itself. In the second mode, the truth is the correspondence (accordance) of the appearance with the idea. Appearance, consequently, is only true insofar as it accords to the idea. Truth here becomes correctness instead of being the disclosure. In the first case *physis* itself is that which assembles all the things into their 'somethingnesses' by throwing them into their boundaries; *physis* is *logos*. In the second case, idea is that which assembles all the things into their 'somethingnesses'; idea is *logos*. *Physis* as *logos* is itself the fundamental thinking as the assemblage of everything in the light of *physis*; it (such thinking) arises from the *physis* itself. Whereas, idea as *logos* is thinking which is thrown upon *physis* as matter; it is foreign to *physis*. In the first case *logos* is the 'logic' of *physis*; in the second – *logos* is *ratio*, the basis of conventional logic.

Beginning with Plato, *physis* – that which was beyond all order and

[45] *Ibid.*, p. 139.
[46] *Ibid.*

which was holding everything in an order – itself became merely matter exposed to the ordering principles, ideas; it became that which can be ordered.

When investigating Anaximander's saying,[47] Heidegger translates the word 'necessity' (τό χρεών) as *Brauch* in the sense of spare or sparing. *Brauch*, or spare, Heidegger understands as "to let sojourn, as a sojourner, something-which-sojourns"[48] or "to hand something out into its very essence and to retain it, as thus sojourning, in the guarding hand."[49] 'Guarding,' in German *'wahrende,'* has both connotations: 'making true' and 'guarding.' *Physis* as revelation discloses (makes true) everything which sojourns in the light brought forward by it and guards everything within its light. "The spare [*Brauch*], which ... 'de-fines' that which sojourns, hands out the boundaries; therefore, as τό χρεών, it is at the same time τό ἄπειρον or that which is without boundaries insofar as it 'essentiates' itself by granting the boundaries of sojourning to that which sojourns."[50]

To apeiron (boundlessness), which is *physis*, is *eo ipso logos*, because it brings forward everything in its articulated order. "Τό χρεών [*Brauch*, spare]," Heidegger says, "contains in itself the yet unsettled essence of the lighting-concealing assemblage. The *Brauch* is the assemblage: ὁ λόγος."[51]

The sojourning being which is assembled in *physis* does not sojourn there in its isolated presence as separated from its absence. A sojourning being which is revealed or disclosed (which is true) in the realm of revelation (the ultimate truth or *physis*) is always there as breaking forward into revelation, sojourning there, and withdrawing from there. Coming-forward, as not-as-yet-there, and going away, as already no-longer-there, the sojourning being is present; it is present in its entanglement with its absences. "The sojourning being by taking place in the realm [of Being] 'essentiates' out from its absence."[52] To be absent, as well as present, is only possible in a realm (*Gegend*) of openness. Absence is a mode of presence. Beyond the realm of openness there is neither presence nor absence. A sojourning being which is

---

[47] "The Non-Limited is the original material of existing things; further, the source from which existing things derive their existence is also that to which they return at their destruction, according to necessity; for they give justice and make reparation to one another for their injustice, according to the arrangement of Time." Freeman, op. cit.

[48] Heidegger, *Holzwege*, p. 338.

[49] *Ibid.*, pp. 338–339.

[50] *Ibid.*, p. 339.

[51] *Ibid.*, p. 340.

[52] *Ibid.*, p. 323.

assembled by *physis* as *logos*, on the other hand, in its own way assembles this realm in which it is presently-absently present.

Such sojourning beings which are assembled in *physis* are not just material things. Here also man is assembled – though in a distinct way. Man himself assembles by taking-over and guarding the assemblages of *physis* as *logos*. By emphasizing the idea, Plato stressed perception instead of *physis*, the coming-forward or revelation. 'Understanding' in German is 'Vernehmen.' 'Vernehmen' implies 'perceiving' in the sense of 'receiving' or 'taking-over.' When understanding as perception is emphasized, it becomes the revealing factor which brings an order into disordered nature or matter.

Man for the early Greeks, by standing in *physis* and thus by understanding the assemblages or *logos* of *physis*, was guarding the *logos*, guarding that which was assembled in *physis*; whereas since Plato, man became the true possessor of *logos*. Instead of being located in *physis*, *logos* becomes located in the mind or, as Heidegger indicates, in a statement.

In the beginning *logos* as assemblage is the occurrence of disclosure, and is founded in and servile to it [to disclosure]. Now, on the contrary, *logos* as assemblage becomes the place of truth in the sense of correctness. It results in the Aristotelian thesis according to which the *logos*, [merely] as a statement, is that which can be true or false.[53]

Here *logos* gradually becomes logic. With the upsurge and dominance of logic, as Heidegger indicates,[54] the primary phenomena, such as *physis* and *aletheia* are lost. Therefore these phenomena cannot be thought of logically; on the contrary, logic, whose essence is *logos*, is grounded in these phenomena.

Logos, as that which assembles, is that which governs and holds sway. Heidegger defines it as "the established sway of assemblage held in itself." [55] *Physis* as revelation is the ultimate truth, and *physis* as *logos* is the ultimate reason or understanding. The 'ultimate' is the first or the most primary. "Being, as the assembling-securing letting-to-come-forward, is that principle from which anything whatsoever comes forward only by sojourning in its [Being's] assemblage and breaks forward within the arisen revelation." [56] Therefore the foremost *logos* is *arche*, principle.

On the other hand, since *logos* is "the assembling letting-lie," it is

53 Heidegger, *Einführung*, p. 142.
54 *Ibid.*, p. 92.
55 *Ibid.*, p. 98.
56 Heidegger, *Satz*, p. 182.

that which founds everything and is its ground.[57] Everything which *is*, is indebted for its being to *logos*. Debt in Greek is *aition* which in Roman translation is *causa*, the cause.[58] Hence, *logos* or *physis* is the principle and cause, in the sense of the ground of everything. In the post-Socratic philosophies, this situation becomes reversed: nature becomes determined by the principles and causes, instead of being their ground. The articulations or assemblages, the language of *physis*, *logos*, accomplished by *physis* within *physis*, has been replaced by the sterile universal concepts by which a logical subject was enabled thereafter to order and to control nature.

Physis is the coming-into-light, appearing. Anything which is, stands in this light and is laid in the articulating order of *physis*. *Physis*, by laying everything into its order, perceives, in the sense of receiving, everything into it. This receiving, in German *Vernunft*, is the understanding. To *physis* "*belongs* understanding; its sway [the sway of *physis*] is co-sway of understanding." [59] 'Belongs' here is italicized to emphasize its connotation of 'listening to' (*gehören*); Understanding listens to *physis*, stands under the sway of *physis* ('under-stands') – it belongs to *physis*.

Man stands in *physis* in a distinguished way: he partakes in the sway of *physis*, in its *logos*. By 'under-standing' the orderings of *logos*, he guards them, i.e. he holds or keeps up the order of *physis* or the order of *logos* as an order by letting everything appear in its light or assemblages the way everything is laid or assembled in this light. Man's understanding, and accordingly his intellect, owes its light to the light of *logos*; and its ultimate destination is the guarding of the truth of *physis*. "Truth is the fundamental presupposition of all human understanding. Modern thinking, however, maintains that intellectuality in itself is already carrying the light." [60] Understanding is a mode of the breaking-forward of *physis* itself, and man becomes man by partaking in the understanding of *physis*. "Understanding is not a mode of conduct possessed by man as his property, but, on the contrary, understanding is that event which possesses man." [61]

Heidegger sees the belonging of understanding to nature illustrated in the Hölderlinian poem *Wie wenn am Feiertage*.[62] Here Hölderlin

[57] *Ibid.*
[58] *Ibid.*, p. 183.
[59] Heidegger, *Einführung*, p. 106.
[60] From the course "*Grundfragen der Antiken Philosophie*," held by Eugen Fink in the fall semester of 1947–48 at the University of Freiburg (Germany).
[61] Heidegger, *Einführung*, p. 108.
[62] Heidegger, *Hymne*, pp. 2–4.

indicates the awakening of nature. "In the awakening it comes to itself," says Heidegger. "The light lets everything come forward in its appearance and glow, into which everything real, set aflame by it, stands in its own contour and measure." [63] Such an articulation of everything real and its illumination in the light of nature, the *logos*, is its thinking. Even in the conventional understanding, thinking is the procedure of illuminating and 'de-fining' in the sense of holding everything apart by setting everything in its limits and at the same time holding it in the unity of concept. Now, since nature assembles all the sojourning beings to themselves, it holds them in the unity of its light. Nature is thinking, and by the thoughts of nature everything has its place. By standing in nature, and thus in the thoughts of nature, man guards these thoughts – he thinks.

Physis as *logos* is the ultimate essence of thought as well as of language. It renders thought and language possible. Thinking and talking are merely man's responses to the thinking and talking of *logos*, the language of Being. In Heidegger's *Sein und Zeit*, *Dasein* as the to-be-in-the-world is a continuous illustration of man who stands in the world – in the articulation, in the setting-in-boundaries, and in the unification of everything in the light of Being, the *logos* of *physis*.

J. Glenn Gray, referring to *Sein und Zeit*, says: "In that book he [Heidegger] was the philosopher of human history and culture, as far removed as it might be from the early Greek concern with *physis*." [64] Such a statement cannot be made after a thorough study of the phenomenon of to-be-in-the-world as a standing in the *logos* of *physis*.

III. LANGUAGE

'To say' (*legein*) ultimately is 'to let lie' all that which is assembled in the openness of *physis*. This indicates man's subordination in his sayings to the assemblages of *physis* in its *aletheia*. Language is in no wise originated or invented by man. 'To say,' *legein*, means that "the speaking of language comes to itself from the disclosure of that which sojourns; and it determines itself according to the being-laid of the sojourning beings by letting them lie in assembly." [65]

The letting-lie of that which is assembled or laid in the *logos* of the

---

[63] *Ibid.*, p. 14.

[64] J. Glenn Gray, "Heidegger's Course: From Human Existence to Nature," *The Journal of Philosophy*, LIV, 8: 201, April 11th, 1957.

[65] Heidegger, *Vorträge*, p. 213.

physis, means to guard it in its disclosure or truth. A word ultimately
sets a being back into Being and thus preserves it in the openness of
Being. Man as a talking being is the guardian of the language of Being.
"He overtakes and fulfills the trusteeship of the sway held by that
which overwhelms him." [66] Man as a talking being stands in the
service of the language of Being, the *logos* of *physis*. "Language really
speaks and not man. Man only speaks insofar as he responds to
language." [67]

When language becomes a language of signs, it is under the control
of man and is merely his instrument. With the elimination of *logos*
from *physis* or of idea from *aletheia*, the covering-up and the falling-
into-forgottenness of *physis* and its language, the *logos*, took place.
Man no longer stood in the service of language, but language became
the instrument of man.

Today the conception of language as an instrument of information goes to
extremes. Although there is an awareness of this fact, there is no attempt to see
its meaning. Everyone knows that now in the field of constructing electronic
brains not only accounting machines but also thinking and translating machines
are being built. However, all calculation in the narrower and broader sense, all
thinking and translation, occur in the element of language.[68]

The interest in symbolic logic is not accidental but highly characteristic of our times: it expresses the mechanization of our thinking and
talking. When words are merely signs, they can be replaced by symbols,
and thinking or language can thus become a mechanical procedure.
Then it stands in man's service like any other apparatus or instrument.

Such a mechanization of language goes right along with the mechanization of the earth (the harnessing of earth to the slavery of man).
Just as the mechanization of language cannot reveal its essence, so the
mechanization of earth cannot reveal the essence of the earth. For the
modern man, however, the calculation of nature "is the only key to
the secrets of the world." [69]

According to Heidegger, the controlling or calculating attitude of
the modern man is a typically subjective attitude, and to experience
the essences of language and the earth, a respectful attitude is needed.

Besides the understanding of nature in the sense of the physical
sciences, there is a 'natural' understanding of nature. The rising and
setting sun, changing phases of the moon, the starry sky, and the

[66] Heidegger, *Einführung*, p. 132.
[67] Martin Heidegger, *Hebel – der Hausfreund* (Pfullingen: Günther Neske, 1957), p. 34.
[68] *Ibid.*, p. 35.
[69] *Ibid.*, p. 30.

serene mountains or wild forests still give a glimpse of the once overwhelming *physis*. The 'nature' of the physical sciences cannot give
such a glimpse because it is not appropriate to it. Everything that such
'nature' teaches was previously placed in it by the system of the
science as one of the possible factors, data, or answers within such a
system. Mathematically approached nature cannot give any other but
mathematical, i.e. quantitative, answers.. An answer of essence
(*Wesen*) can only be obtained by guarding or preserving the language
of nature in human words.

The subjective man with his controlling attitude is a man who has
lost his hearing – the hearing of the *logos* of *physis*. Hearing here
means the being open to that which is assembled in the articulation
of *physis* and which approaches us in the *logos* of language. In hearing,
man assembles himself upon the assemblings of the *logos*. "Hearing
really is this assembling of oneself in which one gathers himself together upon the him-appealing and him-addressing language" [70] of
Being.

Since man belongs to or partakes in the *logos* of *physis*, he can hear
its language. The German words for 'belonging,' '*zugehören*' and for
'hearing,' '*zuhören*' are neighboring words, and Heidegger refers to
both of these words as to a single phenomenon when expressing man's
implication in Being.

True hearing always involves the hearing of *logos*, even when
listening to the words of man. When a philosopher speaks, he responds
to the *logos*, the language of *physis*. Therefore his words are in a certain
sense *logos*. Elucidating Heraclitus' fragment 50, Heidegger says:

'Not to me,' namely this speaker, not to the divulgence of his speech need you
listen. You do not really hear at all as long as you only direct your ear to the
sound and stream of a human voice in order to pluck a kind of speech from it
for yourselves. Heraclitus begins the saying with a rejection of hearing merely
for aural delight. However, such rejection is based on an indication of true
hearing.[71]

In his investigation of various philosophies in history, Heidegger
often indicates that such investigation cannot limit itself only to
what has been said by this or that philosopher, but also must hear the
unsaid of the philosophy, which nonetheless belongs to the assertions
of this philosopher. For this reason, Heidegger's historical interpretations seem to be inadequate and often appear to, or rather do, say
more than what was said by such a philosopher.

[70] Heidegger, *Vorträge*, p. 214.
[71] *Ibid.*, p. 216.

IV. WORLD AND EARTH

Physis as the breaking-forward from concealment and withdrawing into concealment has the dark aspect dominant; while *logos* as the assembling of everything in the light has the light aspect dominant. Such a duality of Being is reflected in Heidegger's problems of the earth and the world.

For Heidegger, the earth is that which constantly opposes the world and which stands in strife with it. In the essay on the artwork he indicates that *physis* is the earth as he understands the earth.[72] Often he also shows *physis* as world. When investigating Heraclitus' phenomenon of fire, Heidegger denotes fire as "the everlasting breaking-forward" [73] as *physis*, which by breaking forward holds onto itself and thus stands in a reservation. By doing this, *physis* holds an open realm for anything whatsover to appear or to be present. "But this is the χόσμος," [74] Heidegger says and he remarks immediately that world here cannot be understood cosmologically or scientifically. World is not the sum or framework of all the beings, but is that which enables the beings to be beings. World is the openness of Being itself. Hence, the Heraclitian phenomenon of fire, the *physis*, is the earth as well as the world. It is the strife of the world and the earth.

Heidegger's earth opposes the world; but by indicating that they are in a constant strife, he shows at the same time their necessary reference to each other and their necessary belonging together. Hence, the opposition of these two phenomena is really their togetherness. The world and the earth are truly one and the same phenomenon when taken ultimately; they merely express the structure of *physis* or Being, just as the to-be-in-the-world expresses the structure of *Dasein*. "When Heraclitus speaks of fire," says Heidegger, "he thinks, above all, the lighting sway, the ordering reference [*weisen*] which gives and withdraws the standards [*Mass*]." [75] Because these standards are the boundaries of everything whatsoever, they make everything something. 'The lighting sway, the ordering reference' represents worldness, and the 'withdrawal' – earthliness. By distinguishing the earth and the world, Heidegger is merely trying to peer into *physis*, into the "lighting

---

72 Heidegger, *Holzwege*, p. 31.
73 Heidegger, *Vorträge*, p. 275.
74 *Ibid.*
75 *Ibid.*

EARTH 153

sway, the ordering reference, which gives and withdraws the standards."

By showing the structure of *physis* or of the openness of Being as the strife between the earth and the world, Heidegger is ultimately showing the strife between concealment and the revelation, between truth and untruth. Properly understood, truth is nothing static, but is a dynamical breaking forward of the revelation from the concealment. It is a strife between truth and untruth. How Heidegger arrives at such an understanding of the truth and how such understanding of the truth is related to the traditional understanding of the truth is shown in his *Vom Wesen der Wahrheit*.

The traditional understanding of the truth ultimately rests on the proper understanding of the truth but has forgotten these foundations upon which it is resting. By considering the basic problems of traditional philosophy, Heidegger generally reveals the lack of fundamentality in them and uses them merely as indications and roadmarks for finding the more fundamental phenomena. He calls such a method of dealing with traditional philosophy the destruction of traditional philosophy. 'Destruction' here is not a negative but a highly positive pursuit. It "does not have any other concern but the regaining of the primary Being-experiences of metaphysics through demolishing the conventional futile conceptions." [76]

Heidegger attempts such a 'destruction' in his *Vom Wesen der Wahrheit* where he tries to rediscover the ultimate foundations of truth. With the very first words of his *Vom Wesen der Wahrheit*, he indicates that a philosophy which is inclined to generalizations is a philosophy of groundlessness. The truth for such a philosophy is the truth which embraces the diversity of different types of truth, namely: the truth of practical life, of technical calculation, of political cleverness, of scientific or economical research, of artistic creation, the truth of thinking, religious truth, etc. An attempt to establish a formula which satisfies all varieties of truth is a process of abstraction, a generalization which is a drifting away from concreteness, away from seeing man on his way through history – man struggling to reveal the standards which keep his life and his whole essence in unity.

In all the problems he investigates, Heidegger reaches for the deepest phenomena. Such phenomena are anterior to any theory and have their own stance outside the framework of such a theory. A theory is always subjective by being established by man and used as

[76] Heidegger, *Seinsfrage*, p. 36.

an instrument in man's hand; whereas that which is prior to all the theories belongs in the hand of Being itself.

The tendency to go down to that which is prior to all theories is not a return to the commonsense level, and is not an attempt to see things with the eyes of the commonsense man. Common sense bases everything upon self-evidences, and it does not see any need of going into the foundations of these self-evidences and of questioning their ontological firmness. "Philosophy, however, can never refute common sense since common sense is deaf to the language of philosophy. Nor may it even wish to do so, since common sense is blind to the things which philosophy sets before its own essence-seeking eyes." [77]

That which stands at the beginning is prior to any theory as well as to the standpoint of commonsense understanding. However, in order to trace back or rediscover that which stands at the beginning, there is no need to reject all these theories and the standards of common sense. On the contrary, they can serve as guides to lead us back to the sources from which these theories and the commonsense understanding emanated and were later lost.

Heidegger indicates in his *Vom Wesen der Wahrheit* that that which is real is commonly considered as true. In this way, we can talk about true gold as distinct from that which looks like gold, which is not gold and only appears to be gold. However, even that which is not gold, by not being gold, nevertheless is real. Hence, to be true and to be real are two distinct phenomena. When we talk about gold as true, we indicate that it corresponds to that which is understood by the concept or idea of gold; whereas, that which only looks like gold has something in it which does not correspond to that which is known as gold. Consequently, truth implies correspondence or agreement.

In addition to the correspondence of a thing to the concept or idea, we also apply the phenomenon of truth to a saying or a statement. If something is said about something, it is true only if such a saying accords to that about which it is said. If it does not accord to it, it is considered as false.

Consequently, truth implies a correspondence of a thing to the idea and can be referred to as the thing-truth (*Sach-wahrheit*) or – of a statement to a thing, the statement-truth (*Satz-wahrheit*).

The true then, be it a true thing or a true proposition, is that which is correct, which corresponds. Being-true and truth here mean correspondence, and that in a double sense: firstly, the correspondence of a thing with the idea as pre-

---

[77] Heidegger, *Wahrheit*, p. 6.

conceived of it, and secondly the correspondence of that which is intended by the statement with the thing itself.[78]

Tradition formulates this with the *veritas est adequatio rei et intellectus*.

For the majority of medieval philosophers, truth ultimately was the *adequatio rei ad intellectum divinum*. As far as the human mind is concerned, truth was the correspondence of the human mind to the things or beings, namely: *adequatio intellectus ad rem*.

In the beginning of modern times, the interest in the *adequatio rei ad intellectum divinum* diminished, and human truth became of more interest. However, the thesis *veritas est adequatio intellectus humani ad rem* gradually was transformed into the thesis *veritas est adequatio rei ad intellectum humanum*. Already Descartes saw the pre-eminence of human ideas over the material things as far as the truth is concerned. With Kant this pre-eminence was remarkably emphasized. For him, the intellect did not dance to the time tapped out by the things; but, on the contrary, the things danced to the time beaten by the intellect and the other cognitive powers. All of Kant's basic philosophical works tried to show that the whatness of a thing depends on the structure of our cognitive faculties. This turn from *adequatio intellectus ad rem* to *adequatio rei ad intellectum*, called by Kant himself the Copernican turn in philosophy, was nothing but radicalization of the subjectivization of the truth.

The traditional formula of truth as applied in either way (as thing-truth or as statement-truth) expresses its basic characteristic, namely: the characteristic of directing or accordance; either a thing directs (accords) itself to the idea or an idea directs itself or accords to the thing. The German word for the 'directing of oneself' is '*sich richten*,' and therefore Heidegger uses the word '*Richtigkeit*,' which in English could be translated either by 'correctness' [79] or by 'rightness,' to indicate truth understood in such a way.

After he discloses the basic characteristic of traditionally understood truth, namely, correctness, Heidegger raises the question, whereupon is truth as correctness founded, or what is that which makes correctness possible? By raising such a question in his *Vom Wesen der Wahrheit*, Heidegger attempts to go into the foundations of the traditional formula of truth.

---

[78] *Ibid.*, p. 7.
[79] 'Correctness' originates from Latin *corrigere*, and this from *com-regere*, meaning the straightening of something in accordance with something – directing.

Two silver dollars are totally in accordance to each other; nevertheless, there is a difference between saying 'this is a silver dollar' and an actual silver dollar. Two silver dollars or two bricks can lie beside each other, and a truth will never take place, even though they accord to each other. Only when these things are considered by man, does truth take place or rather does correctness take place. The human attitude or his approach to the things makes correctness possible.

By our attitude we let a thing stand in front of us as an object. By having an insight into a thing, we can face it as an object; and thus we can have an accordance or disaccordance with it, or we can indicate its accordance or disaccordance with another thing.

Such a placing of a thing in front of us and its representation (*Vorstellen*) in our mind or in our statement is again only possible if there is an openness, i.e. an open realm within which we can place a thing in front of us and have an insight into it or represent it in us. The placing of a thing in front of us and its representation in our mind or statements do not create a realm of openness, but merely presuppose it, use it, or overtake it. What is this openness?

When Husserl in his *Ideas* [80] retreated from all theoretical interpretations of reality (bracketed them), he showed the remaining natural standpoint as the 'world out there.' Heidegger thinks of this 'world out there' as the to-be-in-the-world and understands it as to be open to the openness of Being (*Offenständigkeit*). The open attitude enables things to be objects of accordance even though it does not create them.

A silver dollar has no open attitude; therefore it cannot agree or disagree with another silver dollar. Only man with his open attitude to things or beings raises them into a realm within which such an agreement or disagreement can take place.

Only because there is an open realm, the world, can we encounter things, handle them, deal with them, know them, and misunderstand them, ignore them or fail to grasp them. Openness renders the open attitude possible, and the open attitude makes correctness possible. An open attitude enables a thing to become an object, and in addition this same attitude enables man, as a subject, to accord or disaccord with these objects. Our open attitude is ontologically more fundamental than the known objects as well as the knowing subject. "But if correctness (truth) of a statement is merely made possible by the open

[80] Edmund Husserl, *Ideas* (London: George Allen & Unwin Ltd. and New York: The Macmillan Co., 1952), pp. 110–111.

attitude," says Heidegger, "then it follows that this open attitude that alone makes correctness possible must have a more original claim to be regarded as the essence of truth." [81] From this Heidegger concludes that "truth is not primarily at home in the statement." [82] This means that truth primarily is not located in the mind or in our subjective cognitive powers directing themselves in accordance with the things or determining the quiddities of things, but in our open attitude as the to-be-in-the-world. Hence, our open attitude, our worldness, is ontologically prior to our intellection.

What is the open attitude, this truth more basic than correctness? It is the standing in the openness of Being; it is a "submitting of oneself to the binding criterion" [83] of this openness. Man's open attitude is his being-free to the openness and to all that which can be revealed within the horizon of this openness. Man's open attitude is his freedom. Freedom here is the freedom toward the bindings of that which is assembled for the appearance (disclosure) within the realm of the openness itself. Since man is free towards everything which appears in the world, he lets it stand in front of him as an object, represents it in his mind and his statements, and accords or disaccords with it. "The open attitude, as that which makes correctness possible, is grounded in freedom. The essence of truth is freedom." [84]

By subordinating truth (as correctness) to freedom, Heidegger in no wise makes truth subjective in the sense that man determines truth in his fully unrestrained way according to his will or whims. That which appears on the horizon of openness is not an object of our unrestricted freedom; yet by being free to that which is assembled on the horizon of openness, we let that which is assembled there remain the way it is. "Freedom reveals itself as the letting-be of beings." [85] This point in Heidegger resembles that of Husserl where he brackets all the attempts of theorizing interpretations (subjectivistic interpretations in the Heideggerian sense) of the things or beings. By suspending the attempt at theorization, we let the things be the way they are.

Yet, such a suspension is not mere inactivity (passivity) or indifference. On the contrary, "the letting-be is the letting-oneself into the midst of beings." [86] Such a 'letting-oneself-into,' Heidegger interprets

[81] Heidegger, *Wahrheit*, p. 12.
[82] *Ibid.*
[83] *Ibid.*, p. 13.
[84] *Ibid.*
[85] *Ibid.*, p. 15.
[86] *Ibid.*

as "the letting-oneself-into the Open [87] and its openness [88] into which any being, whatever *is*, stands in and which it necessarily brings with itself." [89]

Freedom as letting-oneself-into-the-openness is that which in *Sein und Zeit* was called *Dasein*, the to-be-in-the-world. *Dasein* is the being free or being open to Being and to that which is assembled in the openness of Being; it is the 'ec-sistence.' Freedom is 'ec-sistence.' [90]

The truth of Being is the basis of freedom. Freedom, as the standing in the truth of Being, is prior and ontologically anterior to a subjective freedom which is merely a property of man. "Man does not 'possess' freedom as a property; it is the contrary that is true: freedom, or 'ec-sisting' disclosing *Dasein*, possesses man." [91]

The great men in history in diverse fields of culture are not those who cling anxiously to certain formulated rules or regulations, but those who are free *from* these, and free *towards* the coordinations and assemblages of Being – those who receive directions and standards from Being itself. From here only, from the ultimate source of truth, the great turns of history are begun.

Since truth is freedom, as letting-things-be, it (freedom) may also let things be not the way they are, but the way they only appear to be. In such a case beings or things are concealed or distorted. Yet, since freedom is not a property of man, but rather man is a property or a possession of freedom, even the concealment or distortion of truth, i.e. the untruth, is based and grounded on the openness or truth of Being. "Truth and untruth are not indifferent in their essence, but they belong together." [92] Just as truth ultimately is not correctness of a statement but revelation of Being, so also the untruth ultimately is not mere falsity of a statement but the concealment of Being.

In freedom, man is open to the things as assembled by Being itself and not as related to a subject (i.e. not as objects). Man's openness to the things lets them be the way they are. Man can be open to the things because primarily he is open to the openness of Being, to the world. Man's openness to the openness of Being is interpreted by Heidegger as man's being tuned (*gestimmt*) in harmony with Being in its totality. "The whole behavior of historical man, whether stressed or

---

[87] Being.
[88] World, the openness of Being.
[89] Heidegger, *Wahrheit*, p. 15.
[90] Cf. pp. 72–73 for the meaning of 'ec-sistence.'
[91] Heidegger, *Wahrheit*, p. 17.
[92] *Ibid.*, p. 18.

not, whether understood or not, is tuned, and by this attunement, raised up into Being in its totality." [93] Since man ultimately is in accordance with Being, or rather with the truth (openness) of Being, he can be in accord or can be directing himself in accordance with the things. In other words, due to the truth of Being man can have rightness or correctness – a scientific or also a commonsense truth.

Being in its totality is not the sum of all beings. It can never become a matter of scientific calculation or investigation. For science it is merely nothing. That which grants to everything its 'somethingness,' itself is undetermined and concealed; it is not a something. Being is that which brings everything into light – discloses or makes true – and which itself is not illuminated but concealed, is untrue. "The letting-be is also a concealment. In the 'ec-sistent' freedom of *Dasein* there is accomplished a concealment of Being in its totality – *is* the concealment." [94] 'Is' here can be read as 'takes place.'

It is important to stress and to see that the concealment (untruth) of Being is not a lack of disclosure (truth); concealment is not something secondary or merely an after-effect. "The concealment of Being in its totality, the most proper untruth, is anterior to any revelation whatsoever of this or that being. It is anterior also to the. letting-be which by disclosing holds concealed and stands in relation to concealment." [95] In the Greek word *aletheia* the *a-* denies the concealment (*letheia*) and thus indicates the anteriority of the concealment of Being.

Being is often compared to light. Light discloses everything which can be seen, yet light itself always remains concealed: cannot be seen. By dealing with the things which are revealed in the light, man forgets the light itself. Man forgets the ultimate standard of truth (Being itself), and takes his norms or measurements from the beings; he directs himself in accordance with them by placing them in front of him. In his decisions man ordinarily guides himself by cleverly calculating the beings and not by Being. Such a way of man's existence is ignorance of Being, and therefore, according to Heidegger, it is really not 'ec-sistence,' not standing out in the light of Being, but 'insistence.' 'In-sistence' is the being-closed-in of oneself within the realm of mere beings and the being-closed-off from Being as such. 'In-sistence' is non-transcendence.

[93] *Ibid.*, p. 19.
[94] *Ibid.*, p. 20.
[95] *Ibid.*

Man 'in-sists' only because ultimately he 'ec-sists.' "The 'in-sistent'
turning towards the practicable and accessible and this 'ec-sistent'
turning away from the mystery, go together. They are the same." [96]
Man is characterized by his being exposed to Being. Even his ignorance
of Being is ultimately a mode of his being determined or tuned by
Being.

In his *Vom Wesen der Wahrheit*, Heidegger shows the difference
between the conventional understanding of truth as correctness and
the truth as disclosure. He also shows that the truth as disclosure is
more fundamental or more ultimate, i.e. truer, truth. It is significant
for the truth as disclosure that it is not placed in the mind. The place
of truth as disclosure is Being, *physis. Physis* as coming-forward is
revelation. Yet, it comes forward as concealed. *Physis* then is revealed
concealment or the strife between truth and untruth. The ultimate
truth is world as the openness of Being. Since Being reveals itself as
concealed, the openness of Being, world, is also its concealment. World
is truth-untruth. Such an awkward statement 'truth is truth-untruth,'
however, shows the inner structure of truth or the inner structure of
the world, which is the strife between truth and untruth or between
world and the earth as it is shown in Heidegger's essay on the artwork.

Art is "the truth's placing of itself in the work" [97] of art. Truth
here is not truth as correctness but truth as disclosure. Heidegger
indicates that 'placing' in the above definition of art "means the
bringing to a stand." [98] Here he remarks that truth is not created by
the artist and is not born in an artwork as something which never was.
An artwork brings to sight that which already is 'hanging in the air.'
The 'hanging in the air' indicates the assemblage of everything in the
light of *physis.* Art or the truth of art in Heidegger's essay on art is in
no wise an aesthetical problem. For Heidegger, beauty is the appearing
or breaking forward into the openness of *physis* itself; it is an ontological problem par excellence.[99]

An artist is not the maker of the artwork and, hence, of the truth
which is revealed by it. Truth as that which is located in the *physis*
belongs to *physis* rather than to the artist. An artist merely spells out
that which is already assembled into words in *physis.* "In great art
especially – and only such is had in mind here – the artist remains
something indifferent in respect to the artwork, something like a

---

[96] *Ibid.*, p. 23.
[97] Heidegger, *Holzwege*, p. 25.
[98] *Ibid.*
[99] Cf. p. 139.

channel destroying itself in the procedure of the creation in order that the work may arise." [100]

An artwork is not at all an object or a thing which has some specific characteristics or properties distinguishing it from other objects or things. To know what a thing is, does not mean to be on the way of knowing an artwork by acquiring some additional specific characteristics belonging to an art-thing. We cannot approach an artwork from a thing, but, on the contrary, we approach the 'thingness' of a thing from the artwork.[101]

With this Heidegger indicates that the essence of an artwork or of its truth – since an artwork is that wherein truth is brought to a stand – is beyond the realm of mere things. It is thus a transcendental problem. Transcendence for Heidegger is not a leap from one being (subject) to another being (object), but a leap over all the beings into worldness itself.[102]

What an artwork is, can only be understood in the realm where it belongs, the realm which is arrested by the artwork in the sense that it is brought to a stand. This realm is its world. "The work [of art] as such belongs only in a realm which is opened by it. The 'workness' of the work consists in such an opening." [103] The cathedral of Bamberg, even though it is well preserved and stands on the same place as it did years ago when it was built, is not the same thing it was, because the world in which it belonged and which had been brought to sight by it is gone. The cathedral of Bamberg today is merely a something in our modern world, a something which stands in front of us as something had-been, something which can be, or is, a historically interesting object of art investigation. It can be an object of admiration in many different ways; nevertheless, it is no longer what it was. "κόσμος οὗτος does not indicate one range of beings as demarcated from another, but this world of beings as distinct from the other world of *the same* beings." [104] The same thing in a different world is a different thing.[105]

An artwork is that by which truth is brought to a stand and by which a world is opened – a realm within which anything whatsoever

---

[100] Heidegger, *Holzwege*, p. 29.
[101] *Ibid.*, p. 28.
[102] Cf. p. 117.
[103] Heidegger, *Holzwege*, p. 30.
[104] Heidegger, *Vom Wesen des Grundes*, p. 22.
[105] To the question, whether a thing is or can be between two worlds, the only answer is that to be or not to be is only possible in a world; between the worlds a thing neither is nor is not. On the other hand, a multitude of worlds can never be thought of as a multitude of beings, because a world is not a being, is 'no-thingness.' A world is merely a mode of openness of Being, a mode of *physis*, a mode of *the* world.

can take a place and sojourn. How such a bringing to a stand of truth
takes place, can be illustrated by the full moon throwing light upon
a village below and thus bringing it into light. The light of the moon
is not its own. The moon merely assembles it and brings it to a stand.
By assembling the light unto itself, the moon assembles everything
in the realm of this light: the moon opens up a world. If there were no
moon in the sky (if there were no artwork), the light of the sun (the
light of truth or the light of *physis*) would not be brought to a stand,
and the village below would lie in darkness (a world would not be
opened).

A Greek temple shows the strength of the rock by sitting on it, the
stormy sea by opposing it calmly, the height of the sky by towering
into it.[106] An artwork (temple) brings the earth to appearance in the
light of the world, and thus opens up a world. "The standing temple
opens up a world and sets it at the same time back upon the earth
which itself thus comes forward as the native ground." [107]

Previous to the temple in this same essay, Heidegger investigated
the Van Gogh painting which shows a pair of peasant shoes.[108] Here
Heidegger has shown that the shoes 'assemble' into appearance within
a world the wide fields, rough winds, dampness and richness of the
soil, country roads, bare winter fields, and the crops of autumn; they
show man as living his life on his native ground, in his world. A shoe,
by being dependable (*verlässlich*), takes the peasant into his world.
The German word '*verlässlich*' (dependable) has a root of '*lassen*' or is
related to '*ein-lassen*,' i.e. the 'letting' or 'letting-into.' Because of its
dependability "this implement lets the peasant into the silent call of
the earth. By the efficacy of the dependability of the implement, the
peasant is aware of the world." [109]

An artwork as that which brings forward the earth and erects the
world is not something symbolic. It indicates the real or true earth
and the world in which man dwells. A work grants space for man to
inhabit. However, this space is not something like mathematical space,
but real (mathematical space is mere abstraction). Space opened by
an artwork is living space – experienced and not just speculatively
comprehended. The Greek temple by towering into the sky manifests
the height of the sky; by being seen from distant seas or far mountains,
it brings these into its space; it grants space to them – spaces-in a

[106] Heidegger, *Holzwege*, p. 31.
[107] *Ibid.*, p. 32.
[108] *Ibid.*, pp. 22–23.
[109] *Ibid.*, p. 23.

space. "The spacing-in means here the releasing of the free range of openness and the organizing of this range in its structure." [110]

In his *Sein und Zeit*, Heidegger has shown space as presupposing the directing and distancing *Dasein*. Space is possible only because *Dasein* grants space (*einräumt*).[111] *Dasein* as the to-be-in-the-world is to-be-aware of the world. By such an awareness of the world man can be aware of different implements. This awareness of the implements is *eo ipso* awareness of their belonging in one or another place in reference to other implements and in reference to the 'whole works,' to the living surroundings (*Um-welt*). Such awareness is awareness of what is near and what is far, of what goes in what direction or goes in what place with respect to others and to all. Such awareness, the distancing (*ent-fernen*) and directing (*ausrichten*) of *Dasein*, renders space possible and is rooted in the knowledge of the world. And again, the knowledge of the world is only possible through an artwork which arrests or brings the world to a stand.

An artwork erects the world and brings forward the earth. The temple brings forward the whiteness of marble, the blueness of sky, the strength of the rock, the range of the sea. Artwork consists of stone, wood, color, tone or word. All these are educed by the artwork and revealed in their true earthliness. The earth appears or comes forward in stone, wood, color, tone or word. Nevertheless, in all this appearance it clings to itself and remains unexplained and concealed. A ponderous rock on the slope of a mountain or a brightly colored flower in the grass is educed into a world by the artwork; the earth appears. Yet, what is this ponderousness of a rock? – What is the very 'rockness' of the rock? And what is the bright color of a flower? We cannot reveal the rock by shattering it or by weighing it. We cannot reveal the color of the flower petal by breaking it apart or by jabbing it with a fingernail, or by measuring the color's frequency of oscillation. Even though we have an exact number indicating the weight of the rock or the frequency of oscillation of the color, we do not have the very essence of the ponderousness or of the color in their true emphaticness. The earth "shows itself only when it remains concealed and unexplained." [112]

All the scientific or systematic explanations, calculations, and analyzations of matter – even though they are precise and of great

---

[110] *Ibid.*, p. 34.
[111] Cf. p. 40.
[112] Heidegger, *Holzwege*, p. 36.

importance to modern society – do not reveal the earth. The earth retreats and is lost in all these attempts to seize it. Only where the earth is guarded and preserved as essentially undisclosed, does it appear openly-lighted and as itself. "The earth retreats from any attempt to disclose it. It holds itself constantly concealed." [113]

The concealedness of the earth is not a stubborn clinging to itself in the sense of not coming to appearance at all. The earth appears. It is real and can be experienced. It can be experienced in divers modes and in an inexhaustible variety of forms in which the earth comes forward as essentially reserved and concealed. The earth, as coming forward in its concealment, develops a richly articulated language by which it announces its reservation or concealment.

The concealedness or reservation of the earth is that which cannot be penetrated, which refuses any invasion into itself; it is a firm foundation on which a world can rest and be a world. World is world by holding the richly articulated language of the earth in the openness. The earth with the tendency to reservation or concealment and the world with the tendency to total revelation are distinct and opposed, but they can never be separated. "The world grounds itself upon the earth, and the earth breaks into the world." [114] They both stand in a strife in which neither of the two tends to the annihilation of the other; by standing in the strife they help each other to be what they are.

An artwork brings forward or assembles the truth of the world. This truth consists in the strife between the earth and the world.

Heidegger's theory on truth is based on the Greek phenomenon of *aletheia* which means 'revelation.' Revelation is the disclosure and the coming-forward from concealment. Without concealment, the truth – and without disclosure, the untruth – is not thinkable. The 'essentiation' of truth ultimately is the strife between truth and untruth. Such a strife stirs up a clearing or a realm into which things can stand-in and appear; it stirs up a world. The strife between the truth and untruth is represented by the strife of the world and the earth. The ultimate disclosure, the truth par excellence, is the world. The more extensive formulation of truth is the strife between disclosure and concealment, between truth and untruth; the more extensive formulation of world is the strife between revelation and concealment, between the world and the earth. Untruth as well as truth is truth.[115]

[113] *Ibid.*
[114] *Ibid.*, p. 37.
[115] 'Untruth' here is 'concealment' and therefore, in no wise is it falseness.' Falseness or wrongness belongs in the realm of de-rooted truth, correctness.

The earth as well as the world is world. The context of truth and untruth is merely the shown structure of truth, just as the context of the earth and the world is the shown structure of world. By replacing the first 'world' in the formula 'world is the strife between the world and the earth' by '*physis*,' we may make that formula sound clearer: '*physis* is the strife between the world and the earth'; however, the most important thing to remember here is the fact that this context, 'the strife between the world and the earth,' indicates the structure of appearing Being, structure of *physis*, structure of world. In the late part of his third phase of thinking, Heidegger has developed greatly the understanding of the structure of the world in his phenomenon of foursome which will come up frequently in the latter part of this study.[116]

The world is not merely revelation and the earth is not just concealment. In its world a nation is faced with obscure tasks and dangerous decisions. In all these decisions in the various turns of history which befall the life of a nation, the nation is exposed to the unknown, the undecided, the misleading and the concealed. On the other hand, the earth on which a nation dwells is not merely "the concealedness but that which comes forward as self-concealing." [117] An artwork discloses the earth in its diversity. The earth comes forward as a nation's native grounds with rocks and stones, hills and valleys, creeks and lakes, plants and animals. An artwork leads a nation into these articulated modes of the earth's coming forward and thereby brings such a nation to respond to them – to find its ways on its earth. These diverse modes of the earth's upcoming also give foundations to the nation's language.

According to Heidegger, the Greek word *techne* primarily does not mean a technical performance in producing an artwork or an implement. It primarily indicates the mode of knowing. However, this knowledge is not a practical knowledge as opposed to theoretical knowledge. It is the primary knowledge presupposed by the practical as well as the theoretical knowledge. It is the standing in the *aletheia*, in the openness of the strife of the world and the earth, in the *physis*. An artwork can be created because *physis* is constant-coming-forward, is *logos*. The knowledge (*techne*) as the standing out in the openness of the strife of the earth and the world, is the response

---

[116] The ambiguity which still remains in the interrelation of the earth and the world will be diminished in the investigation of foursome.

[117] Heidegger, *Holzwege*, p. 44.

to the *logos* of *physis*. An artist by creating an artwork merely guards
the coming-forward *physis* in its *logos*.

The *logos* steps as λέγειν in front of φύσις. In such a dialectic, *logos* as the
occurrence of the assemblage becomes the ground which founds the being-
man ... To be man means to *overtake* the assemblage – the assembling understanding of the Being of beings, the knowing setting-into-work of appearance
– and thus to *administer* over the revelation and to *guard* it against the concealment and covering.[118]

The word 'guarding' in German '*Bewahren*' denotes not only the
preserving of something but also the maintenance of it in its truth,
in its disclosure, and thus the showing of it the way it is assembled
in *logos*.

The act of the artist is rooted in *physis*. The artist stands in the
attunement of *physis*, and his work is his response to such an attunement.[119] By his response an artist helps the strife between the
world and the earth take a stand in the artwork, and thus he partakes
in the disclosure of a world.

Even though an artwork becomes real only during the procedure of
creation; nevertheless, the strife between the world and the earth,
rather than the creator or his act of creation, is that which primarily
determines the artwork. The strife between the world and the earth
uses the creative artist to let its truth be captured in his work.

The artwork in the first place is not a work insofar as it is brought about or
made, but insofar as it realizes Being in a being. This realization means the
bringing into work of that in which – as in that which appears – the coming-
forward, the φύσις, comes to shine. Whatever else appears or is found is only
by the artwork, as being-Being, confirmed *as being*, or also as non-being, and
also only by the artwork is it made accessible, explainable, understandable.[120]

An artwork, as that which assembles the world and the earth, assembles Being and thereby is that whereby being *is* – is being-Being.

Truth ultimately is the strife between truth (disclosure) and untruth
(concealment). Truth as strife stirs up an open realm for anything to
come forward and to sojourn. Truth stirs up such a realm, and thus
truly is truth, only if it takes a stand within the stirred-up openness.
Its stand is the artwork. By taking a stand within the openness, it
holds it open and grants a world for things to appear and for man to
live his history.[121]

118 Heidegger, *Einführung*, p. 133.
119 Compare with the phenomena of 'thrownness' and 'projection' on pp. 45–46.
120 Heidegger, *Einführung*, p. 122.
121 Heidegger, *Holzwege*, p. 49.

With the investigation of the essence of an artwork, Heidegger did not intend to contribute anything to aesthetics; he merely brought the problem of truth back to where it belongs, back to where it was prior to Plato, back to *physis*.

Physis is the utmost truth. This truth in no wise is an agreement of a subject and object. Such a truth, correctness, can take place in a given open realm, in a world; and therefore such a truth is not the ultimate truth. The ultimate truth is the truth of *physis*: it reveals a realm and holds such a realm open; it grants a world in which a subject as well as an object can take place and be in accord or in discord with each other. Such a truth cannot be proven; nevertheless, it can be experienced. "Something can be true," says Bäumler in his introduction to Bachofen's works, "even if it is not proven or 'documented.' There is a criterion of truth which should not be overlooked – profundity." [122] The truth as the strife between the world and the earth is the truth of profundity. Such truth is the foundation which cannot be reached and experimentally investigated by scientific or syllogistic methods. Science can never give any information or make any judgments about primary truth because such truth builds the realm in which science can be born. Science never can reach beyond its birth-bed because it is 'progressive,' looking ahead. Science presupposes an already opened or stirred-up realm in which it can take a section and therein proceed with its exact methods. "Science is not a primary event of truth, but always merely a cultivation of one section of already opened truth, and that by the grasping and founding of all that appears as possibly or necessarily correct." [123] A scientific man does not accept anything as true which is not reasonably founded, in the sense that it is represented in his mind. Consequently, a scientific man only considers as true a subjective truth (a truth representable in the mind), truth subordinated to man. Whereas truth, which opens a world for things to appear and for man to live his life and make his decisions, is a truth that exceeds man. Such a truth is no longer "merely a human truth, but the truth of Being itself." [124]

Modern man faces nature as a field of forces which are servile to man or are in the process of being made so. "The earth itself can only show itself as an object of an attack, which can only adjust itself to

---

[122] Bachofen, *op. cit.*, p. XC.
[123] Heidegger, *Holzwege*, p. 50.
[124] Walter F. Otto, *Die Gestalt und das Sein* (Düsseldorf-Köln: Eugen Diederichs Verlag, 1955), p. 3.

the will of man as an unconditional objectivization. Nature appears everywhere . . . as an object of technology." [125]

Heidegger with his efforts to think earth in a great mode, the way it had been thought by the early Greeks, attempts to restore respect for the earth and thus to free us men from the handicap of our subjectivism. Heidegger's earth, as Egon Vietta indicates,[126] is not "an earth suppressed, totally lost in the production-procedure which mobilizes the entire powers of the earth," but is an earth "which is closer to the stars."

V. HÖLDERLIN'S UNDERSTANDING OF NATURE

The early Greek *physis* stands at the beginning; yet, it does not stand still. It is the constant coming-forward and assembling of everything in its open realm. *Physis* is *logos*. The earth stands in the strife with the world. This strife, like a whirlpool, stirs up a realm for things to appear and for man to live his history. In Hölderlin's poetry, or rather in his poetical thought, to the phenomenon of nature is given as highly a respectable place as to *physis* by the Greeks and to the earth by Heidegger. Hölderlin "prayed to the divine, primeval world, over which the rule of Zeus has been established, and called it nature." [127] Nature for Hölderlin is holiness itself. Gods are holy because they stand in the realm of holiness, in nature. Holiness is not a property of a god.

Heidegger indicates in one of his late works that gods as well as men are not casting their own light, but they stand in the service of light by serving it in their own way: gods as its carriers and men as its guardians. "Just as those who are distant [*Entfernten*] belong to the distance [*Ferne*], so these [gods and men], as revealed, are entrusted, in the indicated sense, to the lighting which secures them, holds them, and retains them." [128] This lighting is nature in the grand manner of its understanding by Hölderlin.

"Nature is older than the gods," says Jean Wahl, [129] when commenting on Hölderlinian thought. Nature is older than gods not because nature is beyond time, but because it is time itself. Hölderlin

[125] Heidegger, *Holzwege*, p. 236.
[126] Vietta, *op. cit.*, p. 127.
[127] Otto, *Gestalt*, p. 193.
[128] Heidegger, *Vorträge*, p. 279.
[129] Wahl, *Hölderlin*, p. 27.

calls nature "older than the times" [130] to indicate that the times of man or his history can only take place because nature is the all-present, the presentation and temporization, time itself. "The first aspect of holiness is the all-present nature: nature as far as it is older than all the times, as far as it is time itself, as far as it is that which makes all the beings be present in the openness, also as far as it is the unity of opposition, and as far as it befalls us gently in its might." [131]

Hölderlin calls nature the all-living, the wholly alive. That which is alive is more present, whereas the dead is somehow absent. The all-present is *eo ipso* the all-living. However, life here cannot be understood biologically. Nature as all-living should be thought of as the Greeks thought of their *aeizoon*. Here "the verb 'to live' speaks from a most broad, most extreme, and most inward meaning, of which also Nietzsche is thinking in his 1885/86 notes when he says: ''being' we do not have any other notion for it but 'living' – How could anything dead be?' " [132]

According to Heidegger, in the above Greek word (*aeizoon*), or rather in the root of that word, there are connotations of light, divinity, holiness, fieriness. Therefore Homer and Pindar, according to him, referred to mountains, shores and rivers as living. Ultimately life for the Greeks was the same as *physis*. Thus, when Hölderlin indicates nature as all-living, he uses the word 'all-living' in its primary, profound meaning.

All-living nature, in the sense of the most open and the most true – just as *physis* is the most *aletheia* – is that which enables everything that can be to get into the openness and be illuminated or disclosed, i.e. become true. "Nature appears to us as the creative light. It is creative in respect to all because it permits all the beings to appear in their contours and in their measurements." [133]

Nature, as all-living, as most illuminating, itself is not a static light, but it is dynamically and constantly rising out of the veils of darkness. In one of his poems, *Wie wenn am Feiertage*,[134] Hölderlin portrays nature as awakening. Just as *physis*, the constant-breaking-forward into revelation, is breaking out from concealment, so also the a-wakening nature, in the above indicated poem, awakes into light from

---

[130] Hölderlin, *op. cit.*, p. 8.
[131] Wahl, *Hölderlin*, p. 51.
[132] Heidegger, *Vorträge*, p. 273.
[133] Wahl, *Hölderlin*, p. 28.
[134] Hölderlin, *op. cit.*, pp. 7–9.

the darkness of sleep. It arises "out from the holy chaos." [135] Chaos
here is not disorder, but the source of everything. Chaos is "that chasm
from which the openness opens itself," says Heidegger and adds that
"chaos is the holiness itself." [136] The most illuminating nature is
ultimately darkness.

Here again it must be noted that Being, which illuminates everything by making it visible and which is the base of everything as far
as it is, itself is not visible and is baseless; it is an abyss, a chaos.

The chaos is the beginning of everything, even of gods. "Hesiod's
basic postulate is that even the gods have come into being." [137]
Hesiod refers to gods as "sprung-out from Earth." [138] He also indicates
that the earth originated from chaos.[139] That the gods are not the
highest of all is often shown in the ancient Greek literature. When the
chorus-leader asks Prometheus whether there is anything more powerful than Zeus, he answers: "He may not avoid what is destined." [140]
That in whose hands destinies are lying is above all those who are
destined by these destinies.

'Destiny' in Greek is *moira*. Heidegger explicates *moira* as "the
imparting of destinies." [141] That which imparts destinies is that which
bounds everything into its boundaries. *Moira* and *logos* and thus
physis are the same.[142] Zeus, just as any other being, is assembled by
Being or *physis*.

On the other hand, as Heidegger indicates,[143] Zeus is referred to in
Heraclitus as *logos*. He seems there to be above all the assemblages of
the *logos* without himself being assembled within the *logos*. However,
since by being illuminated by the light of *physis* – assembled in *logos* –
everything *is*, the more anything is illuminated, the more it is a carrier
of light itself. Zeus, as the highest being, is the most illuminated and
therefore the most 'logical' in the sense of *logos*-like. Hence, he can be
considered as *logos*. He is the concentration of light. As the god of
thunder, he is the messenger of *physis*. He brings the light of *physis*
and thus opens up a realm of light; he is *logos*. Hölderlin, when speaking
about the awakening of nature, indicates that "out of the hot night

[135] Heidegger, *Hymne*, p. 17.
[136] *Ibid.*
[137] Jaeger, *op. cit.*, p. 11.
[138] Hesiod, *Sämtliche Werke* (Wiesbaden: Dieterich'sche Verlagsbuchhandlung, 1947), p. 9.
[139] *Ibid.*, p. 10.
[140] Aeschylus, *Prometheus Bound, Greek Dramas*, Vol. I, p. 141.
[141] Heidegger, *Holzwege*, p. 340.
[142] *Ibid.*
[143] Heidegger, *Vorträge*, p. 222.

refreshing lightning falls and ever the thunder sounds from afar." [144]
A god of the light and revelation is here shown as related to the
night (concealment) of *physis*, of nature.

Gods are mighty and full of light. Yet they have their might and
light from the realm of nature. "The powers [of nature] do not originate from gods; but gods are by virtue of these powers, which, as "all-
living, hold everything, even gods, in life.' " [145] The German word for
'light' is *'Helle'* which resembles – and also is close to in its meaning –
the *'Heil,'* the 'holiness.' *'Heil,'* just as also the English 'holy,' is
related to 'whole.' We can encounter something wholly, if it is standing
in the light. Gods are illuminated par excellence; they *are* in a whole
or a holy way because they are the carriers of the light of wholeness,
of holiness, of nature itself.

Even though nature makes everything accessible, it is itself, the
source of accessibility, inaccessible. This can be compared to Heidegger's earth, as essentially concealing itself. In his Hölderlinian
commentaries, Heidegger indicates this concealment as *ent-setzlich*,
'dis-missive.' *Entsetzlich* also means horrible. "As 'dis-missive,' holiness
is the horrible itself. Yet this horribleness is concealed in the mildness
of its gentle encompassment." [146] Mild becomes this light when it is
arrested in a song or work of art. Here it becomes safe as taken from
the horrible immediacy of the holiness. Those who enjoy song, called
by Hölderlin "the sons of the earth," [147] are secure, and only the poet
is exposed to the danger of the holiness. Hölderlin dramatically
portrays the poets as standing with their heads bare under the thunders
of a god and with their bare hands taking his lightnings and handing
them safely to the folk. "And from there the sons of the earth can
drink the heavenly fire without any danger." [148]

The dismissiveness and the horror of nature hints or drives man to
an artwork, as the only place where it (nature) can appear. Light
cannot be seen itself; it can only be experienced on an illuminated
object. The song of the poet is the place where gods and men and
holiness itself can appear.[149] Without a poet humanity would be living
an unholy (un-whole, lacking awareness of all-comprising Being) life.

The song of a poet is a work of gods and man: Zeus brings the light

144 Hölderlin, *op. cit.*, p. 7.
145 Heidegger, *Hymne*, pp. 19–20.
146 *Ibid.*, p. 18.
147 Hölderlin, *op. cit.*, p. 9.
148 *Ibid.*
149 Heidegger, *Hymne*, p. 20.

of the heavens and the poet turns it into a word. Nevertheless, neither
the poet nor a god is the author of the word of the song. That which
is named by the loftiest words of a poet is holiness. Holiness itself
comes to a word. Holiness is nature's beauty. "All true poetry has its
beginning in an encounter with the divine, but in Hölderlin the
poetical world cannot even be distinguished from the religious one;
'the most beautiful is also the most sacred,' says Hyperion." [150]

Physis as constant-coming-forward is beauty.[151] Therefore the word
of a poet naming the beauty of nature is primarily the word of nature
– is *logos*. The poet talks merely by responding to the *logos* of nature.
Everything is held in the womb of nature, and a poet's words merely
reflect everything as already brought forward in the boundaries of
logos. "Composing is finding." [152] "When a poet salutes the things,
ultimately the things are those that salute him." [153] Things salute him
from their unifying whole of *logos*, from the holiness of nature's beauty.

By finding the things which are assembled in the *logos* of nature,
the poet is not merely copying them as objects standing in front of
him and disposed to him. To do this would mean to show them as they
are in their relation to man, who faces them, and not the way they are
in the assemblage of *logos*. By singing things as in the light of sacred
wholeness, in the light of holiness, a poet sings the hymns of holiness
itself. The words of a poet primarily are words of holiness. "The
holiness denotes the word and itself comes into this word, and the
word is the event of holiness." [154]

Hölderlin faces nature deeply, religiously. That seems strange to us
modern men because "we do not let it be what it is; but we violate it
or rather – since it does not let itself be violated – by our technical
thinking and mechanization, we erect between it and us second, dead
nature as a partition. How then, according to Hölderlin's words,
could the divinity dwell in between the two?" [155] The place of gods
is between nature as holiness and us men. Since, as has been said in
the above quotation, we moderns erect an artificial nature in this
place, we no longer encounter either gods or holiness. Hölderlin's
religious attitude towards nature seems strange to us because we have
reversed our attitude toward nature: instead of openly responding

150 Otto, *Gestalt*, p. 288.
151 Cf. p. 139.
152 Heidegger, *Erläuterungen*, p. 13.
153 Wahl, *Hölderlin*, p. 60.
154 Heidegger, *Hymne*, p. 31.
155 Otto, *Gestalt*, pp. 202–203.

to its *logos*, we dictate to it our 'logical' *logos*; we force it to answer our subjective questions and we make it subservient to us; we control it. Nature, in the Hölderlinian sense of holiness or in the Greek sense of *physis*, Heidegger compares to a country road.[156] Not man but the road assembles everything and lets everything stand in relation to everything else. When everything, even man, stands in the assemblage of the road (*logos* of nature) and not of man (logic, *logos* of subjectivity), everything stands then in serenity (*Heiterkeit*). And when serenity thus is experienced or known, it leads to eternity. "An understanding of serenity is a gate to eternity. Its door swings on the hinges which once were forged by a skilled smith from the riddles of *Dasein*." [157]

---

[156] Heidegger, *Feldweg*, pp. 5–6.
[157] *Ibid.*, p. 6.

CHAPTER V

GODS

In the previous chapter an attempt was made to bring out the importance of the problem of nature as *physis*, as the strife between the earth and the world, and as holiness – the way it is thought of by the early Greeks, by Heidegger, and by Hölderlin. However, the earth, as standing in strife with the world, did not sufficiently show how the earth has to be thought of in its relation to man; and again, what is its relation to the world when man and gods are brought into play. All this may become clearer in the consideration of the foursome (*Geviert*), the problem of supreme importance in Heidegger's late philosophy.

For reaching the problem of foursome and for looking into it properly, it is necessary to consider the problem of gods. In Heidegger's works, the passages dealing with the problem of gods are scarce and rather obscure. Perhaps this is so because Heidegger presumes that the reader has acquired sufficient knowledge of the Greek religion or because he expects his brief passages concerning gods to be more easily comprehended by the reader than they really are. In any case, for a more extensive understanding of gods, it is necessary to go to some additional sources.

A man possessing an exhaustive knowledge of Greek religion and, at the same time, having a deeply philosophical insight into Greek gods, is Walter F. Otto. His field is the fully developed Greek religion, namely, the Olympian religion as it is pre-eminently shown in Homer's works.

For a long time the Olympian religion was considered as the only religion typical of the Greeks and even as the only one known to them. However, in recent times more and more discoveries have been made by the ethnologists and the mythologists concerning the pre-Olympian Greek religion, the so-called Chthonian religion. The best authority for this period of Greek religion is Johann Jakob Bachofen, a man of philosophical aptitude and at the same time a man of deep feeling for the mythical world. His knowledge of myths is not merely limited to Greek myths but also embraces those of the Roman and the Oriental nations.

These two scholars and, of course, Hölderlin and Heidegger will be sufficient sources for acquiring an understanding of the phenomenon of a god in the sense of a god in Greek religion or in Heidegger's philosophy or Hölderlin's poetry. This chapter will contain six sections. The first one of these sections will consider the Olympian gods, and the second, the Chthonian ones. A separate section will be dedicated to the god Dionysus due to his importance not only in the Greek religion but also in the Hölderlinian-Heideggerian understanding of a god. The fourth section will deal with chaos which also is an important phenomenon for Greek religion as well as for Hölderlin and Heidegger. The fifth section will show the relatedness of gods to *logos*, and the last section will fix gods as the ultimate realities.

I. OLYMPIAN DEITIES

The most characteristic feature of Greek religion is its worldliness. Due to its worldliness, the Greek religion does not seem to even be religion because a religion, in the conventional understanding, has to do with the beyond-the-world realm. On the other hand, the abundance of gods and man's subordination and dependence on them indicate the 'religious' character of Greek religion.

Gods in the Oriental religions reveal themselves to a chosen person and reach him in his soul. From the soul of a seer such a religion is carried to the community of believers. A Greek prophet finds a god in the world. A deity "does not reveal itself to a sight which is turned to inwardness, to the depths of the soul, which [this sight] then, dazzled by the mysterious inward light, turns to the things; but it [the Greek deity] reveals itself to an open eye, which directs itself to the outwardness, to the world." [1]

The Greek gods approach man in his world. They themselves belong to the world and are not thinkable beyond the world or nature. "The Greek gods are stationed *inside* the world; they are descended from Heaven and Earth, the two greatest and most exalted parts of the universe; and they are generated by the mighty power of Eros, who

---

[1] Otto, *Gestalt*, p. 121.

likewise belongs within the world as an all-engendering primitive force." [2]

A Greek god does not disturb the natural order; he never is in conflict with nature. A deity for the Greeks "is neither a justification nor a disruption or elimination of a natural course of the world; it is this natural course of the world itself." [3] When in his *Odyssey*, Homer narrates Telemachus' trip home from the Greek mainland, he says: "And grey-eyed Athene sent them a favoring breeze, rushing violently through the clear sky that the ship might speedily finish her course over the salt sea." [4] In an Orientalistic religion, a god would have made the ship run against the wind. By disturbing nature, such a god would reveal his power, his super-natural power. "There had never been another creed in which a miracle in the true sense, namely, a rupture of the natural order, would have played such a small role in the divine revelations as it did for the ancient Greeks." [5]

Things themselves, the way they naturally are, were somewhat divine for the Greeks. Not that which is supernatural but the very natural was wonderful for them. A god did not have to distort the natural order in order to reveal himself. On the contrary, the very natural, as such, revealed the divinity as that which supports the natural in its being. In the Greek world "the divinity is placed above natural events not as a sovereign power: it reveals itself in the forms of the natural itself, as its essence and being." [6]

As Walter Otto indicates,[7] the events of the *Iliad* and the *Odyssey* could just as well be related without the interference of the gods. This shows how complete is the accordance of the gods and nature in the world of the Greeks. The Greeks saw the acts of gods in the simplest events because they were living a great life and saw reality in a mode of greatness.[8] Just as they were in their plastic arts, so they were everywhere else: they were able to see and show the very concrete and natural in full mergence with the eternal, the divine.

By showing the hand of a god in an event which can be explained naturally, they showed this event as backed by the divine reality. "By

---

[2] Jaeger, *op. cit.*, p. 16.
[3] Walter F. Otto, *Die Götter Griechenlands* (Frankfurt a.M.: Verlag G. Schulte-Bulmke, 1947), p. 168.
[4] Homer, *Odyssey*, p. 235, *The Complete Works of Homer* (New York: The Modern Library, 1950).
[5] Otto, *Götter*, p. 12.
[6] *Ibid.*, p. 13.
[7] *Ibid.*, p. 211.
[8] What is meant by a greater mode of living will be dealt with in the chapter on 'Dwelling.'

introducing the divine, everything accidental disappears. The singular events and their totalities reflect themselves in the eternal, and yet none of the blood and breath of living presence is lost." [9]

The Greeks did not look beyond nature or world, and yet they were living a great life. Nothing would be more wrong than to say that the Greeks ignored the spiritual and lived merely an animal-like life. The Olympian gods were considered as highly spiritual. Nevertheless, they belonged to the world, to nature. Only an Orientalistic attitude either fully succumbs to the animal way of living or totally scorns the natural and tends to the beyondness of nature. The Greek spirit was turned to reality which – even though concrete – was divine.

A Greek deity in no wise stresses itself. By supporting a hero, such a deity makes natural events favorable to the hero (Athene strengthens the wind for Telemachus). It does that by letting the natural event be what it is or be more so. Only by stressing the natural as the natural does such a deity bring itself into appearance as that which does not let the natural fall into meaningless chance, but holds it in a greater unity: gives life to it by letting it help a hero. The deity remains in the background, and only the natural stands on the façade. The Oriental deity commonly breaks through the natural and shows itself as itself by breaking the natural laws and directly emphasizing itself. "To a Greek god the self-accentuation which is not willing to see anybody else beside himself, was always foreign." [10]

The Greek gods backed up the natural order. By doing so they prevented such an order from disintegrating into unholy meaningless-ness. By stressing such an order or by backing up that which was right, they stressed also themselves, but only indirectly. They never forced their way through the natural and never emphasized just themsel-ves. "Zeus gives, reveals through Apollo's oracle that which is right and in no wise himself." [11] Very often, as Otto indicates, such an oracle advises the inquirers to be true to their own gods.[12]

Man was left by such gods to live in a free way and see things and events in their true essences: he was not coerced to scorn them and surrender himself to mere gods. The worldly religion of the Greeks showed clearly "that this nation was far removed from any kind of dogmatism or fanaticism, that it respected divinities without falling into dust." [13]

[9] Otto, *Götter*, p. 218.
[10] *Ibid.*, p. 233.
[11] *Ibid.*
[12] *Ibid.*, p. 234.
[13] Otto, *Gestalt*, p. 98.

Since gods were the very being of the things and events, as holding
them in unities by backing them, they were the most real realities.
And the Greek man, by turning full face to these realities, was a true
child of the world. He did not see anything disdainful or ugly in the
world. He saw the true beauty. Beauty of the world and divinities
were for him the same. From such a world no redemption was necessary, and cognition to him was the sight of being and beauty and thus
the divinity of nature.[14] Contrary to an Oriental man, cognition to a
Greek was in no wise a way to salvation.

Even though worldly, the Greek man was constantly reaching the
utmost limits of worldliness; he lived in the neighborhood of eternity.
That into which the Oriental man was so hasty to leap by abandoning
and despising the real, was totally beyond the interest of the Greek
man; he never crossed the limit into the beyondness of nature (the
super-natural) and always remained true to the natural.[15] Nevertheless,
he was constantly facing the gods and thus lived in a fully exalted
nature.

Nature as implying gods can never be identified with the conventionally understood nature, formed essentially by scientific
patterns. In other words, nature for the Greeks was not a nature
distinct from spirit. It was not something which is formed or acted
upon by spirit; nature for the Greeks was rather forming and bringing
forward itself in its full divine beauty.

These few general remarks about Greek religion and their gods
cannot give sufficient insight into the problem of gods. The importance of the phenomenon of gods for the basic problem of Heidegger's late philosophy – the problem of foursome – demands much
better acquaintance with the Greek gods. It is therefore necessary to
investigate several figures of Greek deity in order to see what a god is
in his very essence. These few remarks, however, may be helpful
before considering a particular god. They will focus the attention on
the typically Greek god-characteristics.

Athene

One of the chief deities in Greek religion is the goddess Athene. She
is generally known as the goddess of battle and is portrayed with a
spear and a helmet. Nevertheless, she is an arch-enemy of senseless
passionate eagerness for war. She is a goddess of energy, vigorous

[14] *Ibid.*, p. 95.
[15] Otto, *Der Europäische Geist und die Weisheit des Ostens*, p. 20.

activities, and pursuits; she is never merely a deity of battle. Her activities are accompanied by prudence and thoughtfulness. Not only heroes of war, but also men of great enterprises, strong and forceful personalities, are such because of their association with Athene, the goddess of vigor and wisdom. "She is a divine sister, a friend, an attendant of the hero in his undertakings. Her heavenly proximity fills him with enthusiasm, enlightens and inspires him always in the right instance." [16] In the first book of his *Iliad*, Homer describes the quarrel between Achilles and Agamemnon. The warlike Achilles was already drawing his sword to strike Agamemnon for his insolence, but Athene stopped him saying: "Cease from strife, and let not thine hand draw the sword." [17] Presence of mind or prudence stayed passion. To modern sight this act of Achilles was merely his own thoughtful decision not to let himself be overpowered by his passion. For the Greeks, who saw man as subordinated to the higher realities, such an act of Achilles was backed up by the higher reality, the reality of Athene. Thoughtfulness belongs to the world of Athene. "She is not a mere admonisher. She is, strictly speaking, decision itself, namely, the decision of the reasonable against mere passion." [18]

Athene as a deity of curbed passion is symbolized as handing the golden bridle to Bellerophon by which he becomes a master of the flying horse, Pegasus.[19] A horse in symbolic language always means the wild, fiery passion. Such passion is the extreme opposite of the cold, clear-sighted wisdom of Athene.

Athene is marked by the presence of mind in an instant of danger during great pursuits, or by the rapid and clear finding of one's way in a critical situation of war or of great enterprises. She is often referred to as an owl-eyed goddess. According to Otto, the most significant characterization of Athene is that she is the constantly near deity.[20]

This feature of nearness is shown not only by presence of mind in the crises of great undertakings, but also in the many practical activities in the everyday life of men and women. The presence of mind is *eo ipso* the presence of the goddess herself in the events, as of the reality which is backing up such events. Athene, accordingly, is the one who inspires or helps in finding the ways of doing things right for

[16] Otto, *Götter*, p. 47.
[17] Homer, *Iliad*, p. 7, *Complete Works*.
[18] Otto, *Götter*, p. 49.
[19] *Ibid.*, p. 51.
[20] *Ibid.*, p. 54.

a carpenter, a wheelwright, a smith, a potter or for girls and women in housework.[21]

By being a goddess of nearness, Athene is a contrast to Apollo, the god of distance. Even though Athene is the goddess of wisdom, her wisdom is of action and practical pursuits, whereas Apollo's wisdom is more spiritual and speculative. Athene does not approach a situation from distant ideas, but from an immediate grasp of what the instant demands – which demands Athene meets in action.

This quality of practical wisdom is the basic feature of Athene's being a female deity. A woman does not tend to speculative distances, but is typified by an understanding of the living situation and its needs. A man with his far-reaching speculative insights is often merely a dreamer in an immediate, practical, living situation, whereas a woman usually is clear-sighted and wise in proximate everyday doings.

Apollo

Just as Athene is characterized by constant nearness, Apollo and his sister Artemis are referred to as the constantly distant deities.

Apollo is the most typical deity of Greece, of the nation which managed to curb the wild and barbarian world and to bring it into a higher, spiritual order. According to Otto, Apollo in the temple of Zeus in Olympia is portrayed as rising up in the midst of a wild uproar and as bringing everything into a calm order merely by stretching out his arm. "Majesty radiates from his countenance; his wide open eyes command in the superior power of his slightest glance; around his strong and noble lips, however, plays a fine, almost sad feature of higher knowledge." [22] In the wild passionate world Apollo commands order with hardly any attempt at active interference with it. He acts by his mere presence from his spiritual distance. He acts like a ray of the sun which removes the veils of night and sets the world into the clearness of light. Very frequently Apollo is referred to as Phoebus. 'Phoibos' means 'pure' and 'holy.' According to Otto, the word 'phoibos' indicates sunshine or the glare of waters.[23]

Apollo and his sister Artemis are often portrayed with bows and arrows, indicating them as the deities who can reach everything from a distance. Artemis resides in the lonesome, undisturbed forests and mountains; and Apollo lives in retirement part of the year: like the

[21] *Ibid.*, p. 57.
[22] *Ibid.*, p. 62.
[23] *Ibid.*, p. 63.

sun (his name Phoebus indicates sun) Apollo withdraws for the winter months.

Apollo, as the god of higher knowledge, knows what is right and knows the future. From the far distance of such knowledge, he indicates through oracles what is right; he is a god who knows the order of *logos*. He brings forward or reveals this order as lying in *physis*, just as the rising sun brings the order of the world out of the darkness of night into the light of day.

The bringing of order and harmony into the boundless confusion is symbolized in the golden lyre which Apollo holds. Apollo, the tamer or subduer to superior harmony of that which is wild and boundless, is expressed in Euripides' *Alcestis*.[24] "Here the sound of Apollo's lyre enchants the wild animals and takes their wildness away" by assembling them into the harmony of beauty. The sound of his music, just as the arrows of his bow, brings the distant order of *physis* into appearance or beauty.[25] Even a bow, when releasing an arrow, sounds like music. "So-called musical bows are well known to ethnology, and we hear that in ancient times warriors' bows were used for the generation of musical tones." [26] The paradoxical fragment 51 of Heraclitus [27] is not so paradoxical after all when the sameness of the bow and the lyre is seen. Apollo's bow and lyre are the same; both bring forward or reveal a higher order of reality. An arrow hits and kills to fulfill that which is destined in the higher order or to restore justice; and the tones of music act as the rays of the sun which throw everything into the harmonious light of the higher order.

Artemis

Like Apollo, Artemis is also a deity of distant purity and clearness. "O maiden – goddess chaste and pure!" Aeschylus calls her in his *Suppliants*.[28]

Artemis is the goddess of free nature in "its innocent purity and its strange duskiness." [29] While Apollo represents the *physis* as in the light of *logos*, Artemis stands for *physis* in its retirement and avoidance of any approach or disclosure. Apollo is the world tending toward revelation and Artemis is the earth blocking the path of any invader.

---

[24] *Greek Dramas*, Vol. I, p. 698.
[25] Cf. p. 139.
[26] Otto, *Götter*, p. 77.
[27] Freeman, *op. cit.*
[28] *Greek Dramas*, Vol. I., p. 11.
[29] Otto, *Götter*, p. 81.

Industrialism may break into a wild and undisturbed nature; it may conquer and control it; but it can never disclose its essence. "The proud conqueror may gain ground as far as he wants, the mystery remains unrevealed; the puzzle persists unsolved. It flees away from him without being noticed by him. It comes back again where he is absent. This sacred unity of untouched nature might be torn apart or destroyed by the conqueror, but never comprehended and rebuilt." [30]

In the diverse forms of plants, trees, and animals, in anything that glares, steams, grows, rots, jumps, flies, streams – in all this seemingly confused disunity, this realm of Artemis can be felt and experienced. Artemis by backing up all this variety makes it unique and the same. The reality of undisturbed nature is gentle and mild, is beautiful and alluring, and on the other hand, it is distant and reserved, cold and dreadful.

> It dwells in the clear aether of the mountain summits, in the golden gleam of mountain meadows, in the glitter and glare of ice crystals and snow flakes, in the silent astonishment of fields and forests when the moonlight illuminates them and sparklingly drops from the tree leaves. Everything becomes transparent and light. The earth itself has then lost its weight, and blood knows nothing about its dark passions. Above the ground it floats like dancing white feet. That is the divine spirit of sublime nature, the tall glimmering lady, the purity who overpowers everything with her enchantment but nevertheless cannot love – she, the dancer, the huntress, who takes a cub on her lap and runs a race with deers. She is death-bringing when she draws her bow. Strange and inaccessible like wild nature, she is nonetheless all charm and fresh motion and lightning beauty. *It is Artemis.*[31]

In this description of untamed nature, if one abstains from everything that he knows theoretically and scientifically about it and gives in to it openly, he then will be able to see that there is a reality, literally *real* and the *same* in all the modes and diversity of wild nature. He will know that it is not merely something emotional, stirring only within him, but a great reality, highly spiritual, which holds a whole world open and grants meaning and realness to everything.

The typical feature of virgin nature, the goddess Artemis' reality, is the constant eluding of any attempt to grasp or to possess it; and even though such a nature is experienced and real, it is always in the distance, always beyond reach. It is ghostly and in a certain sense dreadful. Therefore, night in the unexplored wild regions is very suitable to express Artemis-reality: beautiful and fascinating; frightful

[30] *Ibid.*, p. 82.
[31] *Ibid.*, pp. 82–83.

and mysterious with mountains, meadows, and forests lying in the
silvery light of the moon.

Artemis, the goddess of unexplored nature, does not exclude man.
In a certain sense man, too, belongs to such a nature. According to
Otto, Artemis teaches man many skills: making shelter, finding food,
starting a fire, finding the way in uninhabited areas. Man learns all
this by responding to the demands of wild nature (response here
ultimately means being taught). In ancient Greek literature, she is
often referred to as the guide or rescuer.[32] She is also known as the
deity who teaches how to rear children and who cares for orphan
daughters. When there is no father or mother, nature takes care of the
children just as it takes care of the wild animals. This nature is Artemis.

There is hardly any better way to think of virgin nature – beautiful
and fascinating, full of danger and insecurities, gentle and mother-like,
rough and forsaking, smiling and charming, wild and furious – than
the way Greeks understood it in the form of the goddess Artemis.

Aphrodite

Aphrodite is the goddess of love, joy, and beauty. According to
Hesiod, she was born from seafoam. Nevertheless, she is not a sea
goddess. Yet the sea in its full beauty, gleaming in the sunlight, is the
smiling Aphrodite. Also the land, blossoming meadows, and the wide
sky with golden clouds belong to Aphrodite's realm of beauty. Not
only the flowers of a meadow but also garden flowers, and especially
roses, reveal Aphrodite's divine reality. According to Otto, she has
been known as the "goddess of flowers." [33]

In the Greek myths, Aphrodite is related to an apple, which is a
well-known symbol of love, or more specifically, of erotic love. Wherever she goes, Lucretius tells us,[34] she fills the hearts of birds, animals,
and everything living with love and desire. However, the full reality
of Aphrodite is revealed only in man.

As the goddess of sinful love she does not support wedded love. She
fills hearts with blind desire. Man here breaks all the ties of fidelity,
forgets the whole world, and only strives to be in unity with the one
he loves.

Beautiful women are the heart of Aphrodite's reality. These reveal
Aphrodite in her basic essence. The beautiful women here are not

[32] *Ibid.*, p. 87.
[33] *Ibid.*, p. 95.
[34] *Ibid.*, p. 96.

brides or wives but simply the beautiful, desirable, and lovable women. Aphrodite is a goddess of love, desire, and union.

To the realm of Aphrodite's reality also belong association and friendship, and all the activities or gestures which attract and gain friends, and even words – the charming, kind, and winning words.[35]

Aphrodite, like Athene, Apollo, or Artemis, evidences that an understanding of the gods as anthropomorphic – the way they are represented in the plastic arts – is naive and inadequate. Aphrodite is a reality which is brought forward by the charm of the sea and sky, by the flowers of the meadows and gardens, by the joyful songs of the birds, by the beauty of animals, and most fully by humans and their desirous love. Thus manifested, the reality of Aphrodite can be maintained in its completeness, placed in sharp relief and grasped, only by letting its light elements accompany the shadowy ones, like the valleys along the mountains. The lure of the sea is really charming and calm after a fearfully raging storm. The sky is high and blue when heavy grey clouds have cleared away and given gloss back to the sky. Mountain meadows can be seen and noticed in the full harmony of their colors after a season of drought, when they lay in clouds of dust, is ended by rain, or after the barrenness of winter is replaced by the verdure of spring.

Aphrodite does not merely bring charm and bliss but often disaster into human life. Helena, who left her husband Menelaus and fled her native Lacedaemon to become the wife of Paris of Troy, often regretted her imprudent, passionate act. In Euripides, Medea ruined her life and happiness by her excessive love of Jason. Therefore, to be favored by Aphrodite's gifts may be considered a disaster. The women-chorus in *Medea* sings: "Never may Cypris, the goddess dread, fasten on me a temper to dispute, or restless jealousy, smiting my soul with mad desire for unlawful love." [36] The goddess of unification in bliss and in the harmony of love, is at the same time the goddess of separation and of fearful destructive disunity. "No power can so terribly disunite and confuse as that whose work is the most brilliant and blissful harmony, and only thanks to these dark shadows does Aphrodite's charm of light become a complete creation." [37]

All that which brings forward the reality of Aphrodite is real in its full charm and harmony or is real in its distortion or disharmony because it is carried or backed up by the reality of Aphrodite. Aphrodite

[35] *Ibid.*, p. 101.
[36] *Greek Dramas*, Vol. I, p. 737.
[37] Otto, *Götter*, p. 104.

is more fundamentally real than all this. She is *physis* which breaks forward and appears in the Aphroditian world.

Hermes

Another example of a deity, who backs up a multitude and variety of forms and reveals them with their light and shadows, is the reality or world of Hermes. He is the god of stones along the road, of servants, merchants, thieves, and herdsmen. He is god of night and a guide for souls. In superficial consideration, all these characteristics of Hermes seem to be without unity. Nevertheless, they belong in the togetherness and reflect each other in Hermes' world when approached and considered not merely logically or psychologically but with a sight for essences.

The name of Hermes is related to a 'pile of stones.' [38] Along the roads of ancient Greece there stood stone columns, the 'columns of Hermes,' and, as an act of piety, travelers used to throw stones at them in ritual of the cult of Hermes.

Hermes was known as the god of travelers. A traveler is a man of chance. He may find something on the road or discover on his way some good opportunities. Therefore Hermes is known as the god of opportunities and luck. Often he is portrayed wearing winged shoes and the cap of invisibility. Such a cap is comparable to a traveler who seems to suddenly appear from nowhere into a community of stable people.

A traveler is usually one who has learned many different tricks and is handy at various arts. Such features are characteristic of servants and also of thieves. Thieves, like travelers, appear all of a sudden in a place as if they had walked in with the cap of invisibility. Thus they often seize an opportunity and then disappear as though with winged shoes. Hermes is the god of servants and thieves, and he himself is the servant to the Olympian gods.

Hermes as a god of opportunity is the god of merchants. These people, too, just as servants on their service trips or thieves on their prowls, belong to the roads and are travelers. An ability for calculation is a gift of Hermes, and he is present where money is involved. Often he is portrayed by the Greek artists with a bag of money in his hand. Hermes is a god of the sudden gains by which merchants or thieves, or men of luck are indicated. "Who finds a valuable thing on a road or to whom sudden luck occurs, gives thanks to Hermes." [39]

[38] *Ibid.*, p. 107.
[39] *Ibid.*, p. 109.

As the stones along the roads would indicate, Hermes is the guide
of travelers. When Priam went from Troy to the camp of the Achaeans
to get the body of his dead son Hector from Achilles, Hermes was the
guide who led the way safely.[40] Hermes is a guide. "He is the lord of
the roads." [41] Man, the traveler, ends all his travels with a journey
into the beyondness. Here, also, Hermes is his guide. He leads the
dead into the world of Hades. The guiding Hermes also led Oedipus
to the place of his death.[42]

Herdsmen, too, consider Hermes as their own god. Herdsmen, just
like the travelers, are men of the outdoors; they are away from their
homes. Hermes brings increase to their herds. According to Otto,
Hermes is shown on ancient Greek vases carrying a ram on his
shoulders.[43] Hermes, as the god of sudden gains, multiplies the herds
not by generation but by suddenly bringing animals from somewhere
else.

These favorable acts that Hermes does for men constitute or disclose
just a part of his essence. Any increase in herds or any discovery on
the road means a loss for someone else. Hermes is thus the god of loss.
This is well indicated by his being the god of thieves. The gain of
thieves means the loss to robbed people.

Thieves work under the cover of night which hides them like the
cap of invisibility. And also travelers or merchants are often exposed
to the night when on the road. Night belongs to the realm of Hermes.
Also the night of after-life belongs to his reality: he guides the souls
of the dead into it.

"The demoniacal night can be goodly protection as well as perilous
misleading." [44] In the night, proximity and distance lose their meaning.
Everything becomes near and far at the same time. Everything is here and
nowhere at the same time. Night in its trickiness is a typical mode of
disclosure of Hermes' reality. He is the god of roads. As the god of
roads, he does not belong anywhere: he is always on his way, and
therefore really nowhere. Nevertheless, as the god of the roads, he
seems to be everywhere.

In all the various modes in which Hermes' reality is reflected, he
maintains the same unique face. He is the power which holds everything which partakes in his world in unity; he grounds it. Hermes is a

---

[40] Homer, *Iliad*, p. 451, *Complete Works*.
[41] Otto, *Götter*, p. 115.
[42] Sophocles, *Oedipus at Colonus, Greek Dramas*, Vol. I, p. 663.
[43] Otto, *Götter*, p. 11.1
[44] *Ibid.*, p. 117.

world. "All things belong to it; however, they appear in a different light than in the realms of the other gods." [45]

Gods as worlds

These few contours of the Greek gods with their characteristic features are sufficient for the conclusion that they are unique and real. They are real in the sense that they are not products of imagination; their characteristic features are in no wise accidentally assembled and put together in various historical determinations or mere chance occurrences in a nation's life. The Greek gods are real in the sense that they grew with the Greeks as a tree grows with its roots, trunk, branches, and leaves of the same element. Each figure of Grecian deity reviewed above maintains its sameness, its true essence in every mode of its appearance. Beyond the multitude of modes in which these deities were revealed, the Greek spirit felt these deities as real and mighty. These divine powers "carried the riches of the world in their hands." [46]

It is quite possible that the diverse authors who emphasized one or another feature of a certain deity did not have an exhaustive theoretical insight into the necessary coherence of such features. They merely unfolded these features from their knowledge of them as real in their living world and from their experience of them in their *Dasein*. When Hesiod describes Hermes as placing lies and deceptive words in Pandora's heart,[47] and when Homer relates Hermes as giving to Odysseus a herb which protects him from the magic of Circe,[48] they are both disclosing Hermes' sly nature. Men like Hesiod or Homer did not create the personages of Grecian deity. They merely responded to the gods as to the powers of Being of their living world and revealed them in their works. These realities can be considered as the basic articulations of *logos*, the language of *physis*.

A Greek deity is not merely real. It is *ultimately* real because anything whatsoever can be real or not real only on the grounds or against the background of deity. To comprehend and experience a deity is more than merely to comprehend or experience something real. "The visage of each true god is a visage of a world." [49] A world is not something real but is the reality itself which is presupposed by any-

---

[45] *Ibid.*, p. 122.
[46] *Ibid.*, p. 127.
[47] Hesiod, *Werke*, p. 76.
[48] Homer, *Odyssey*, p. 153, *Complete Works*.
[49] Walter F. Otto, *Dionysos* (Frankfurt a.M.: Vittorio Klostermann, 1933), p. 126.

thing real and which enables anything real to be real. A god as a world supports everything real with his own fundamental reality. Without such a fundamental reality, anything whatsoever would be groundless and would disintegrate. A god as a world holds everything real in the unity and thus makes it real. "To be god means to carry in oneself the whole reign of being and to rest in splendor and majesty upon each of the forms belonging to this reign. The divine essence is near to all the appearances of its domain, and all these appearances from the inanimated to the human reflect themselves in it." [50] Such a reflecting of these appearances is not something accidental to them: it constitutes their essences.

In the worlds of two different gods, a thing is not the same in each because by reflecting a different essence of a god, it itself becomes different. Night in the world of Artemis and night in the world of Hermes are different phenomena because they disclose different worlds. Artemis' night is serene in its frightfulness and beauty, and Hermes' night is advantageous or disadvantageous cover in one's pursuits. Similarly love in the world of Hermes and in that of Aphrodite are different loves. Love in the world of Hermes is a matter of luck or opportunity. It is the kind of love a traveler knows – suddenly coming and going, found, enjoyed, and forgotten. A love in the world of Aphrodite is a blissful unification breaking all bounds and upsetting the former mode of living. Such a love brings a revolutionary change in human life, like a sudden spring in which meadows burst into blossoms overnight. Or such love may bring disaster by destroying a happy wedded life like a storm which ruins a settlement beyond repair. Such a love is not a coming-and-going love but is a powerful phenomenon in the world of Aphrodite.

Gods as worlds never merely dominate or support a section of reality; they dominate everything whatsoever. However, everything is shown and seen in a different light by a different god and therefore is different. The reality of Artemis seems to be confined to merely a section of a world, and not to be a whole world. It is not so. Artemis, the reality of wild nature, holds sway over all things including men. The essence of Artemis is "narrated by earth, waters, and air; by day and night, by plants and animals, and also by man. In a virgin woman, in her charm and her reservation, her motherly instinct and harshness, in her lightness, grace, and tenderness, coldness and cruelty – everywhere here features of Artemis are vividly coming forward." [51]

[50] Otto, *Gestalt*, p. 130.
[51] *Ibid.*

All the forms or phenomena in which a god brings his reality forward are not identical with him. A god is beyond them as their background. From this background they draw their realness. It supports and carries them. This background is not there as if it were one of these forms. It also is not present for itself somewhere in the beyondness. In the presence of these forms, their background, the god, is present. All the forms are either present or absent; they start, last, and pass away in the realm of the deity. The deity itself does not start but is eternal – not because it is beyond time but because it is time itself.

Mythos relates that all the Olympian gods have had their beginnings. The beginning of a god as a world can never be thought of as the beginning of a being. A god becomes present all of a sudden. When a god arises he seems always to have been. All the things then immediately appear in a different light, in the light of this god, by reflecting his reality. Instantly that god is older than all the things because he is presupposed by them, and they merely *are* by reflecting his reality. The birth of a god is not a birth of a within-the-world or intra-temporal thing. It is the birth of a world.

If gods are worlds, there seems to be again a world of gods or a world of worlds. For the Greeks many gods were present simultaneously. Hence, a Greek was simultaneously present in many worlds. Since this cannot be (the Greeks did not live in a multitude of worlds), gods are worlds in such a way that they are the modes of *the* world.

The worldness of a world is Zeus. Zeus, the god of lightning, is ultimately the reality of light, of revealing, of disclosing, of *logos*. All the other Olympian gods are modes of this light. Since a god is a world, he brings himself forward in diverse forms without being identical with any of these forms; nevertheless, being present in them, he reveals himself. He reveals himself by disclosing the forms or appearances of his world. A god is disclosure or truth. He assembles all the forms that reflect him in his world; and by reflecting the truth of a god, these forms are true. They are in the *logos* of this god. Zeus then is the *logos* par excellence.

Since, as was indicated at the beginning of this chapter, Olympian gods are not beyond-nature gods, but are the essences of nature, therefore gods as *logoi* are the coming forward *physis* itself. *Physis* may come forward in diverse modes or diverse *logoi* – in the *logos* of Athene, Apollo, Artemis, Aphrodite, or Hermes. In each of these modes of coming-forward, *physis* comes forward into light and thus is *logos*. Anything which belongs to the world of a god, *eo ipso* belongs to the *logos* of *physis*; it stands in the light of Zeus. A Greek by standing in the worlds of diverse deities, ultimately stood in the *logos* of *physis*.

II. CHTHONIAN RELIGION

The Olympian religion, the way it is clearly and vividly shown in both of Homer's famous epics, is not the complete picture of the Greek religion. Previous to the Olympian religion, the so called Chthonian religion flourished in Greece. As much as the Olympian deities were deities of heaven and light, the Chthonian deities were deities of earth and night. Without an acquaintance with the Chthonian religion, it is impossible to understand the Greek religion sufficiently. "He who begins with the Homeric Olympus, is on the way toward missing the primeval beginnings of the religious life in Greece," [52] says Creuzer, quoted by Alfred Bäumler, in the introduction to J. J. Bachofen's works. And that is not all: the Olympian religion is hardly thinkable without the Chthonian. By combating it, the Olympian religion grew and reached its full development. To be more exact, it never ceased to be in combat with it; the Olympian religion was constantly forced to secure its position in renewed combat. The Chthonian religion was never fully conquered. "In spite of their antithesis to the Olympians, the primeval powers always remained acknowledged in their being and venerableness." [53] It is this struggle between the Olympian and Chthonian powers that constitutes the Greek religion.

Not only for a better acquaintance with the Greek religion is it necessary to consider the Chthonian religion, but also the Hölderlinian-Heideggerian mode of understanding gods demands it. Hölderlin is more attentive to Dionysus, a god who stands in both realms and is the god of twilight. Even though Heidegger does not discuss Dionysus in his philosophy – he hardly comes upon any of the gods singularly – the spirit of his thought is in many aspects Dionysian.

The Chthonian world is an order in whose center stands the earth. Here the earth is Earth because she is the most prominent deity. All the other gods have their beginnings in her. Earth is mother and specifically – Mother. Everything whatever lives (in the broad sense of the word: to live – to be) comes from Earth, sojourns in her order, and goes back to her.

---

[52] Bachofen, *op. c t.*, p. XXXII.
[53] Otto, *Götter*, p. 133.

The order of Earth, the Chthonian order, is guarded by the spirits or powers of Earth, called Erinyes, Furies or Eumenides. These powers are protective and friendly to all who live and respect the primeval order, but they are frightening and merciless to all who break this order. Therefore, in the Olympian times they were awesomely referred to as the 'angry,' whereas in earlier times they were known as the 'venerable,' or the 'friendly.' [54] These *friendly* deities become *angry* in respect to all who dare to break the laws of Earth.

The greatest crime in Chthonian society was matricide. The blood of a murdered mother drops down to Earth and raises or awakens the Erinyes for the persecution of the murderer. Such a case is dramatically shown in Aeschylus' *Oresteia*. Any mother is considered as representative of Mother Earth. To plot against a human mother is *eo ipso* to offend Mother Earth.

The great respect for mother in gynecocratic society, a society ruled by women (Chthonian society basically was gynecocratic society), is indicated by the fact that children were named by the mother. Daughters remained with the mother, whereas the sons were married out. Not the oldest but the youngest daughter, as the nearest to the mother, obtained the heritage.

In Chthonian society the dead are real and powerful – even more powerful than the living. They can act upon the community of the living favorably or destructively. The Olympian religion is wholly a religion of the living. Olympian "gods belong fully to life, and by their own essence they are separated from everything dead." [55] Olympian gods often help the heroes in their enterprises, but as soon as the destiny of death comes upon a hero, an Olympian god forsakes him because anyone marked by the mark of death is already beyond the realm of the Olympians. Apollo frequently helped Hector, the hero of Troy, but in his duel with Achilles, in which he was destined to die, Apollo deserted him.[56] Athene herself said to Telemachus: "But lo you, death, which is common to all, the very gods cannot avert even from the man they love, when the ruinous doom shall bring him low of death that lays men at their length." [57]

During the battle of Troy, Zeus several times threw the lots of heroes on the scale to see to which one of them Moira, the goddess of destiny, intended death. Moira designates to everything its own place. Moira

[54] *Ibid.*, p. 22.
[55] *Ibid.*, p. 30.
[56] Homer, *Iliad*, p. 406, *Complete Works*.
[57] Homer, *Odyssey*, p. 36, *Complete Works*.

is the Chthonian order itself. Zeus, who replaces the Chthonian order with the Olympian, never is an absolute monarch: "by the side of Zeus rules μοιρα, an impersonal, dark, totally non-Olympian power." [58]

Even though the Chthonian religion was not totally suppressed by the Olympian, still in Homeric times its importance diminished. This is shown by the fact of the altered attitude toward the dead. The dead were excluded from the community of the living, and they were no longer considered as having the power to interfere in any way with the events of the living. They were not considered as real anymore but merely as having been. The dead were not looked upon in their own realm or their own reality, but they were considered merely as what they no longer were as compared with the still living. To speak of the dead in terms of the living is inadequate. This inadequacy character-izes the world of Homer. "Death is the greatest evil for the Homeric man," says Alfred Bäumler, "only because it is the end of life. Neither death nor the dead have any spiritual reality. Since death for Homer is merely an end and nothing else, therefore the Homeric world is so brilliantly light." [59]

Homer often talks of the kingdom of Hades where the dead continue their life as mere shadows of the living, i.e. not as real but merely as the had-been-living. The custom of cremation clearly expresses this attitude toward the dead: the burned dead become smoke, the mere shadow of what they were.

This changed attitude towards the dead goes right along with diminished respect for the Chthonian gods, the gods of earth, and with an increased reverence to the gods of light and heaven, to the Olympian gods. In his work, *The Greeks and their Gods*, W. K. C. Guthrie gives a few facts of the rites of sacrifice which indicate this changed attitude.[60] According to him, an animal was sacrificed throat upward to the Olympians and throat downward to the Chthonians. High altars were built for the Olympians, and low or none for the Chthonians. For these a pit or a trench was dug to gather the blood. A white animal (custom-arily an ox) was sacrificed to the Olympians and a black one (usually a ram) to the Chthonians. The shrines of the Olympians were temples, and those of the Chthonians were subterranean caves which probably had some relation to tombs. Olympian sacrifice usually took place in the morning in the open sunlight, while the Chthonian was held in the

---

[58] Bachofen, *op. cit.*, p. XLI.
[59] *Ibid.*, p. XXXIX.
[60] W. K. C. Guthrie, *The Greeks and their Gods* (Boston: Beacon Press, 1955), pp. 221–222.

evening or at night. The gesture of prayer to the Olympians was the hands raised palm upwards, and to the Chthonians, the hands lowered palm downwards.

According to Bachofen, the primeval society in Greece was gynecocratic, a society ruled by women. It is quite natural that a woman first curbs brutal power with her motherly hand. Nature is not mere blind power, threatening and malicious. It is mild, protective, and constructive. A woman stands much closer to nature and has an intuitive understanding of its *logos* or law by which nature brings itself to appearance. "Woman bears the law in herself," says Bachofen, "it speaks from her with the necessity and certainty of natural instinct." [61]

Another significant feature of a woman is her stability. Man is a warrior, traveler, hunter. With her stability she resembles the earth and home. From all his errands man comes back home, and thus his dynamic strides are kept in balance and curbed.

Like the earth, a woman brings a new life from the darkness of her womb. She is the representative of great Mother Earth. Everything is brought forward into the light by Earth, and everything goes back into her. "What comes from her is perishable; she alone remains eternal and enjoys that immortality which she cannot share even with those to whom she gives birth, even with the most beautiful among them, the godlike men." [62] A woman, the representative of Earth, in a certain sense is Earth herself in the belief of primeval society. Therefore a man of this society who respects nothing else will bow his head to a woman and accept her rule. "Who harms a woman, offends the primeval Mother, who infringes on her right, must suffer punishment. Mother Earth becomes the avenger of the misdeed." [63]

A woman is not only a ruler in the gynecocratic world, but also a priestess. With her intuitive knowledge, or with her nature, by which she partakes in the nature of Mother Earth, she is the possessor of wisdom. In pre-Olympian times Delphi was the seat of Mother Earth, and in times of disaster people sought there the decrees of wisdom. Therefore, "it stands as a symbol of the great revolution, when Apollo, the god of the most paternal spirit, takes possession of Delphi, the seat of the ancient oracles of Mother Earth." [64]

Woman, the ruler and priestess, is the possessor of primeval knowledge. This feminine knowledge, the wisdom of Earth, is signified

[61] Bachofen, *op. cit.*, p. 124.
[62] *Ibid.*, p. 126.
[63] *Ibid.*, p. 167.
[64] Otto, *Gestalt*, p. 126.

by passivity. Woman's intuitive grasp of the laws of nature is not obtained by a creative dynamic approach and active disclosure but rather passively, receptively, as if nature itself would bring its laws into light. In this early stage of civilization not man but *physis* itself is the place of *logos*.

In a period of advanced civilization, when human knowledge becomes more active and virile, when the light of *physis* is to a greater extent brought forward by active and creative human works, it may seem that *logos* is not primarily located in *physis*, but in man. Then, it may also seem that *physis* does not bring itself forward in its *logos* or language, but that man disclose *physis* or forces it open in his own *logos* or language. Such a shift, or rather perversion (in the sense of *pervertere*, to reverse), of *logos* gave a start to the history of Western thought, the epoch of metaphysics.[65] However, in the early, pre-metaphysical man there were already seeds for such a 'de-*logos*-ization' of *physis* by its 'logic-ization.' [66]

Some simple examples may help to illustrate this shift, or better the inclination to a shift, of *logos* from *physis* to man even in primeval society. When a prehistoric woman finds some nutritive plants, roots out the weeds and loosens the ground around them, she lets nature fully ripen its fruit. She lets nature thus reveal itself in its care-taking, fruit-giving modes. Nature comes forward as that which holds everything in its order, and distinguishes everything from everything else – assembles all things upon themselves alongside the others. She lets nature appear as laying everything in its order, in its articulated language, in its *logos*.

When a man makes a bow from a branch of an ash tree – a strong and elastic wood – by his insight he has used nature and thus has disclosed it or has urged it to speak. In a certain sense, nature here was something potential, exposed to man's active, forming, disclosing principle. Yet, in the mode of thinking of early times, including the age of the early Greek philosophers, nature was not disposed to man, but man to nature: man helped nature come to its words. By having made a bow, man was thereby stating that this wood is strong and elastic and thus suitable for a bow. Nature brings itself forward in diverse modes. One of these modes is the elastic strength of the ash tree. By using it for

---

[65] Cf. p. 93.

[66] 'De-*logos*-ization' here means the ceasing to treat *physis* as dynamically coming forward in its own *logos*, as speaking.

'Logic-ization' means the subordination of *physis* to generalizations and rules. By being exposed to such generalizations and rules, *physis* becomes mere matter.

his bow, man merely emphasizes it as what it is; he merely helps
physis to come forward to its *logos* in the bow. The human *logos* is
merely a response, and as a response it ultimately belongs to the *logos*
of *physis*.

These examples, however, are too much on a human level to be of
any great importance for the religious problems. A gynecocracy *primarily* is not merely a society ruled by women, but by the higher
reality, Mother Earth. Similarly in Olympian times, the rule was not
in man's hand, but in the hands of the higher realities, the Olympian
gods. Nevertheless, the above examples may have some illustrative
value for the higher realities too. Earth, as that which brings everything to light and takes everything back to herself, is the possessor of
light and is not mere darkness or concealment. She rules the light, has
logos in her hands. When light becomes of great importance and sets
itself off from darkness, it makes Earth appear as mere darkness; it
begins to rule her as exposed to its disclosing might. The *logos* of the
Olympians, as an ordering, ruling, active principle, places Earth in an
order by holding her in its light. Such Olympian holding of Earth in
the light raises her into a higher level, brings her into the Olympian
logos. This makes Earth appear as not having any *logos*, but merely
as that which is exposed to a *logos*. The Olympian religion then is
truly 'spiritual' and the Chthonian becomes merely a 'natural' religion.

These few remarks are not intended to stress the Chthonian religion
as superior to the Olympian, nor vice versa. The aim of this discussion
is only to consider gods and their place in Greek religion. The Greek
religion is neither Chthonian, as cut off from the light of the Olympian,
nor Olympian with the total elimination of the Chthonian. "Disagreement and reconciliation of both principles constitute the history
of the Greek religion." [67] Walter F. Otto maintains that the combat
between the old and the new gods is the central motive in the Greek
religion.[68]

The Greek religion, as the strife between the Chthonian and the
Olympian powers, the strife of the higher realities, cannot be thought
of in the terms of merely something that is real. A something which is
real presupposes the higher realities enabling it to be real. Two beings
standing in combat tend to destroy each other, whereas the higher
realities in their strife strengthen themselves. The strife of Greek
religion develops and brings to its proper place each of the striving

[67] Bachofen, *op. cit.*, p. L.
[68] Otto, *Gestalt*, p. 195.

sides. The Olympian religion is truly Olympian when it rests on Chthonian grounds, and the Chthonian religion is truly Chthonian when it stands in the Olympian light.

Such a strife stirs up an openness which gives a realm to the Greek *Dasein*, and sends the Greek nation on its historical mission. 'Mission' stands here for the Heideggerian word *'Geschick'* which besides 'mission' has also the denotation of 'suitability' imparted by destiny. *Geschick* makes *Geschichte*, history as befalling, possible.[69]

The Chthonian and Olympian religions, as the structural elements of the Greek religion, are the early prototypes of *physis* and *logos*, the phenomena of the early Greek philosophers. *Physis*, when properly thought of, is unthinkable without *logos*, without the assembling appearance, beauty.[70] *Physis* is the breaking-forward or *logos* itself. *Logos* is always the *logos* of *physis*, i.e. that by which *physis* comes into light. *Logos*, as cut off from *physis* and standing by itself or for itself, becomes perverted *logos*, logic. *Physis*, on the other hand, when thought of separately from *logos*, becomes perverted *physis*, matter. Matter is exposed to the de-rooted *logos*, logic.

Heidegger's problem of the strife between the earth and the world reflects the Greek religion as the strife between Chthonian and Olympian powers. Also the structural phenomena of *Dasein*, the 'thrownness' and projection,[71] reflect this strife. 'Thrownness' stands for the Chthonian principle, and projection, for the Olympian.

The most typical representative of the Olympian religion, the religion of light, is Apollo. Even he, Phoebus, the god of the sun, has his Chthonian past. Ultimately he is the son of Mother Earth. According to Bachofen, the "Apollonian name Lykios is derived from λύχή, twilight." [72] In the early stage of Greek religion, Apollo appeared as the god of twilight. Hence, he was related to night or the earth, to the early birth of the sun out of the womb of night.[73]

Another one of the most prominent Olympian deities is Athene. She in her early stage also was a Chthonian goddess. According to Bachofen, her Chthonian character was indicated by the symbols which were related to her in early times. These symbols were water, moon, and agrarian fertility. In the Greek colonies of Southern Italy, Athene was respected as the guardian of customs and rights. "Athene was repre-

[69] Cf. pp. 64–65; also pp. 88–89.
[70] Cf. p. 139.
[71] Cf. pp. 45–46.
[72] Bachofen, *op. cit.*, p. 101.
[73] *Ibid.*

sented in most towns of her oldest cult as seated: an obvious picture
of the highest matronal dignity which manifests itself in the maintenance of discipline, of peace, and of any social order whatever." [74] In
guarding the customs and rights in the early stage of Greek religion,
Athene resembled the Erinyes, "the daughters of Earth and
Darkness." [75]

The Olympians ultimately belong to Earth; they bring forward the
logos of *physis*. And the Chthonian powers are these powers when they
break forward into the light of Olympus, into *logos*. '*Physis* is *logos*'
ultimately expresses the oneness of the Chthonian and the Olympian
reality.

It would be wrong to consider the Chthonian religion as the religion
of mere darkness and of the dead. It was the religion of the living as
well as of the dead. In the Chthonian world the dead are not excluded
from the community of the living. In the greater events of human life,
such as birth, wedding, or death, the dead are somehow present and
can bring either blessing or disaster. They may influence the crop of
the fields, decrease or increase the herds; they may cause success or
failure in hunting, war, and other enterprises. The living, again, with
their sacrifices or prayers can reach the dead and attract their favors,
or they can fulfill their will and take revenge on those who caused their
death.

In the Greek Chthonian myths the symbol of a grasshopper often
appears, which in these myths is believed to breed in the earth and
nourish on the morning dew. According to Bachofen, such an understanding of the grasshopper indicates the darkness of night as coming
forward into light.[76] The grasshopper is known for its peculiar, sad
song. Here lies the reason for relating the grasshopper to a broken
string in these myths. According to Bachofen, the ancient Locrians
believed that "with the rising sun a joyful tone is heard and with the
setting sun a sad tone." [77] This again shows the grasshopper as related
to the sun at the instant of its rising from the night or going down into
night; it is the symbol of the light as being born from the womb of the
night or dying down into it. The night as coming forward into the light
is the procedure of revelation, of truth. Hence it is understandable that
the grasshopper was considered the symbol of wisdom in the same
myths. In the old days of Locris the men of wisdom carried a golden

[74] *Ibid.*, p. 483.
[75] Sophocles, *Oedipus at Colonus, Greek Drama,* Vol. I, p. 614.
[76] Bachofen, *op. cit.,* p. 485.
[77] *Ibid.*, pp. 486–487.

grasshopper in their grey hair.[78] In Plato's *Phaedrus* the grasshopper
is shown as "always singing, and never eating or drinking." [79] The
grasshopper here, according to Bachofen, is "the model of a philosopher
who, disregarding the body, constantly strives for knowledge of divine
things." [80]

The symbol of the grasshopper shows the earth (the grasshopper is
earth-born) as rising toward the sun and almost becoming weightless
(the grasshopper living by song alone). It was previously shown that
the early Apollo was related to twilight. The rising sun as emitting
the sound of a broken string, again, is related to music, and Apollo
is known as the god of music. The Chthonian grasshopper thus becomes highly Olympian in its relatedness to Apollo. Bachofen quotes
Anacreon who, when talking about the grasshopper, says: "Phoebus
himself loves it and gave it the light-sounding song." [81]

The famous Olympian national plays of Greece, which flourished in
the time of the fully developed Olympian religion, were descended
from the funeral rites of the Chthonian times.[82] After the death of a
hero, plays and races were held at his tomb to honor the dead. In the
Iliad, Achilles holds such games in honor of his friend Patroclus after
the cremation.

In the early beginnings the funeral rite games consisted of chariot
races in an oval arena. At the end of an arena, large egg-shaped objects
were erected. Each time, after one cycle, one of these eggs was removed.[83] According to Bachofen, an egg is the symbol of Mother Earth.
Even though the egg is an expression of total rest, it is such only as the
unity of extreme dynamism. The racing chariots express this unity by
going away from the egg and coming back to it at full speed. Bachofen
relates such races to the myth of the Dioscuri Brothers, according to
which, the two brothers, one dark and one white, come out of the egg
in chariots and race with great speed. "Both are distinguished by the
enormous speed with which they fly away with the horses and chariots.
As mighty runners and charioteers, they come out of the motherly
primeval Egg. As in this Egg the germ of all things lays in concealment,
so now the visible created things come forward out of its opened
shell." [84] The Egg is concealment – total rest surrounded by a shell.

---

[78] *Ibid.*, p. 486.
[79] Plato, *The Dialogues of Plato* (New York: Random House, 1937), Vol. I, p. 263.
[80] Bachofen, *op. cit.*, p. 489.
[81] *Ibid.*, p. 490.
[82] *Ibid.*, pp. 431–432.
[83] *Ibid.*, p. 443.
[84] *Ibid.*, p. 441.

The Egg is extreme dynamism – enormous speed of charioteers in the arena, which being oval, stands also for the Egg. Egg, as concealedness and disclosedness, is untruth and truth; Egg is truth as the strife of untruth and truth.[85]

The Egg implies life which is indicated by the running away of the white brother as being born and developing; the Egg also implies death which is indicated by the coming back of the dark brother as returning to the darkness of death. Destruction is necessary to feed the new life. "Death thus is not the opposition but the helpmate of life." [86] In these races, strictly speaking, neither life nor death is emphasized, but that which comes forward in any life or death, the Egg itself. The Egg is that which comes forward into high dynamism from total rest or rather it is this coming forward itself; the Egg is the procedure of concealment-disclosure itself. The Whole, the Egg, is that which holds all life and death in unity; it is the total rest, as well as total movement. The Egg is *physis* which emerges into its own light, the *logos*.

The Egg, as the peak of rest and the peak of movement at the same time, is well reflected by *physis* which is at once being and appearing. Interestingly, Bachofen shows that in gynecocratic society the *prima origo*, the biological coming into being, was considered the moment of birth. This indicates the simultaneity of being and appearing. Whereas in paternal society the *prima origo* takes place in the instant of seeding. Hence, "*prima origo* lies before the completion; being lies before the appearance." [87] With the stress of paternal *prima origo* the supremacy of Mother Earth was discredited and that of Father Zeus accepted. In Aeschylus' *Eumenides*,[88] Apollo emphasizes this paternal supremacy:

> This too I answer; mark a soothfast word
> Not the true parent is the woman's womb
> That bears the child; she doth but nurse the seed
> New-sown; the mate is parent;

The simultaneity of being and appearing, of birth and completion, according to Bachofen,[89] is often expressed in Chthonian myths, where the instant of birth is *eo ipso* maturity, just as the Egg is the very beginning and the total completion. The emphasis of the *prima*

---

[85] Cf. pp. 164–165.
[86] Bachofen, *op. cit.*, p. 442.
[87] *Ibid.*, p. 408.
[88] *Greek Drama*, Vol. I, p. 294.
[89] Bachofen, *op. cit.*, p. 409.

origo at seeding instead of at birth in no wise was a cause introducing a new mode of living but was merely a consequence of the shift of emphasis from the Chthonian realities to the Olympian, from *physis* to *logos*.

The Greek religion, as the strife between the earthly and the Olympian powers, shows man not as the ruler of nature and of his own fate, but as a being who is exposed and dependent on the higher powers. Everything is held in the hands of Moira who sends everything unto its destiny. The destiny of man, however, is not totally determined in the sense that there are certain things which, when done, have certain consequences and, when avoided, escape these consequences. If Laius and Jocasta should have a child, this child will commit patricide – according to destiny. If Aegisthus should wed Clytemnestra, he will be killed by Orestes – according to destiny. Even in the instances of their decisions to avoid or to chance what is destined, men are deeply influenced by the gods, the higher powers. Hence, freedom seems to be a necessity. Yet, it is not. It is not so, because necessity is blind, whereas freedom is the being-open to the higher powers or being-exposed to them. According to Heidegger, freedom is not disposed to man, but man is disposed to freedom.[90] Freedom is the being-open to the higher powers, letting them appear and guarding them in their appearing the way they are. Freedom is the subordination of man to gods. "When something must be decided among men, debate must take place among the gods before men decide." [91] And when man in his life and works brings forward the works of the higher powers, he is free in the ultimate sense. Freedom is not freedom toward this or that, but toward the backgrounds of any 'thisness' or 'thatness' whatsoever – freedom toward the world, transcendence.

The Greek religion in its mythical language indicates the same problems which thereafter were thought of by the early Greek philosophers in their philosophical language. According to Otto, even though *mythos* means "the thing as said, the truth of being and becoming in the word,"[92] nevertheless, *mythoi* primarily are not 'sayings' but 'knowings.' The knowing here is knowledge of the superior or divine *logos*. By being aware of the language of the higher realities, man is a knower and can be a sayer. He is then entitled to and can say a word in the grievous situations of the life of a nation. He is a man of wisdom.

---

[90] Heidegger, *Wahrheit*, p. 17.
[91] Otto, *Götter*, p. 25.
[92] Otto, *Gestalt*, p. 69.

Mythos is the saying or the *logos* of the gods. As far as man is concerned, *mythos* primarily is the knowledge of that which is assembled in the *logos* of gods.

According to Otto, mythos, "as compared with λόγος, is not merely an older expression but it also stands for the older form of the essence of 'word'; it is the 'word' as the ultimate witnessing of that which was, is, and will be, as the revelation of being itself in the ancient venerable understanding which does not distinguish word and being." [93] *Mythos* is *physis* as well as *logos*.

Since *mythos*, as far as man is concerned, is knowledge, as the response to the word of gods, it is cult. "*Mythos* and cult cannot be separated. To say that cult demands *mythos* is not enough. Rather it is of great importance to stress the opposite, namely, that *mythos* demands cult." [94] A word of a god is necessary for cult to become cult. When Heidegger says that *mythos* is not as much "the saying as rather the calling bringing-to-appearance," [95] he indicates that *mythos* is the word of the gods which demands a response from man in the mode of man's knowing, and thus god brings himself forward in cult.[96]

III. DIONYSUS

In his *Theogony*, Hesiod indicates chaos as that from which Earth, Night, Eros, Uranus – the first Chthonian deities – came forth. The Chthonian world was based on the order of Mother Earth, often thought of as the order of Moira, daughter of Night. Hence, it was not chaotic in the sense of orderless. When describing the struggle of the Olympian gods with the Chthonians, Hesiod again mentions the chaos which filled the universe.[97] Of course, as soon as the Olympian order was established, there was no more chaos. Hence, at the beginning of an era and also at the end, chaos comes forward. In the era of an established Olympian order, chaos withdraws. It withdraws; nevertheless, it is never totally absent. "The Greek world rests on the dark,

---

[93] *Ibid.*, p. 71.
[94] *Ibid.*, p. 76.
[95] Heidegger, *Vorträge*, p. 248.
[96] 'Knowing' here has to be taken in a broad sense, namely, as standing-in-the-world, as 'ec-sistence,' as dwelling. This will become clearer in the discussion of the problem of dwelling in a later chapter.
[97] Hesiod, *Werke*, pp. 46–47.

subterranean grounds from which it was wrestled. These grounds, even though they are mastered, nevertheless remain threatening." [98]

Such a threatening became reality with the mighty entrance of the god Dionysus from Thracia into Greece in post-Homeric times. Dionysus brought forth again the chaotic subterranean powers and shook the Olympian order. The very essence of the deity was highly chaotic. Dionysus is marked by contrasting features of lightness and darkness, of life and death, of creation and destruction.

In the myth, Dionysus' mother was the mortal Semele, daughter of the king Cadmus, and his father was Zeus. Semele upon conception was burned in the flame of Zeus. Zeus then took Dionysus, the fruit of his love, into his leg, from which Dionysus was born for the second time. Since woman is the representative of Mother Earth, of the Chthonian order, and Zeus is the peak of the Olympian world, Dionysus then possesses the features of these two great worlds, and is the god of contrasts.

Otto has said that "the central motive of Greek religion is the combat between the old and the new gods." [99] Since Dionysus implies in himself both worlds, the Chthonian and the Olympian, he is not so much a Chthonian power rebelling against Olympian powers, but rather he is the representation of the combat itself of both these worlds.

Since the Chthonian religion is thought of as the religion of night symbolized by the earth, and the Olympian, as the religion of light, symbolized by the sun, the Dionysian religion is the religion of the twilight, symbolized by the moon. Mother Earth commissions everything to life and thus to light [100]; in herself she is then the fullest life and light. On the other hand, the earth is that into which everything returns and dies and becomes extinguished. Earth is the bed of death; she is darkness. Analogically Heidegger thinks Being as that which is the ground of everything and which thus is the most being; on the other hand, he thinks Being as that which is groundless, an abyss.[101] When Bachofen was investigating the origin of the national games, he explained the Egg as both: total rest, that signifies lifelessness as well as lightlessness, and extreme movement, expressed by the racing charioteers in the egg-shaped arena, that signifies life and light. This shows that Dionysus, as the god of the twilight, god of life and death,

---

[98] Words of Eugen Fink taken from the notes of the course of *Vom Wesen der Menschlichen Freiheit*, held during the summer semester, 1947, at the University of Freiburg, Germany.
[99] Otto, *Gestalt*, p. 195.
[100] For the Greeks 'life' has the connotation of 'light'; cf. p. 169.
[101] Heidegger, *Satz*, p. 185.

is the representative of Mother Earth, the basic power of the Chthonian religion.

Even though Zeus, the god of lightning or lights, is opposed to Night, he, just as everything else, originated from Night. Night here, just as the Egg, ultimately is Mother Earth. "O Zeus," sings the chorus of *Suppliants*, "thou king of the earth, and her child." [102] Even though Zeus is the ruler, he does not create what he rules; he merely holds it in the light. Everything is already assembled in the Night, and the light of Zeus merely shows it the way it is in the Night. Fragment 9 of Orpheus says: 'The Theologoi generate all things from Night. The ancient poets agree that the Ruler is not Night and Heaven or Chaos or Ocean, but Zeus." [103] Zeus does not destroy Night. He strengthens her in her 'nightness.' He needs her as the realm from which he wrestles everything to light. "The Night is the concealed *physis*," says Eugen Fink, "it is the creative grounds which prepare everything which comes to light." [104]

In ancient Greece, Zeus sometimes was referred to as Moiragetes, the leader of Moiras.[105] Zeus as Moiragetes is backed up by the Moiras, the daughters of Night, and he leads them into light. Zeus is not exclusively a god of light. As the god of light, he is necessarily related to night which lets his light stand out as light. Many ancient sources indicate light as having originated from night. "From the womb of Night springs forth, with promise fair, the young child Light." [106]

Hence, Dionysus is in a certain sense the representative of Zeus. Dionysus stands for night and light at the same time; he "reconciles the day with the night." [107] Night can only be revealed in its darkness by the day. "Only in opposition to light, does darkness acquire its deepest depth." [108] And the day can only be day when it rests on the impenetrable foundations of night. Dionysus, as the god of twilight, is the testimony for the necessary togetherness of day and night, of life and death, of the spiritual and the earthly.

The natural may retain its entire fullness and liveliness and yet be one with the spiritual, which wants nothing but the completion. Immediate corporal presence and eternal validity as being one and the same is the miracle of Greek

[102] Aeschylus, *The Suppliants, Greek Drama,* Vol. I, p. 37.
[103] Freeman, *op. cit.*
[104] Cf. footnote 60 on p. 148.
[105] Otto, *Götter,* p. 277. Some ancient sources indicate three Moiras, the daughters of Night.
[106] Aeschylus, *Agamemnon, Greek Drama,* Vol. I, p. 176.
[107] Hölderlin, *op. cit.*, p. 61.
[108] Otto, *Götter,* p. 159.

form-creation. And in this unity of spirit and nature the earthliness comes forward with freedom of proportion and a sense of elegance as complete nature.[109]

The spiritual in the Greek religion in no wise is supernaturality but naturality itself in its ultimate truth as revelation. The light of Zeus does not come from beyond the realm of nature, but is born in nature itself and brings nature's riches and depths into sight. The Homeric religion is "a great revelation of nature." [110]

Even though Dionysus is a deity who shows the combat of light and darkness, he is often considered as a representative of night, as having more dark features than light ones. In *Bacchae*, Dionysus says: " 'tis majestic thing the darkness." [111] Nevertheless, Dionysus never is merely the power of darkness. Even when he is considered as a Chthonian deity, he stands at its extreme limits and is tangent with the Olympian light. On the Delphian sepulchral vases, Dionysus is often shown together with the most prominent Olympian deity Apollo.[112] Apollo, too, in his early stage was considered the god of twilight. In the union of these two deities, the interrelation of chaotic boundlessness with the sharply clear distinctions is expressed. "Nature is in need of the spirit to be open, clear, articulate and thus to be the object of respect and understanding. And the spirit is in need of nature as the motherly grounds on which it rests." [113] Dionysus, as standing for nature as well as for spirit, ultimately is a chaotic deity – not in the sense of disorder but of primevalness. He is, just as the early Greek phenomenon of *physis*, a reality which cannot be properly thought of in terms of 'nature' and 'spirit' because he is presupposed by these. With his primevalness, Dionysus brings forward the most profound features of Greek *Dasein*. "Bacchus remains the center in which all the radiations of the circles of gods from above as well as from below run together." [114]

Dionysus may appear as a deity of lesser ontological importance to all those who see the criterion of truth in the clarity of classification by abstract principles or ideas. Such thinkers take the distinction of nature and spirit as fundamentally valid in the sense that in their conviction there is no realm of greater ontological primacy than that of such a distinction. This tendency characterizes all the basic thinkers

[109] *Ibid.*, p. 246.
[110] *Ibid.*, p. 160.
[111] Euripides, *Bacchae, Greek Drama*, Vol. II, p. 244.
[112] Bachofen, *op. cit.*, p. 397.
[113] Otto, *Gestalt*, p. 196.
[114] Bachofen, *op. cit.*, p. 398.

of metaphysics from Plato to Nietzsche. Even Nietzsche, who has a great admiration for Dionysus, sees him in his unity with Apollo merely as the will of creation and destruction. In such a will the creating and destroying subject is emphasized. This subject is not a god, nor God, but basically the higher man, the superman.

The early Greeks did not know the distinction of nature and spirit, and for them their gods in no wise were merely psychological realities.

> The religions of the Chthonian deities and the Olympian gods were not at all mere idle inventions of imagination ... That which was expressed by these divinities or gods are powers which always have determined and will determine the human way of being. The conflict of the religious phenomena is not a collision of phantasy images but of the forces of life.[115]

In the struggles of gods the Greeks experienced that which carries and holds everything, that which is darkness even though it be the source of light, that which is concealed even though it be the source of revelation, that which is chaos even though it be the foundation of everything whatever is – they experienced that which was called *physis* by the early Greek philosophers.

Physis is that which is never concealed because it is constantly coming forward from concealment. To be constantly coming forward from concealment means constantly still to be in concealment. Revelation and concealment are not thought of "as two distinct adjoining events, but as one and the same." [116] *Physis* as constant revelation and concealment is that which constantly *is* and *is not*. Any being, even a god, presupposes *physis* as revelation. Hence, *physis* is more fully being than any being. On the other hand, any being can be fully disclosed in the revelation of *physis*, but *physis* reveals itself as concealed. *Physis* never *is* the way beings *are*; it is rather nothingness.

The Chthonian phenomenon of Mother Earth or of Egg represents *physis* as concealment and revelation in one. Zeus as Moiragetes brings forth *physis* as coming-forward concealment into revelation. Dionysus as the god of twilight also shows *physis* as chaos or concealment which ultimately supports and carries any order or revelation.

Concealment and revelation (as shown in the previous chapter) are untruth and truth for the Greeks. Truth and untruth are the very *physis* which comes forward by holding itself in reservation. Hence, truth is never an accordance or discordance between two realms with

[115] *Ibid.*, p. XXXIV.
[116] Heidegger, *Vorträge*, p. 270.

one determining and the other determined, one of them spiritual and the other natural.

In the Greek myths, the Chthonian side of Dionysus is emphasized by the swarms of women who accompany him. These women with their hair wildly floating in the wind leave their homes and orderly lives and follow the god into the mountains and forests. Here Dionysus is shown as the god of chaos. He acts as a storm which destroys the established order and fills everybody with wild joy and unrestrained freedom.

Dionysus is considered as the god of noise and freedom, of joyful disregard for any rules and boundaries – god of high activity and liveliness. Man in this divine noise and freedom is being taken as by a storm from all the orders and restrictions; he is taken out of order and thrown into the face of dreadful chaos where noise instantly turns into total silence. Consequently, Dionysus, the god of noise, is known as the god of dreadful silence. This dual face of Dionysus is expressed by the maenads, the women who follow Dionysus, who "affected by him, storm away, twirl around in a raging whirl or stand still as though turned to stone." [117]

Such rapid movement and immobility indicate the togetherness of extreme mobility and the total rest shown in the myth of the Dioscuri Brothers who leave the Egg and race around the oval arena in chariots. In this myth, life and death and their togetherness was thus indicated. Dionysus, too, is a god of life as well as death. Maenads are often shown as wet nurses, taking care of children or young wild animals. On the other hand, they are also shown as slaying these children and animals, tearing them apart, and swallowing them.[118] That which grants life to someone also grants death to him. "The wisdom of nations says: where something living stirs, death, is also near." [119] In the Dionysian myths, even the god Dionysus himself is pursued by Titans, torn apart, and eaten.[120] The god of life is the god of death; the god of joy is the god of suffering; the wild Hunter is hunted.

Dionysus often appears surrounded by animals. They may be bulls, bucks, asses – animals of fertility and originators of life; or sometimes they may be lions, panthers, lynxes – the beasts of prey, the destroyers of life. With these symbols also, Dionysus is shown as the god of life and death.

[117] Otto, *Dionysos*, p. 88.
[118] *Ibid.* p. 178.
[119] *Ibid.*, p. 127.
[120] *Ibid.*

In several instances in the Greek myths, Dionysus is related to water.[121] Water is a well-known symbol of primevalness and of the source of life. It is light and transparent, lively and vividly changing in form. On the other hand, water may be still and calm, deep and dark, frightening and dangerous. Water reflects the dual nature of Dionysus, his light and nightly sides.

Waters were impressive to early man because of their swift currents. According to Bachofen, the arena of chariotraces was often situated on the banks of a river. Fast running charioteers reflect well the same reality as the running waters.[122] This fast running denotes strength and power. Strength meant nobility and divinity for early man. Then too, racing chariots in the arenas reflected the cyclical paths of the heavenly bodies, the sun and the moon, which also have been thought of as divine. Waters, just as well as the sun and moon, were not only demonstrations of strength but also of life. In both of these phenomena lightness is apparent: waters shine from far distances as if they were filled with light, and also the sun and moon are significant for their brightness. Just as Bachofen has shown water as expressing strength, light and life, so similarly in the Greek word *aeizoon* (life) Heidegger has indicated, as it was shown,[123] the connotations of 'strength' and 'light.' Water with all its connotations gives a rich modulation and reflection of the Dionysian nature.[124]

One of the many other characteristics of water is its looseness. It cannot be curbed, caught, or bound. It escapes everything. It is a symbol of freedom and unrestrictedness. Dionysus too has as one of his names 'the loosener.' [125]

This feature of looseness is well expressed by another Dionysian symbol, wine. Wine is sweet; it loosens man's tongue for sweet talk; it brings joy and liveliness to him, and makes him friendly and sociable.

> In the dancing and the prayer,
> In the music and the laughter,
> In the vanishing of care,
> And of all before and after;
> In the Gods' high banquet, when
> Gleams the grape-blood, flashed to heaven:

---

[121] *Ibid.*, p. 150.
[122] Bachofen, *op. cit.*, p. 204.
[123] Cf. p. 169.
[124] Bachofen, *op. cit.*, p. 205.
[125] Otto, *Dionysos*, p. 90.

Yea, and in the feasts of men
Comes his crowned slumber; then
Pain is dead and hate forgiven! [126]

On the other hand, wine may loosen man's moral bindings and take
all the restrictions from his words and behavior. Wine may turn man
wild. These dual phases of the symbol of wine are again a thrifty
reflection of Dionysian nature.

Dionysus is a god of drunkenness and ecstasy. Ecstasy means the
stepping out of all restrictions and boundaries. The spirit of Dionysus
"glows in the intoxicating drink, which has been called the blood of
the earth. The joy of the primeval world, ecstasy, dissolution of
consciousness into boundlessness come stormily upon his companions,
and the kingdom of earth opens its riches for them in their trance." [127]

Ecstasy, symbolized by wine, is more than mere intoxication, is
more than mere breaking of the established order or conventional
laws. It has a positive side. Disintegrating order or laws deprived of
their power are not the aim in ecstasy but merely a consequence.
Ecstasy mainly is the taking of man into the face of the source of all
the orders and all the laws. This source itself is the ultimate order and
the ultimate law. When Antigone refuses to obey the ruler and his law,
she is following the primeval law, "the unwritten and unfailing statutes
of heaven." [128]

The true face of Dionysus is not lost beyond all the contrasts by
which his nature is so abundant. He is even referred to as the god of
the mask. All the contrasts and thus the seeming disunity of his nature
merely belong to his mask. The unique Dionysus is behind the mask,
behind the contrasts. In the extreme tension of these contrasts "the
great mystery and the ultimate being announces itself." [129] Beyond
the daylight of all the variety of contrasts, lies the unique world, the
hidden and dark face of Being.

Dionysus is a god of growth and decay. Growth and decay afford a
glimpse of that which holds growth and decay in unity. "To grow
means to open oneself up to the broadness of the sky and at the same
time to be rooted in the darkness of the earth." [130] Dionysus brings
together the broad sky and the dark earth, the Olympian gods and

---

[126] Euripides, *The Bacchae*, *Greek Drama*, Vol. II, p. 239.
[127] Otto, *Götter*, p. 154.
[128] Sophocles, *Antigone*, *Greek Drama*, Vol. I, p. 434.
[129] Otto, *Dionysos*, p. 112.
[130] Heidegger, *Feldweg*, p. 3.

Chthonian powers, and thus he announces something which is difficult to grasp, easy to lose, and which, nevertheless, is more real than anything real. The enormous elasticity and liveliness of Dionysian nature can only manage to bring forward the sparks of that which is incessantly living and shining and yet constantly hidden. This is the primeval chaos. Heraclitus thought of it as fire.

IV. CHAOS

In its primary meaning chaos is never a disorder or confusion. In such a case, chaos would not be that which stands at the beginning. It would merely be a result of the denial of an order. "Apparently the idea of chaos belongs to the prehistoric heritage of the Indo-European people," says Jaeger, "for the word is connected with χάσκω ('gape'), and forms the same stem *gap*. Nordic mythology has formed the word *Ginungagap* to express this same notion of the gaping abyss that existed at the beginning of the world." [131] Similarly Burnet indicates in his *Early Greek Philosophy* that chaos "is not a formless mixture, but rather, as its etymology indicates, the yawning gulf or gap where nothing is as yet." [132]

Chaos as gap indicates the supportlessness. Hesiod in his *Theogony* places chaos at the beginning of everything. Chaos is the ground from which everything begins. Jean Wahl quotes Hölderlin as saying: "There is a desert sacred and chaotic which stands at the roots of the things and which prepares all things." [133] The ground from which everything starts is 'thingless,' is empty, is a gap.

Chaos is that which prepares all the things. Such preparation makes things to be what they are. Such preparation is the assembling of the things upon themselves. The Greeks thought it as *logos*.

Being 'is,' as its primeval name λόγος indicates, ultimately the same as ground. As far as Being 'essentiates' itself as ground, it itself has no ground. It is so not because it grounds itself, but because any grounding – not excluding, but rather certainly including, the one done by itself – remains inadequate to Being as ground. Any grounding, even merely an appearance of groundability, would demote Being to merely something-being. Being as Being remains groundless. Ground – namely as ground which grounds Being – stays away from Being. Being is an abyss.[13]

[131] Jaeger, *op. cit.*, p. 13.
[132] John Burnet, *Early Greek Philosophy* (London: A & C Black, LTD, 1930), p. 7.
[133] Wahl, *Hölderlin*, p. 15.
[134] Heidegger, *Satz*, pp. 184–185.

Chaos which stands at the beginning of all the things is the abyss.

That which stands at the beginning and which grounds everything whatsoever deserves the most attention. "Chaos is holiness itself." [135] It is not merely that which stands at the beginning, and thus is the most anterior, the oldest; but also it is that which is the most posterior, the youngest. "It is the oldest of all antecedents," says Heidegger in his Hölderlinian commentaries, "and the youngest of all subsequents." [136] As applied to the Greek religion, such a Hölderlinian understanding of chaos would mean that chaos is anterior to all the Chthonian deities and posterior to all the Olympian gods. In either way, chaos, holiness itself, is beyond the deities or gods for Hölderlin.

Otto says, referring to Hölderlin: "The Olympian reign of gods, whose victory and eternity the pious singers of Greece glorified, for him was resolvedly retreating. He prayed to the divine primeval world, over which the lordship of Zeus had established itself, and called it nature." [137] Even though Otto does not state so explicitly, Hölderlin's greater attention to nature and his turning away from the Olympians is a sign of his lack of understanding of the Olympians. "Only by the appearance of the heavenly gods in the clear, close-to-man forms is the temple of nature opened." [138] For him the heavenly gods, the Olympians, are ontologically superior. In their light of sacredness, nature can become holy. He did not see, what Hölderlin always kept in sight, that the heavenly gods have their light from the primeval source of everything, from chaos or holiness itself. Gods or deities are sacred because they are the carriers or the vehicles of the holiness of nature. Even though the gods are powerful beings, their "powers do not originate in gods themselves, but gods themselves *are* because of these 'all-living' powers which hold everything, even the gods, in life." [139] In spite of Otto's great insight into the Greek religion, the distinction of nature and spirit was ultimately valid for him. Therefore, he inevitably had to lose the adequate understanding of chaos. A proper understanding of *physis* and of the Hölderlinian phenomenon of nature is rooted in the adequate understanding of chaos.

Hölderlin is not merely inclined to the Greek Chthonian religion as such, but to primeval chaos or holiness itself. To see or to experience the Chthonian night, the Olympian day is necessary. Therefore, he

---

[135] Heidegger, *Hymne*, p. 17.
[136] *Ibid.*
[137] Otto, *Gestalt*, p. 193.
[138] *Ibid.*, p. 194.
[139] Heidegger, *Hymne*, pp. 19–20.

highly respects Zeus, not as an unrestrained ruler of gods and men, but as one who "announces what secret twilight secures in itself."[140] Not a lack of insight into that which is spiritual, but the sight of that which carries and which renders possible any spirituality inspires this great poet Hölderlin to sing hymns to nature as holiness. For this same reason, Dionysus, the god of chaos, is for him the greatest god. He calls him the god of wine,[141] thus indicating him as the god of ecstasy.

Dionysus approaches us from chaos itself, and draws us out of our narrow and detailed boundaries into the breath-taking abyss of chaos. Here is the place of the most joyful freedom, the enthusiasm of being in the captivity of gods, and of the most dreadful danger, the madness of more divine light than a mortal can bear. The abyss of chaos is the realm from which the Olympian light has been carried out, and at the same time it is the realm from which we moderns can expect a light in our godless night. The god of wine is the god who "returns when the time is right." [142]

Chaos as an abyss is not merely a groundlessness which swallows everything. An abyss or gap is essentially openness. Openness means light; it opens a realm in which free movement is possible. Openness is that which sets everything free, assembles it unto itself. Therefore, chaos is for Hölderlin and Heidegger that which stands at the roots of everything.[143] Chaos, the dark abyss, is at the same time the most lightful *logos* which illuminates all things. It is the Heraclitian fire. Heraclitus thought of nature (*physis*) as fire. Fire 'essentiates' itself by shining. *Physis* is the shine, the *logos*.

V. GODS AND *LOGOS*

According to Guthrie, in the word 'Zeus,' as well as in the terms by which all Indo-European languages indicate the god of the sky, the stem of the word 'to shine' is implied.[144] Zeus is known as the god of lightning or of light, but also all the Olympians in general indicate light or shining. *Physis* is the shine, therefore gods shine; they are the carriers or the messengers of the light of *physis*.

Zeus as the god of lightning "lays suddenly, in one blow, everything

[140] Otto, *Gestalt*, p. 189.
[141] Hölderlin, *op. cit.*, p. 61.
[142] *Ibid.*
[143] Wahl, *op. cit.*, p. 15.
[144] Guthrie, *op. cit.*, p. 222.

sojourning in the light of its sojourn." [145] Such a lightning directs and drives everything into its proper place. Thus this lightning assembles everything unto itself. In this sense Zeus, the god of lightning, is "the assembling placement, the λόγος." [146]

Since Zeus is not *physis*, but merely a being; he himself is sojourning in the light of *physis*, i.e. he is assembled in the *logos* of *physis*. Hence, Zeus as *logos* is a mere trustee or vehicle of the *logos* of *physis*.

Logos is the foundation of language. According to Heidegger, λόγον διδόναι means "to offer something which sojourns in its suchandsuch sojourning and in its being-laid, to offer it to the assembling understanding." [147] To talk or to think means to let something be the way it is in the *logos* of *physis*, and not the way it is in relation to the human mind.

In the conventional understanding, a saying is posterior to knowing. For the Greeks, the way Heidegger interprets them, the saying, *legein* is anterior to knowing, *noein*. However, *legein* here is not human 'speech' but that which renders speech possible; it is a more fundamental mode of saying. *Legein* is the letting-lie and *noein* – the taking-into-attention.[148] The taking-into-attention is such a taking which lets that which is taken into attention, lie the way it is laid. The anteriority of *legein* is indicated by the fact that this letting-lie, by letting something lie, is already taking that something into attention. "The λέγειν, the letting-lie, develops itself into νοεῖν." [149] On the other hand, *noein* is not possible without a simultaneous *legein*. "Whenever we take into our attention something laid, we respect it as being-laid." [150] By letting lie a sea, we take it into attention, we let it lie the way it is laid (we may also take something into attention not the way it is laid).

The letting-lie as well as the taking-into-attention indicates the being-laid-already. This means that human thinking or saying presupposes the *logos* of *physis*. The *logos* of *physis*, again, is brought to us by the *logos* of Zeus. Hence, human thinking or saying implies nature and gods. Human speech or language presupposes the divine *logos*; we talk and can talk because gods assemble words for us in their worlds. To know what language is ultimately, is to know the gods, to know the world.

145 Heidegger, *Vorträge*, p. 222.
146 *Ibid.*
147 Heidegger, *Satz*, p. 181.
148 Heidegger, *Was heisst Denken?*, p. 125.
149 *Ibid.*
150 *Ibid.*

Otto has shown that the gods are worlds. Hence, when properly
considered they cannot be treated as singular beings alongside the
other beings or things. They are at the roots of all the things. They
have a transcendental character; even though transcendence here does
not mean that they are beyond the world or nature. Instead, a god is
a mode of nature in the sense of *physis*; he is a world.

A deity is always a totality, a whole world in its completion. This concerns
also the supreme gods: Zeus, Athene, and Apollo, the bearers of the highest
ideals. None of them merely represents a singular virtue, and none of them is
found merely in *one* direction of vividly moving life; each of them fills up the
whole extent of human life with his peculiar spirit – forms it and illuminates it.[15]

If a god would merely represent a singular virtue, he would merely
be a part of a certain totality, of a world. A god carries a whole world
in himself, and thus he decides what things are and how they are
related to the world and interrelated among themselves; what is man's
place in the world and how he has to live his history; what is reasonable, what is foolish; what is a virtue and what is a vice.

Everything which belongs to the world of a god reflects his essence
and is held in his totality, the world. A thing becomes a thing by being-
held in a world. A thing becomes a thing by reflecting a god in the
world. As reflected by everything, a god is always near, but since he
is not a particular thing himself, he remains far in the distance, in
remoteness. "Close but hard to grasp is a god," [152] says Hölderlin.

All those things which disclose and reflect Hermes' essence – a road,
a bag of money, winged shoes, a traveler, a thief, the night – are not
Hermes, the god himself. All that is familiar to us and foreign to a god,
according to Heidegger,[153] reflects the essence of a god and brings him
near us even though as always remote. "In that which is familiar to
us, even though foreign to a god, the unknown [god] brings himself
forward, and he must be guarded in the familiar as unknown." [154] As
unknown, a god stands behind everything which reflects his essence;
he stands behind in the sense that he is the firm essence-granting
background which holds everything in its place and supports it.

To hold something in a unity and support it ontologically, means
to assemble it into a something. Everything which reflects the essence
of a god is assembled by that god in his assemblage, his *logos*. To know
a god as unknown, to know a god as reflected by that which is not a

[151] Otto, *Götter*, p. 161.
[152] Heidegger, *Erläuterungen*, p. 19.
[153] Heidegger, *Vorträge*, p. 200.
[154] *Ibid.*

god, means to stand in his *logos*, to stand in his world. 'To stand' here
is 'to understand,' 'to know.' The knowledge of the divine *logos* makes
us '*logos*-ical' beings, i.e. thinking and talking beings, while ignorance
of *logos* makes us merely 'logical' beings, i.e. correctly and precisely
calculating beings.

To illustrate a god as *logos*, an example may be helpful. The most
controversial and seemingly the most disunified deity is Dionysus. The
chaotic nature of Dionysus has already been shown in section III of
this chapter. By looking back into the Dionysian nature and by adding
a few supplementary aspects here, we will attempt to illustrate Dionysus as a world-sustaining *logos*.

In the Greek myths, Dionysus is reflected by various things, most
of which do not seem to have anything in common with the others, for
instance: a bull, a buck, a mask, wine, ivy, a snake, a child. All these
things explicitly refer to Dionysian nature and are held in unity by it.

A bull is known as a powerful animal symbolizing fertility. The
power of a bull is not merely productiveness or fertility; the bull also
stands for a destructive, blind, and passionate power. These characteristics reflect the stormy, vigorous, chaotic Dionysian nature.

In symbolic language a buck is known as meaning sexuality and
lewdness, passionate liveliness and gaiety. On the other hand, there
is something sinister in a buck. According to Otto, the ancient myths
relate the buck to the reign of ghosts or the dead. Also "the strange
leapings of young bucks seem to have something ghostly about
them." [155]

Dionysus, the god of fertility and gay life, is at the same time a
frightening god of death. Like the swiftly whirling dances of the
maenads which, when interrupted by pauses of total motionlessness,
reveal the speed and power of the dance, or like a noise, when broken
by total silence, is emphasized as noise – so life and fertility, when cut
off by death and destruction, are strikingly revealed to their full
extent.

Dionysus, as the god of oppositions, is shown by the symbol of a
mask. A mask always makes an impression of immediate nearness. The
eyes of the mask seem to bore directly into the spectator. Also the
motionlessness of the face of the actor wearing a mask, as set off from
all the vividly moving surroundings, gives an impression of inescapable
proximity. A mask brings the masked person into oppressing immediacy and at the same time it holds him in remoteness. The near and the

[155] Otto, *Dionysos*, p. 158.

far have the aspects of life and death. This can be shockingly felt after the death of an intimate friend. He seemed to have belonged to the joys and sorrows of the immediate present, and all of a sudden, he is unattainably removed from them by his death.

Immediacy and remoteness, reflected by the mask, are closely related to ecstasy, to the being-taken-out from here-and-now into the beyondness. Dionysus, the god of wine, brings joy and takes away sorrows; he removes all restrictions and boundaries. The far and near becomes the same, and chaos enters into man's life.

In intoxication or ecstasy man is taken to chaos, the never aging source of youth; he is made a child. A child, too, is a symbol of immediacy and remoteness at once, as being here and having the future of an adult. A child is a symbol of the here and the not-here at once. Mask, wine, and child are typically Dionysian symbols.

Wine takes away man's sorrows and gives him joys. It makes him live in a happy remoteness even though remaining in the present. A drunken man is in a 'here' and in a happy 'there' at the same time. The grapevine, the plant of wine "is a child of warmth; it gives birth to a stream of fire with which, by drinking, the body and the soul start to glow." [156]

Totally opposed to a grapevine is ivy which is not 'a child of warmth,' but of the cold. It does not need an excess of sun to grow. It is barren and useless. It does not bring any fire or life to the soul, but rather belongs to the realm of death. It is even used for the decoration of graves. As staying green through summer and winter, it stands for life and death and indicates the connection between the living and the dead. Ancient superstition has it that ivy by its cold nature protects from fire, and, according to Otto, Dionysus and the companions of his feasts crowned themselves with ivy to keep themselves sober, to protect themselves from the fire of the wine.[157] These Dionysian plants, grapevine and ivy, are clearly related in spite of their opposition. They, when brought together, express the interrelation of warm and cold, of far and near, of life and death, of light and dark – they indicate the chaotic nature of the god Dionysus, the god of chaos.

Ivy crawls on the ground and vines around the trunks of trees as do the maenads who whirl around Dionysus, the god "from the ivy-mantled slopes of Nysa's hills, and from the shore green with many-clustered vines" [158]; they whirl around him in their ecstatic dances.

[156] *Ibid.*, p. 144.
[157] *Ibid.*
[158] Sophocles *Antigone, Greek Drama*, Vol. I, p. 453.

The cold and crawly nature of ivy relates itself closely to snakes. The dancing maenads used to tie their hair with snakes or carry them in their hands, as Otto indicates.[159] In one of the ancient myths a maenad is described as having thrown a snake against a tree. The snake twisted around the tree and turned into ivy.[160]

Ivy, easily and lightly crawling on the ground and elastically twisting around the trees, reflects the dancing maenads or the leaping young bucks.

Just as these few phenomena manifestly and explicitly reflect the world of Dionysus, so everything whatsoever reflects Dionysus less explicitly and thus also becomes a something in his world. All these phenomena cannot be thought of as something for themselves before they enter the world of Dionysus. By entering his world and by reflecting his essence, they become assembled into 'somethingnesses.' They are held in unity by the god, and without him they would be disintegrated into meaninglessness. By reflecting the world of Dionysus, they are assembled in the Dionysian *logos*, and thus they are there as a foundation for the human *logos*.

The Greek gods are not the products of imagination. And all their features are not the accidentally gathered characteristics of a divine person. The figure of a god is unique, and all the facets of a god not only reflect him as the basic reality, but they also reflect each other; as for instance, a mask reflects wine.[161] In scientific consideration the relation of a mask to wine could only be accidental or poetical. It would be so because science does not aim to let nature appear the way it is. A scientific attitude is controlling, dictating, demanding, hence – a subjective attitude. To measure or to weigh and express in easily calculable and controllable numbers does not necessarily mean to reveal something in its essence. For the revelation or disclosure of the essence of a thing, it is necessary to let it lie the way it is laid in the *logos* of a god. A thing is a thing when it is held in unity by a god. "God holds the beginning and end and the middle of all existing things." [162]

A god means stability or "equilibrium which holds the world together, which prevents it from eluding or pouring forth into all." [163] Just as the gravity of the astronomical earth prevents everything from flying away into nothing and thus keeps it where it belongs –

[159] Otto, *Dionysos*, p. 144.
[160] *Ibid.*
[161] Cf. pp. 214–215.
[162] Orpheus, Fragment 6, Freeman, *op. cit.*
[163] Wahl, *Hölderlin*, p. 60.

so a god as world assembles everything into his *logos* and holds everything upon itself: keeps it apart from everything else and yet holds it in unity with everything else by relating it to the world, to himself as a god.

In the 'godless' periods of history, the lack of a god (lack is a mode of presence) is that which holds the world in place. The 'godless,' subjective, modern man does not let everything lie the way it is assembled by a god, but places it in his 'objective' system which is his instrument. By doing that he controls it by technical-mathematical means. The rapidly developing symbolic logic can itself be considered as a symbol of subjective *logos* which replaces the divine *logos*. The authentic human *logos* is such by letting everything lie the way it is assembled in the divine *logos*; and logic, the inauthentic, subjective *logos*, becomes logic by violating and distorting the divine *logos* – by assembling everything not upon nature but upon itself as facing all the things as its objects, i.e. as those which are or can be represented in the mind or as far as they are representable in the mind. Logic, the subjective *logos*, is an ontologically posterior mode of the authentic human *logos*, the *logos* of man who is open and responding to the divine *logos*.

Even replacing the world, *logos* of a god, by logic,[164] man is not totally independent from the divine *logos*, because everything, which is taken into the control of the modern man, was previoulsy obtained from the disclosed world of a god, obtained by responding to the *logos* of the god by man's authentic human *logos*. Logic thus presupposes the divine and human *logoi*, which in the course of time have fallen into forgottenness; and logic thereby has become an unrestrained dictator in the modern man's spiritual life. The modern man faces everything as his object disposed to him. With the precise methods of deduction and abstraction, he builds up the general concepts which enable him to keep under his hand the rich, concrete life that tends to spread apart chaotically after the bindings of *logos* have been concealed. The modern man has become the master and molder of the universe. The universe as responding to logic, in its broad sense, is matter.

With logical means man can master and control the universe; however he can never reveal any essences – he cannot reveal things the

[164] Logic here is meant in a broad sense as implying the mathematical-technical means of controlling the universe and also as implying all the calculated and reinforced rules and regulations prescribing the ways of modern man in his social life, and also as implying all the scientific ways of looking at the things. Briefly, logic is understood here as *ratio*.

way they are assembled in *logos*. A shattered rock or a pierced leaf of a blossom does not give out its essence. Neither the weighing nor the calculating of wave-lengths discloses any essences. Essences escape the logical ties. "No idea, no law, no obligation, but merely that which itself is in the highest degree essential can bind the essences." [165] That which is in the highest degree essential or real is a world, a divinity.

VI. GODS AS REALITIES

The bonds which bind all the essences, which assemble everything unto itself and assemble everything within the *logos*, do not concern merely things, in the sense of the material things, but everything whatsoever. The laws governing man in his private and social life are not of his making; they are gifts of the gods as indicated in Aeschylus' *Eumenides*.[166] The Greeks, who have amazed the world with their genius, never thought highly about man. All his works are primarily works of the gods. Without the gods, man is only "a shadow of a dream," as Pindar says in his eighth Pythian ode.[167] Man, a being not fully determined by biological nature, can only persist as man with the help of the gods. "Whoever has wrestled himself from the coercion of nature, has also lost its motherly protection; and only the strong spirit of a god can help him to persevere and remain in the light."[168]

When Hector at the walls of Troy, just before his duel with Achilles, was left and abandoned by Apollo,[169] he knew immediately that his lot was to die; man cannot long persist without a god. "All men stand in need of the gods." [170] All the successes of man in war as well as in the national games, according to the Greeks, are mainly the works of gods. In his odes for the heroes of the national games, Pindar often indicates that the garlands of victory primarily belong to the gods and only secondarily to man. "Wherever strength or skill is shown, eyes are raised to the gods who alone grant success or withhold it." [171]

Man's subordination to gods is not his total determination. On the contrary, the bindings of gods set man free. "Let no man live uncurbed by law nor curbed by tyranny," says Athene in Aeschylus' *Eume-*

[165] Otto, *Gestalt*, p. 280.
[166] *Greek Drama*, Vol. I, p. 284.
[167] Pindar, *Odes* (Chicago: University of Chicago Press 1947), p. 80.
[168] Otto, *Götter*, p. 81.
[169] Homer, *Iliad*, p. 406, *Complete Works*.
[170] Homer, *Odyssey*, p. 30, *Ibid*.
[171] Otto, *Götter*, p. 188.

nides.[172] To be subordinated to gods means to be open to the world or to be in the world, and the to-be-in-the-world means to be free toward everything which sojourns in the world. Without gods there is no freedom. To be free for that which is utterly real (god, world) is *eo ipso* to be open to anything whatsoever. "World holds sway and is more being than that which is seizable and graspable." [173] Everything within a world is in a lesser degree real than the world or deity itself. Since everything *is* by reflecting the deity, the deity itself is more *being* or appearing than anything else within its world. For the Greeks the hills, the meadows, and the banks of the river were appearing, were living, and were holy, because they were reflecting deity. The god himself was looking into their world from their hills, meadows, and river banks and was coming forward into it.[174]

A Greek god was looking forward or coming forward from the things of the world. He did not break into the world by omitting or even upsetting things in the sense of breaking natural laws as if he were an arrival from beyond-the-world. He approached man by holding things assembled upon himself, by backing them as their grounding reality, their *logos*.

> The other religions have worshipped the ruling powers in which one may believe or not. The sense of the Olympian gods, now, is the being of the world. Whether we believe in them as gods or not, the fullness of their meaning and concreteness can be justified even for us. Zeus, Apollo, Athene, Artemis, Hermes, Dionysus, Aphrodite – with each of these names a great reality of the world rises before us.[175]

Gods are realities which have the character of ultimateness, i.e. they are realities which serve as foundations for everything to sojourn and for us to live our life. They can never be expressed and exhausted with abstract concepts logically or scientifically. Gods can be experienced by one who lives or dwells open to them or they can be told about by one who has an eye for them – by a poet. The poet here is not a poet in the narrow sense, but a man with the knowledge of the beauty of gods as the fundamental appearances of *physis*. To have an eye for the beauty of *physis* is *eo ipso* to have an ear for its *logos*. The poet brings *logos* to words in his poetry.

Otto in one of his works [176] gives an example of a scientist who, at

---

172 *Greek Drama*, Vol. I, p. 295.
173 Heidegger, *Holzwege*, p. 33.
174 Heidegger, *Vorträge*, p. 274.
175 Otto, *Der Europäische Geist und die Weisheit des Ostens*, p. 21.
176 Otto, *Gestalt*, p. 216.

dusk, after a day's work with his instruments and tables, takes in his hands Hölderlin's poems and reads a few lines concerning night. Here Hölderlin lets the sound of the evening bells, the wind over the hills and groves, and the moon proclaim the approaching night. Night, full of stars and little worried about us men, shines astonishingly above the mountains in her sad and serene beauty. All of a sudden the scientist feels that here is something which cannot be detected or forced into words by instruments or tables – something which, nevertheless, can be experienced, something which is real. "Down upon this sounding world looks amazingly the great face – the Night!" [177]

Such an experience is too powerful to be merely imaginary; it is an experience of what is real, even though scientifically irrelevant. Night in scientific understanding is the lack of light, which is true just as $2 + 2 = 4$ is true. However, by merely indicating night as the lack of light we do not disclose its essence. Whatever science has to say about night, earth, stars, plants, winds, rains, stones – is correct; but for an attempt to penetrate reality deeply in its essence, the scientific answers avail nothing. Science does not reveal reality but merely presupposes it. All that which can be investigated and calculated scientifically presupposes the realities themselves which cannot be so investigated or calculated. Such a reality or divinity "is the same with all the appearances of the reign of life which it governs. However, as the highest essence and persisting being, it stands for itself high above earthliness in the shine of aether." [178]

Even though a god appears himself in the appearances of the things, still he appears as unknown or as concealed.[179] In one of his novels, Knut Hamsun portrays the life of people in Sellanraa, a remote mountain place in the Norwegian wilds. Talking about these people Hamsun says:

> They had this good fortune at Sellanraa, that every spring and autumn they could see the grey geese sailing in fleets above that wilderness, and hear their chatter up in the air – delirious talk it was. And as if the world stood still for a moment, 'til the train of them had passed. And the human souls beneath, did they not feel a weakness gliding through them now? They went to their work again, but drawing breath first; something had spoken to them, something from beyond.[180]

Who spoke to them? Not merely geese and sky; not their chatter and talk, but that which is brought forward or reflected by these

[177] Ibid.
[178] Otto, Götter, p. 163.
[179] Cf. p. 213.
[180] Knut Hamsun, Growth of the Soil (New York: Alfred A. Knopf, 1953), p. 179.

geese and their chatter, the reality which backs them and holds them in the world – the unknown. These people were shaken by the realness and serenity of this unknown which brought itself forward by the flight of the geese even though it remained in the distance – reality deeply real and yet ungraspable and unknown as if it were nothingness.

The treating of gods as realities of the utmost importance has been confirmed in Greek history in that the conquering Greeks respected the deities of the defeated land.[181] Hearing the news of the victory of the Greeks in Troy, Clytemnestra says:

> Yet let them reverence well the city's gods,
> The lords of Troy, tho' fallen, and her shrines;
> So shall the spoilers not in turn be spoiled.[182]

It is up to the gods whether Achaeans will rule the Trojan land.

For traditional philosophy realities can only be dealt with as objects in relation to the investigating subject. Truth is truth in the mind or in statements. A god, or a world, the ultimate reality, cannot be disclosed adequately in terms of the traditional philosophy. A god as reality is that which, in the diverse appearances of the within-the-world beings, is looking from these appearances into the world. These diverse appearances and phenomena bring a god forward into the world by reflecting him, or rather the god himself comes forward into the world from concealment by letting appearances or phenomena appear. Gods do not come forward into the world as if the world would be standing there and waiting for them. Gods, by coming forward and appearing, light up the world. God is the appearance of the world.[183]

God as lighting up a world has the character of guidance. The lightning of Zeus guides. "It brings everything in advance to its appointed essence-place. Such a bringing is the assembling, the laying down, the λόγος." [184] As has been indicated previously,[185] a god is not his own *logos*. He is rather a vehicle which carries the *logos* of *physis*, the light of Being (*Lichtung des Seins*). God is a mode in which *physis* comes forward in its *logos*.

Gods, even though they appear in the light of Being, are not merely sojourning beings which sojourn in the light. Gods belong to the light

[181] Guthrie, *op. cit.*, p. 29.
[182] Aeschylus, *Agamemnon, Greek Drama*, Vol. I, p. 178.
[183] 'Appearance' here is 'beauty'; cf. p. 139.
[184] Heidegger, *Vorträge*, p. 222.
[185] Cf. p. 170 and p. 212.

itself. Gods are light or *logos*. And not only gods, but also men, as to-be-in-the-world, belong to the light of Being or to the structure of the world. The relation of gods and men "to the light is nothing other than the light itself in as far as it assembles gods and men into the light and retains them in it." [186] A sojourning being stands in the light as in a circle illuminated by this light and in which circle such a being is securely placed. Gods and men "are not only illuminated by the light, but lit up by it and for it. Therefore they have the power to accomplish the lighting (to bring it into the full extent of its essence) in their own way and thus to guard the light." [187] Gods and men belong to the light of Being; therefore gods and men are the only beings which are incorporated into the structure of the world itself. *Sein und Zeit* shows man as *Dasein*, the to-be-in-the-world,[188] and gods are shown by Otto as worlds.

Gods and men belong to the lighting or *logos*; therefore there is the divine and the human *logos*. Gods as the carriers of the light of *physis* are glancing into the world (*Hereinblickenden*).[189] By glancing in from the beings into the world, the gods place and guide these beings in the world and thus assemble them in their divine *logos*. Such an assembling demands man's response. The response of man is the letting-lie of that which is assembled the way it is assembled (*legein*) by taking-into-attention (*noein*). The divine *logos* as a demand and the human *logos* as a response belong to or are incorporated in the *logos* of Being (of *physis* or of world).

The divine *logos* is *mythos*. According to Otto,[190] *mythos* is the older form of *logos*. The Greek myths to a superficial understanding are diverse stories concerning various events in the life of gods. The myth of Dionysus, for instance, implies diverse symbols, such as bull, buck, mask, child, wine, ivy. A myth as a story does not assemble these diverse symbols as mythological-psychological images, but the reality of the god Dionysus assembles them as real phenomena belonging to his world. *Mythos* is not a told story, a myth; it is located in the reality itself, in the *logos* of one or another god. *Mythos*, in the sense of the

[186] Heidegger, *Vorträge*, p. 278.
[187] *Ibid.*
[188] In *Sein und Zeit*, world necessarily belongs to the structure of *Dasein*, and here it is said that man belongs to the structure of the world. *Dasein* is the essence of man. For Heidegger essence is that which makes something to be something without being itself a something. However, in the case of man, *Dasein* belongs to man because man is an 'ec-sisting' being; he stands out into the openness of Being, into the world. To the 'essentiation' of the world, or to the 'worlding' of the world, belongs man.
[189] Heidegger, *Vorträge*, p. 277.
[190] Otto, *Gestalt*, p. 71.

divine *logos*, is *aletheia*, the truth; and truth for the Greeks is not placed in the mind or in statements. Hence, a myth as a story is not identical with *mythos* as *aletheia*. When man, by being open to the truth of a god, responds to this truth with his human *logos*, then the divine *logos* or *mythos* may, and often does, become a myth.

A response to mythos is a cult, and cult ultimately is the naming of a god. By the naming of a god, a world is opened for man and his history. Gods approach man with their word, the *mythos*. Such an approach is powerful and overwhelming. It tears man from his familiar everydayness, and carries him into the enthusiasm of gods. Dionysus takes man into the ecstasy of divinity, into his chaos from the orderliness of everydayness. "Man has to relinquish everything finite in order to be able to become the prey of gods." [191] From such being-taken-away into the remoteness of gods, man approaches himself; he advances towards himself. 'Advancing' in German is *Zu-kunft*, i.e. future.[192] By being an 'adventist,' a comer upon himself from the remoteness of gods, man can have a past. "The past as such can only manifest itself because there is future" [193] in the sense of advancing. The adventistic past brings out the present. Heidegger concludes *Sein und Zeit* with the indication that time is the "horizon of Being." [194] With the erupting time, world opens itself.

Since a world is opened by a response to *mythos*, a word of gods, and the responder is the namer of gods and narrator of their life, and since such naming and narrating is cult – the poet for the Greeks, as well as for Hölderlin, is a prophet.

---

[191] Fink, *op. cit.*, p. 26.
[192] Cf. p. 62.
[193] Biemel, *op. cit.*, p. 125.
[194] Heidegger, *Sein und Zeit*, p. 438.

CHAPTER VI

FOURSOME

As stated in Chapter III of this study, in the third phase of Heidegger's thought the problem of world, when brought to its completeness, is the interplay of the foursome. These four are earth, sky, gods, and mortals. The need to understand foursome properly necessitated studying each member of the foursome. Man as *Dasein*, which in the terms of Heidegger's late thought is man as mortal, has been dealt with in Chapter I. In this and in the remaining chapters it will only be necessary to indicate a few aspects of man in his mortal essence.

The earth and the sky have been presented in Chapter IV. However, the sky has not been dealt with explicitly, but it has been present implicitly throughout the whole chapter inasmuch as the problem of *physis* implies the sky just as well as the earth. Since Chapter V had gods for its theme, the individual considerations of each member of the foursome can be regarded as completed. This chapter is to conclude the investigation begun in Chapter III, an investigation of the world. Here the problem of the world will be treated under the aspect of foursome by showing the places of earth, sky, gods, and mortals in the world and their reciprocal interrelation. Generally, this chapter will recapitulate and organize materials already presented instead of introducing any wholly new elements.

The foursome (*Geviert*) is the interplay of earth, sky, gods, and men as mortals.[1] In this interplay the world as openness is stirred up in the sense of being opened up. All four of the foursome are not the parts of the world; nor are they four things or beings which produce a fifth thing, the world, but each of them necessarily refers to the other three. All four stand in a friction or strife which by setting them apart at the same time unifies them. Strife is the world itself. World is a dynamic process.

---

[1] By 'man as mortal,' or briefly by 'mortal,' the essence of man is indicated. For traditional philosophy, man in his ontological structure is *animal rationale*; for Heidegger man in his ontological structure is mortal. *Sein und Zeit* can be considered as a work which results in showing man as mortal.

Such dynamism characterizes not only the world as the interplay of foursome, but also the world as the to-be-in-the-world and world as the openness of Being. *Dasein* in its ultimate sense has been shown as the resolute running forward into the possibility of the impossibility of *Dasein*, which can be stated briefly as the openness to death.[2] This openness to death characterizes *Dasein*, the extreme openness itself, in a highly dynamic mode. Since Dasein is the to-be-in-the-world and since the to-be-in-the-world is the way in which the world 'essentiates' or 'worlds' (*weltet*) itself, dynamic openness is the typical indication of the world. Hence, world in the first phase of Heidegger's philosophy already is a highly dynamic phenomenon.

In the second phase of Heidegger's thought, world has been considered as the openness of Being. Since openness or revelation is truth for Heidegger, and truth is the strife between truth and untruth, the world as openness of Being is the constant-coming-forward from concealment (untruth) into revelation (truth); it is a highly dynamic phenomenon also.

World is not something which is dynamic, but is dynamism itself. This dynamism is the coming-forward from concealment into revelation – it is an event of truth. Event, again, indicates not merely a taking place in time, but the becoming what one is, the entering into one's own self. In German '*eigen*' is 'own' and '*Er-eignis*' is not only an 'event' but also the 'entering-into-one's-own-self by gathering oneself into unity or self-possession.' "The event of lighting is the world." [3] In this 'event' everything whatsoever comes to itself; and also each of the foursome comes to itself; and, finally, the world itself comes to itself. The grammatical character of 'foursome' (*Geviert*) also indicates the dynamism of the event of the world. '*Geviert*' is the past participle of '*vieren*,' 'to four.' '*Geviert*' as translated literally would be 'foured.'

To be in the world means to stand in the openness of Being. To stand in the openness of Being, again, means to sojourn on the earth as a mortal. "But 'on the earth' already means 'under the sky.' Both imply 'abiding in front of deities' and include 'belonging to the to-getherness of men.' From their primary unity the four – earth, sky, gods, and mortals – are one." [4]

As to what these four are, Heidegger gives only brief indications in

[2] Cf. p. 57.
[3] Heidegger, *Vorträge*, p. 276.
[4] *Ibid.*, p. 149.

two of the essays included in his *Vorträge und Aufsätze*, the "*Bauen Wohnen Denken*" and "*Das Ding.*" According to these indications, "the earth is that which constructively supports; cherishingly bears fruits; preserves waters and rocks, plants, and animals." [5] The earth is such when it is upheld and sustained as such and not when it is made a field of subjective exploitation.

"The sky is the motion of the sun and the course of the moon, the shine of stars, the seasons of the year, the light and twilight of the day, the darkness and clearness of night, the grace and inhospitability of weather, the passing of the clouds, and the bluish depth of aether." [6] The sky, too, is such when it is taken as such by man, the dweller on earth. The sky also can be disregarded as such and seen merely as another area for subjective interpretation.

For us moderns, the sky as described by Heidegger seems to be either a primitively or a poetically viewed sky. We are inclined to consider the earth as well as the sky positivistically. The sunrise or sunset, for instance, is an illusion dependent upon the revolving of the earth on its axis. Heidegger, by describing the earth and the sky phenomenologically (*logos*-like), does not proclaim the scientific way of considering them as false. However, what is not false, is not *eo ipso* true – true in the ultimate ontological sense, namely, in the sense of the disclosure of essences. Science does not have the ultimate and the final word as far as the essence of the earth and the sky is concerned. Essence for Heidegger is that which *ultimately* makes possible that which stands in question. Hence, earth and sky, as the objects of scientific investigation, presuppose the essences of the earth and the sky as that which is beyond the scope of scientific investigation. Science is not an instrument for knowing the essences.

According to Heidegger, traditional philosophy also does not answer the question of essence because what it means by essence is opposed to existence, while for Heidegger 'essence' (*Wesen*) is a verb and expresses the mode of being by which whatever-is reflects the world, the whole, in which it becomes what it is. Essence necessarily indicates world – that which makes it possible for whatever is to be what it is.

Heidegger tries to let the sky and the earth appear the way they are in themselves and not the way they become when conceptually controlled by man. The thunder of the sky, when left the way it is, causes fear, astonishment, or an experience of man-exceeding powers. How-

---

[5] *Ibid.*, p. 176.
[6] *Ibid.*, p. 177.

ever, when science explains in detail that thunder is caused by a col-
lision of two opposite charges of electricity on the clouds and on the
earth, the overpowering mystery is solved. When this purely theoretical or 'logical' control of such an event is followed by the construction of a mechanical device which takes away the danger of being
struck by the lightning, the logical control becomes enriched or
supplemented by physical control, and man becomes fully released
from exposure to the elements of the sky. However, at the same time
he is released from being exposed to Being too. The control of thunder
and of the earth and the sky does not reveal the essence of thunder
and of the earth and the sky. Essence can only be revealed by letting
the thunder and the earth and the sky be the way they are by being
exposed or open to them. Of course, this does not mean that the
erecting of lightning-conductors is the wrong thing to do. No! But it
is wrong to replace the openness to essences by scientific explanations
of them and thus to let our spiritual sight be stunted at the point of
controlling nature and to remain blind to the essences which are
beyond this point. What are these essences and what is exposure to
them, are the direct interest of this study which intends to throw some
light on them.

The earth and the sky, when allowed to be the way they are, necessarily refer to gods. "The deities are the nodding messengers of
the divine. From its concealed rule appears a god in his essence,
which eludes any comparison with that which sojourns. "[7] The 'divine' here is that which Hölderlin calls 'holiness' or 'nature.' Gods
appear and approach us from the realm of holiness or nature in
the sense of *physis*. As appearing from the rule of *physis*, gods are the
bearers of this rule to everything which is or to everything which
sojourns. That which sojourns becomes that which sojourns by being
ruled by this rule of *physis*. Gods in their essences, as the messengers
of the divine, are totally different, and thus incomparable to that
which sojourns. They belong or are implied in the all-ruling divine
itself; they are standing in the outskirts of that which sojourns – the
outskirts which are grounding that which sojourns – they are implied
in the worldness of the world.

Earth, sky, and gods necessarily refer to mortals.

The mortals are men. They are called mortals because they can die. To die
means to be capable of death as death. An animal expires. It has death as death
neither before nor behind itself. Death is a shrine of nothingness, i.e. of that
which in any aspect whatsoever is not merely something which is and which,
nevertheless, 'essentiates' specifically as a safeguard of Being itself.[8]

[7] *ibid.*
[8] *Ibid.*

By indicating man as a mortal, Heidegger does not deny life after death; he, however, does not confirm it either. By man as mortal, Heidegger indicates the very essential ontological structure of man. "Metaphysics, on the contrary, represents man as animal, as a living being. Even though the *ratio* penetrates and rules animality, man remains determined by life and living experience. The rational living beings must become mortals." [9] They must become mortals in order to be ultimately, essentially men.

In *Sein und Zeit*, where the ontological structure of man is exhaustively analyzed, Heidegger shows death as the very basic stroke in the ontological make-up of man. Man is shown there as a being of possibilities. Man is a being who can always be more than he is, who has possibilities that stand out beyond him and that nevertheless belong to him. Man is fully thought of when he is thought of as implying his ultimate possibilities. Man's extreme possibility is death, the possibility of the impossibility of *Dasein*. Man, as thought of ultimately, implies death, is mortal.[10] To imply a possibility does not mean to realize it because in that case possibility would cease to be a possibility. To imply a possibility here means to guard possibility as possibility, to be open to it.

Death, as the possibility of the impossibility of *Dasein*, indicates man's transcendentality, i.e. his capability to stand beyond himself and beyond everything which is – to stand into nothingness. "*Dasein* means the being-held-in-nothingness." [11] Here to-be-held-in-nothingness is the same as to-be-in-the-world; more specifically, it is the authentic way of to-be-in-the-world. World is the openness of Being. Hence, to stand in the world is to take part in this openness or to let it be openness. When Heidegger (in his *Sein und Zeit*) stresses death – or rather when he stresses the being-towards-death as running-forward-into-the-possibility-of-impossibility-of-*Dasein* – he shows death as a highly opening factor. Death reveals *Dasein* in its fullness. Death, as extreme to-be-in-the-world, is extreme truth, extreme revelation.

In his *Vom Wesen der Wahrheit*, Heidegger has shown the open, revealing attitude of man as being-free, namely, the being-free to all which is. Such being-free is letting all which is be the way it is. The letting-be of all which is, is only possible by standing somehow beyond all which is: *Dasein*, as being-held-in-nothingness is *eo ipso* being-

9 *Ibid.*
10 Cf. pp. 54–55.
11 Heidegger, *Was ist Metaphysik?*, p. 32.

beyond-all-which-is. Only from this beyondness, from this transcendence, can a being be known as a being. An animal, who expires
but does not die, cannot know a being as being. A dog can know that
a bone tastes good, but he does not know that bone *is*. If we lived
constantly in the day, i.e. if we did not know the night, we would not
know the day either. In order to know that a being *is*, it is necessary
to stand beyond that which is, to stand in that which is not, to stand
in the world. Hence, dying is not an experience which takes place when
we are about to die or expire as living beings: our way of being itself
is dying. "As long as man *is*, he stands in the inescapability of death."[12]
The essential feature of man is his standing out into nothingness. Man
"can become a shepherd of Being insofar as he is the agent of
nothingness."[13] Death is man's extreme possibility which marks the
manness of man. Man is mortal.

Mortality or death, as the standing beyond the totality of that which is,
is the factor which gives a unity to the totality of that which is. Death
is the shrine of nothingness which surrounds and holds everything in
unity. "Death as the shrine of nothingness secures the 'essentiation'
of Being itself. Death, as the shrine of nothingness, is the highland of
Being."[14] 'Highland' in German is *'Gebirg.'* *'Gebirg'* has the connotation of *'bergen,'* namely, 'to include or surround securely.' Death
as the shrine of nothingness secures and surrounds the totality of that
which is and thus death is the highland of Being. To be dying for Heidegger in no wise means to be retiring from life or being. "Mortals are
what they are as mortals, by their 'essentiation' in the highland of
Being. They are the 'essentiating' relation to Being as Being."[15]

Being needs man to bring itself into being. Being is not thinkable
without its approach towards man or withdrawal from him. Man
'essentiates,' exists as man, by being open to the approach or the
withdrawal of Being, i.e. when he guards Being in its modes of breaking
forward. Being 'essentiates' by approaching man and man 'essentiates' by responding to the approach of Being. It would be wrong to
think of Being and man as two separate beings who have as their
properties certain interrelations with each other.[16] It is also wrong to
think of them as one identical being. Neither Being nor man fundamentally is a being but they are the world or worldly reality.

[12] Heidegger, *Einführung*, p. 121.
[13] Heidegger, *Holzwege*, p. 321.
[14] Heidegger, *Vorträge*, p. 177.
[15] *Ibid.*
[16] Heidegger, *Seinsfrage*, p. 27.

To indicate Being as the nothingness which grounds everything which is and to show that Being is not something separate from man in his essence, Heidegger in one of his late works (*Zur Seinsfrage*) applies a peculiar way of writing the word 'Being,' namely as '~~Being~~.' ~~Being~~ as crossed hints at nothingness, and the four branches meeting in the heart of Being (the world) indicate the four of the foursome. Just as man as a mortal is implied in Being or world, so are the earth, sky, and gods.

Man in Heidegger's philosophy is shown in the dark backgrounds of nothingness, of dread, and death, while gods are backed by holiness, which refers to light, to joy, and to serenity.[17] Gods, as the messengers of Being, are the carriers of light. Gods, as immortals filled with the light of Being, need the realm of darkness to reveal their light; they need man because, as Hölderlin says, "mortals can better reach into the abyss." [18] And mortals are in need of light which they cannot receive directly from holiness, but merely from the hand of gods. In the reciprocal need of gods and men the love between them is grounded. "By the mediation of this love they belong, however, not to themselves but to holiness." [19] Being or holiness brings itself to openness or to the world by availing itself of the immortality of gods and the mortality of men.

In Heidegger's early works, man is shown as the to-be-in-the-world which, when thought radically, is the being-held-in-nothingness.[20] For Glenn J. Gray this seems to be a natural conclusion of the extreme subjectivism by which, in his opinion, Heidegger's early works have been marked.[21] For this reason, according to Gray, Heidegger's thought in his late works shifted from the subjectivistic to the objectivistic standpoint, "from self-assertion to self-submission, from transforming to letting-be, from the delusion that man conditions things to the truth that things condition him." [22] Gray misunderstands Heidegger by considering him as a subjectivistic and anthropocentric thinker in his early period and as a naturalistic thinker in his late period. Such misinterpretation of his philosophy is not unusual since Heidegger's thought is so fundamental that it easily eludes us.

In the early, as well as in the late works, Heidegger ultimately is a

[17] Heidegger, *Erläuterungen*, p. 16.
[18] Heidegger, *Hymne*, p. 23.
[19] *Ibid.*, pp. 23–24.
[20] Heidegger, *Was ist Metaphysik?*, p. 32.
[21] Gray, *op. cit.*, pp. 201–202.
[22] *Ibid.*, p. 205.

philosopher of the world, the openness of Being. In his early works, Heidegger treats world as the to-be-in-the-world and in the late works as the interplay of the foursome. Man as a mortal belongs to the foursome which means that he is standing in the world, namely, that he is the to-be-in-the-world. Here the to-be-in-the-world as the be-longing-to-the-interplay-of-the-foursome is broadened and developed to-be-in-the-world. To be in the world *eo ipso* means to dwell on the earth, beneath the sky, and to stand under the gods. Not a change or a shift characterizes Heidegger's late thought but the development and the enrichment of the same thoughts.

Earth, sky, gods, and mortals necessarily belong together. "Each of the four reflects in its own way the essence of the rest. Each reflects its own nature in its own way within the conflux of the four." [23] In such a reciprocal reflection each of the four appropriates itself in its own essence and becomes bound with the rest in the conflux of their togetherness. "None of the four stiffens itself upon its separated particularity. Rather each of the four is expropriated within the uni-fication to its own peculiarity. This expropriating unification is the mirror-play of the foursome." [24] The world expropriates or grants properties to each of the foursome; and each of the foursome receives these properties, appropriates them.

The mirror-play of the foursome in which all the four become what they are in their togetherness, is the procedure of the 'worlding' of the world. "We call the appropriating mirror-play of the conflux of earth and sky, of deities and mortals, the world." [25] World is not posterior to the four of the foursome. The interplay of the four *is* world. The four are incorporated in the worldness of the world; they belong to its structure.

Any attempt to explain, to ground, or to causally relate one of the four to the other three is impossible, because any grounding or causing presupposes the world and thus is posterior to the foursome. The interplay of the foursome is the ground on which any grounding, any explanation, or any cause-effect relation can take place. The four of the foursome are transcendent, i.e. they are beyond the realm of mere beings; they are held or implied in the worldness of world.

The mirror-play of the four – Heidegger stresses it repeatedly never can be thought of as the play of four beings. "The mirror-play

[23] Heidegger, *Vorträge*, p. 178.
[24] *Ibid.*
[25] *Ibid.*

of the world is the round-dance of appropriation." [26] The four of foursome do not enter the round-dance as something in themselves already;
but they becomes what they are, they appropriate their essences, only
in this round-dance of the world.

The world mirrors. It founds and grounds everything and is itself
an abyss: it is not grounded but chaotic. World as chaos is not disorder; it is an orderly mirror-play of foursome in which any order
whatsoever is grounded. For our modern 'sober' times, such an understanding of the world seems strange. For us the earth is de-divinized;
it is subordinate to us, and it becomes what we make of it. In itself it
is merely a complex of blind powers from which anything reasonable
can result merely by chance. The modern world is basically a godless
world.

World, as seen by Heidegger, highly resembles the world of the
Greeks. "There is no other picture of the world," says Otto referring
to the world of the Greeks, "in which the earthly and human realities
were filled with the presence of deities to such a great extent; no other
human society would think of a divinity with such faithfulness and
veneration even in the less important instances of their existence." [27]

The earth, as related to the gods, and man, as belonging in a necessary interrelation with them, indicate the religious character of being
and living in the world, similar to that of the Greeks as shown in Otto's
words. When we approach things or events from the whole of the world,
we let things be in their full essence, i.e. as that which sojourns in the
openness of world. When things are let be the way they are, they
reflect the four of the foursome; and by doing that they bring or assemble these four in the world. A thing or an event thus has a religious
character. To dwell on the earth – which *eo ipso* is to be under the sky,
be near gods, and belong in the togetherness of the other mortals –
primarily means to treat with consideration, to spare everything
whatsoever,[28] i.e. to let-it-be-reflecting earth, sky, gods, and mortals,
which, again, means to let-it-be-assembled in the openness of world or
in the *logos* of *physis*. To dwell on the earth means to be exposed to
gods. Every act of man's dwelling on the earth – manifestly or con-
cealedly – has this religious implication. "Man as man has always
measured himself already by and with something heavenly." [29] Such
measuring, when expressed in the language of the early Greek phi-

---

[26] *Ibid.*, p. 179.
[27] Otto, *Gestalt*, pp. 120–121.
[28] Heidegger, *Vorträge*, p. 149.
[29] *Ibid.*, p. 195.

losophers, is the response of man to the divine *logos* in his human *logos*. This response to the divine *logos*, the *mythos*, is ultimately a cult. Dwelling ultimately is a cult.

In the everyday life of peasants, even today there are remnants of such religious implications. W. S. Reymont in his *Peasants* depicts "the sower whose hand-motion of sowing was pious, blessing-the-earth motion." [30] The sower "dispersed the grain with a sacred spread." [31] 'Earth' and 'bread' in the language of peasants are often accompanied by the epithet of 'sacred.' They consider rain in the time of drought as a gift of God. Reymont dramatically describes the death of the peasant Borina, the main personage of his novel. Borina, deliriously ill and driven by a love of the earth, walks out into the fields in the middle of the night and has the illusion that he is sowing grain in his "ancestral fields," as though he were sowing "all the days of his life, all his human existence, which he had received and which now he was returning to these sacred fields and to the Lord of Eternity." [32] Exhausted he falls to the earth and dies. Man is shown here in a deep implication with the earth heightened unto the realm of the heavens.

Modern man, because of his too great 'sobriety' is losing the firm foundations from under his feet. 'Sobriety' here indicates man's highly articulated explanations and clear scientific insights into various phenomena of nature and life. The foundations which carry us and hold us in unity are not revealable scientifically because science has sight only for the within-the-world beings and not for the world itself. When explained or controlled scientifically, the worldly phenomena (earth, sky, gods, mortals) elude us and leave us without support. Not the control of them but the being exposed to them by letting them be the way they are frees us for our authentic way of being and supports us in our stand. Such a being-exposed to the higher powers (response to *mythos* or to *logos* of *physis*) indicates the necessity of a religious attitude for man. Only such an attitude grants to man strong backgrounds or world. "Every great step in the development of the human race lies in the field of religion, which is always the most powerful – in the primeval times the only – carrier of civilization." [33]

When the higher powers of the foursome elude us and fall into forgottenness, the world in which we live becomes disintegrated, and *eo ipso* thrown out from the assembling power of *logos*; this means our

[30] W. S. Reymont, *Kaimieciai* (Chicago: Nemunas, [n.d.]), I, p. 21.
[31] *Ibid.*
[32] *Ibid.*, III, p. 469.
[33] Bachofen, *op. cit.*, p. 271.

disintegration as well. The only thing in modern times which replaces the lost foundations of foursome is logic in the broad sense.[34] Logic in this sense is rather the mechanical means of unification. For example, in the life of modern society the enforced laws are the means of holding such a society together. While *logos* is the grown, inward power of unification. Such a power, for instance, is expressed in the unwritten laws of the life of a nation. Logic ultimately is rooted in *logos*, like the written laws which have developed from the unwritten ones.

Man, as subordinated to the higher powers and as merely a responder, seems to be excluded from them and not to have a notable part in them. However, it is not so. As one of the four of the foursome, man has a highly important place in the world; he essentially belongs to the structure of the world. An insight into the structure of the world can give an answer to this seeming contradiction. Being (world is openness of Being) is signified by the turning-toward. The turning-toward is not the property of Being as though Being were a substance. Being *is* the turning-toward. The turning-toward is an invocation or appeal. Invocation is never a calling without someone to whom the call is made, i.e. without a responder. A responder is not something for himself before he responds; by responding he becomes a responder. An invocation makes a responder possible; it creates room for a response.

An invocation is a language. A language is fully a language when answered. Man, as responding to the *logos* of Being, stands in the service of Being and thus makes *logos logos*. Man responds to the *logos* of Being by letting lie what is laid. By letting lie he is taking-into-attention; *legein* (letting-lie) is *noein* (taking-into-attention). Similarly *logos* as being-laid is *eo ipso* being-assembled. *Logos* as being-laid founds *legein* as letting-lie, and *logos* as assembling founds *noein* as the taking-into-attention, assembling, understanding.

Being is in no wise something standing for itself and then coming occasionally into a relation with man. Man "is not only implied in 'Being,' but 'Being,' as demanding the human essence, is assigned to abandon the seemingness of for-itself." [35] Man is incorporated into the structure of Being; he belongs to the worldness of the world indicated by ~~Being~~ which signifies Being in its openness, in its breaking forward into light at the intersection – the interplay – of earth, sky, gods, and mortals.[36]

[34] Cf. footnote 164 on p. 217.
[35] Heidegger, *Seinsfrage*, pp. 30–31.
[36] *Ibid.*, p. 31.

Being as turning-toward is coming to itself in the sense of coming to appearance. This coming to appearance expresses itself by the diversification of everything which is in its boundaries and structure, and thus it discloses everything in the light of Being. "Such a diversification is essential thinking," [37] the thinking of Being, the *logos*. Thinking primarily belongs to Being. "We do not come to thoughts. They come to us." [38]

By the thinking of Being (thinking in which Being thinks), by *logos*, everything is diversified and at the same time unified or assembled. "Reality is not a disordered pile of objects but reveals itself in a certain structure." [39] *Logos* as diversified assembling is the ultimate truth as revelation. Truth as revelation is not located in the mind, as responding to an object or as that to which an object responds, but in the world itself. Since the world is the interrelation of earth, sky, gods, and mortals, this interrelation, the mirror-play, is the primary revelation, the primary truth.

A world can never be opened or a truth can never take place without a thing which undergoes the interplay of foursome or which is exposed to the light of Being. "The openness of that which is open, i.e. the truth, can only be what it is, namely, this openness, when it establishes itself and insofar as it establishes itself. Therefore, in this openness there has to be a being in which the openness takes its stand and steadfastness." [40] For light to be revealed as light, an object is necessary which is illuminated by the light and which reflects light in its lucidity.

The importance of a thing in the world can be illustrated by the fact that an artwork (a thing) establishes a new world and upsets the old one.[41] However, it would be wrong to consider an artwork as the cause of a new world. An artwork becomes an artwork merely by reflecting the interplay of foursome in the way an object reveals light by reflecting it when illuminated by it. The artwork has world-opening significance in the beginning of Heidegger's third phase of thought. In the latter part of it, such significance is given to a thing as a thing. By reflecting the light of the world, a thing 'things.' By introducing the verb form of thing (*dingen*), Heidegger indicates that the

---

[37] Heidegger, *Hymne*, p. 14.

[38] Martin Heidegger, *Aus der Erfahrung des Denkens* (Pfullingen: Günther Neske, 1954), p. 11.

[39] Stephan Strasser, "The Concept of Dread in Heidegger," *Modern Schoolman*, XXXV (November, 1957), p. 31.

[40] Heidegger, *Holzwege*, p. 49.

[41] *Ibid.*, p. 54.

'thingness' of a thing consists in bringing the world into nearness. "The thing 'things.' By 'thinging,' it detains the earth and the sky, the deities and the mortals; by detaining them, the thing brings the four near to each other in their remoteness." [42] To detain the foursome means to 'thing' the world.[43]

A thing 'things' the world, i.e. it brings the world near to us and thus gives us room for an authentic mode of being in the world when we let a thing be the way it is, when we treat it with consideration. "How is this done?" asks Heidegger. His answer is: "By mortals' cherishing and taking care of things which grow, by their expressly erecting the things which do not grow." [44] The German word 'bauen,' 'to build,' indicates the cultivating of growing things, as well as the erecting of buildings. Building-cultivating is a mode of dwelling, i.e. a mode of the sojourn of man on the earth. Dwelling ultimately means the guarding of the foursome in the things.

Sein und Zeit thinks of the world as the to-be-in-the-world. Hence, man in his very essence is the world, the place where Being breaks itself into openness. This does not conflict with man as mortal because man as mortal is a member of the foursome, and he belongs to the round-dance of the world – he stands out in the mirror-play of the world and thus is the to-be-in-the-world. In Sein und Zeit, world is approached through man in his essence without developing all the implications which man in his essence entails.

With the essay "Der Ursprung des Kunstwerkes" in his Holzwege, Heidegger shows the earth as being necessarily related to the world. He also indicates therein [45] that he understands the earth the same way as the early Greek philosophers understood physis. In physis the earth and world, although implied, have not been distinguished. Just as Dasein is man (as mortal) in the world, so physis is earth in the world. Earth necessarily implies sky, gods, and mortals. Therefore earth, just as Dasein, can be regarded as the 'worlding' of the world.

In the previous chapter, gods were shown as worlds. Since gods – the way they have been thought of by the Greeks and by Hölderlin – are the powers of Being or physis, they too can be considered as modes of physis or modes of world, just as Dasein or earth. An approaching god brings forward the holiness (physis or world) in which his divinity is grounded.

[42] Heidegger, Vorträge, p. 176.
[43] Ibid., p. 179.
[44] Ibid., p. 152.
[45] Heidegger, Holzwege, p. 32.

In all these cases the sameness of *Dasein*, of earth, of gods, and, analogically, of sky with the world in no wise means their identity with the world. Identity can only be applied to the within-the-world beings but not to the transcendental phenomena, i.e. the phenomena implied in the worldness of world. Their sameness indicates their inseparability even though it does not deny their distinctiveness.

CHAPTER VII

THING

The attention of this study is directed toward the earth and the gods. World, as the interplay of earth and sky, of gods and mortals, gave a better insight into these two basic phenomena in Heidegger's late thought. However – as indicated near the end of the previous chapter – world, as the interplay of foursome, necessarily refers to a thing which, by standing in the light of the world, 'things,' i.e. brings into nearness, the four of the foursome. A thing 'things' when it is treated with consideration. Such a treating, a letting-be, is done by dwelling as a mode of being of mortals. Hence, to complete the investigation of world, which *eo ipso* means to complete the investigation of the phenomena of the earth and the gods, it is necessary to consider thing and dwelling.

These two remaining chapters, "Thing" and "Dwelling," are in a certain sense practical whereas the previous four chapters in a certain sense were theoretical. 'Theoretical' here indicates the establishing or expounding of the whole, the world, which serves as the background for a thing to appear in its full 'thingness' and for man to live his life in full authenticity, to exist as mortal. The 'practicality' of the two remaining chapters consists in showing that earth and gods are reflected in things and dwelling. By doing so a better understanding of the phenomena of the earth and the gods will be achieved which is the aim of this study.

The first section of this chapter will briefly indicate the traditional approaches to the problem of the thing. The second section will show that Heidegger's understanding of an artwork can be considered as his attempt to disclose the 'thingness' of a thing. The third section will present the fully developed understanding of a thing as the assembler of foursome. In the fourth section of this chapter an attempt will be made to compare the Heideggerian and the traditional modes of thinking the 'thingness' of the thing. The fifth section will deal with the consideration of the problem of space, since 'thingness' in-

volves 'spaceness.' The sixth and last section will give an outline of
the Heideggerian philosophy of thing.

I. TRADITIONAL UNDERSTANDING OF THING

The 'thingness' of a thing for Heidegger does not consist in its objectivity, i.e. in its relation or correspondence to a subject, but in its
sojourn in the world. A thing sojourns when it "has arrived to an
abidance within the realm of revelation." [1] A sojourning being within
the realm of revelation is never an object. Objectivity indicates the
possibility of a being to be represented in a subject. The representability by a subject, and not the sojourn in the revelation itself, is
considered in traditional philosophy as that which constitutes the
'thingness' of a thing.

In traditional philosophy the thing is grounded by the intellect.
The representability in the mind (either human or Divine) is the
foundation of a thing.

> Representation supplies sufficient ground for the sojourn of that which
> sojourns, as of an object in returned relation to a subject. By supplying sufficient
> ground, the representation becomes the sole mode by which the relation of
> modern man to the world is determined and thus by which modern technology
> is made possible. [2]

Heidegger goes down to the foundations on which the modern
approach to a thing rests and tries to bring out the deeper roots of the
'thingness' of a thing. In his *Sein und Zeit*, Heidegger does not develop the 'thingness' of a thing directly but deals with the implementality of an implement which consists in its reference to the
world. [3] In his *Holzwege*, he goes deeper into the problem of 'thingness'
by investigating the problem of an artwork.

"What is then really a thing insofar as it is a thing?" asks Heidegger
in his *"Der Ursprung des Kunstwerkes,"* the first essay of his *Holzwege*. [4]
Heidegger enumerates here different things, such as a stone on a
country road, a clod, a pitcher. Milk in a pitcher or water in a well are
also things. Things are clouds in the sky, a thistle in the field, a leaf in
the wind, a hawk over the forest. There are also things which themselves do not appear. Such is the Kantian *Ding-an-sich*. Even God is

[1] Heidegger, *Holzwege*, p. 319.
[2] Heidegger, *Satz*, p. 148.
[3] Cf. p. 35.
[4] Heidegger, *Holzwege*, p. 10.

considered as a thing. "To say it briefly," says Heidegger, "the word 'thing' names here everything whatever which is not a nothing." [5]

Such a broad concept of a thing does not give any hold for a firm starting point and makes it impossible to investigate the 'thingness' of a thing. "Besides, we also shun," Heidegger says, "calling God a thing. We shun likewise taking the peasant on the field, the janitor at the boiler, the teacher in the school for a thing. Man is no thing." [6] Even a deer in the forest and a bug on the grass is not merely a thing. Heidegger concludes that, most positively, things are the so-called things of nature, such as: stone, clod, wood, and things of usage, the utensils, such as: a hammer, a shoe, a belt.

What is the 'thingness' of a thing? Before proceeding to determine the 'thingness' of a thing, Heidegger first indicates that in previous philosophy the 'thingness' of a thing has not been properly determined. He shows it in a brief critical review of the traditional theories concerning the thing.

A piece of rock is hard, heavy, extended, massive, formless, rugged, colorful. These are the characteristics which this thing has. Hence, the thing is not these characteristics but rather that which is underlying them. A thing is a substance and the characteristics of the thing are accidents. Such an approach to a thing is clear, planned, systematic, but therefore artificial. According to Heidegger, the substance-accident structure of a thing is not natural, in the sense that it does not reflect the true structure of a thing, and only seems to be natural because of long use.[7]

Another attempt to determine the 'thingness' of a thing by traditional philosophy was made by the consideration of a thing as the unity of sensual data. According to Heidegger, we never just perceive singular data and then combine them into unities. On the contrary, things themselves are closer to us than these sensual data. We do not first of all see the patches of colors and then unite them into a unity of a human face, but rather we first see such and such a person and only in the margin of our observation do we perceive this or that feature of his face.

The third approach of traditional philosophy to the 'thingness' of a thing tries to do justice to the inner structure of a thing as well as to its external characteristics. In this approach a thing is considered

[5] *Ibid.*, p. 11.
[6] *Ibid.*
[7] *Ibid.*, p. 14.

as formed matter. That which persists in a thing, i.e. the 'thingness' of a thing, is the context of form and matter. Such an approach is orientated by the looks or the appearance of a thing and it can be applied to natural as well as to man-made things.

Is the distinction of matter and form sufficiently founded? Heidegger doubts it. Also the broad applicability of the matter-form formula makes it doubtful whether this formula is the proper way of disclosing the 'thingness' of a thing. This formula in a broadened sense can be applied to any being whatsoever.

Are the principles of matter and form really the ultimate principles in the 'thingness' of a thing? Things such as a ewer, an axe, a shoe are made. The making of them is determined by the 'what-for' of these things. The 'what-for' expresses the serviceability of the thing. Serviceability "is that principal feature from which this being views us, i.e. throws a ray on us, and therewith sojourns and is a being at all." [8] By the serviceability of a thing its matter and form are determined.

Since a shoe is used for walking, leather or rubber is selected for its durability, toughness, and flexibility. The form, too, is determined in response to the serviceability of the shoe, depending on whether these shoes are for the field, for dancing, or for playing. Matter and form are not the primary determinants of an implement (a shoe, a ewer, an axe); they are subordinate to serviceability. Serviceability, again, is not the ontological structure of a thing, but of an implement. Hence, matter and form in no wise express the 'thingness' of a thing but merely presuppose it.

These three theories or their combinations dominate the whole of the traditional philosophy of a thing. Instead of revealing the 'thingness' of a thing, they merely cover it and prevent any attempt to think the 'thingness' of a thing by the pretense that the answer is already given. Heidegger's phenomenological method is for the greater part an attempt to approach things without the interference of the traditional thing-interpretations. Such an approach is much more difficult than it may seem to be.

If one is acquainted with the different scientific insights, the understanding of a simple thing – such as a blossoming tree in a meadow – the way it is in itself may become more difficult than if one is without such an acquaintance. "Does the tree stand 'in consciousness,' or does it stand in a meadow?" asks Heidegger. "Is the meadow lying in the soul as an inner experience, or is it spread out on the earth? Is the

[8] *Ibid.*, p. 18.

earth in our head, or do we stand on the earth?" [9] Various 'exact' sciences would 'prove' that what we seemingly think to be a tree is "an emptiness with randomly interspersed tiny electrical charges which whizz about with great speed." [10] Accordingly, the tree is only in our head.

Heidegger does not try to say that these sciences are false, he only indicates that what they discover and 'prove' is not the 'thingness' of a thing but one of the many possible cases which can respond one way or another to a system which is already established before the approach to a thing. Depending upon the system, the answers received from the thing vary. "One who asks psychological questions," says Stephan Strasser, "will receive psychological answers; one who proceeds as a biologist will arrive at biological insights; one who searches as a sociologist will propose sociological solutions, and so on." [11]

The phenomenological method means an attempt to free the question from all such prejudicial systems and thus to let reality itself say its word. This means letting things be the way they are assembled in the *logos* of Being. Such letting-be is responding to the *logos* of Being. The question thus becomes a response.

II. ARTWORK AS AN ASSEMBLER

A phenomenological approach to reality can be illustrated by an art student who tries to draw the real things. For such a student one of the most important things to overcome is the temptation to put in the drawing not what he really sees but what he knows should be there. Such a student may constrain himself to draw all five fingers of a hand while he may be seeing only one finger, and the others only partially, on his model.

Sciences and traditional philosophy presume that the 'thingness' of a thing consists in the representability of the thing in the mind, i.e. in its objectivity. "The 'thingness' of a thing, however," says Heidegger opposing the understanding of a thing as of an object, "neither rests in the fact that a thing is a represented object, nor is it all determinable from the objectivity of an object." [12] For a thing to become representable, it is necessary for it to be already revealed or to appear

[9] Heidegger, *Was heisst Denken?*, p. 17.
[10] *Ibid.*, p. 18.
[11] Strasser, *op. cit.*, p. 3.
[12] Heidegger, *Vorträge*, p. 165.

in reality. "Regardless of which way we represent it, we can only represent that which previously from itself has ignited itself and has shown itself in the light it brings along with it." [13]

Since Plato, traditional philosophy has maintained that the source of light, and thus of revelation and being, is intellect. For the early Greek philosophers *physis* brings forward itself in its own light. To disclose the 'thingness' of a thing properly is only possible by letting the thing appear in its own light – by letting it appear the way it is laid in the *logos* of *physis*.

In his essay on artwork, after having indicated the insufficiency of the traditional approaches to the 'thingness' of a thing, Heidegger begins a totally different mode of investigating a thing. This mode is the previously indicated so-called phenomenological method by which things themselves are allowed to come into word. In this manner Heidegger describes a pair of peasant shoes:

> Out of the dark opening of the worn-out interior of the shoes stares the toil of work-paces. In the firm massy heaviness of the shoes, the tenacity of tardy walk is stowed – the tardy walk over the far–spread and uniformly matched furrows of the field, over which the harsh wind halts. On the leather lies the dampness and the saturation of soil. From under the soles slips the loneliness of the country-road in the fading evenings. In the shoes reigns the suppressed call of earth, its silent giving away of ripening grain and its unexplained refusal in the barren fallows of wintry fields. All through this implement the uncomplaining anxiety for the security of bread, the wordless joy of an overcome distress, the shiver at the arrival of a birth and the shudder at the threat of death are drawn. To earth belongs this implement and in the world of a peasant is it preserved.[14]

For a thinker trained in the traditional philosophy, such thinking does not even seem to be philosophical thinking, but merely poetical utterance. Whoever knows Heidegger, would never suspect him of taking cover under poetic thinking because of his ineptness for rationalistic thought. Not because of his insufficiency to think rationalistically does he abandon rationalistic thought, but because of the insufficiency of rationalistic thought to disclose the fundamental realities.

On the other hand, the above description of peasant shoes is not so strange after all. To say simply and soberly that shoes are for the protection of the feet may raise a series of implications, such as: the feet need protection because of the hardness of the ground and the length of the fields; shoes have to be sturdy and water-repellent because of the muddiness of the soil or because of deep snows in the winter;

---

[13] *Ibid.*, p. 169.
[14] Heidegger, *Holzwege*, pp. 22–23.

the long walks are required by the need to prepare the soil and to take care of the plants needed to feed oneself and the family – those who are helpless either at their birth and several years thereafter or when facing death or in the distress of illness. To approach anything in the best and most complete way, it is necessary to indicate many other things to which it refers. Here we can recall how Heidegger's *Sein und Zeit* investigates the implementality of an implement.[15] The structure of an implement, as is indicated there, is the 'for' (*um-zu*); for instance, a hammer is *for* driving nails, a saw *for* sawing wood, etc. An implement essentially refers to something beside itself; it "does not manifest itself as a particular being, it enters into an implemental complex which as such is at *Dasein*'s disposal." [16] By referring to the totality of the implements, a singular implement *eo ipso* refers to us as the to-be-in-the-world, i.e. it indicates the world.

With his description of the peasant shoes, Heidegger does not claim to have disclosed the 'thingness' of a thing, but merely the 'implementness' of the implement. The 'for' (*um-zu*), Heidegger calls here serviceability (*Dienlichkeit*). However, serviceability is not yet the ultimate ontological structure of an implement. As the ultimate ontological root of an implement, Heidegger sees the dependability (*Verlässlichkeit*). Shoes can serve the peasant because they are dependable. They are dependable because they enable the peasant to go into raw fields, to go on the long roads, to go out in harsh weather. In the German word '*Verlässlichkeit*,' besides 'dependability,' Heidegger indicates an important connotation of 'letting' (*lassen*) which for him is the primary meaning as far as the ontology of an implement is concerned. A shoe is dependable because of its 'letting-ness.' "Because of it, the peasant is being-let-into the silent call of the earth; because of the dependability of the implement the peasant knows his own world." [17] A shoe with its dependability assembles the earth and the world at the feet of the peasant.

Another thing, which Heidegger describes phenomenologically in the essay on artwork, is the Greek temple.

It simply stands there in the midst of a rugged, rocky valley. The edifice surrounds the statue of god and lets it, in its concealment, stand out through the colonnade into the sacred sphere. Because of the temple, god is present in the temple. This presence of god is in itself the unfolding and confining of a sphere as sacred. The temple and its sphere do not float away into indefiniteness.

[15] Cf. p. 35.
[16] Biemel, *op. cit.*, p. 30.
[17] Heidegger, *Holzwege*, p. 23.

The temple-edifice disposes and at the same time assembles around itself the unity of those paths and relations in which birth and death, disaster and blessing, victory and disgrace, endurance and recession acquire their form and course in the destiny of human essence. The realm holding sway over these open relations is the world of this historical [placed into its destined mission] nation. From the world and within it, the nation comes back to itself for the accomplishment of its destiny.

Standing there the edifice rests on bedrock. This repose of the building draws out the darkness of the huge, and yet suppressed to nothing, supporting character of the rock. Standing there the edifice withstands the raging storm and thus shows the storm in its power. The gloss and gleam of the stone, even though it seems to be such because of the kindness of the sun, nevertheless, brings primarily to appearance the light of day, the breadth of the sky, the darkness of night. Its steady towering makes the invisible space of air visible. The unshakableness of the edifice opposes the waves of the sea and, because of its own calm, lets them appear in their fury. The tree and the grass, the eagle and the steer, the snake and the cricket enter the shape provided for them and thus they come forward as what they are.[18]

In these two paragraphs, a thing – this time not an implement but an artwork – is shown as that which opens a world for the nation to live its history as befalling and at the same time brings the earth forward into the world of the nation. The first paragraph of the description of the temple considers the world. God here is indicated as that which brings forward the holiness (the holy whole) itself. In this light of holiness the unity of diverse relations is made possible which gives to man "the prospect upon himself," [19] and which thus enables man to find his ways in his world.

The world is never an object which stands before us and can be observed. The world is the ever unobjective to which we are subordinate as long as the paths of birth and death, of blessing and curse hold us thrust into Being. Where the essential decisions of our history befall us and which are taken over and abandoned, misunderstood and again sought by us, there 'worlds' the world.[20]

An artwork is essentially that which erects a world. Such an erecting of a world is only possible when the world grounds itself upon the earth. The lucidity of the world is stabilized by the weightiness of earth.

An artwork always consists of some material such as stone, wood, color, word, tone, etc. In an implement such materials are consumed; they are set back into the implement and disappear in its serviceability, while the materials in an artwork are splendidly revealed. Stone comes forward with its gloss, colors gleam, and tones sound. In all this

[18] *Ibid.*, pp. 30–31.
[19] *Ibid.*, p. 32.
[20] *Ibid.*, p. 33.

coming-forward of materials, the artwork itself retreats and seems to disappear. The earth is "the concealing coming-forward." [21] The artwork, by retreating, "holds the earth in the openness of a world." [22]

The earth, as held out into the openness of the world, even though it appears in stone, in color, in tone, never discloses itself. Any attempt to penetrate stone or color or tone with the intention of disclosing its essence fully and clearly fails. The earth discloses itself as closed. The earth "shows itself when it remains concealed and unexplained." [23]

The world, as that which throws everything into light, and the earth, as that which conceals, are interrelated and can never be separated. "The world grounds itself upon the earth and the earth projects itself through the world." [24]

The strife between the world and the earth is the procedure of truth. Truth is never merely victorious revelation; "truth is the primeval strife in whose procedure a mode of openness is obtained into which everything stands and from which everything receives itself and comes forward as that which is." [25] This strife between the world and the earth can only be truth when it takes a stand within the realm of openness obtained by it. This taking-stand is realized by the settling down of the truth into a thing, the artwork. "The clearing of an openness and the settling within the openness belong together." [26]

The fundamental feature of an artwork is the guarding of the earth and the world in their strife, i.e. letting the truth take place. An artwork assembles the earth and the world and, by guarding them in their strife, guards the truth as the openness which is obtained by the struggle between the earth and the world. This openness ultimately is world. The strife of the earth and the world merely expresses the structure of the worldness of world. Just as to-be-in-the-world is world where man in his essence (mortality) expresses the worldness of world, so the earth as standing in strife with the world is the structure of world shown in another way. A completely expressed structure of world is given in Heidegger's consideration of the thing as an assembler. Here not just a partial structure of world is shown, a structure which involves merely the mortals or the earth, but a complete structure which explicitly shows all four transcendental or worldly phenomena, namely: earth, sky, gods, and mortals.

[21] *Ibid.*, p. 35.
[22] *Ibid.*
[23] *Ibid.*, p. 36.
[24] *Ibid.*, p. 37.
[25] *Ibid.*, p. 49.
[26] *Ibid.*, p. 50.

III. THING AS ASSEMBLER

Heidegger's philosophy of an artwork can be considered as one of the stages of his philosophy of thing which, when fully developed, treats thing as the assembler of foursome. An artwork is that whereby truth in taking a stand accomplishes a disclosure of a world. Truth is disclosure. Ultimately it is world as revelation of Being. Since an artwork is that wherein the light of Being breaks into revelation from concealment (and that is exactly what makes an artwork an artwork), the artist is never the cause of an artwork, but merely a helping hand in the procedure of its creation. By creating the artworks, artists serve Being. They let Being take a stand and thus appear in their works. "They throw the block of work in front of the overwhelming order and detain the world thus disclosed in it. With these works comes principally the order, the φύσις, to a standstill in the sojourning beings." [27] An artwork thus assembles the world by reflecting it in openness; and world, again, in a different manner assembles the work securely in its order or light and thus makes it a work.

In *Vorträge und Aufsätze*, where he reaches the full development of his problem of thing, Heidegger sees in the very 'thingness' of a thing the assembling of the world. Thing is thing by assembling the world, the interplay of the foursome.

How a thing is an assembler of foursome, Heidegger shows by his description of a pitcher or ewer. The essence of a ewer consists in the outpour of a flow of liquid. Even by refusing to outpour this gush, by being empty, the ewer, nevertheless, has its essence in outpouring. Only a ewer can refuse to outpour and not a hammer or a scythe, as Heidegger indicates.[28] A ewer outpours water or wine. Heidegger thu begins the description of a ewer:

"In outpoured water sojourns the spring. In the springwater sojourns stone and in stone the dark slumber of earth which receives the rains and dew of the sky. In springwater the nuptials of sky and earth sojourn. They likewise sojourn in wine from the fruit of the vine in which the cherishing of the earth and sun of the sky are mutually engaged. In the outpour of water, in the outpour of wine always the sky and the earth sojourn. But the outpour of a gush is the ewerness of a ewer. In the essence of a ewer sojourn the earth and the sky." [29]

[27] Heidegger, *Einführung*, p. 47.
[28] Heidegger, *Vorträge*, p. 170.
[29] *Ibid.*, pp. 170–171.

The gush from the ewer quenches the thirst of men; it refreshes their leisure days.[30] In the days of festivities, ewers are used in devotional exercises to gods. The offerings of liquids in sacrifice to the gods are, according to Heidegger, the most essential outpourings.

The word 'gush' truly means sacred drink – offering and sacrifice. 'Gush,' 'to gush' sounds in Greek χέειν, in Indo-European – *ghu*. This means to sacrifice. To gush, when properly accomplished, sufficiently thought, and genuinely said, is to offer, to sacrifice, and therefore to outpour. And only then does gushing – as soon as its essence is stunted – become mere tapping until finally it degenerates to ordinary bar-tapping. Gushing is not mere pouring-in or pouring-out.[31]

This description of a ewer shows that a thing, when thought 'non-systematically,' i.e. when not approached from a well-articulated and worked-out subjective order, but when allowed to be in its own order, brings or reveals all four of the foursome. A thing assembles earth, sky, gods, and mortals. A thing, when approached 'systematically,' is over-powered by the system and does not show its true face, does not reveal itself in the *logos* of the world. To approach a thing non-systematically does not imply here disorder or passivity. To think, in the sense of *legein*, means to see and understand a thing the way it is laid in the order of *logos*.

A thing, when let to be the way it is in itself, brings the structure of world to light. This structure is the interplay of foursome. To bring the interplay of foursome to light means to let the four sojourn. Such sojourning "brings the four into their own light." [32] An illuminated object, even though it brings forward and lets the light sojourn upon itself, in no wise is anterior to the light. A thing lets sojourn the light upon itself by sojourning itself in this light.

A man who makes a ewer – analogically to what previously has been said regarding an artwork – is not the maker of the ewer; he merely stands in the service of the higher powers and by responding to them helps them to come to appearance. This can be applied to all man-made things such as buildings or bridges.

A bridge connects two banks of a river. It brings them together and reveals them as banks. Not only the banks of the river but also the provinces on both sides of the river are brought together and assembled along its stream. A bridge "brings the stream and the banks and the land into a reciprocal neighborhood. The bridge *assembles* the

---

[30] *Ibid.*, p. 171.
[31] *Ibid.*
[32] *Ibid.*, p. 172.

earth as lands along the stream." [33] The pillars of the bridge withstand the power of the stream when the storms of the sky or melting snows raise the waters; "the bridge is prepared for the weathers of the sky and their changeable nature." [34]

A bridge holds an open path for the stream and secures a way for mortals. Bridges guide man in multiple ways: some of them connect sections of the town, some lead the way to neighboring villages, to churches or markets, some carry a harvest wagon from the fields to the barns, some direct the trail into the fast traffic highways. "Always and in different manners the bridges guide to and fro the lingering or hasty ways of man, so that they can get to the other banks, until finally as mortals they go to the other side." [35] Mortals are always en route to the last bridge. Whether they are aware of it or not, they are always tending to "surmount that which is familiar and profane in order to bring themselves before the sacredness of the deity." [36]

A bridge, just as previously a ewer, "*assembles*, in *its* manner, the earth and the sky, the deities and the mortals unto itself." [37]Heidegger admits that in ordinary understanding, a bridge is thought of as something for itself. Besides being a bridge, it may also express symbolically or parabolically something else. Ordinary understanding thinks of things as substances, and therefore it does not think of them primarily. 'Thingness' primarily is assemblage – assemblage of the diversified structure of the world (the interplay of foursome) and the other things as grounded in the world.

In *Sein und Zeit*, the understanding of an implement can be considered as the forerunner of the understanding of a thing. There, too, an implement is never treated in its isolation. Implement essentially indicates, and thus assembles, the other implements and the whole perplexity of their indications, the to-be-in-the-world or the world. In *Sein und Zeit*, too, things indicate and assemble the earth and the sky, even though this is not shown explicitly. "In the roads, streets, bridges, buildings – in a certain way nature is discovered by care-taking.[38] A covered platform of a railway station takes into account bad weather; the public lighting of streets – darkness." [39]

---

[33] *Ibid.*, p. 152.
[34] *Ibid.*
[35] *Ibid.*, p. 153.
[36] *Ibid.*
[37] *Ibid.*
[38] The care-taking is a mode of dealing with the things or handling them in the every-dayness; cf. pp. 32–33.
[39] Heidegger, *Sein und Zeit*, p. 71.

IV. SUBJECTIVE AND ESSENTIAL UNDERSTANDING
OF THING

The centuries-long habit of thinking of things in isolation gives an impression that "all that belongs to the assembling essence of a thing is a decoration supplementally added to it." [40] For scientific or so-called exact thinking, the Heideggerian way of thinking of things as the assemblers of the foursome appears as poetical or arbitrary thinking. Such thought, when considered from a 'sober' scientific viewpoint, would seem to be inferior, not as yet developed to the proper height, poetizing, or even subjective – in scientism's understanding of subjectivism – thinking. However, scientific thinking itself is fundamentally subjective thought in the sense that only what accords to the mind of the subject, only what is representable in his mind or intellect, is true. Even though – as it is in the positive sciences – our mind or understanding corresponds to the thing and not the thing to our mind, nevertheless, we affirm as true or real not what a thing really is, but how far it is representable in our mind. The subject still remains the central factor in spite of the fact, or rather exactly because of the fact, that such sciences are highly objective. Ultimately so-called objective reality is subordinate to man and is fitted to his requirements. It is ultimately an instrument in man's hand.

Heidegger does not consider exact scientific thinking as superior; nor does he consider it inferior. According to him, sciences do not think at all. Thinking is not that which makes discoveries leading to an extension of our control of reality. Thinking discloses essences. Essences are disclosed by virtue of disclosure, and they are always on the way to the ultimate disclosure or revelation, the light of the world, the *logos*. The light of the world, and not the light of the mind, is the disclosing factor. Man's disclosing activity consists in letting the essences appear the way they are in the light of the world, in *logos*. By responding thus to this light, man is in the disposition of the world as *physis*; and his thinking, human *logos*, is merely a response to the *logos* of *physis*. Essential thinking is servile thinking in respect to reality, while scientific thinking is dominating thinking in respect to reality.

Essential thinking, in scientific conception, is thinking in gener-alities or abstractions, whereas for Heidegger essential thinking is

[40] Heidegger, *Vorträge*, p. 154.

"radical [going down to the roots], turned-to-reality thinking." [41]
Radical thinking is thinking as rooted in the soil of Being. Such
thinking is a primary or a transcendental thinking in the sense that it
reaches the worldness of the world. To say something essential about
a within-the-world being means to show it as bringing forward the
source of 'thingness,' the world, into light. To make a comparison, an
illuminated object is essentially thought of when it is thought of as in
its own visibility bringing forward or emphasizing the light itself
which as such is invisible. A thing is essentially thought of when it
reveals or assembles the interplay of the foursome – the world. Essential thinking for Heidegger is thus concrete and transcendental at
the same time. In no wise is it opposed to existential thinking; rather
it is existential thinking in the sense of 'ec-sistential,' i.e. referring to
the world, thinking.

Realities, as approached and explained scientifically, are diverse
groups of within-the-world beings. Here realities are 'freed' from their
background, the world; they have become uprooted realities. By
explaining diverse phenomena in the world – starry skies, thunder,
rock-formations, growths, and animals – science releases man from
thinking of essences, i.e. from being disposed to the transcendental
powers, and thus make him, too, an uprooted being. When the exact
answers concerning diverse realities are given, we become indifferent.
'There is nothing more to look for,' we say; and instead of turning to
the essences of the things, we occupy ourselves with the things as
servile to us and as having their meaning merely from such servility.
Neither things nor we ourselves are then held in unity by the transcendental powers of the world, but merely by interpretive scientific
systems; *logos* becomes replaced by logic. [42]

The essential thinking given in Heidegger's phenomenological de-
scriptions of the ewer, of peasant shoes, or of the Greek temple, is
merely an explicit mode of the thought common to men who live an
earthly life. Their thinking is not explicit, is not formulated; it is not
'mental' thinking but rather 'lived' thinking.

Such 'lived' essential thought can be illustrated by an example. One
of the most important implements in the life of a peasant is the wagon,
and especially the wagon wheel which is the most important and most
difficult part to make. The wagon wheels are made of a tree which is

[41] Heidegger, *Wahrheit*, p. 5.
[42] 'Logic' here stands for 'rationality.' The word 'logic' here is preferred to '*ratio*' because
it connotes *logos* and is a perverted *logos*. '*Ratio*', too, is the Roman translation of Greek *logos*.

tough, weather-resistant, and flexible. The ash tree is such a tree.

When seeing a well-grown, straight ash tree, the peasant necessarily thinks of the felloe, or by seeing wheels or felloes, he thinks of the ash tree. For making wheels great skill and care are needed, because wheels have to be made to withstand the roads of the country, bumpy with rock and stone, or the forest trails with hard, protruding roots of trees. Often in the rainy spring days wheels sink deeply in the mud. When such wheels are being made, the rugged country roads and weather conditions have to be taken into account.

In addition, these wheels often have to carry heavy loads of crops from the field; they have to be dependable for man to care for his everyday interests, to reach towns or other distant places speedily. They also have to be attractive because on holidays they take man to the church for his religious homage. Wheels do their share in carrying a newborn baby, often from remote rural areas, to the church for christening, and the very same wheels often carry a coffin to the graveyard.

Even though the peasant when making these wheels does not think of all this explicitly, however, it is known and taken into account. He knows it the way a man knows the world in which he handles the things of everydayness and solves his problems. Such thinking is not under his full control: it is responsive to the various requirements of reality.

Wheels 'assemble' roads and different sections of the country; by their very 'thingness' they refer to the weather, to dry and rainy seasons; somehow they bring man into unity within the diverse ways of his life, from birth to death. By showing man as assembled in his full being-man, they show him as facing God and giving Him an account of his life.

V. THING AND SPACE

When a bridge is built, the place on the river becomes a place. Previously it has not been a place. It merely was one of the many spots along the river for a possible bridge. For a place to be a place a thing which takes place is necessary. "The place cannot be known independently from a being which occupies it." [43] Hence, "a bridge never comes to be at a certain place but from the bridge itself arises a

43 Biemel, *op. cit.*, p. 69.

place. A bridge is a thing: it assembles the foursome; it assembles it, however, in such a manner that it grants steads to the foursome. From these steads the sites and ways by which a space is spaced-in determine themselves." [44]

According to Heidegger, space or room primarily meant the "cleared site for a settlement or a camp." [45] Such a site can become a site if there is something which takes place there. A thing as place assembles a site to itself – to a site. A thing which is a place, i.e. which can assemble a site and space, is a building. This may be a bridge, a house, a hut, a temple.

A thing ultimately is the assembler of foursome. Also a thing as place primarily is the assembler of steads of the foursome. By taking these steads, the four fundamental realities of foursome break into space and thus give a start or found a space; they space-in a space. A thing assembles the steads of the foursome and therefore it can also assemble the site and many diverse localities; in its own way a thing-place spaces-in a space. Localities become localities by their being in a certain nearness or farness from a place. A bridge as a place holds in its spacing-in order different localities such as: parts of a town, markets, factories, stadia, resort areas, etc. Such localities are charac-terized by their distance from their assembling bridge; they are brought into the area of the bridge, into its orbit. They are spaced-in by the bridge.

Localities as belonging to the space of the bridge can thus come to be treated as standing in a certain distance from the bridge or from one another. These distances are *spatia*. Distance or *spatium* tends to become indifferent from where and to where it extends. When it becomes totally indifferent, totally something for itself, it is then an extention. Extensions are tridimensional, and they are the foun-dations for acquiring a purely mathematical understanding of space. *Spatium*, extension, and mathematical space are rendered possible and ultimately grounded by the things as places. When various things and their places are approached and expressed in calculating mathematical dimensions, this approach may give an impression of grounding, whereas truly a dimension as such is grounded in the things as places. That which ultimately founds everything, may itself appear as founded by what it founds. A thing can be made clear and precisely determined

---

[44] Heidegger, *Vorträge*, p. 154.
[45] *Ibid.*

mathematically, but in no wise can its essence ever be revealed mathematically.

An example may help to illustrate Heidegger's understanding of space. Let us pretend that an airplane crashes in the forest mountains. Passengers survive. To protect themselves from the weather they build a shelter. They gather dry wood for their fireplace. They discover a spring which supplies water. From the mountain stream they get fish and on some sunny mountain slopes, wild strawberries for their food. On a high bare cliff they make smoke signals for possible searching airplanes.

Before these people crashed by chance into these mountains, the mountains were known as a wooded area remotely located from such and such cities. Here with these people this region becomes in a certain sense a world.

Their shelter is a thing which is a place. The shelter standing in the middle of the camp makes the camp a camp. Camp here is a site as assembled by the shelter as a place. By their shelter or camp different localities are held in variously correlated unity. These localities are: firewood locality, spring, fishing spot, strawberry slope, and their signal cliff.

The camp with all its localities is the space where these people live through their days of distress; it is their world. The earth appears in such a world with all its rugged genuineness. When walking on their paths, these people have to take into account various rocks and jutting cliffs, rough slopes, fallen logs, thick bushes or brush; they have to detour to avoid them. Firewood, fish, water, and strawberries are the gifts of the earth.

Assembling all the localities and paths leading to them, the camp assembles the earth and brings it forward into the world of the survivors. It gives stead to the earth. The shelter protects these people from winds and rain, from their being-exposed to the inhospitability of the sky. By thus indicating the sky, the shelter assembles it into the space of these survivors; it gives stead to the sky.

Assembling the earth and the sky, their camp assembles the people as struggling for survival. Here in this camp, where their lives are endangered by their being confronted with death, their lives are revealed in their full extent. Man in this camp is pulled from the securities of ordinary life and placed on his own feet; he is gathered together into unity from his dispersedness or disunity of previous irresponsible and secure modes of living. To be exposed to death (*Sein zum Tode*) is to live fully or to be disclosed fully, to be revealed. The camp grants stead to men as mortals.

Exposed to the elements of nature in this camp, man experiences his dependency. Here he has lost control of the situation and is left to the mercy of other powers. Here – even if he may not have done it in his previous life – he raises his eyes to the sky with hope not only for possible searching airplanes but also for the grace of the heavens. Such a camp of survival necessarily has religious implications, and God, by guiding human fate, somehow is present here – has His stead.

After their rescue, as long as they live, these people will refer to their sojourn in this camp as a world, where earth, sky, gods, and they themselves, in their essence of mortality, were near and real in their experience, as having steads in their space.

What is such a camp? A man, skilled in mathematical and geographical sciences, would tell these people it is a region of uninhabited mountain forests, situated in such and such geographical latitude, having a certain geological formation and climate peculiarities. And that is just about all that can be said objectively about it. These people would know then that not all was said. There was something overpoweringly real in that camp of survival. The earth appeared there not merely as a certain geological formation but as an impenetrable might which was protective and nourishing, endangering and merciless at the same time. The sky was higher, and especially in the night with the stars shining it appeared fearful and threatening, and a great deal more real than the ordinary sky in the city above the lights of the street. Their own lives out there were shown in a totally different light. This place in the wilderness brought up questions and gave hints for answers never thought of before – questions and answers concerning the human essence. God, too, was not something to think about on holidays, something more or less vague, but frightfully real as holding the reins of everything in His mysterious hands.

A camp, as described by the scientist of geography, is approached from a planetary viewpoint. A camp is a spot on a map or globe. Our planet is a member of the solar system in the universe. Everything is a point in the universe which can be exactly determined. The distance between stars can be precisely calculated and masses of planets or their weights can be expressed in exact numbers. A camp, too, can be determined mathematically with precision. Even though things thus exactly and precisely determined are known with certitude, such knowledge is not primary knowledge, i.e. not the knowledge of ultimate realities which let them be in our space.

The distance between the shelter of the camp and the signal cliff expressed in exact numbers can be abstracted from the shelter and the signal cliff and be considered as a line from Point A to Point B. Such an indifferent line can become the basis for constructing an indifferent, universal space. When such a universal space is established, it becomes an easy medium to determine everything possible within such a universe. Thus determined, things may seem to be well and objectively grounded.

If there were no shelter or any other thing as assembler of the world, no universal space would be thinkable. "Things are places which grant steads to the foursome; these steads space-in a space." [46]

In *Sein und Zeit*, *Dasein* is thought of as that which by distancing and directing grants space or spaces-in everything.[47] Here the situation seems to be reversed, because a thing becomes that which spaces-in *Dasein*, the interplay of the foursome. Even though it seems so, there is no reverse or shift in Heidegger's understanding of space from his early to his late works. A thing as an assembler does not let space out of itself; it merely reflects the interplay of the foursome or the world and lets it take stead in it, just as an illuminated thing lets light sojourn or take stead upon itself. By sojourning at the thing, or by being assembled by the thing as place, foursome or *Dasein* breaks into space by taking stead in the thing.

Things as granting steads are buildings.[48] Man, when building a building, is partaking in the spacing-in procedure. Man can never be thought of without space, and space is not thinkable without man. "Space is never opposite to man. It is neither an external object, nor an inner experience. There are not men and beside them *space* ... By naming 'man,' I already name the sojourn in the foursome with the things." [49] Such sojourning is dwelling.

In *Sein und Zeit*, Heidegger analyses the phenomenon of the to-be-in-the-world. This same phenomenon in his late works comes forward as dwelling. To-be-in-the-world is in constant commerce with the things of its surroundings, the implements. Implements in their essential structures are the indicators of world as thought of in the mode of everyday to-be-in-the-world. Hence, implements are assemblers of the world, and *Dasein*, as standing in commerce (*Umgang*) with the implements, dwells.

[46] *Ibid.*, p. 155.
[47] Cf. p. 40.
[48] Heidegger, *Vorträge*, p. 155.
[49] *Ibid.*, p. 157.

The human way of being is dwelling. "The mortals *are*. This means that by their dwelling they penetrate [*durchstehen*] the space on the grounds of their sojourning with the things and places." [50]

The essential feature of dwelling for Heidegger is the treatment with consideration or the sparing (*schonen*) of things by letting them assemble the foursome. Such a mode of being (*dwelling*) is then a response to the *logos*, or to the assemblage of *physis*, or it is *Dasein* as 'ec-sistence,' the standing-out in the openness of Being. Since Being in his late works is ~~Being~~ , therefore the standing-out in the openness of Being is the standing in the interplay of the foursome and letting it appear as assembled by the things – it is dwelling.

VI. PHILOSOPHY OF THING

According to Heidegger, the German word '*Ding*' (thing) was in archaic German '*thing*' and its meaning was 'assemblage.' [51] Only by a coincidence this Old German word is spelled identically to English 'thing.' A thing when thought primarily and essentially is not an object with such and such features, but an assemblage of foursome. The 'essentiation' of a thing – a thing as let to be what it really is – Heidegger calls 'thinging.' "The thing 'things.' The 'thinging' assembles. It assembles the sojourn of foursome by letting it take place in something which sojourns – to take place in this or that thing." [52]

The Old High German word '*thing*' in the sense of assemblage was often used to express a convocation of men for the consideration of public affairs. With similar meaning the Romans used their word '*res*.' Therefore *res publica* primarily did not mean the state but a thing of public importance. [53] Interestingly, the Lithuanian word '*dalykas*' indicates similarly, as does the Roman '*res*,' the matters of public importance and also expresses 'thingness.' The root '*dal-*' of Lithuanian '*dalykas*' indicates 'part,' 'taking part,' 'participating.' 'Participate' in Lithuanian is '*dalyvauti*.' Participating is a mode of assembling. The Old High German *thing*, just as the Roman *res* or Lithuanian *dalykas*, means assemblage as the basic and essential stroke of 'thingness.' According to Heidegger, the English word 'thing,' too, in some usages has preserved the meaning of the Roman '*res*.' [54]

---

[50] *Ibid.*, p. 158.
[51] *Ibid.*, p. 172.
[52] *Ibid.*
[53] *Ibid.*, p. 173.
[54] *Ibid.*, p. 174.

The Roman *res* has been used interchangeably with *causa*, which
did not primarily mean 'cause,' but the matter of consideration or
decision. The French *chose* originated from the Roman *causa*.[55] Consequently, *chose* also indicates the assembling character of things.

All these implications of assembling and dynamism in the early
meanings of the word 'thing' in various languages show that a thing
has not always been understood statically as an object of representation. The early Greeks indicated the dynamism of things by understanding them with temporal connotation as the sojourning beings.
A sojourning being takes place in the openness of Being by coming
forward into it, sojourning there, and retreating from it. A sojourning
being thus, by being itself assembled in the openness of Being, on its
part assembles this openness by indicating it as the realm of its
sojourn.

A thing as a sojourning being has the temporal character of being
present. However, presence here is presence in the realm of openness
and has spatial implications as well. The German word by which
Heidegger expresses the 'being present' is *'gegenwärtigen'* which literally means 'to sojourn in front of.' However, the *'gegen'* of *'gegenwärtigen'* for Heidegger is not understood conventionally as 'in front
of' but essentially as *'in der Gegend,'* 'in the realm.' Therefore, he says
that *gegen* is not "the 'in front of' a subject, but the open realm of
revelation into which and within which the sojourner sojourns." [56]

A thing is not a static object. A thing 'things.' " 'Thinging' is the
approximation of the world. Approximation is 'essentiation' of proximity. As far as we spare thing as thing, we inhabit this proximity.
The approximation of proximity is the proper and the only dimension
of the mirror-play of the world." [57] This proximity is the proximity
to the things. Proximity to the things is *eo ipso* proximity to the world
as the interplay of foursome. The proximity to foursome is proximity
to the earth and gods. Heidegger is a realist, but his realism indicates
the proximity to gods, and therefore is deeply religious realism.

In his essay on an artwork, Heidegger has shown an artwork as the
assembler of the earth and the world and thus as an opener of a world.
The artworks are comparatively rare things made by the great men.
In his essays on building and on thing, Heidegger shows a thing as an
assembler of foursome and thus as an opener of world. Here not just

[55] *Ibid.*
[56] Heidegger, *Holzwege*, p. 319.
[57] Heidegger, *Vorträge*, pp. 179–180.

an artwork assembles a world but anything whatsoever. This may give an impression that each thing grants, 'things,' or approximates a new world. Truly, however, each thing approximates *the* world; each thing, when thought of in its most profound essence, 'essentiates' or 'things' the world in its own way. Just as each being sojourning in the light of Being reflects the light of worldness, so each thing in its own way 'things' the interplay of foursome, approximates the earth and the gods.

Heidegger's way of thinking things returns their religious aspects to them which have been taken away by 'clear-sighted' scientific approaches. "God holds the beginning, and end, and middle of all existing things," says Orpheus fragment 6.[58] According to Jaeger" the founders of mysteries knew well that the deepest secrets are found only in things that are seemingly obvious." [59]

Things had religious implications not merely in the Orphic teachings, but they were such for the Greeks in general. The Greek gods do not reveal themselves by omitting things or nature; on the contrary, they look at man from the things themselves. "A deity does not act here from a beyondness into the inwardness of man by a mysterious contact with the human soul. The deity is one with the world and advances to meet man from the things of the world. .... Not by turning into himself does man experience the deity but by going out, by seizing, by acting." [60]

Things as backed by the world or by worldly realities – earth, sky, gods, and mortals – are themselves held in unity by these realities. Without being backed by these realities, things would be lacking 'thingness.' A feeling for that which backs things is experienced when reading Hamsun's description of cow-mushrooms. "Even the big cow-mushrooms are not altogether meaningless; not a mere white emptiness to the eye. The big mushroom does not flower, it does not move, but there is something overturning in the look of it; it is a monster, a thing like a lung standing there alive and naked – a lung without a body."[61] In this strange and rather vile description it is hinted that things are not merely the effects of sensual perception, they are backed by a power of reality not sensually perceivable, but nevertheless real and experienceable. The worldly realities are real there in the things – assembled and brought forward by the things. And a thing consists

58 Freeman, *op. cit.*
59 Jaeger, *op. cit.*, p. 99.
60 Otto, *Götter*, p. 172.
61 Hamsun, *op. cit.*, p. 180.

in assembling these realities by letting itself be assembled by these realities.

Only a couple of decades ago the older generations of Lithuanian peasants referred to fire as 'sacred.' The women, when starting the fire in the morning or putting it out at night, made the sign of the cross upon it. The earth and bread for these people was 'sacred earth' and 'sacred bread.' To sell land even though in time of great distress was somewhat sacrilegious in their eyes. A peasant worked or performed his acts on his land somewhat like a priest performing his acts at the altar of God. In just such a spirit, Hamsun describes Isak, the sower, in his *Growth of the Soil:*

> For generations back, into forgotten times his father before him had sowed grain; solemnly, on a still, calm evening, best with a gentle fall of warm and misty rain, soon after grey-goose flight. Potatoes were a new thing, nothing mystic, nothing religious; women and children could plant them – earth apples that came from foreign parts, like coffee; beets. Grain was nothing less than bread; grain or no grain meant life or death.
>
> Isak walked bareheaded, in Jesu name, a sower. Like a tree-stump with hands to look at, but in his heart like a child. Every cast was made with care, in a spirit of kindly resignation.[62]

Whoever has been living on a self-sustaining farm knows that, depending upon whether rye grows in a sandy section or in a clayey field, the taste of bread is somewhat different. If the weather is favorable in the rye-harvest season and the shocked rye dries out without getting a drop of rain – that year, the bread is light brown and has a better taste. If, when drying in the field in shocks, the rye is soaked by rains, the peasant family eats dark and inferior-tasting bread all year. Here bread, its texture and taste, assembles the earth and the sky. In the appearance of bread and in its taste are reflected and sojourn the earth and the sky.

Bread also assembles gods and mortals. Bread is called 'holy' because it is a gift of God. A peasant is dependent upon weather conditions, which he cannot influence. After the grain has been sowed in the earth, a peasant can only raise his eyes to heaven and pray for more favorable weather. When rye grows well, the peasant thanks God. When rye on the field is dying, it is a sign of God's wrath. In either way God is present here.

In the previously quoted passage of Hamsun, it was said that 'grain or no grain meant life or death.' Here grain is that which reflects man in his struggle for survival, and thus it shows him as mortal.

[62] *Ibid.*, pp. 30–31.

According to Bachofen, in prehistoric Greece "just as everything in the state and in life was a religious act, so also were garments. Its change meant an offense against a deity." [63] Even the change of clothing-styles in primeval society is not pending upon human disposition, but abides in the hands of gods. When such a change actually took place in ancient Megara, it was not an act of human decision but the result of the struggle of religious powers. Here a thing (clothes) is shown as backed by the higher realities which are reflected in this thing, and thus this thing is meaningfully held in unity by such a reflection or assemblage of these realities. Garment 'things' or approximates the gods who even though inexplicitly entail the other three of the foursome – earth, sky, and mortals.

A thing primarily belongs in the hands of higher realities. A change of the mode of dress is decided by gods, and man accomplishes such a change merely in response to the gods. Similarly a maker of a thing is never the cause of such a thing; he simply stands in the service of the higher realities of the foursome. When, as Heidegger shows in his essay on building, the people in the *Schwarzwald* built their homes 200 years ago, they were responding to the realities of the foursome. This being open to the interplay of foursome was the basic factor which directed the building of such a house. There, when a man built his home near a spring and facing south on a hillside protected from raw winds, it was the earth itself which directed the construction of such a building; and man by being open to the demands of earth was merely a responder. When he extended the roof far down past the wall of the house and gave it a sufficient slope, he had taken into consideration the stormy winter skies and possible accumulations of snow on the roof. Here, too, the weather, or rather the sky, determined the structure of the building. A built-in corner for prayer was a response to God, and a place for a cradle and a coffin reflected man in his mortality.

Man's standing in the foursome is his standing in the service of the foursome: his subordination to its direction and guarding of its truth. By being thus exposed to the superior realities, man brings the foursome into openness or lets it take stead in the thing built. This standing in the openness of the interplay of the foursome is dwelling. *"Only when we are able to dwell, we can build."* [64]

Building is a mode of dwelling. Since building is responsive, it *eo*

---

[63] Bachofen, *op. cit.*, p. 188.

[64] Heidegger, *Vorträge*, p. 161.

ipso is knowledge. To respond to the world or to the foursome means to know them. Only because man has an understanding of a world can he respond to it, i.e. can he dwell and build. Dwelling is thus knowing the world or its *logos*. "*Logos* is the articulated structure of Being," as Eugen Fink states.[65] The most fundamental articulation, upon which all the subsequent articulations are based, is the articulation of the world itself as the interplay of the foursome. According to Heidegger, *logos* primarily does not mean language or saying, as it is commonly accepted, but "the laying of one beside the other, the bringing together, briefly – assembling; all along with this assembling, the distinguishing of one from another is accomplished." [66]

Since dwelling thus is *logos* in the sense of human responsive *logos*, it is *eo ipso* thinking. According to Heidegger, thinking – just as building – is a mode of dwelling.

> Building and thinking are always in their own way indispensable for dwelling. Both however are also insufficient for dwelling as long as they are separated and go on their own instead of listening to each other. They can do this, when both building and thinking listen to dwelling, when both remain in their limits and know that one as well as the other comes from long experience and incessant practice.[67]

Here it is clearly shown that dwelling, which in the first phase of Heidegger's thought is to-be-in-the-world and in the second 'ec-sistence,' is ontologically anterior to technical performance as well as to speculative intellection – anterior to practice and theory. A wise man thus is not a speculative man with intellectual or spiritual capacities by which he orderly forms and subdues reality, but a man turned to the things as the assemblers of the ultimate realities which constitute the world, and by being subordinate to which, man is man. By knowing things and by letting them 'thing' the world, man guards the truth of the world; he is the "shepherd of Being." [68] To be aware of the superior realities and to guard them in one's thoughts and in the things one makes and cultivates, is to dwell and be wise all in one.

---

[65] Cf. footnote 60 on p. 148.
[66] Heidegger, *Einführung*, p. 95.
[67] Heidegger, *Vorträge*, p. 162.
[68] Heidegger, *Holzwege*, p. 321.

CHAPTER VIII

DWELLING

In *Sein und Zeit*, Heidegger is not primarily a philosopher of man but of the world. World here is dealt with as *Dasein*, the to-be-in-the-world. Authentic *Dasein* – *Dasein* as disclosed in its wholeness – is the running-forward-toward-death. In the to-be-in-the-world, as well as in the running-toward-death, *Dasein* is shown as transcendence. For Heidegger, transcendence means a stepping over the beings and thus a standing in the worldness of the world. Whereas the to-be-in-the-world basically is the inauthentic transcendence, the running-toward-death is the authentic transcendence. The authentic transcendence in Heidegger's *Was ist Metaphysik?* is shown as the being-held-in-nothingness.[1] Nothingness here is world. Transcendence, the standing in the world, is the basic feature of man's being-self. The running-forward-to-death *eo ipso* is the coming-into-self, into the very essence. Mortality is the essence of man. When man lives a 'deathless' life, he is not his own self but merely common-man's self; he lives inauthentically.

The coming-into-self, the mortality, is advance. In German 'advancing' is '*Zu-kunft.*' This word for Heidegger stands for 'coming-into-self' as well as for 'future' (*Zukunft*). The English word 'advancing' beside the 'coming-towards' also has the connotation of 'future.' The running-toward-death by disclosing the authentic self discloses *eo ipso* the concealed self, the self of everydayness – discloses it in its concealment, in its withdrawal from the authentic self; discloses it in its past. Advancing thus is the withdrawal into the past. Transcendence, as the stepping over the beings into the worldness of world, is not escaping from beings but a return to them to face them from one's authentic self instead of from a common-man's self. Such a facing is the presence in the situation. This presence is the presence among the things facing them from the worldness, from the being-held-in-nothingness, from the mortality.

˙.¹, Heidegger, *Was ist Metaphysik?*, p. 32.

It would be wrong to think of time as a phenomenon for itself, knowable without the *Dasein*. *Dasein* by its transcendence, by its advancing from the self of its mortality, initiates time. Man as mortal renders it possible that time becomes time or world becomes world. "As long as *Dasein* temporizes itself, there *is* a world ... Without an existing *Dasein*, there is no world there [*da*] either." [2]

In *Sein und Zeit* world is investigated as the to-be-in-the-world, i.e. as world brought into openness or time by man in his mortal essence. Man in his mortality necessarily is interrelated with earth, sky, and gods. In Heidegger's late works, as well as in his early ones, world is not thinkable without man in his essence, without man as mortal. Being and man are not two separate beings. Being essentially turns towards man as mortal. Being is not something which, besides being this something, now and then can turn toward man; but Being is the turning-toward-man itself. Being and man belong together, just as a call and a response belong together. [3]

Man is the shepherd of Being. In this littleness man does not lose anything but gains by being admitted to the truth of Being. He gains the essential poverty of the shepherd, whose dignity rests in his being-called by Being itself into the guardianship of its truth. This call comes as the throw from which originates the 'thrownness' of *Dasein*. Man is, in his being-sent essence, a being whose being, as 'ec-sistence,' consists in the fact that he dwells in the proximity of Being. Man is the neighbor of Being. [4]

This dwelling in the neighborhood of Being is not something symbolic or something rare and exceptional. It simply indicates man as dwelling – dwelling in his real concrete world. Even though dwelling means 'living-in,' to dwell is not something very easy and simple; care is needed to maintain dwelling in the proper heights, i.e. as sojourning in the neighborhood of Being. Dwelling may become perverted; it ceases then to be 'ec-sistence,' the openness to Being, and becomes 'in-sistence,' the closing of oneself away from Being.

At the end of the previous chapter [5] it was indicated that building and thinking are modes of dwelling. To see how building and thinking are related to dwelling, it will be necessary to study these phenomena. An inquiry into these phenomena will also give a better insight into the phenomenon of dwelling. The first section of this chapter will treat with the problem of building, and the second one will study the problem

² Heidegger, *Sein und Zeit*, p. 365.
³ Heidegger, *Seinsfrage*, p. 28.
⁴ Heidegger, *Humanismus*, p. 29.
⁵ Cf. p. 262.

of dwelling in its relation to *logos*, as the ultimate foundation of thinking. Since *logos* is brought to man by gods in their divine *logos*, man when responding to *logos* is a prophet. For Hölderlin-Heidegger, just as for the Greeks, a prophet is a poet, a namer of gods. The third section will deal with the poet as a prophet, in which man will be shown in essential interrelation with gods. Such interrelation is cult; and cult, again, is not a matter of everydayness, but of festivities occasionally taking place. The fourth section thus will reflect upon the festival as the time when man receives the standards of dwelling from the gods. Festivity, as the coming together of men and gods bares the godless man as opposed to the godly man. Therefore the fifth and last section will be occupied with the problem of godless and godly man.

I. BUILDING AND DWELLING

According to Heidegger, the German word '*bauen*,' 'to build' primarily meant 'to dwell.' The archaic forms of '*ich bin*,' '*du bist*,' and '*bis*' (*sei*), i.e. 'I am,' 'you are,' and 'be,' were '*buan*,' '*bhu*,' '*beo*.' These are the forms of the archaic '*bauen*.' [6] Hence, '*bauen*,' 'to build' primarily meant 'to be.' Such 'to be' in no wise was an abstract mode of 'to be' but a very concrete mode of being which implied the taking care of things. This care-taking, again, means the concern or heed for things which already exist in man's natural environment such as plants and animals; or it means the making of the things which do not exist without man. The mode of being, as care-taking and making of things, is suitably expressed by dwelling.

'To cultivate' and 'to build' are expressed in German by one and the same word '*bauen*.' "Both ways of *Bauen, bauen* as to cultivate in Latin *colere, cultura*, and *bauen* as to erect buildings, *aedificare* – are implied in the proper *Bauen*, 'dwelling.' " [7]

Heidegger relates the German word '*wohnen*,' 'to dwell' from the Old Saxon *wuon* or Gothic *wunian*. These words have meant 're-maining' in the sense of 'residing' or 'detaining oneself' or 'dwelling.' The Gothic *wunian* expresses more explicitly the meaning of such remaining. "*Wunian* means to be peaceable, brought to peace, re-maining in it." [8] The word 'peace' in German is '*Friede*' which has the

---

[6] Heidegger, *Vorträge*, p. 147.
[7] *Ibid.*
[8] *Ibid.*, p. 149.

connotation of 'freedom' in the sense of undisturbing, letting be free. *'Zufrieden sein,'* 'to be brought to peace' means "to be guarded from mischief and threats." ⁣ To be guarded from means to be spared. To be spared here does not merely indicate to be left alone, but has a positive aspect of taking care or of being taken care of. "To dwell, to-be-brought-to-peace, means to be freed within the *Frye*, i.e. within the openness that spares everything in its essence. *The principal feature of dwelling is sparing.* It penetrates dwelling in its full extent."[10]

When man is dwelling in the above indicated deep, richly concrete sense, he is sparing everything within the openness of Being, the world. Such a sparing lets things be the way they are, and when a thing is allowed to be the way it is, it is the assembler of the world, the interplay of the foursome. To spare a thing means *eo ipso* to spare the foursome – the earth, sky, gods, and mortals. Hence, dwelling is being open to the world, to the ultimate realities.

Things are spared when they are taken care of in the sense of being cultivated or being built. To cultivate and to build – as it was already indicated – in German is *bauen*. The German word *'Nachbar,'* 'neighbor,' according to Heidegger, in its archaic form was "the *Nachgebauer*, one who dwells nearby." [11] To dwell nearby means to cultivate and to build things in the neighborhood. Hence a neighbor is one who is open to the higher realities next to us. In the modern world the 'neighbor' merely indicates someone who is spatially dwelling next door. Not the higher realities hold modern men in unity and thus make them neighbors, but merely spatial proximity. Such ties tie loosely and break easily. This is often exemplified by modern neighbors who may live next door for years without even knowing what the neighbor is cultivating or building.

Just as is neighborhood, so also are the building and making of things and the care-taking of not man-made things brought into a highly respectable place by considering them as the assemblages of foursome. To make a thing does not mean primarily to cause something as far as its form or construction is concerned or to mold a disposed reality according to some idea possessed by us, but it rather means our own being-disposed to the higher realities and standing under their directions.

Building brings foursome forward in a thing. A built bridge or a

⁹ *Ibid.*
¹⁰ *Ibid.*
¹¹ *Ibid.*, p. 146.

made ewer – as was shown in the previous chapter – assembles the world as the interplay of the foursome and shows or allows the four of the foursome to appear in their true essence.

A thing, even though it assembles foursome, in no wise is anterior to foursome. By reflecting the foursome, a thing itself is held in the unity of the 'thingness.' The foursome, as the ultimate realities, hold things in the unity of their 'thingnesses' and in the unity with the other things in the world. The builder or the maker of the things, too, is exposed to these realities. By building or by making the things, the builder or the maker of them lets these realities come forward into a thing. The being-exposed to the realities of the foursome means to be used by them, to be implied in their holding or backing-everything-up activity. The world, the mirror-play of the ultimate realities of the foursome, brings itself forward to appearance by using man. Man is the spot (*das Da*) of Being (*des Seins*), therefore his essence is *Dasein*, to-be-in-the-world.

By sparing things we are open to earth and sky, to gods and mortals. By sparing things we spare these ultimate realities. Things approximate these realities to us. "The thing lets the foursome sojourn. The thing 'things' world." [12] " 'Thinging' means approximating the world." [13] Hence, by making or sparing things, i.e. by standing under the directions or the standards of the foursome, we ourselves sojourn in the neighborhood of that in which everything whatsoever takes its start by being held in unity by it. This neighborhood is the ultimate root of 'homeness.' "The most proper and the best feature of 'homeness' rests in the being-near to the source, and nothing but this. Therefore, faithfulness to the first source is innate to such a 'homeness.' " [14]

Home, as the neighborhood to Being, can only be properly realized by sparing things. When we rule things, as the modern man does, we are homeless; we are homeless even though we have a place to live. Home for the modern man is something subordinate to him just as any other thing or instrument he possesses. Inasmuch as any other instrument is easily exchangeable or replaceable, so also is a home. A home becomes identical to a house.

"With difficulty forsakes a place one who dwells near the first source," says Hölderlin.[15] When a home is the proximity to the first

12 *Ibid.*, p. 179.
13 *Ibid.*, pp. 179–180.
14 Heidegger, *Erläuterungen*, p. 21.
15 Hölderlin, *op. cit.*, p. 62.

source, it is the standing in the interplay of foursome, the to-be-in-the-world. This neighborhood of Being is not 'homeness' in merely a symbolic or figurative sense. To be in the neighborhood of Being is to take care of things and to dwell in one's home with a respectful or with an open attitude to the worldly realities. Man is homeless not because he has no house, but because he does not spare the things and thus does not dwell in the proper sense of dwelling.

Someone who is born and reared in a country home,[16] and who for a succession of years has been living in a city where he moves from one section of town to another and constantly occupies different 'homes,' knows – when he comes back to his country home – what 'homeness' as neighborhood to foursome means. He knows it when he sees the weather-beaten dwellings and barns of his ancestral country home; when he hears the rustling trees protecting his home from winds and sun; when he walks on the paths on which he used to run as a child. Home for him is the place where he has seen the earth bearing fruits for him and his people in the blessed years or failing to give sufficient crops in the lean years. Here he has learned to understand the mild summer skies which send the warmth of the sun and the blessing rains to the earth, or the stormy and disastrous autumn and winter skies tearing the roofs of the dwellings or breaking the branches of the trees. Home for him is the place where he has learned to pray to God and where he has heard his parents' clamorous words to the heavens in the days of calamities and their grateful words in the days of favor.

Home is the neighborhood of gods and earth,[17] and to dwell means to sojourn in this neighborhood. In this neighborhood, the neighborhood of men is also rooted. It has been previously [18] indicated that a neighbor is the one who spares things and thus spares the higher realities nearby. The sparing of the higher realities, as is shown here, is the neighborhood of the foursome. Hence, the neighborhood of man is founded in the neighborhood of the foursome. The neighbor is the one who dwells nearby in the sense that he sojourns in the neighborhood of gods and earth; and he is not the one who only spatially lives next door.

Anyone who merely exploits nature can never *be* in nature's

[16] The example of a country home is used here because the country home better than the city home has preserved the proper dwelling.

[17] Gods and earth stand here as an abbreviation of the four of foursome. Such abbreviation is justifiable because any one of the four of foursome necessarily indicates the other three.

[18] Cf. p. 266.

neighborhood. He lives godlessly which also means inauthentically. By not being his own self, he can never be anyone's neighbor. His homelessness rests in his being closed away from, being not a neighbor of, Being. "It is one thing, only to abuse the earth, and another to receive the blessing of the earth and to become at home in the law of such reception in order to guard the 'homeness' of Being." [19]

To dwell is to be exposed to earth and gods. Since modern man rules the earth, and since the things which he handles are the rationalistically determined results of his planned activities, he no longer knows the earth as worldly reality but only as matter which is disposed to his planning and forming activities. Neither does he see any traces of gods in the things – of gods as the powers of reality, which by backing the things, hold them in their 'thingnesses,' and which themselves are reflected by these things.

The things of modern man do not reflect anything any more because they are fully controlled and thus suppressed things in the sense that they are not allowed to be what they are – to assemble the fundamental realities. When a thing is not suppressed, it 'things,' i.e. approximates the world to us so that we can become at home in its neighborhood. Modern man, since he is essentially homeless, is also a worldless man. The world he lives in is a perverted world because it is a man-made world. In such a world everything succumbs to the human rule, everything reflects man in his self-centered happiness. A man who is the center of his world can no longer have great aims (greatness necessarily points to the more-than-man; it is 'ec-sistence'). His aim is the establishing and securing of his 'world-centric' position. In such an aim lies his subjective or egocentric happiness. Nietzsche calls such a man, the last man.

"Alas!" says Nietzsche, "there cometh the time when man will no longer launch the arrow of his longing beyond man – and the string of his bow will have unlearned to whizz!" [20] For such a self-centered man anything great is nonexistent. He has no sense for it. "What is love? What is creation? What is longing? What is a star?' – so asketh the last man and blinketh." [21] 'In-centric' or 'in-sisting' man does not know what a star is because stars are above man. He does not know what a star is because everything is subordinate to him, and what is not subordinate to him – what is above him – is not really there; it is

[19] Heidegger, *Vorträge*, p. 98.
[20] Friedrich Nietzsche, *The Philosophy of Nietzsche* (New York: The Modern Library, 1927), p. 11.
[21] *Ibid.*

nothing. Without being open to what is greater than man, without 'ec-sistence,' man is condemned to be small. Things which surround the small man in his artificial world, the suppressed things, are small, too, because they reflect only man in his smallness. "The earth hath then become small, and on it there hoppeth the last man who maketh everything small." [22] The small man, lacking a sense for greatness, knows, however, 'in-centric' happiness. " 'We have discovered happiness' – says the last man and blinks thereby." [23]

Only by being subordinate to realities which exceed him can man be great. In the first volume of his *Weltgeschichte*, Friedrich Christoph Schlosser describes Cynegirus, Aeschylus' brother, who in the Persian War held a boat with both of his hands and refused to give it to the enemy. When the Persians chopped off both his hands, he held the boat with his teeth until he died. The Greek was fighting for his world which exceeded him and to which he subordinated himself. In his combat and death the greatness of his world was reflected. To be man means to guard the truth of man's world in works. A world cannot be a world without someone who is in the world and who guards it in its worldness, just as a road cannot be a road without a traveler who, by traveling on the road, guards or helps to bring forward the 'roadness' of the road. We can talk about the Greek world because the Greeks in their works spared the ultimate realities, earth and gods, by letting them appear in their works. The works of men are their answers to the demands of world-realities, the foursome. These answers are the being-exposed to the demands of the foursome and are not godless self-satisfaction which disregards any higher realities and simply makes everything servile to oneself. These answers constitute the 'man-ness' of man.

The works of man are not only his works of art, but also the things built or made by him, and also his words, his language. All human works are grounded in the language of Being, in *logos*.

II. DWELLING AND *LOGOS*

Language ultimately is rooted in *logos*. To say something is to bring it into the light. *Logos* has the character of disclosing light. To sojourn in the light of *logos* means to appear, to be disclosed or revealed, to be true. *Logos* is revelation, is truth.

[22] *Ibid.*
[23] *Ibid.*

Logos, by holding everything in its disclosing light, sustains, articulates, and grounds everything in this light, the order of Being. *Logos* is fundamental *ground*, ultimate reason. *Logos* is the primary language. The human saying, human *logos*, is based in the primary *logos*, in the bringing-itself-forward *physis*. "The saying and talking of mortals," says Heidegger, "already from the early beginnings take place as λέγειν, as laying. Saying and talking 'essentiate' themselves as the letting-lie in the realm in an assembly all that which sojourns as laid in revelation." [24] Since our human saying or talking is letting-lie what already is laid or assembled, what is already disclosed, it never is founded in us, and never is an instrument in our hands, but is supported and grounded in the *logos* itself, the primeval language. Language arises from the revelation, the truth of the world, from reality itself, and not from the inwardness of man. It grows like a tree and is not a product of man.

The light of human speech is not in the possession of man; everything is revealed or appears in the light of *logos*, and the human *logos* rests and has its light from the primary *logos*. "Human reason," according to Eugen Fink, "is not fire but rather coal which can burn only in contact with *sophon* [*logos*]." [25] Reason *ultimately* is not a power located in us, given to our disposition, but is our standing in the *logos* of Being. The most significant feature of reason is the standing in the light, being-exposed to the light of fundamental realities – it is 'under-standing' in the sense of standing under.

Our standing in the light of *logos* is not merely standing by. "We stand in the light of Being subsequent to our essence: we stand in the mission of Being given to us by Being." [26] Heidegger indicates here [27] that the problem of understanding treated in his *Sein und Zeit* was misinterpreted by various philosophers and understood as the representation of reality in the human mind, whereas the basic element of understanding is the standing-in-the-light of reality, of Being. This standing-in-the-light *eo ipso* is the standing in the mission of Being. Being is in need of man as the guardian of its truth.

Physis as having come forward from concealment into revelation is *logos*. *Logos* is "the assemblage of Being (φύσις)." [28] The mission of man is the guarding of *physis* as that which emerges into the light of

[24] Heidegger, *Vorträge,* p. 212.
[25] Cf. footnote 60, p. 148.
[26] Heidegger, *Satz*, p. 146.
[27] *Ibid.*
[28] Heidegger, *Einführung*, p. 129.

its *logos*. Man guards *logos* in his words and thoughts. "That which is great and which persists in the thinking of the thinkers consists in the bringing to word that which always is sounding already." [29] *Logos*, as the language of *physis* is always 'hanging in the air.' By putting it into his words or thoughts, the thinker speaks or thinks. Language ultimately is not there for our disposition; it is not subordinate to us, but we stand in the service of language, and this service makes us men. "Language speaks and not man," says Heidegger. "Man speaks only by responding to the mission of language. Such responding is the proper mode by which man belongs to the light of Being." [30]

Why Being breaks into openness, we do not know. For Being to come into openness a response of man is needed to make the demand of approaching Being a demand, just as a traveler is needed for a road to be a road. Inasmuch as a road is never the possession of a traveler, but rather the traveler as traveler belongs to the road, so also language is not the possession of man, but man with his words and thoughts belongs to language.

In *logos* are rooted all the essences which hold everything in unity. "Language secures the treasure of everything essential in itself." [31] The openness of man to *logos* thus frees man to this treasure of all the essences and frees him thereby to his proper place in *physis* as the guardian of its treasures; moreover his freedom to the treasure of *physis*, freedom to its language, is man's awareness of this language. By such an awareness, man stands together with others on the same ground – on the ground of *logos* – and is in the same world with them; he can therefore understand and communicate with the others. *Logos* is placed out there in *physis*, in the world, and is never man's possession; therefore by standing in the world (to-be-in-the-world), man has the understanding of language and is understood by others as by those who stand with him in the same world. "The moral teaching of Heraclitus," says Burnet, "is summed up in the rule 'Follow the common,' .... the one wisdom which is fire. That is what is really 'common,' and the greatest fault is to act like man asleep." [32]

All the thinkers of the history of thought ultimately belong together because they are responding in their own manner to the *logos* which is common to all of them. Therefore an interpretation of a thinker cannot be proper which takes him from the road of *logos* and treats

[29] Heidegger, *Satz*, pp. 47–48.
[30] *Ibid.*, p. 161.
[31] Heidegger, *Hebel*, p. 33.
[32] Burnet, *op. cit.*, p. 168.

him in isolation. Often when the writings of great thinkers are hard to decipher, an approach to them from the road of *logos* helps, "because it guides the foot on a twisty path quietly through the broadness of sterile land." [33]

On the road of *logos* tripping or even being-lost is possible. The cause is not in the traveler, but in the road itself. Hard, rocky, winding sections of a path emphasize and make strikingly noticeable the level and comfortable stretches. Light can be revealed in its lucidity when interrupted by intervals of darkness. Truth as revelation already refers to the concealment from which it arises. Great living words or thoughts can only glare brightly in the midst of grey, dead, abused words; by upsetting these they reveal their full power. The trippings and being-lost from the way of *logos* belong to this way and do their share in building it.

To build the way of *logos* does not mean to make it, but to respond to it, i.e. to be open to it and to all the essences assembled within it – to listen to it. The human *logos* is the listening *logos*, and only the primary *logos* (*logos* of *physis*) is truly talking *logos*. However, listening as responding belongs to the talking which demands a response. The primary *logos* and the human *logos* are not two separate *logoi*; they belong together and are the same even though distinct. *Logos* is responded *logos*, and only the responded *logos* is truly *logos*, i.e. "the assembling laying-down" [34] or the articulation as such. Such articulation, the ultimate language, brings everything into its assemblage and thus makes it something. With a naming of a thing such a thing comes to being. This primary naming is not done by human words; however, it is not done without a man. Naming, as bringing into being, takes place in *logos* itself in which man takes part merely as a responder. This is not done by the ordinary human language, but by the primary, which is poetical language.

Poet and poetry in this sense are in German *Dichter* and *Dichtung* which are distinct from the mere poet and poetry of literature. *Dichtung* is the founding or grounding of a language of a nation. Such grounding is done by *logos* which uses a poet, the *Dichter*, to lay down its words in the realm of its light. 'Poet' and 'poetry' in the course of this chapter will be used in the above indicated sense of *Dichter* and *Dichtung*. Poetry thus will not have anything to do with verse-making; on the other hand, poet and poetry in the conventional sense will have

---

[33] Heidegger, *Feldweg*, p. 1.
[34] Heidegger, *Vorträge*, p. 215.

a lot to do with the poet and poetry as *Dichter* and *Dichtung* – those
are founded and grounded in these; the conventionally understood
poetry presupposes poetry as *Dichtung*. Poetry as *Dichtung* is the
primeval poetry as rooted in the primeval language of *logos*.
"Language is poetry [as *Dichtung*] not because it is the beginnings of
poetry [in the conventional sense], but poetry [in the conventional
sense] comes to being in the language because language guards the
primeval essence of poetry [as *Dichtung*]." [35] Not poetry makes
language poetical, but the poetic (*das Dichterische*) of language enables
poetry to become poetry. Poetry as *Dichtung* is the primary saying as
bringing to word the saying of Being. Since Being itself comes here to
word and appears, this primary saying, the poetry as *Dichtung*, is the
primary place of beauty, in the sense of the appearance of *physis*, and
thus is the foundation of poetry in the conventional sense.

Language, as the primary poetry, is that which is laid by Being, the
logos of *physis*. *Logos* founds the language of a nation and *eo ipso* it
grants things to it: it opens up a world.

> Poetry is the naming which founds Being and the essence of all things; it is
> not unrestrained speech, but such speech by which principally all about which
> we converse or discuss in our everyday language enters into openness. From
> here it follows that poetry never receives language as working material disposed
> to it, but poetry itself principally renders language possible. Poetry is the
> primeval language of a historical nation. Therefore, the essence of language,
> against the conventional opinion, has to be understood from the essence of
> poetry.[36]

Such subordination of human language to the language of Being,
is in no wise a fatalistic determination of man in his talking and
thinking. On the contrary, it frees man within his world; it frees man
to his word by granting him his world. Being uses a poet for this
granting of a world to a nation. A poet stands in the midst of the
birth of a world; he is the true to-be-in-the-world. In his *Hebel – der
Hausfreund*, Heidegger compares the poet to the moon. "The moon
brings light into our nights. However, the moon did not itself ignite
the light which it brings. It is merely a reflection which the moon has
previously received from the sun." [37] The *logos* of the poet is the reflection of the primary *logos* to which the *logos* of the poet primarily
belongs.

The to-be-in-the-world in Heidegger's late works – as has already

---

[35] Heidegger, *Holzwege*, p. 61.
[36] Heidegger, *Erläuterungen*, pp. 44–45.
[37] Heidegger, *Hebel*, p. 21.

been shown [38] – is dwelling. Dwelling is the sparing of the things in their 'thinging' of the world.[39] Since poetry is the ultimate to-be-in-the-world which grants things and language to a nation, it renders dwelling possible. "Poetizing is the real letting-dwell." [40] A poet is the one "who brings to language the house of the world for the dwelling of man." [41] The 'bringing to language' Heidegger explains as "the raising principally to a word that which previously has not been discussed, never said, and the letting appear that which so far has been concealed – letting it appear by saying it." [42]

Logos, the primeval language, is that which grants being. Anything which is, *is* by being assembled in the *logos*. To be means to belong to the language of Being. Language is the house of Being. "Since language is the house of Being, therefore we attain that which-is by the constant going through this house. When we go to the water-well, when we go through a forest, we always go through the word 'water-well,' through the word 'forest' already even though we do not pronounce these words or even think of anything linguistic." [43] We can go through a word because a word primarily is not a sound-word, nor a mental idea or image, but the word of *logos* which is the ground of being.

To dwell means thus to belong to the house of Being. The knowledge of the language of Being is nothing theoretical or mental; it is a very concrete mode of being, dwelling. Dwelling, again, is nothing prosaic; "poetically man dwells on this earth." [44] To dwell poetically does not mean to wander in an ideal, fairy-tale land, but to be on the very earth. "Poetizing principally brings man on the earth and for the earth – brings him thus to dwelling." [45]

Dwelling can only take place because of poetry. Poetry gives standards, grants things in their essences and thus enables men to be open to whatever is and to become at home in this world. Man becomes at home by building in the sense of *Bauen*, i.e. by cultivating plants and erecting buildings. Poetry is the first step in such building. "Poetizing, as the proper measuring of the dimension for dwelling, is the foremost building." [46]

[38] Cf. p. 264.
[39] Cf. pp. 265–266.
[40] Heidegger, *Vorträge*, p. 189.
[41] Heidegger, *Hebel*, p. 32.
[42] *Ibid.*, p. 33.
[43] Heidegger, *Holzwege*, p. 286.
[44] Heidegger, *Vorträge*, p. 192.
[45] *Ibid.*
[46] *Ibid.*, p. 202.

Poetry and dwelling do not exclude each other. A prosaic, as a totally unpoetical mode of dwelling, is rendered possible by·man's drifting away from the primary poetical mode of dwelling. "Dwelling can be unpoetical only because dwelling in its essence is poetical."[47]

Poetry, as disclosure of the essences of the things in the world of a nation, is the procedure of truth as revelation and is analogous to the procedure of thinking which also is a response to the *logos* of Being. A poet names the assemblages of *logos*, whereas a thinker thinks them. Both of them are subordinate to *logos* and stand in its service, in its procedure of revelation. "Thinking poetizes the truth of Being," [48] says Heidegger expressing the belonging together of thinking and poetry on the road of *logos*. Even though poetry and thought are distinct, they are not separated. Poetry ultimately is thinking by showing the articulations and interrelations of the essences in the assemblages of *logos*. As the world opener, poetry is the standing-in-the-world and thus 'under-*standing*.' On the other hand, thought, as the guarding of *logos*, the language of Being, is poetry. "The thinking of Being is the primary mode of poetizing. In it, language principally comes to talking, i.e. it comes into its essence. Thinking is primeval poetry .... The poetizing essence of thinking guards the rule of the truth of Being." [49] Thought, just as poetry, extends the rule of *physis* as *logos* within the world of a nation; and such extension is the disclosure of the nation's world.

Thinking as well as poetry is rooted in *logos* and stands in the service of *physis*.

Λόγος is a name for Being. But λόγος, namely that which lies as the basis, simultaneously is a supporter on which others lie and rest. We say – the basis, the ground. Λόγος names the ground. Λόγος is being and ground at once. Being and ground in λόγος belong together. Λόγος names this belonging together of being and ground. It names it by saying simultaneously: ¹) the letting-lie as letting-come-forward, the coming-forward-from-itself, the φύσις, Being; *and* ²) the letting-lie as laying-down, the building of the basis, the grounding, the ground. Λόγος names all at once Being and ground.[50]

The coming-forward has the aspect of beauty, is poetical; and the laying-down has the aspect of grounding, is thought-like. Both of these aspects – primeval saying or naming and primeval thinking – are implied in the primeval *logos*.

With *logos* as Being and Ground, Heidegger shows again that *logos*,

47 *Ibid.*, p. 203.
48 Heidegger, *Holzwege*, p. 343.
49 *Ibid.*, p. 303.
50 Heidegger, *Satz*, pp. 179–180.

the ultimate language, is the ground which is given to us by poetry
and thought and on which we find our ways (walking through the
forest, we walk through the word 'forest') in our world in which we
dwell. The thinkers and the poets do not dwell and besides, at a
certain part of the day, keep themselves busy with thinking or saying-
naming things in verses; but their thinking and poetizing ultimately
are the first steps of dwelling, the primary mode of being-man. The
road of thought, the *logos*, "remains to the stride of the thinker as
close as to the stride of a countryman who walks to mow in the early
morning." [51] *Logos* is the ground on which we dwell.

Dwelling is ultimately the response to *logos*, just as travelling is a
response to the road. The peak of dwelling is poetry. When dwelling
is taken in the sense of cultivating plants and of erecting buildings,
such a response to *logos* is posterior to the response to *logos* in thought
and poetry; and dwelling then is subordinate to thought and poetry.
However, if dwelling is taken in its ultimate sense, it is poetry as well
as thinking (letting-lie and grounding). In this sense poetry and
thinking are modes of dwelling, just as building is.[52]

Poetry and thought are the first steps of the opening of a world for
a nation. Therefore they are the first steps of its history. The German
word for 'history,' '*Geschichte*,' connotes the 'being-sent,' the 'being-
on-the-mission.' By responding to *logos*, human thought or saying,
called by Heidegger "mortal λέγειν," [53] places itself in history as in the
mission of *logos*. *Logos* guides man in his world through his history.

History is the realm held open ultimately by *logos*. Within this
realm man lives his history, goes through his decisions and omissions,
victories and failures. All these are the modes of man's response to
logos. The mortal *legein* brings (or fails to bring) within the *logos*
articulated essences of whatever-sojourns within the light of *logos*.
Such bringing is guarding. "In as far as λόγος lets that, which is laid
in the realm, lie as such in the realm, it discloses that which sojourns
in its sojourn. But the disclosure is ἀλήθεια. This and λόγος are the
same." [54]

Since *logos* is that which guides man in his history, grants to him
his words and thoughts, and assembles for him essences of everything,
in Heraclitus' fragment 64, it is referred to as lightning, the thunder-

[51] Heidegger, *Feldweg*, p. 2.
[52] Heidegger, *Vorträge*, p. 162.
[53] *Ibid.*, p. 218.
[54] *Ibid.*, p. 220.

bolt.[55] According to Heidegger, lightning here means the god of lightning, Zeus. Zeus guides and holds everything in an order within the realm of his light. *Logos* thus is Zeus.[56] The Greek myth refers to Moira as she who holds everything in her order. The order of Moira, the goddess of destinies, cannot be changed by anyone, not even by gods. Gods do not change Moira's order, but rather bring it into light. Zeus as Moiragetes [57] represents Moira's order as brought into light. Zeus thus is backed by Moira's order; he holds this order in the light. Zeus as Moiragetes in the early Greek philosophy was thought of as *physis* which as the constant coming forward into light is *logos*.

Logos assembles things in its light and thus holds them in meaningful unities. Even though *logos* primarily is the *logos* of *physis*, in the course of this study gods, too, have been considered as worlds and thus as *logoi*. Zeus as the god of light explicitly stands for *logos* as the all-disclosing reality. As Moiragetes he has been shown as the carrier of the light of Moira, which by the early Greek philosophers (Parmenides) [58] has been thought of as that which by granting destinies primarily brings itself forward – as *physis*. In this study gods frequently were indicated as the modes of *physis* or as the carriers of its light, its *logos*.[59] The *logos* of gods has been referred to as the divine *logos* or as *mythos*.[60] Man as the responder to *logos* is himself marked with the human *logos* which can be, or rather was, treated as the to-be-in-the-world, as 'ec-sistence,' as mortality, as dwelling. Dwelling, as the response of mortals to the demands of *physis'* or gods' *logos*, is done by poetizing, by thinking, by human works in history, by sparing things.

Things as assemblers reflect the *logos* which assembles them, i.e. they assemble *logos* in their own way. Since things are the assemblers of the realities of the foursome, they reflect the *logos* of *physis* which assembles them. This *logos* of *physis* is the *logoi* of earth and sky brought to man by the *logos* of gods and responded to by man's mortal *logos*. There are not four *logoi:* the *logoi* of earth and sky and the immortal and mortal *logoi*, but there is rather an interplay of *logoi* – *the logos*, the world. *Logos* as the demand of the *logos* of *physis* is brought to man by the gods in their divine *logos* and given to him with the hints of responses; and these responses are: the human language and

[55] Freeman, *op. cit.*
[56] Heidegger, *Vorträge*, p. 222.
[57] Cf. p. 346.
[58] Heidegger, *Vorträge*, pp. 251–252.
[59] Cf. pp. 189–190, p. 212, p. 221, p. 227, and p. 236.
[60] Cf. pp. 200–201 and pp. 222–223.

thoughts, man's works in history, and his dwelling by sparing things.
When thus responded to by man, *logos* is *logos*. There is no *logos* in itself.
To *logos* necessarily belongs language, dwelling, and history of man.

Perverted *logos*, logic, grounds and founds everything on the suppressed things, i.e. not on the things as the assemblers of ultimate
realities, but on the things as treated in their isolation or in their mere
objectivity – the things in their representation in a subject. Even
such suppressed things ultimately are obtained from the interplay of
the ultimate realities by ignoring such realities and thus by considering the things as suppressed.

Since a poet or a thinker with his mortal *legein* grants a world for
a nation to live,[61] he does it by responding to the *logos* of earth, sky,
and gods. In the *legein* of the poet *physis* and *mythos* are talking. The
framing-in of a world is a work of the founding *physis*, carried by
mythos and spelled out by poetry, the mortal *legein*. The work or word
of a poet is actually the work or word of the ultimate powers of the
world, and such a work or word primarily reflects these powers. "A
god always stands at the beginning," says Otto. "Through him is an
aim and a way and also a want given which must be gratified by
him." [62] A poet frames-in a world by naming a god. To name a god is
eo ipso to name earth, sky, and mortals. By the naming of foursome,
a world is named and given to the nation. Such naming, of course, is
not simply pronouncing the name of a god, but is the bringing of god
to utterance whereby earth and sky and the destiny of man is brought
to light. Such bringing does not force the god to utterance or to
appearance, but merely helps him to come forward by responding to his
approach — it is the being-exposed to the approach of higher realities.

When gods are primarily named, and the essences of the things come to words
so that the things can start to shine – when this happens – the human *Dasein*
[dwelling] is brought to a firm structure and placed on firm ground. The saying
of a poet is the establishing, not only in the sense of free granting, but also in
the sense of firm grounding of human *Dasein* on its ground.[63]

The framing-in of a world for the dwelling of man is accomplished
by taking the measure from gods to lay out the dimensions for the
dwelling. Man founds his dwelling on the divine standards. A deity
"is 'the measure' with which man measures his dwelling, his sojourn
on the earth under the sky." [64] In such a measuring consists the mortal

[61] Cf. pp. 273–274.
[62] Otto, *Dionysos*, p. 31.
[63] Heidegger, *Erläuterungen*, p. 43.
[64] Heidegger, *Vorträge*, p. 195.

legein. "To poetize is to measure." [65] Here is the responding character re-emphasized: the realm for human dwelling is measured with the standards of Being brought to us by gods in their divine *legein.* In the history of Greek cultural life this is confirmed in the Greek works and achievements in various fields. Literature, plastic arts, architecture, forms of social and political life, thought and understanding of things and nature were ultimately the results of their responses to their *mythos.* Here they got their standards to construct their dwelling, their *Dasein.*

In the *Iliad* Homer describes Skamandrius, son of Strophius, as "the mighty hunter, whom Artemis herself had taught to shoot all manner of wild things that the mountain forest breedeth." [66] Since dwelling, the manner of human existence, is formed by divine standards, all that man knows and can achieve is ultimately obtained from the gods. Gods are the teachers of men. "To poetize is to take measures for the dwelling of man." [67] The song of a poet is an attempt to respond to the standards of gods. "Zeus, father," says Pindar, "I pray that with the Graces' aid I may sing his excellence and on many occasions honor success, throwing my spear right close to the Muses' mark." [68] The spear of a poet here is his word, and the mark of the Muses is the divine standard.

Logos is not mere words but the interplay of the ultimate realities, the world. *Logos* holds human *Dasein* (dwelling) in a unity. The standards of human dwelling are backed by *logos.* By ignoring the standards of *logos* and by replacing them with 'logical' (rationalistic) standards, man endangers his *Dasein*: his dwelling comes in constant danger of falling apart. If we were to take away all our 'logical' (rationalistic) ties, i.e. the laws and regulations holding our modern dwelling in mechanical unity, we would instantly be in the midst of disorder. When *logos* is gone, 'logic' is merely a mechanical device holding together men and the things.

III. POET AS PROPHET

A poet is the peak of 'man-ness' – not because of his inner content or spiritual development but because of his openness ('ec-sistence') to

---

[65] *Ibid.*, p. 196.
[66] Homer, *Iliad*, p. 76; *Complete Works.*
[67] Heidegger, *Vorträge*, p. 198.
[68] Pindar, *op. cit.*, p. 123. (9th Nemean ode).

the higher, the wordly realities. Openness to the world is openness to *logos*, which enables man to speak a word. The poetical word is the primary word; it stands at the beginning of the language and history of a nation. "Only where there is a language, is there a world, i.e. the constantly varying extent of decisions and works, of deeds and responsibility but also of caprice and noise, of decline and confusion. Only where the world holds sway, is there a history." [69] Without a poet and his word there is no world. However, a poet or his word does not cause a world, but rather the poet and his word are needed for a world to be a world. *Logos* as demand is in need of a human response to be *logos*.

A poet and his word here are not a poet and his word in the narrow sense as a man pronouncing poetical sound-words, but a poet and his word here imply an artist and artwork in general. "Art in its essence is poetry [*Dichtung*]." [70] Poetry as *Dichtung* is the *logos* of *physis* as brought into the nation's world by the works of a man who is aware of *logos* – the fundamental language – and who lets it appear in his works. Not just artworks but also any thing as *thing* [71] reflects or assembles the world. A statesman, a sculptor, a thinker, a bridge-builder, and even a potter or a shoemaker – all of them are with their works ultimately responding to *logos* and letting it appear in their works. However, these prosaic modes of poetry presuppose the more fundamentally poetical mode. The making of a thing is a mode of dwelling, and poetry is the finest mode of dwelling. Poetry measures the dimensions for dwelling and the various modes of dwelling – cultivating, building buildings, and making implements. For making or building anything whatsoever, the world of dwelling has to be already experienced and outlined; it gives the standards for makings and buildings. Poetry, the fundamental mode of dwelling, does not receive the standards from an already framed-in world, but takes these standards as though from nothing, because it frames-in a world which renders possible anything whatsoever. "Poetical projection comes from nothing in the sense that it does not derive what it gives [truth of the world] from familiarities and things hitherto existing." [72] A work of art stands under different standards than those which are familiar to everybody. The truth of poetry "establishes the unfamiliar

[69] Heidegger, *Erläuterungen*, p. 39.
[70] Heidegger, *Holzwege*, p. 62.
[71] Cf. pp. 257–259.
[72] Heidegger, *Holzwege*, p. 63.

and at the same time upsets the familiar." [73] By doing this a poet rescues man from his being lost in inauthentic everydayness and brings him into the authentic mode of existence. Poetry founds a world. "The act of poetry is the basis which carries history; it is also the basis which renders language possible." [74]

Poetry can give the standards for dwelling – found history and historical language – because it is an explicit mode of the to-be-in-the-world; it is the being-held-in-nothingness. Such being-held-in-nothingness is the belonging to the 'worlding' (*Welten*) of the world, the standing in the service of Being – the coming forward *physis*. "Being is φύσις, that which from itself announces itself. This means that the revelation of itself is the basic feature of Being." [75] It is however misleading to say 'basic feature,' because then it may seem that Being is something besides this feature, i.e. something which carries such a feature. Therefore, it is more adequate to say that "Being belongs to the basic character of the self-revelation." [76] The self-revelation is the coming-forward, approach, demand. A demand creates room for an answer. When a demand is raised in the midst of nothingness, then room is given which anticipates an answer, an island is created to stand on and to reach into the abyss of nothingness. By taking this stand man becomes responder, and more than that – he principally becomes man. "To be able to hear is not a consequence of the fact that we are men, but its presupposition." [77] Being-able to hear is being-open to world, to not-a-thing, to nothingness; it is transcendence, mortality. "The most mighty [Being] is in need of the most finite [man as mortal]. By receiving the man-calling voice of Being, man acquires his own being." [78]

A poet, as standing in or being held in the worldness of world, himself is 'worlding,' i.e. he stands in the procedure of erecting the world for a nation to dwell. "To poetize is to take the measure for the dwelling of man." [79] From where does a poet take the measure? From a god. The essence of a god is holiness. Holiness is not a property of a god but rather vice versa: god is the property or is in the possession of holiness. Holiness as brought by a god is *mythos* in the sense of the divine *logos*.

[73]. *Ibid.*, p. 62.
[74] Wahl, *Hölderlin*, p. 75.
[75] Heidegger, *Satz*, p. 120.
[76] *Ibid.*, p. 121.
[77] Wahl, *Hölderlin*, p. 63.
[78] Eugen Fink; cf. footnote 60, p. 148.
[79] Heidegger, *Vorträge*, p. 198.

Holiness, often referred to as nature by Hölderlin, was called *physis* by the early Greek philosophers. *Physis* is the constant-coming-to-appearance, is *logos*. Previous to the early Greek philosophers, *physis* was apparently thought of as Moira, the deity of earth, and often identified with Mother Earth. Parmenides thought of Moira philosophically, namely, as nature or *physis*. According to Heidegger, for Parmenides, *moira* is "bestowal which protectingly imparts," [80] is "the imparting of destinies" [81] to everything. Such imparting is the assembling of everything upon itself by granting its share of 'beingness' to it. By imparting its share of 'beingness' to everything, Moira makes everything distinct from everything else and, at the same time, she holds everything in the unity of her order. Such distinguishing and unification of everything is *logos*. Even logic, the late outcome of *logos*, still obviously retains this distinguishing and unifying character by its abstract concepts or generalities. *Moira* in Parmenides' philosophy, just as *logos* in Heraclitus,' is not logical but ontological. It is the Being of the sojourning beings. [82]

Even though the *physis* in the early Greek philosophies refers more obviously to earth and sky, it actually retains the character 'above all,' namely, above men and gods. This character is clearly seen in Moira. "Gods and men are subordinated to μοῖρα." [83] *Physis*, even though primarily referring to earth and sky, implies ultimately *mythos*, the immortal *logos*, and poetry, the mortal *logos*. *Mythos* and poetry in their own way imply the *logoi* of earth and sky, that is the *logos* of *physis*. The world as the interplay of the four of foursome is *logos* as the interplay of *physis* (*logoi* of earth and sky), of *mythos* (*logos* of gods), and of poetry (*logos* of mortals). World as approached from earth and sky is *physis*; world as approached from gods is holiness (or Moira); and world as approached from man is *Dasein*, the openness to death, the mortality. *Physis* as well as holiness (immortality), as well as *Dasein* (mortality) is world. To see any one of the foursome as necessarily interrelated to the other three is to see it in its worldliness. When Hölderlin refers to the gods as subordinate to nature, he shows them as belonging to the foursome, i.e. as wordly. Also a poet, when he is thought of as taking the measures for dwelling from the gods, is shown as mortal, i.e. as worldly (in the sense of belonging to the round-dance of the world).

[80] *Ibid.*, p. 251.
[81] Heidegger, *Holzwege*, p. 340.
[82] *Ibid.*, p. 342.
[83] *Ibid.*, p. 340.

"A poet cannot name holiness by himself," says Heidegger in his commentaries on Hölderlin.[84] Gods are higher and stand closer to holiness than does man; they bring a ray of light and set the soul of a poet aflame. Only then can the poet name holiness, only then can his song succeed. A song is "the work of gods and men." [85] Gods bring the light of Being to men, and only when penetrating the darkness of mortality can this sacred light reveal the immortality of gods. The eternal refers to man in his mortality. "The eternal needs him so that it would be felt and expressed." [86]

Only someone whose mode of being is the being to death (*Sein zum Tode*) can really experience what life is. Neither an animal nor a god ever experiences death. Only a being who is exposed to the possibility of not-to-be-in-the-world-anymore experiences death – is mortal. Such a being is the being whose essence is mortality. To be open to death means to live and to feel, to express oneself in a song. Without gods who carry the light of holiness to men, man would expire like an animal without ever experiencing life and death; no song would sound then, and dwelling would not be poetical, nor could it be prosaic.[87] Since gods are deathless, they lack a feeling for life. They depend on 'another,' namely, on a poet, to express the feel of eternity[88]

Living, feeling, and expressing oneself are characteristics of personality. Personality is signified by 'self-ness.' In the beginning of his *Sein und Zeit*, Heidegger indicates *Dasein* as having the character of personality, the *Jemeinigkeit*, the 'very-my-ness.' [89] Such a personal character is emphasized by the mode of being of man, the being-toward-death. Even though a man may live his life inauthentically, he has to die his death himself. Death throws him upon himself.[90] The 'I' ultimately is rooted in death. Without mortality I would not know that I am I.

A god, being immortal, is not personal. He is "an eternal stability of the living world." [91] Anything which changes or endures is such within a world. A god does not rise or perish within a world; he comes forward and retires with a world itself. Due to an impression from the

---

[84] Heidegger, *Hymne*, p. 23.
[85] Hölderlin, *op. cit.*, p. 9.
[86] Otto, *Gestalt*, p. 206.
[87] Without Being or gods man would not be mortal: he would not be 'ec-sisting.' Without 'ec-sistence,' 'in-sistence' is not possible either.
[88] Otto, *Gestalt*, p. 200.
[89] Heidegger, *Sein und Zeit*, p. 42.
[90] Cf. pp. 54–55.
[91] Otto, *Götter*, p. 232.

Greek plastic arts, their gods often have been thought of as very personal. However, Walter Otto has shown them as worlds which by backing everything, assembling and holding everything upon itself, themselves remain beyond the immediacy. A buck, a child, wine, ivy, a snake, water, and everything in greater or lesser degree are what they are because the god Dionysus brings himself forward in those things. Nevertheless, he is not identical with any one of these things. Dionysus is the basic reality which makes all these things real, and yet they are foreign to him.

That which is foreign to a god, is familiar to man. Everything that shines and sounds, comes and goes, rises and falls – in all this "familiar to man and foreign to god, the unknown [god] brings himself forward in order to be guarded in it as unknown." [92]

To see things as assembled by gods or by *physis* is to see them as assembling in their own way their own assemblers – is to stand in the *logos*, to be open to truth. "The truth is there not for everybody but only for the strong." [93] The strong are those who can bring the world of a nation, its *Dasein*, to a stand. The world is brought to a stand by the works of the great men. In these works steads are given to earth and sky, to gods in their holiness and men in their mortal essence. Such great men are poets and thinkers.[94] A poet's openness to the *logos* of a god, as being struck by his holy ray, fills him with the experience of the fullness and bliss of the god and endangers thus his own poetical essence.

Being 'struck' he may be inclined to 'mis-measure' himself [on the god] by merely following this bliss and to lose himself in the possession of god. But this would be a misfortune because it would mean the loss of the poetical essence, since the uprightness of the poetical essence is not grounded in the reception of the god but in the being-embraced by holiness.[95]

The taking of the measure for dwelling from the gods is ultimately the living under the gods or living in the fear of the gods. Such a living under the gods, however, is not a bending of one's head and a personal surrender to a divinity with the resignation of oneself by trying merely to please and to serve the divinity. To live under the gods is to be open to the realm ruled by such a divinity, to be open to its *logos*. Athene is known as the companion of the men of great deeds. "Where a great heart knocks stormily, where a thought flashes liberatingly, there is

[92] Heidegger, *Vorträge*, p. 200.
[93] Heidegger, *Einführung*, p. 102.
[94] *Ibid.*, p. 101.
[95] Heidegger, *Hymne*, p. 24.

she present, called hither more by heroic readiness than by devoted entreaty." [96] To live under the standards of gods does not mean to resign from being man but rather to be more radically man. To be man is to be open and to respond to the higher order, to listen to the divine *logos*. Such listening is the awareness of the presence of a god in every event and every *thing*, however merely as of a carrier of the light of holiness, of the *logos* of *physis*.

This living under the *logos* of gods is the standing in an interplay with the gods and thus letting the world flash into light; it is the granting of a world for the dwelling of a nation. To be open to the familiar things by letting them be the assemblers of gods, the unfamiliars, is to poetize. "Poetizing is the taking measure for the dwelling of men." [97]

Poetry as a response to *logos* is the conversation which gives birth to a world. Language is primarily and essentially not a means of communication but a "dialogue with the divine." [98] In such a dialogue, a god comes into language and is present in his divinity; a god breaks into the world, into the life of a nation. A deity can truly be a deity only in the world of mortals.

A poet thus is not an aesthetician but a prophet, and a prophet, again, is not a resigned and surrendering servant of the gods, but the guardian of the truth of Being. By not submerging into the divinity, and thus remaining himself, the poet guards the *logos* of the world. To be a prophet is to know the truth, to guard it and to hand it to others. A poet is a mediator between gods and men. "Hesiod is appointed a poet by the Muses. Pindar calls himself in one of the Delphian Paeans the 'prophet' of the Muses. As a poet he was in an intimate connection with Apollo and entered his priesthood in Delphi." [99]

The knowledge of *mythos*, the divine *logos*, is knowledge of that which stands at the beginning of everything whatsoever. It is the knowledge of the gods themselves in their holy essence. "Poetry is primarily the naming of gods." [100] To name gods is to open a world and the history of a nation. A god for the Greeks is not a superior person but the power of Being, a world which holds things assembled in its light and which grants to men the standards of dwelling. "The prime source of all development lies in *mythos*," says Alfred Bäumler.[101]

[96] Otto, *Götter*, p. 234.
[97] Heidegger, *Vorträge*, p. 198.
[98] Otto, *Gestalt*, p. 45.
[99] *Ibid.*, p. 290.
[100] Heidegger, *Erläuterungen*, p. 47.
[101] Bachofen, *op. cit.*, p. CLXXXIX.

To know *mythos* is to know the principles and to be wise. A poet for the Greeks "was not merely the singer of things past –

> 'of old unhappy far-off things
> and battles long ago' –

but he also was the prophet of things to come, and the wise man in whom was enshrined the wisdom of the ages, the highest adviser in things present whether material or spiritual." [102] The poet as a priest is the wise man; he knows *mythos*. *Mythos* is the language of the higher realities to which the language and the works of men are subordinated. *Mythos* is the source of the standards for dwelling; *mythos* makes man man and never is itself a result of man, a product of his imagination. "*Mythos* does not mean ... a play of dreamy imagination but the highest solemnity, sacred knowledge and with that the standard for the direction and rightness of all thinking and doing." [103] The one who knows *mythos*, knows the standards of dwelling. "Gods implant reason in men." [104] Reason is the *logos* – the ground on which we dwell; it is a gift of gods. Language or dwelling ultimately is a response to the approach of gods – is cult.

Otto sees the essence of cult in man's response to the most sublime presence of a god. Such presence determines "the solemn stride, the grandeur of all gestures, all acts. Here is also the beginning of all hymnal poetry which wants to be nothing but the salutation of the god." [105] Poetry, as the highest mode of dwelling, is cult-like; but also all the other modes of dwelling such as the cultivation of plants, building of temples and other edifices, and even the making of things for everyday use are ultimately responses to the divine *logos* and thus have a religious or cult character. Not only the Greek temple but also a bridge, a ewer, and even a pair of peasant shoes have religious implications. Such implications can be revealed by a highly respectful attitude toward things – by sparing them in their assembling essences and thus letting them assemble the order of the higher realities. Things then bring man in front of the gods, and dwelling becomes cult.

The prosaism of modern times is rooted in the lack of a true dwelling, the lack of being exposed to the higher realities. The lack of a true dwelling is primarily the lack of true words and true sayings – lack of poetry as *Dichtung*. To be a true poet in modern times demands an

---

[102] Words of A. W. Mair in the introduction of Hesiod, *Poems*, pp. VI–VII.
[103] Otto, *Gestalt*, p. 218.
[104] Sophocles, *Antigone; Greek Dramas*, Vol. I, p. 441.
[105] Otto, *Gestalt*, p. 22.

enormous strength – strength to see the things and to say the words by not succumbing to the modern logical, scientific way of seeing them and saying them. To talk poetically (in the sense of *Dichtung*) and to dwell naturally (in the sense of sparing things) in the highly prosaic and artificial world of modern times requires enormous strength and solitude. A man who tried it – Hölderlin – collapsed into insanity.

Dwelling, and not atomic energy, is the real, even though hidden as yet, problem of modern times. Finding ways for a true dwelling is more important than harnessing atomic energy. The modern times are in need of men "who know that man cannot live but rather can perish by atomic energy, i.e. can lose his essence even when atomic energy is used for peaceful purposes and when such purposes are considered as the only determinants and aims of man." [106]

IV. FESTIVITY

A poet opens a world by responding to the divine *logos*. The birth of a world is *eo ipso* the birth of a language. The first words are the names of gods. The naming of gods cannot be accredited to the poet but rather to the gods themselves, who approach the poet with their demands. "The word which names gods is always an answer to such demands." [107] A poet's answer is not merely words but an existential entering into a destiny made possible by the demands of gods.[108] "Since gods bring our *Dasein* to speech, we can enter the realm of decision by meeting the demands of gods or by refusing ourselves to them." [109] Whether we follow their demands or fail to follow them, in either case we find ourselves in the realm created by their invocation; we are in a world which supports and backs our ontological constitution. Without the gods we would be floating around empty in the emptiness – we would not be. "Since the time of conversation with gods, we are," [110] says Hölderlin as quoted by Heidegger.

The conversation with the gods is carried on by a poet. "The poet, according to Hölderlin, is a mediator between god and man." [111] A

---

[106] Heidegger, *Hebel*, pp. 31–32.
[107] Heidegger, *Erläuterungen*, p. 42.
[108] Being sends man into his destiny. Gods are the messengers of Being. They bring the *logos* of Being to man. Man by responding to the mission of Being stands in his history as befalling.
[109] Heidegger, *Erläuterungen*, p. 42.
[110] *Ibid.*
[111] Otto, *Gestalt*, p. 233.

poet's openness to gods does not indicate an intensity of his inwardness, his highly articulated personal life and the richness of the nuances of his soul. A poet in the sense of Hölderlin-Heidegger and the Greeks is the one who is open to the real – to the ultimate realities which found the *Dasein* of man and of nations. "A poet principally brings man to the earth, brings him to dwelling." [112]

The world of a poet is a world of a community, and since a poet names gods and brings their *logos* to men, he is the priest of the community. Not inward intensity, but a sharply opened eye and being fully awake to the real, to the world of dwelling, marks a poet. "To those who are awake, there is one ordered universe common (*to all*), whereas in sleep each man turns away (*from this world*) to one of his own," says Heraclitus. [113] A poet is fully awake and sober. Therefore he not only sees what is superficial, but also he can penetrate the superficial down to the great backgrounds, the ultimate realities or gods. "A poet is most enlightened. He sees the events down to their depths, even though the participants themselves may only see the surface." [114]

"Blind is the heart in the multitude of men," says Pindar in his seventh Nemean ode, [115] indicating that only a few are chosen by the gods and open to them. The blindness of the multitude of men is not accidental: it is needed to set off the clear-sightedness of the poet. An intense sound is heard in its full intensity in a large hollow space, and the stars twinkle brightly because of the dark sky beyond them. The poet as the seer is the heart of the community; he is its priest. Without a community a priest could not be a priest, just as a heart could not be a heart without an organism.

A community is not totally blind. If it were, it could not enter the world of the poet. A community knows the words of the poet. Such knowledge is not a theoretical knowledge. It is nothing mental. A community knows the world and words of the poet by standing in his world and in his words. It knows them by dwelling in them – by dwelling under the godly standards given to it by the poet. Such dwelling is rightly called 'knowing' because the words of a poet or an artwork of an artist is truth as revelation. To know the truth ultimately is not merely to possess it in one's mind but to stand in it.

A poet, as the mediator between gods and his community, "is an

[112] Heidegger, *Vorträge*, p. 192.
[113] Freeman, *op. cit.*, Heraclitus fragment 89.
[114] Otto, *Götter*, p. 194.
[115] Pindar, *op. cit.*, pp. 114–115.

outcast: he is cast out into the *between* of gods and men." [116] From this *between* he can determine the stand of man. He determines this stand with his poetical words.

Using Hölderlin's expressions, Heidegger indicates that language is "the most dangerous of all the goods" and at the same time it is "the most innocent of all occupations." [117] The poet's proximity to the gods does not manifest his blessedness or security. "The poet is exposed to the lightnings of god," [118] says Heidegger in his Hölderlinian commentaries. To be exposed to the lightning-bolts of the gods is certainly less than security. It is to stand in extreme danger. "To us poets," says Hölderlin, "it is allotted to stand under the storms of god with head bared, to seize the father's thunderbolt itself with our own hand and to pass it on, the divine gift, wrapped in a song to the nation." [119]

In spite of such a danger, the poet's work is 'the most innocent of all the occupations.' It is like a child's play. It stands aside and does not interfere with the actualities of the day, with the points of interest of the crowds.

Gods can be highly destructive. The arrival of the Dionysiac religion in Greece brought with it much of such destructiveness in respect to the previous religious, social, and moral orders. Through the Homeric epics we know the destructive deeds of Aphrodite who breaks the most sacred bonds in human life and brings disaster. "Everything great is dangerous," says Otto.[120] Gods mean danger. Besides being dangerous for a hitherto fixed life of men, gods are dangerous in a deeper sense involving man as man.

A poet, when exposed to gods, is hit by the thunderbolt of gods and set aflame. Such instance is the greatness of man's being man. Man is not god, but in the supreme instances of his life he becomes divine. These instances of being hit by the divine flame are the greatest exaltations and at the same time the greatest horrors. "There is not only glorifying grief but also a horrible glory." [121] A poet is capable of withstanding this horrible glory only because it does not last long. The gods spare us, according to Hölderlin, by not being too close to us.[122]

---

[116] Heidegger, *Erläuterungen*, p. 48.
[117] *Ibid.*, p. 45.
[118] *Ibid.*
[119] Hölderlin, *op. cit.*, p. 9.
[120] Otto, *Götter*, p. 243.
[121] Otto, *Gestalt*, p. 17.
[122] *Ibid.*, p. 85.

The gods themselves, since they are strong, can endure their constant being in the flame of holiness. Nevertheless they are in this flame and are suffering. "O my deity!" says Hölderlin, "that you could suffer as much as you are blessed, I could not understand for a long time." [123] Everything which is great has something tragic in itself. "Is not perfect beauty itself surrounded by a breath of grief?" [124]

Where is the suffering of gods and hence of a poet ultimately grounded? In Being itself, in the holiness. "Suffering is the standing fast in the beginning," [125] Heidegger says. The beginning is Being itself, called in one of the Hölderlinian poems (*Wie wenn am Feiertage ...*) 'the eternal heart.' The eternal heart, the holiness itself, is the standing-fast-in-the-beginning. Such standing-fast-in-the-beginning is not a static rest but a constant shudder as constant coming. "Standing as coming is the 'un-pre-thinkable' 'beginningness' of the beginning." [126] Being does not begin, but *is* constant beginning. Therefore, holiness or Being is "older than the times" [127]; it is time itself as the constant 'beginningness' of the beginning. The eternal heart is the constant shudder. This shudder grounds gods as its carriers and also the poet as exposed to the shudder of gods. Therefore, the gods and the poet are suffering.

The suffering of the gods, as well as of the poet, is not opposed to blessing or joy. "The primary essence of joy is the coming to be at home in the proximity of the beginning [Being]," [128] whereas suffering is indicated as "the standing fast in the beginning [Being]." [129] Thus joy is not plain joy as distinct and opposed to sadness or grief. The joy of a poet "is the knowledge that in all joyfulness – whatever befalls him – the most joyful greets him by detaining itself." [130] The most joyful is the holiness itself. Being as constant shudder, constantly beginning 'beginningness,' is never a fully accomplished beginning, statically lying in front of us. The constant beginning is the constantly detained beginning. To face Being is *eo ipso* to face nothingness, and the highest joy is *eo ipso* the shuddering grief. Bliss and suffering ultimately are the same. "The tranquility of our pains," says Otto in his commen-

[123] *Ibid.*, p. 308.
[124] *Ibid.*
[125] Heidegger, *Hymne*, p. 30.
[126] *Ibid.*
[127] Hölderlin, *op. cit.*, p. 8.
[128] Heidegger, *Erläuterungen*, p. 23.
[129] Heidegger, *Hymne*, p. 30.
[130] Heidegger, *Erläuterungen*, p. 23.

taries on Hölderlin's *Hyperion*, "is more closely related to the joys of
gods than the rejoicing of our pleasures." [131]

To be exposed to the lightning of gods is to be exposed to the
shudder of Being.[132] Being in its shudder or dynamism makes use of
gods and men to sustain itself in its shudder or dynamism. "Being
founds itself in the turning-toward, which as such applies the human
essence so that it would waste away for Being." [133] Glaring in the light
of gods and transferring this light into the world of a nation, a poet is
on the peak of 'man-ness' as being wasted away for the shudder of
Being. This glaring is like the blossoming of a rose which assembles the
roseness of a rose and holds it in unity: it assembles and founds the
'man-ness' of man. "The divine essence possesses a perfection of which
man is only a reflection." [134]

A poet takes the glare of divinity into his own darkness and shows
it as that which exceeds him. By doing this, he fulfills his mission. To
be man is to be burned in the glare of the gods. To be man ultimately
is not to 'in-sist' in oneself but to 'ec-sist' or to exceed oneself as being
used up for higher realities. To bring the light of these realities down
into one's mortal world is to be great. "Justice does not tower above
humanness [*Allzumenschliches*]. Only greatness does." [135] Achilles in
the *Iliad*, by choosing greatness instead of a long peaceful life, shows
that the meaning of man is not 'in-sisting' self-satisfaction but being
exposed and wasted away for the gods. The heroes of the *Iliad* or the
victors sung in Pindar's odes are great not because they display the
splendor of the very human but the brilliancy of gods and of that
which is above man.

The brilliance of the lightning of gods is displayed when drawn into
the world of man. Such drawing-in is possible by man's 'ec-sistence,'
by his ability to stand into the more-than-he, by his being-held-in-
nothingness – by his mortality. Gods as immortals need men as
mortals – man as exceeding themselves in their great deeds – to be
revealed in their immortality and thus to bring the holiness of Being
into the world of men. Man dies so that gods may live.

Glaring in the light of gods or being wasted away for Being is the
very essence of man; it is at the same time his standing beyond himself and no longer being himself as a subject – it is his mortality. The

131 Otto, *Gestalt*, p. 307.
132 Cf. pp. 52–53.
133 Heidegger, *Seinsfrage*, p. 31.
134 Otto, *Götter*, p. 227.
135 *Ibid.*, p. 255.

essence of man is his mortality as the standing beyond himself. To be for man is to tend towards death (*Sein zum Tode*), which means his openness to realities exceeding him. "The soul is not infinite, but it is the openness to infinity," [136] Eugen Fink says.

Man as mortal, as being-wasted-away for gods and Being, emphasizes man's tragedy. Such a tragedy is not the failure but the greatness of man. The essence of man, namely, "the *Dasein* of the historical [sent-into-destiny [137]] man means: to be placed as a breach into which the superpower of Being breaks forward into appearance so that the breach is eradicated by Being." [138] Man is placed into the security of his everydayness only because, by throwing him out of such a security, Being could reveal its power and *eo ipso* reveal man's responsive essence.

Man as mortal – man as exceeding himself by being exposed to overpowering-him reality – is man in dread. In *Sein und Zeit*, Heidegger shows man's authentic way of being as dreadful. To withstand dread, to be exposed to the divine realities, is possible only for the strong. Crowds need security. On the other hand, for the 'self-ness' – for the authentic way of being – the everyday 'self-less' mode of being (the self of the common man) is needed. 'Self-ness' is 'self-lessness' modified by authenticity.[139]

The prosaic crowd, which is not strong enough to face the danger of divinity, is in need of a poet who hands to it language and with it the standards for dwelling in a tender form. This tender form is the song. "To us poets," says Hölderlin, "it is allotted to stand under the storms of god with head bared, to seize the father's thunderbolt itself with our own hand and to pass it on, this divine gift, wrapped in a song to the nation." [140] The danger of holiness is abated by a song. "The sublimity in which the highest joy dwells together with fearfulness transforms itself into the 'livingly-near,' into the play of beauty." [141]

A poet spares the prosaic multitude, the nation, from immediate exposure to the divinity and enables it to receive the standards of talking and dwelling in a safe way by the intermediacy of the song. "A poet grants a beautiful life to 'the sons of the earth' [thus Hölderlin

[136] Cf. footnote 60, p. 148.
[137] Cf. pp. 88–89.
[138] Heidegger, *Einführung*, p. 124.
[139] Cf. p. 12.
[140] Hölderlin, *op. cit.*, p. 8.
[141] Otto, *Gestalt*, p. 298.

calls the nation]. But he himself, in order that the others could enjoy
his songs, has to expose himself to the storms." [142]

The position of a poet, the way it is shown in Hölderlin's meditative
poetry, is truly such as it was in ancient Greece, namely, the position
of a priest or prophet. The Greek poet-priest was in a much more
favorable position than the poet-priest Hölderlin. The Greek poet-
priest, the interpreter of the signs and hints given by gods, was surrounded by his true community who received his words and guarded
them in its dwelling; while Hölderlin was totally alone in the midst
of a modern rationalistically 'clear-sighted' society. His society was
blind to the divinities and deaf to his songs. The poet-priest Hölderlin
was a priest without a community which would have served him as a
discharging body, releasing him from his surfeit of divine glare. "He
saw himself alone and felt that anyone in our times the more real and
gifted he is, the more lonely he has to be." [143]

A poet-priest is not truly a poet-priest without the resonance of a
community; and gods without having entered the world of a nation
are distant gods: either they are have-been gods or the gods of the
future. "Only when carried by a community, is humanity in a position to behold the divinity," says Otto and quotes Hölderlin saying:
"We are heartless, shadows 'til our Father Aether recognizes each and
belongs to all." [144]

Hölderlin thus becomes a priest of the future community and a
prophet of the coming gods. The gods of the past are the gods of the
future. They are the gods "who formerly were here and who come
back when the time is right." [145] In the midst of the modern godless
times, Hölderlin has a presentiment of the coming gods. They, "the
ones of the future, shine and speak joyfully from afar." [146]

The godless mode of dwelling by which the dwelling of the modern
man is marked, is a perverted mode of dwelling. Isolated in himself
and ignoring the higher realities, modern man measures everything
with exact, calculable measures. These measures are subordinate to
him and the answers brought to him by them are nothing but the
enrichment and extension of scientifically, rationalistically controlled
fields. Instead of man's being exposed to surpassing reality, all reality
is considered as disposed to man.

[142] Wahl, *Hölderlin*, p. 76.
[143] Otto, *Gestalt*, p. 281.
[144] *Ibid.*, pp. 281–282.
[145] Hölderlin, *op. cit.*, p. 61.
[146] *Ibid.*, p. 75.

Even such a godless mode of dwelling is rendered possible by the perversion of the measuring standards: instead of measuring himself with the divine measures of holy (whole) reality, he measures reality with his 'all-too-human' (*allzumenschliche*), subjective standards. Man cannot *ultimately* dwell or be man without gods. "That the super-humanness, though only for a slight instant is necessary for humanness to be human ... – such is the teaching which is given to us by all truly great men, but none of them expresses it so clearly as Hölderlin does." [147]

A true society is in need of gods. Since in everyday life there is a tendency to forget the divine measures received from the poet and to replace them with measures subordinate to man – the very human measures – there is a constant need for such a society to renew the contact with the divinities. Such renewal takes place by the repeated receptions of the interpretations of the signs of gods, of divine *logos*, from the poet-priest. The poet-priest, as the mediator between gods and men, brings gods and men together. Such a coming together of gods and men is festivity, and the center of festivity is cult.

"Festivity," says Jean Wahl referring to Hölderlin's *Wie wenn am Feiertage*, "is the origin of all civilization and all culture." [148] On the day of festivity, the nation receives its standards for dwelling with which it finds its ways in its world.

In prehistoric times, during such festivities, animal-sacrifices were offered to the gods. According to Otto, the primary meaning of such a cult was the mutual meals of gods and men.[149]

In the primeval time, as the Greek *mythos* says, in the Golden Age, before Toil and Misery had made the human way of existing very-human, gods and men lived together in trusted alliance and sat together at meals. Such a time comes back repeatedly in every sacrificial meal as festivity. Man enters for an instant the higher state and touches upon the divine.[150]

In a truly Hölderlinian-Heideggerian spirit, such Greek *mythos* expresses man's primary belonging or being related to gods and the essential need for him to break repeatedly through the realm of 'in-sistence' out towards the realm of the gods in order to remain essentially man – man as mortal.

Since gods are messengers of holiness, "the day of festivity is an event of salutation in which the holiness is greeted and appears itself

[147] Otto, *Gestalt*, p. 253.
[148] Wahl, *Hölderlin*, p. 91.
[149] Otto, *Gestalt*, p. 257.
[150] *Ibid.*, p. 258.

as greeting." [151] Therefore, the day of festivity is the day of holiness, the holy-day. Holi-day in such a sense is the day when holiness breaks into the life of a nation and grounds such a nation and holds it in unity. The day of festivity in ancient Greece, for instance, were the days of the national games, which ultimately were the days of cult. The national games of Greece even historically were the factors of unification, development, and bringing the Greek nation to greatness.

A nation does not create its religion, its gods, and its *mythos*; on the contrary, it itself is grounded and begun by the realities which exceed it, by *mythos* as the divine *logos* approaching with demands.

Mythos, understood in such a profound sense as the testimony of the appearance of the divine in the world and its everything-ordering, everything-valuating, everything-directing greatness, did not grow from a nation and its culture; but it itself, as the great forming and unifying power without which no true community can be born, created the nation itself.[152]

A nation as determined by *mythos* is not a nation without freedom. *Mythos* frees a nation to itself by granting to it its world. Man as subordinate to the divine laws is man freed for *logos*. To stand in the *logos* is not only to be freed for word and thought but also for dwelling. To be curbed by divine laws is to be freed for an essentially human way of dwelling. Man, whose basic feature is 'ec-sistence,' stands out beyond himself. For man to be curbed by human laws is to be 'insisting,' to exist inauthentically. To be curbed by the higher laws is to be fully man, to exist authentically. "Let no man live uncurbed by laws and curbed by tyranny."[153]

V. GODLY AND GODLESS MAN

Man's determination by the gods is rooted in his worldliness, in the sense of his being implied in the interplay of the foursome. Heidegger's world as the interplay of the foursome is that which Hölderlin thought of as nature in the sense of holiness, and the early Greek philosophers as *physis*, the constant coming forward. Neither world, nor nature, nor *physis* can ever be understood and approached by the conventional concept of nature which indicates nature as opposed either to arts, or to spirit, or to history, or to supernature, or to the unnatural.[154] To

---

[151] Wahl, *Hölderlin*, p. 50.
[152] Otto, *Gestalt*, p. 224.
[153] Aeschylus, *Eumenides; Greek Drama*, Vol. I, p. 295.
[154] Heidegger, *Hymne*, p. 10.

think of nature properly means to go down to the roots of the phenomenon of nature and to think of it as *physis*, as holiness, as world.

According to Heidegger, "φύσις, φύειν means growth." [155] Growth here cannot be considered or understood as merely an increase in size, development, or becoming. "Φύσις is the coming forward as breaking through, opening of oneself which, by breaking forward, at the same time goes back into its forward coming and thus conceals itself in it." [156] This breaking-forward concealment corresponds to what Hölderlin expressed by referring to nature as "older than the times."[157] Since *physis* is the constant beginning, no beginning can ever be thought of as previous to it. *Physis* is the 'beginningness' itself. To be constant 'beginningness' means never really to begin or to be disclosed. Really to begin means to be removed from the source, whereas *physis is* source. To be source means to be 'beginningness' which as much as it leaves the source, so much does it go back to the source. "Φύσις is the forwardly-breaking going-back-into-itself." [158] Therefore *physis* is as much concealment as it is revelation or as much untruth as it is truth. Openness or world, the ultimate truth, is truth-untruth, is a play of light and dark colors. "The clear and the light need the shadow and the dark; otherwise nothing would be there to be clarified." [159]

Since man is the to-be-in-the-world, he is constantly standing in the world, in the truth of Being. This does not mean that he constantly exists authentically, i.e. constantly stands in the approach of Being, the coming forward *physis*, but that he is the truth even when he ignores Being, i.e. when he stands in the withdrawing Being, in going-back-into-itself *physis*. In this later sense the philosophers of metaphysics (philosophers starting with Plato and ending with Nietzsche) stand in the truth of Being by ignoring Being. "The turning-away and withdrawal never are a nothing. They hold sway, even more oppressingly for man, so that they draw him along, suck his strivings and doings till finally they are so sucked into the itself-withdrawing suction [of Being] that man may begin to think he is encountering merely himself." [160]

Such a typically subjective man is the modern man who lives in the realm created by the withdrawing Being and pretends to be alone in

[155] *Ibid.*
[156] *Ibid.*
[157] *Ibid.*, p. 2. Compare nature as 'older than times' with the phenomenon of 'the eternal heart' (p. 291) and with the Dioscuri Brothers (pp. 198–199 and p. 206).
[158] *Ibid.*, p. 11.
[159] Heidegger, *Satz*, p. 24.
[160] Heidegger, *Seinsfrage*, p. 27.

his determinations. He considers, judges, and treats everything in relation to himself. Such a man is a worldless man. However, he can only be worldless because of the lack of world, because of the concealment or withdrawal of *physis*. Man is essentially related to Being either as approaching or withdrawing. "The essence of man rests in the fact that he constantly, one way or another, holds himself or dwells in the turning-toward or turning-away." [161] By the turning-toward or turning-away Being, we are placed or sent into our history as befalling.[162] To be in history as befalling means to dwell in the neighborhood of Being which appears by granting a realm for us to dwell in and which conceals itself by leaving us free in our world to live our history thus befallen on us. "The befalling of Being [*Seinsgeschichte*] is the mission [*Geschick*] of Being which sends itself to us by withholding its essence." [163]

The withdrawing Being, as well as the approaching, is real and ultimately determining us as far as our to-be or not-to-be man is concerned. By determining our essence, by placing us in its order, Being 'essentiates' itself. "Being is no thing which takes us somewhere and removes us, but the withdrawal is the mode in which Being 'essentiates,' i.e. befalls us as the sojourning [*Anwesen*]." [164] Being constantly comes forward in the mode of concealing itself or conceals itself by breaking forward in its concealment. "The way up and down is one and the same," says Heraclitus.[165]

This dual aspect of the world is reflected in each of the foursome. The earth on which we walk and dwell is mysteriously impenetrable and undisclosable in spite of its obviousness. By scraping a flower petal or by splitting a ponderous rock, we end up with nothing. The obvious things of nature in all their obviousness escape our penetrating insights; by an attempt to disclose the earthliness of a thing, we merely lose it instead of possessing it. The only thing which remains in our hands after the attempt to control the earth and things is our formula, or subjective system by which we seemingly had conquered them. The earth "shows itself only when it remains undisclosed and unexplained." [166] The disclosure of the earth is only possible by bringing it into openness as that which conceals itself.[167]

[161] *Ibid.*
[162] Cf. pp. 64–65 and p. 88–89.
[163] Heidegger, *Satz*, p. 108.
[164] *Ibid.*, p. 122.
[165] Fragment 60, Freeman, *op. cit.*
[166] Heidegger, *Holzwege*, p. 36.
[167] *Ibid.*

The sky, too, remains a mystery in the sense of undisclosability in spite of contemporary scientific attempts to conquer space. In scientific consideration, the sky is an empty space with the stars and planets interspersed in it. The empty space near the earth is not totally empty: it is filled mainly with air and known as the atmosphere. Does such an insight give the 'skyness' of the sky? Heidegger would say: no! The sky with winds, rains, storms, and thunder, with the rising and setting sun, moon and stars, with clouds and rainbows – as soon as it is explained by giving experimental, physical, astronomical, psychological, or even aesthetical proofs and principles – becomes mere space, mere nothing. In spite of this, we, as the dwellers of the earth, know that the sky is real. We dwell under the sky exposed to it in our everyday life. It is as real as the earth is real and, like the earth, escapes us when 'explained.'

Gods as the powers of Being, the ultimate realities, stand at the beginning of the world of a nation. Their names are the first words which grant language to the nation and *eo ipso* its outlooks on the things. Homer's works give testimony that every instant, every event in the life of a nation and all the things in its world are in one way or another related to gods. Neither these events nor the things of their world, nor men themselves would be understandable, known, and graspable without knowledge of gods. Gods are the measures by which man measures the dimensions for his dwelling [168] More specifically – not a god, but a god as revealed in his unknowability, is the measure. That by which man measures his world and gets to know it remains unknown.

The measure is the manner in which the remaining unknown god is revealed *as* unknown by the sky. The appearance of a god through the sky consists in an unveiling which lets that be seen which conceals itself. However, it lets it be seen not by an attempt to draw it out from its concealment but merely by guarding the concealed in its concealedness. Thus the unknown remaining god appears as unknown through the appearance of the sky. Such an appearance is the measure by which man measures himself.[169]

Those gods who are not gods of sky, for instance Dionysus, also appear in their own realm or world as ultimately unknown. The gods generally – in Hölderlin-Heidegger's and also Otto's understanding of the Greek gods – are worlds as modes of the world. They are *physis* as the coming forward into the light of *logos* of these gods, and since "φύσις is the forwardly-coming going-back-into-itself," [170] gods, by

[168] Heidegger, *Vorträge*, p. 197.
[169] *Ibid.*
[170] Heidegger, *Hymne*, p. 11.

being reflected by the things of their world, remain unknown themselves in the above sense.

The analysis of *Dasein* in *Sein und Zeit* shows man as a being who essentially is signified by being open to the world and everything which is. And yet *Dasein* as openness is mainly inauthentic and selfless. Man exists not as himself but as oneself (as common man's self); *Dasein*, the openness, thus remains concealed. The authentic mode of being in dread, death, and guilt is unthinkable without the clash with inauthentic everydayness.

Any attempt to entirely explain reality inevitably results in losing it from sight because the untruth as concealment just as necessarily belongs to it as truth or disclosure. An explanation which gives a proper understanding of reality to man is that which lets reality be the way it is in itself; such an explanation is the *logos* as the response to the *logos* of reality. Such an explanation lets reality appear in its revealed concealedness – in its truth. Such an explanation is 'earthly' thinking, a mode of dwelling.

By letting reality be the way it is, i.e. by responding to the primeval *logos* (*physis*), we hold ourselves in its neighborhood – we dwell. In the nearness to the ultimate realities (the four of the foursome), 'homeness' is grounded. "The proximity to the primeval source is 'homeness,' " [171] says Heidegger indicating by 'homeness' not only the being-home but also the guardianship of the ultimate realities in their mystery or concealedness.[172] To dwell in the neighborhood of Being is *eo ipso* to know it, know it as a mystery. "We know mystery not by unveiling and dismembering it but solely by guarding mystery as mystery." [173] A poet guards the mystery of Being by naming it and by naming gods, the messengers of Being; with such naming he namingly calls all the things into their essences. A thinker guards the mystery of Being by thinking it and thinking the world and the essences of everything as rooted and grounded in the world. A mortal in general guards the mystery of Being by dwelling, i.e. by sojourning in the neighborhood of Being in such a way that he spares – cultivates, builds, and makes – things.

In Bachofen's investigation of myths the basic theme is the struggle between the Chthonian and Olympian powers. Since he did not restrict himself to Greek myths alone, but was also dealing with the

[171] Heidegger, *Erläuterungen*, p. 22.
[172] '*Geheimnis*' in German is 'mystery' but Heidegger also regards the same word as 'homeness.'
[173] Heidegger, *Erläuterungen*, p. 22.

Roman and other ancient myths, the struggle between the Chthonian and Olympian powers for him was a mode of the struggle between the gynecocratic and the paternal modes of living. The most interesting aspect in all his investigated myths was the fact that in these myths gynecocracy was always depicted as locked in struggle with paternity. Gynecocracy presumably was the oldest cultural form, and had been in existence for milleniums before it became involved in the struggle with a totally different cultural form and finally was replaced by it. "That which persists quietly without being attacked, does not arouse any attention. Only when destruction approaches, when struggle commences, does the world become aware of that which has ruled it throughout the centuries, without being apprehended by it." [174] For gynecocracy or Chthonian religion to be revealed, to become true, the patriarchal or the Olympian religion is necessary. Neither Chthonian nor Olympian religion alone is a true religion. Truth as revelation is only possible when a coming forward from concealment into openness takes place. The Chthonian world would not have been a true world, if it had not been brought into light by the Olympian world's combat with it which thus placed it into the Greek *Dasein*; and also the Olympian world would not have been a true world without having fought the Chthonian world and thus having placed itself within the Greek *Dasein*. Neither the Chthonian nor the Olympian is the true religion but the struggle of both. This struggle creates an openness in which a nation can dwell.

The Olympian religion attained superiority in Homeric times only to be opposed again by the upcoming Dionysiac religion which was a new upheaval of the Chthonian religion. The struggle of both these man-exceeding religious powers is depicted in the great Greek dramas of Aeschylus, Sophocles, and Euripides. The Greek civilization was true in the sense that it was an openness, a world which gave a rich multitude of diverse great works in various cultural fields. These works reflected the Chthonian and Olympian struggle; they were true. Whenever this struggle was discontinued, the Greek world or *Dasein* fell into disintegration, and ceased to be true.

In this section it has already been shown that the truth-structuring elements of revealedness and concealedness can be seen in all four of the foursome.[175] On the other hand, it has been emphasized several times that any one of the foursome necessarily implies the other three.

[174] Bachofen, *op. cit.*, p. 215.
[175] Cf. pp. 298–299.

Whenever a struggle of the ultimate realities takes place, it always means a struggle or an interplay of earth, sky, gods, and mortals. The struggle between the Chthonian and the Olympian powers, or a struggle between one and another god, can be considered as the interplay of the foursome – the ultimate realities which constitute the worldness of world. Since man ultimately is the to-be-in-the-world, he stands in the midst of such struggling realities. To dwell means to be exposed to man-exceeding realities.

To be exposed to the 'worlding' realities is to be the spot (the *Da*) where the struggle of such realities takes place. For a man to ignore such realities and to act as though he were his own lord, is to fall into *hybris*, conceit. In *Aiax*, Sophocles describes a young hero leaving for war whom his father advised: " 'My son, seek victory by the spear but seek it always with the help of heaven.' " [176] His son manifested his conceit by answering his father: "Father, with heaven's help a mere man of nought might win victory; but I albeit without their aid, trust to achieve a victor's glory." The perilous result of this hero's *hybris* is shown, according to Otto,[177] in the course of the tragedy. "What characterizes a Greek is his constant vivid awareness of the proximity of the divine; such awareness leaves him neither in his planned activities nor in the passionate, sublime bliss of his heroic deeds. The proud and unruly warriors never forget that no cast or thrust can ever be successful without the gods." [178]

The proximity of gods in the life of a Greek can be seen as witnessed in their art and literature. However, man's most striking exposure to the struggling divine powers is given in the great Greek tragedies. The power of gods can be felt beyond the acts of men in these tragedies. All the strivings and acts of man end up, willingly or not, by letting powerful divine backgrounds break into the real living situation and thus by making them manifest.

There are certain things that are as though they were hanging in the air woven by gods or other higher powers (Moira, Erinyes). By performing certain acts, man serves as a trigger to release these things, to initiate events which are often of very disastrous consequences. Such consequences may fall, if not on the doer, on his children.

> Whilome in olden days the sin was wrought,
> And swift requital brought –

[176] *Greek Drama*, Vol. I, p. 339.
[177] Otto, *Götter*, p. 187.
[178] *Ibid.*

Yea on the children of the child come still
New heritage of ill!
For thrice Apollo spoke this word divine,
From Delphi's central shrine
To Laius – *Die, thou childless! thus alone*
Can the land's weal be won! [179]

In Aeschylus' *Seven against Thebes* (from which the above words
are taken) some of the consequences of Laius' disregard for Apollo's
oracle are shown. Hanging in the air was the destiny, woven by gods,
of Laius' child to kill his father, wed his mother and thus to bring
disaster upon his land. By disregarding Apollo's oracle, Laius served
as a trigger to introduce the above destiny which echoed down to the
third generation.

Curses, inherited from long ago,
Bring heavy freight of woe; [180]

Man's acts of disobedience to the destinies ordained by the gods
are the spots (the *Da*'s) where the higher, divine realities flash forward
into the *Dasein* or the world of a nation. Man is exposed to surpassing
realities, and his mission is to help them break forward in one way or
another into his world.

Man often becomes guilty even by obeying the demand of a deity.
When the Greek fleet, ready to sail to the Trojan land, was waiting in
vain for a favorable wind, Calchas, the seer of the signs of gods, indicated that the lack of winds was caused by the wrath of the goddess
Artemis. This wrath could only be gratified by the sacrifice of Agamemnon's daughter Iphigenia. Agamemnon obeyed the will of Artemis and

Thus on his neck he took
Fate's hard compelling yoke.[181]

After the Trojan war, Agamemnon came home and was killed by
his wife Clytemnestra and his cousin Aegisthus. When Agamemnon's
son Orestes, bid by the god Apollo, took revenge on his mother by
killing her, he incurred upon himself the wrath of the Erinyes, the
goddesses of the earth. Ultimately Apollo and the Olympians, and not
Orestes, were opposed to and guilty against the Erinyes: they were

---

[179] *Greek Drama*, Vol. I, pp. 110–111.
[180] *Ibid.*
[181] Aeschylus, *Agamemnon*; *Greek Drama*, Vol. I, p. 174.

struggling with the Chthonian powers. "The standpoint of the old law
is that of the Erinyes. According to it, Orestes is guilty; the blood of
a mother is irreconcilable. Apollo and Athene, on the contrary, are
leading another law to victory – the law of the higher paternity of the
heavenly light. This is not a struggle of dialectics but of history which
is decided by the gods themselves." [182] 'History' means reality for
Bachofen. The real, man-exceeding powers stand in a struggle, and
Orestes is merely the point where these powers cross. His guilt is in
his being exposed to these powers – his being a sacrifice.

   The tragedy of Oedipus is a good example of a guilt which was
incurred without the slightest intention to commit any act which
entails such a guilt. Not only that – when Apollo's oracle told Oedipus
that he was to kill his father and wed his mother, he left his home and
country in order to avoid such a horrible destiny. He did not know
that the parents he fled were his stepparents. His attempt to avoid
his destiny led him to its fulfillment. In Sophocles' *Oedipus at Colonus*,
Oedipus thus answers to the accusations of Creon:

> O shameless soul, where thinkest thou,
> falls this thy taunt – on my age, or on thine
> own? Bloodshed – incest – misery – all this
> thy lips have launched against me – all this
> that I have borne, woe is me! by no choice of
> mine: for such was the pleasure of the gods,
> wroth, haply, with the race from of old.
> Take me alone, and thou couldst find no sin
> against myself and against my kin.[183]

   In spite of Oedipus' unwillingly committed crime, he was guilty in
the Greek world. Why? Because to be means to be guilty. A man has
not made himself, and has not placed himself in the world. The higher
powers have done it and man owes himself to them. Also, all of man's
acts and intentions are nothing but responses to the higher *logos*, to
the orderings of Moira. For what he is and what he can perform, is
indebted to higher powers.

   Man is marked by his openness not merely to this or that definite
thing in his world but to the higher realities forming the worldness of
the world itself. By being exposed to the higher rules (being exposed
to the *logos* of *physis*) man serves these rules by helping them to be-

[182] Bachofen, *op. cit.*, pp. 48–49.
[183] *Greek Drama*, Vol. I, p. 647.

come disclosed within his world. He is exposed to the lightning of gods so that such lightning might become a flame after having struck him. Man's very self consists in his being the breach by which Being brings itself into openness, and it does not consist in his clinging to himself as to an 'I-thing.' Man is in the disposition of Being, and the greatness of man, according to Eugen Fink,[184] depends on the degree of man's availability to Being. The works of man primarily are the works of Being by which "Being founds its stead in man." [185] Therefore, man hardly has any claim to the glory of his deeds. "The nation must admire great thoughts more than the thinker, artworks more than the artist, holy words more than the prophet. The laurel of glory adorns the forehead of the heroes." [186]

Man in the Greek world is not treated in isolation. Therefore, he cannot be judged merely by his isolated acts. Just as in his being, so also in his acts, is he guilty as owing them to the powers which exceed him. Therefore, in the Greek world "there is no such thought that man should not carry the consequences of his perverted acts. On the contrary, they come upon him with an inexorableness which shocks us." [187]

For this same reason man in the Greek world is never a miserable creature. Even in his failure he retains his greatness. "Whatever has happened, even if it must destroy him, ultimately belongs to the higher destiny; the fury which is thus brought forward has, among gods, its wonderful and eternal face unto which he may gaze even from his ruin." [188]

Since a Greek did not dwell under the subjective, 'in-sisting' standards of good and evil, but was dwelling under the divine, 'ec-sisting' standards of greatness – his merits as well as his wrong-doings had to be seen and judged from the viewpoint of greatness. "Whether the act was good or evil, whether man had to be praised or blamed for it, in no wise may he believe that he alone accomplished it, that a sovereign will was dwelling in him on whose goodness or evilness alone depended what he did or omitted." [189] Human works and accomplishments primarily are works of higher powers and only secondarily do they belong to man.

[184] Fink, *op. cit.*, p. 13.
[185] Vietta, *op. cit.*, p. 147.
[186] Fink, *op. cit.*, p. 31.
[187] Otto, *Götter*, p. 173.
[188] *Ibid.*
[189] *Ibid.*

Pindar's odes are a series of confirmations that the deeds and victories of heroes primarily are those of gods. In his sixth Isthmian ode he says:

> Zeus, in
> your own Nemea first
> we held up before you the shining of
> their garlands.　　190

Without the gods man would lack all integrity. In isolation from his standing-out into the interplay of the higher realities, he would be a mere 'shadow of a dream.'

> We are things of a day. What are we? What
> are we not? The
> shadow of a dream
> is man, no more. But when the brightness
> come, and God
> gives it,
> there is shining of light on men, and
> their life is sweet.　　191

Only by being struck by the lightning of a god and thereby set aflame does man receive his integrity and freedom toward his own guilt. His standing under the laws (standards) of gods makes man truly man – frees him into his own essence, whereas man under human laws is neither free nor authentic in the ultimate sense. "Choose thou the hate of all men, not of gods," 192 says Pylades to Orestes when he is hesitant to fulfill his duties demanded by Apollo.

Man, explicitly open to gods, is the wise man, the seer. For the Greeks, the seer was a poet and a priest – the man of wisdom. In the time of disaster everyone's eyes were turned to the seer. He was more than anyone else in a position to tell what are the works of gods as regards men. A seer was not a man heavily learned in the human arts but a knower of the divine things. In his Hölderlinian commentaries, Heidegger remarks that a poet is a poet by being educated by nature, holiness itself. "Mighty nature, because divinely beautiful, because wonderfully omnipresent, embraces the poets. They are brought into this embrace. This bringing-in transfers the poets into the fundamental

---

190 Pindar, *op. cit.*, p. 142.
191 Pythian 8th. *Ibid.*, p. 80.
192 Aeschylus, *Choephori*; *Greek Drama*, Vol. I, p. 260.

features of their essence. Such bringing-in is bringing-up." [193] Bringing-up is used here in the sense of raising, educating. The German 'bringing-in' is '*Einziehung*,' and 'bringing-up' in the sense of educating is '*Erziehung*.' By being brought into the interplay of higher powers, the poet is brought up to be the seer of the divine standards by which the human dwelling is curbed.

The Greek concept of barbarians was not mainly that of non-Greeks but of men not bound by the divine laws, i.e. men who were not fundamentally men. Odysseus indicates or manifests such an understanding of man when, after having awakened on Phaeacian land, he says: " 'Woe is me! to what men's land am I come now? say, are they froward, and wild, and unjust, or are they hospitable, and of God-fearing mind?' " [194]

The god-fearing mind is the mind open to the signs of gods. A poet or a seer is thus the peak of 'manness' because of his explicit openness to gods. Oedipus, as being chosen by the gods to be the spot where divine powers manifest themselves in the world of men and as being himself willing to live a righteous, god-fearing life, was brought into the works of the gods and was gradually brought up to be a seer. When he discovered that he had committed the great crimes of patricide and incest, he inflicted blindness upon himself, abdicated his kingship, and wandered for many long years as a beggar. Having been exposed to the divine powers all his life and having suffered so much, at the end of his life he became a prophet. "Thou winnest my belief," Theseus said to him in Sophocles' *Oedipus at Colonus*, "for in much I find thee prophet whose voice is not false." [195] By being a spot where divine powers were brought aflame, he himself became divine. According to Delphi's oracle the land in which Oedipus will be buried will be a land blessed by the gods. "He has become a kind of vehicle through which the power behind the universe will act," says R. C. Jebb in his introduction to *Oedipus at Colonus*.[196]

Oedipus is an example of a man who dwells under the standards of the gods. Such a mode of dwelling was possible in the world of the Greeks in which gods were present. Is dwelling in the sense of sparing things as assemblers – which *eo ipso* is sparing the fundamental realities of the foursome and thus being exposed to them – is such dwelling possible in our 'sober' modern times? Our "world-age is signified by

---

[193] Heidegger, *Hymne*, p. 8.
[194] Homer, *Odyssey*, p. 90; *Complete Works*.
[195] *Greek Drama*, Vol. I, p. 662.
[196] *Ibid.*, p. 612.

the absence of God, by the 'lack of God,' " says Heidegger in his commentaries on Hölderlin.[197]

Hölderlin's experience of the lack of God, however, neither denies the continued subsistence of Christian relatedness to God in individual cases and in the Church, nor does it condemn it contemptibly. The lack of God means that no god is manifest and unequivocally assembles men and things upon himself and from such assembling ordains the world-history and the human sojourn in it.[198]

It has already been said that the lack of Being, and thus the lack of gods, is not a nothing, but rather a mode of 'essentiation' or presence of Being or gods. The lack of gods is real, and in one way or another it determines human dwelling. Just as to dwell prosaically is only possible because dwelling essentially is poetical,[199] so also the godless way of dwelling is rendered possible by man's essentially being a godly being. A stone or an animal neither is godly nor can it ever be godless.

The lack of gods is shown in Hölderlin by the sleep of nature. Sleeping nature, too, is a mode of nature's appearance. "But how could 'nature' appear as absent if it were not present in the heavenly gods, in the earth and its growths, in nations and their history? 'In the times of the Year' the ever-present nature seems to be sleeping. 'The Year' means here the year of 'seasons of the year' as well as 'the years of the nations,' the world-ages." [200]

Such absence of nature – nature in the mode of lacking – is not known to the man in the street; however, it is known to the poets. "To be a poet in the wanting times [modern times] means to respect by a song the traces of the gods who have fled. Therefore, a poet names the holiness in the time of world-night [time of lack of gods]. Therefore, the world-night, in Hölderlin's language, is the holy night."[201]

Even though the gods are absent in our days, a sensitive and poetical soul, open to higher realities, can have a presentiment of holiness which is the essence of nature for Hölderlin or Being for Heidegger. "Even though at times the holiness can be named and out of its serenity a word can be uttered, these 'holy' words are not naming 'names.' '... the holy names are lacking.' " [202] 'Name' here i n German is written not as 'Name' (name) but as 'Nahme' (taking).

[197] Heidegger, *Holzwege*, p. 248.
[198] *Ibid.*
[199] Heidegger, *Vorträge*, pp. 202–203.
[200] Heidegger, *Hymne*, p. 9.
[201] Heidegger, *Holzwege*, p. 251.
[202] Heidegger, *Erläuterungen*, p. 25.

This indicates that gods cannot as yet be taken or brought into poetical words because they (gods) are not approaching us; they are still lacking, still afar.

Since for Heidegger metaphysics is essentially the philosophy of the forgottenness or ignorance of Being, therefore in Hölderlin's poetical naming of holiness Heidegger sees the times approaching when Being will cease to be ignored and thus metaphysics will be replaced by a more fundamental philosophy (which in Heidegger's thought is actually taking place). However, as long as Being has not become a real problem of our times, we still belong to the world-night. "We come too late for gods and too early for Being." [203]

"Even though holiness appears, god remains afar." [204] Hölderlin cannot name gods as yet; he nevertheless feels them coming. "The 'lack' of god is the ground for the lack of the 'holy names.' " [205] Even though gods are lacking, the fact of their lack is experienced. For Hölderlin the lack of gods is not an empty phrase or mere negative concept but a great reality. The realness of the lack of gods is the world in which Hölderlin stands. In his lack, a god is greeting him already. "Therefore the 'lack of god' is no deficiency." [206] It is the most valuable thing our times have possessed. To guard this treasure and wait until gods appear is to stand on firm ground. This firm ground is that of which the modern man, in his isolation unto himself, in his being cut-off from the higher realities, is no longer aware. The lack of gods is the 'homeness' as mystery (*Geheimnis*) given to a poet to be guarded. "Therefore solely this prevails upon the poet's care: to remain near the lack of God without fear of seeming godlessness and to tarry in this prepared proximity to the lack, until from the proximity of the lacked God the primeval word, which names the High, will come." [207] Even though silent, the *logos* of the contemporary godless world-night is nevertheless the only realm from which man can say a weightier word. "The lack of gods helps." [208]

Considering Shakespeare's tragedy *Hamlet*, Karl Jaspers says: "The tragedy of Hamlet represents man's knowledge trembling at the edge of destruction. There is in it no warning, no moralizing, only man's knowledge of fundamental reality in his awareness of his ignorance

---

[203] Heidegger, *Erfahrung*, p. 7.
[204] Heidegger, *Erläuterungen*, p. 25.
[205] *Ibid.*
[206] *Ibid.*, p. 26.
[207] *Ibid.*
[208] *Ibid.*

and in his will to truth, whereby his life is shattered: 'The rest is silence.' " [209] For Karl Jaspers, the fundamental reality, called in his philosophy transcendence, is only experienced when man breaks apart on his way to truth. The failure of existence brings a glimpse of transcendence but only as that of which we have no knowledge except that it surpasses us. The words of the dying Hamlet: 'The rest is silence!' typically characterize man's knowledge of transcendence.

This side glance into Jaspers' understanding of Hamlet's last words, 'the rest is silence,' expresses something that is meant by the Hölderlinian-Heideggerian lack of gods. The lack of gods is the silence which, even though it cannot be heard, nevertheless can be experienced by a poetical attitude.

The ultimate standards for which Hamlet had been searching remain in the dark, in the silence. Why? Because they belong in the hands of gods, and gods are withdrawn. Hamlet remains in the darkness of silence because gods are lacking. Hamlet's tragedy results in an emphasis of the silence of the higher realities, whereas the tragedy of Oedipus brings the essence of Apollo to light. Oedipus dwells under the gods, and in his life and suffering he reflects their light. The greatness of Hamlet reflects the darkness and silence of the ultimate reality. In his hour of death, the tragic hero Oedipus, led by the god Hermes, merges with the glare of divinity, while Hamlet merges with the vacuum of silence. This vacuum, when properly thought, is a firm support or determining standard for bringing the groundless uprooted modern man to a stand. To be exposed to the lack of gods is a mode of being-exposed to gods, to the silent *logos* of world. However, to a 'sober,' positivistic attitude, whatever is silent or lacking cannot be real, or a standard. It is nothing.

The essence of man consists in being exposed to realities which surpass him. In modern times man himself becomes the ultimate reality and determines the quiddities of anything whatsoever by relating them to himself as the heart of the universe. Man becomes the standard of everything which-is, instead of measuring himself with the standards of higher realities. The modern man as the standard of everything is an 'in-sisting' man, whereas man as exposed to the higher realities is an 'ec-sisting' man. The 'in-sisting' man lacks his own self; he determines himself from the inauthentic common man's self which ignores the higher realities. From the universal standpoint of common man, denuded of any higher realities, from the impersonal scientific

[209] Karl Jaspers, *Tragedy Is not Enough* (London: Victor Gollancz Ltd., 1953), p. 71.

eye, modern human dwelling is determined. Complex rules, schemes, and regulations, well worked-out codes of laws and systems of all-embracing universal concepts take the place of the world for the worldless modern man and thus hold him in unity merely logically and rationalistically, since the *logos*-ties have fallen into forgottenness.

When the superior realities come to be concealed and fail to hold man's essence in integrity, they become replaced by passion or rational rule. Neither gives freedom to man. Freedom in the sense of freeing man for his authentic mode of being or dwelling is only possible by his being determined by gods (or by the lack of gods). "When a Russian, according to Gorki, observed regarding the problem of God's existence: 'If God does not exist, then I can do what I please,' a Greek manner of answering this would have been: 'Because gods exist, man is in the possession of freedom.' " [210] Man as taken from the superior realities is not a free man. On the contrary, the belonging to them frees him for his own essence, for *logos* – word, thought, dwelling.

To be free means to be exposed to the superior realities – earth, sky, gods, and mortals. Such an exposure is a response to the *logos* of the world in grown, meaningful words, authentic thoughts, in created artworks or made implements, in built edifices and cultivated growing things, as the assemblers of the superior realities; briefly – in dwelling under the divine standards. By dwelling under the divine standards we grant steads to superior realities in our words, thoughts, in the things we care for – we spare the realities which exceed us in our living days.

When every-*thing* [211] assembles divinities, every-*thing* then is the place where man meets gods; he stands then in the light of gods – is always in festivity, and all his acts are acts of cult. He then lives under the norms of greatness. *To dwell on the earth means to live in the neighborhood of gods.*

> ... *dichterisch wohnet*
> *Der Mensch auf dieser Erde.*

---

[210] Otto, *Gestalt*, p. 177.
[211] '*Thing*' here is an archaic German word expressing the essence of things; cf. p. 257.

HEIDEGGER AND CHRISTIANITY

The intention of this study was the consideration of gods and earth as the basic problems of Heidegger's late thought. Earth and gods are a mere abbreviation of the foursome, the interplay of earth and sky, of gods and mortals. The investigation of the earth, even though not explicitly, was also the investigation of the sky since the phenomenon of *physis* doubtlessly implies the phenomenon of the sky. Right along with the problems of earth and gods, man was thought of in his essential feature of mortality. *Sein und Zeit* has the essence of man, namely the 'ec-sistence' or mortality, as its fundamental theme. The acquaintance with *Sein und Zeit* and the works of the second phase of Heidegger's philosophy is presupposed to any attempt to consider the problem of foursome, the interplay of man as mortal with earth, sky, and gods. Therefore, in the first two chapters of this study, reviews of the first and the second phases of Heidegger's philosophy were attempted.

Since world is the typical problem of Heidegger's thought – ultimately it is his only thought, known in his first phase as the to-be-in-the-world, and in the second phase as the openness of Being, and in the third phase as the interplay of foursome – the phenomena of earth and gods have been approached in this study from the phenomenon of world which is the only proper way to deal with them. Hence, the third chapter had the problem of the world as its theme.

Whereas in Chapters IV and V earth and gods were disclosed as far as their essential character and their stand in the world are concerned, the attention of the study, in the last two chapters, turned to the phenomena of thing and dwelling. These were not treated as two additional problems, but as a necessary part of the investigation showing how earth and gods belong in the things and in the concrete dwelling of man.

In the course of the study, frequent references have been made to non-Heideggerian sources, especially to Walter F. Otto and Johann

Jakob Bachofen. However, throughout the whole study constant care has been taken to hold the truly Heideggerian line of thought. Therefore, these additional sources have not been given here as what they are in themselves, but have been used as servile material to bring out the essence of Heideggerian thought.

Gods and earth have been shown as the ultimate world-structuring realities which are necessarily related to man. The mission of man on the earth as the shepherd of Being – his word, thought, and dwelling – has been shown as a guarding of the truth of the ultimate realities. Dwelling as a measuring of oneself by the divine standards means the wasting away of oneself for gods instead of for various everyday enterprises subordinate to man. Such a wasting away for gods does not lift man into the ideal realm of the beyond-the-real, but sets man back on the earth for true sojourn on it with respectful, sparing attitude toward things by letting them thus become the mirrors of the divine *logos*. "Poetically dwells man on this earth." [1]

Man's wasting away for gods inevitably is bound to raise the question, what is man's attitude to Christianity and to God? And this is precisely the point on which Heidegger's philosophy, and consequently this study as well, does not present any information. Therefore, these few remarks in the Appendix do not belong directly to the study of earth and gods (the study has been completed), but are merely a few hints which try to justify the silence about God in Heidegger's philosophy.

On the path of his thought, Heidegger does not encounter God in the Christian sense. The fact of such non-encountering is not a judgement against the existence of God. Neither is it a testimony for Him in the explicit sense. "Philosophy is a finite assertion of man and not the voice of God." [2] The finite saying or thinking is for Heidegger a mode of dwelling, and dwelling ultimately is responding to man-exceeding *logos*. To respond to *logos* means to experience it. Thus man experiences the essences of earth, sky, gods, and mortals. Yet this does not say that the ultimate experience of the natural man – man dwelling on the earth – the experience of the four superior realities of foursome, represents all the possible realities. However, to say either positively or negatively that something beyond the experienceable *logos* is real or non-real, would be an attempt to say what in no wise is within the disposition of natural man – man dwelling on the earth. On the other

---

[1] Heidegger, *Vorträge*, p. 192.
[2] Words of Eugen Fink; cf. footnote 60, p. 1.8.

hand, this does not indicate that man cannot say anything which is beyond the experienceable *logos* at all. He can do so: he can say it as a man of faith. Is a man of faith still a man? We hardly can say yes, because a man of faith determines his dwelling from the super-natural, beyond-the-world realm. Is a standing beyond the world still a standing in the world, the to-be-in-the-world, the *Dasein*? This is a problem which cannot be attempted here. Thought cannot reach the beyond-the-world realm. Thought is the under-*standing* of worldly realities; it is not faith, the under-*standing* of beyond-the-world powers. Thought is no faith. "Faith has no room in thinking." [3]

As far as the gods are concerned, they are experienceable realities (the lack of them also is experienceable).

The other religions honored the ruling powers, in the existence of which one can either believe or not. The sense of the Olympian gods, however, is the being of world. Whether we believe in them as gods or not, their meaningfulness and concreteness validate themselves even for us. Zeus, Apollo, Athene, Artemis, Hermes, Dionysus, Aphrodite – with each of these names rises a great reality of the world before us. The powerful ground of all these figures lies not in their artistic perfection, which is often referred to when attempting to explain their eternal youth, but in the truth. Being speaks through it.[4]

How such realities are experienceable and in what way they are the truth of Being has been shown in this study. Here it is important to stress that the admittance of gods in the sense of experienceable realities is not a confession of polytheism, and it does not exclude or deny the validity of Christian monotheism. In fact, the name 'god' for a Greek deity and the Christian God (or even God in the other great religions) is used to a great extent equivocally. Gods are wordly, whereas God is above the world.

Instead of the man, unbounded and 'freed' towards his own bare subjectivism in which he faces the world as the field of objects disposed to the molding activities of his unrestrained intentions or uncontrolled will – instead of this modern man, Heidegger sets his man as the participant in the event of Being, the shepherd, guardsman, missionary of Being, the sufferer whose sufferings are caused by Being which gives birth to itself (comes into openness) in man. In the Heideggerian philosophy of Being, Arland Ussher sees strikingly religious aspects. "Heidegger, the ex-theological student, returns to a sort of piety: a

---

[3] Heidegger, *Holzwege*, p. 343.
[4] Otto, *Gestalt*, p. 107.

man does not anymore 'transcend himself,' [5] rather he 'waits' for the Transcendent," [6] for its call. Karl Löwith also notices that "the power of his philosophical thinking is associated with a religious motive." [7]

In spite of the strongly religious character of his thinking, Heidegger does not come to the problem of God. He is not an atheistic philosopher either. In no way does he give any support to atheism. According to Max Müller, Heidegger is against too great an influence of the philosophical categories on theology. Theology uses philosophical language "instead of talking its proper language which alone is decisive in the experience of the Christian reality." [8] Emphasizing the proper language of theology based on Christian experience, Heidegger hints that the language of philosophy is based on ontic or ontological experience.

Such a philosophical experience is not analyzed in a direction forward toward the Supreme Being, but backward toward the primordial Being. Heidegger thinks the truth of Being, but not that of *a* being and thus not of the Supreme Being. "This does not indicate a negation of God, nor a rejection of God, but simply indicates that on his passage from beings to that which is closer to the foundation of Being, the thinker did not encounter God." [9] Interestingly, Max Müller even reveals that Heidegger in his never-published third major chapter of *Sein und Zeit*, which was supposed to be named *"Zeit und Sein,"* was going to approach the problem of God directly. According to Max Müller, Heidegger was going to treat three kinds of differences:

(a) The *transcendental* difference or the ontological difference in the strict sense: the difference of a being from its aspect of 'to be' (*Seiendheit: etymol.* 'beingness').
(b) The *transcendentel* (*transzendenzhafte*) difference or the ontological difference in a wider sense: the difference of a being and its 'beingness' from the Being itself.
(c) The *transcendant* difference or the theological difference in the strict sense: the difference of a being, 'beingness,' and Being from God.[10]

---

[5] Here Ussher apparently refers to *Sein und Zeit* where *Dasein* is treated as the essence of man, and therefore it seems that man transcends himself, whereas verily *Dasein* is primarily not man but Being, and therefore transcendence is accomplished by Being. Man is only participating in this transcendence.
[6] Ussher, *op. cit.*, p. 91.
[7] Löwith, *op. cit.*, p. 73.
[8] Müller, *op. cit.*, pp. 60–61.
[9] *Ibid.*, p. 61.
[10] *Ibid.*, p. 63.

According to Max Müller, Heidegger dropped this approach because it was based on a rather speculative construction instead of being based on an ontic experience.

That which is beyond experience cannot become a theme of human saying. Since God is beyond experience, any affirmation or negation of His existence or any consideration of his essence is un-human in the sense that it is beyond the reach of human experience. 'Experience' here is used in the broad Heideggerian sense, where it not only means the experience of the intra-world beings, but also of worldly realities to which gods, in the Greek sense, also belong.

When Heidegger, as Müller indicates, has dropped the consideration of transcendant difference – the difference of Being and God – he has done so because God is beyond the reach of human experience and thus beyond human saying. To speak of God from Christian experience is to speak of Him on a level which no longer is a human level. A Christian or a believer lives his life under the supernatural norms, and his experiences, insofar as they are the experiences of a believer or a Christian, are not human experiences.

The *human* problems – the natural phenomena accessible for human experience – are natural problems where, again, 'natural' means '*physis*-like' or worldly. God is not a natural but a supernatural problem, whereas gods are *natural* problems. Therefore Heidegger in his inquiry into gods, as the world-structuring realities, and his silence toward the problem of God in no wise confesses polytheism which *eo ipso* would deny Christian monotheism, but is careful not to cross the realm of human experience. Such care is true respect for the super-natural, and thus superhuman, realm and is not its denial.

In modern times there is an increased tendency to live and to think under the subjective or intra-worldly norms and no longer under the Christian – the supernatural – norms or under the worldly – those of Being, i.e. natural in the sense of *physis*-like – norms. Such modern times can be rightly called godless times because they are times closed off from superior realities – be it supernatural (God) or worldly (gods). Such times are typically indicated by Nietzsche's famous phrase 'God is dead!' Heidegger calls them, in the words of Hölderlin, "the needy times" [11] (*die dürftige Zeit*, where '*dürftig*' means not only 'needy' but also 'dry' in the sense of meaningless or nihilistic). Our times are needy because they lack a god who would "assemble on himself man

---

[11] Heidegger, *Holzwege*, p. 248.

and the things and in this assemblage would arrange the history of the world and man's sojourn in it." [12]

These needy times are becoming more and more needy because man not only lacks a god but also because he no longer notices this lack [13]; they are becoming the "times of the world-night" [14] (compare to completed nihilism!) which stand between the dusk of gods and the dawn of Being. "We arrive too late for gods and too early for Being." [15] Hölderlin, too, calls gods "the gods who fled," [16] and senses the approach of the god of the future who "shines joyfully in his approach from afar." [17]

The approaching god of the future, however, should not be considered as the Christian God returning after the exile of the nihilistic 'God is dead' period, but the god as the messenger of Being. This god is a worldly god because he brings the norms of Being, the norms of world-morning, into modern man's worldless night.

To avoid misunderstanding it has to be said that Heidegger, by interpreting Nietzsche's 'God is dead' as the mark of the end of the era of God and by indicating that the god of the future is a fundamentally worldly reality, in no wise proclaims any slogan against the Christian God as supernatural reality. Heidegger *does not investigate* supernatural reality for the very reason that such reality is unattainable for man. Man as man is or can be aware of natural reality. The realm of super-nature is beyond the scope of man as man. A Christian or a believer is brought up or elevated to a mode of being under supernatural norms. Whether such a man is still man cannot be decided here. In any way, insofar as man is a believer and lives and thinks under supernatural norms, he is not a philosophical-natural man, man of 'ec-sistence,' but a superhuman man, man of 'super-ec-sistence.' Is 'super-ec-sistence' still 'ec-sistence'?

Nietzsche's 'God is dead' proclaims the cessation of God as a philosophical problem, but says nothing about the Christian religion itself. Nietzsche's 'God is dead' is not a religious but a metaphysical problem. By proclaiming the invalidity of supernaturalistic values and their replacement by the values of a strong man, the superman, Nietzsche brought subjectivism to its extremes. Platonic essences (ideas) in St.

---

[12] *Ibid.*
[13] *Ibid.*
[14] *Ibid.*
[15] Heidegger, *Erfahrung*, p. 7.
[16] Hölderlin, *op. cit.*, p. 73.
[17] *Ibid.*, p. 75.

Augustine's and in St. Thomas' philosophies became ideas of the divine mind – they became ideas of the divine subject. Descartes, by stressing the importance of human ideas, brought out the importance of the human subject as well. Kant's nature, as the totality of appearances, was founded in man. Thereby Kant has placed man in the centre of nature leaving for God only *Ding-an-sich*. Nevertheless, God for Kant still was He Who by determining the *Ding-an-sich* of nature and the *Ding-an-sich* of the soul, remained the absolute subject. Nietzsche with his 'God is dead' eliminates this absolute subject and thus gives man, even though a finite being, the post of the infinite being. Such an elimination is not made by Nietzsche; it takes place by the attempt of the sciences to explain reality godlessly, and Nietzsche merely makes such an attitude explicit. By doing this, Nietzsche does not erupt into the path of philosophy with his personal atheistic convictions, but he sequentially continues to build the road of Western thought started long before him in the time of the Greeks. The modern scientifically-disposed man, a finite being, treats reality as totally exposed to himself as though he were an infinite being. He treats reality in a lordly manner without permitting any superior reality – be it natural or supernatural – to interfere with his absolute will to power. The mark of 'God is dead' stands on the life and thinking of modern man.

'God is dead' is nothing but a phase in the inner-dynamics of the metaphysical subject-object realm. Its meaning starts and falls with subjectivism and has nothing to do with trans-metaphysical reality and less yet with God as super-natural reality. Theology, being basically a metaphysical framework for the interpretation of supernatural reality, has not 'explained' but merely subjectivized and thus distorted the understanding of this reality – it has made it an intra-worldly reality which, as such, presupposes a world, a fundamentally natural reality.

Such a distortion took place by letting the ontological difference – the difference between Being and beings – fall into forgottenness. Metaphysics, according to Heidegger, is onto-theo-logy. By such an expression Heidegger indicates that metaphysics is a dual logic – a logic which relates everything to that which stands at the beginning and is the most universal, and, on the other hand, a logic which relates everything to that which causes everything and thus is the highest and the last (ultimate end). Essence of logic for Heidegger is *logos* in the sense of that which grounds and founds.

Logic as onto-logic considers being as ground in which every-thing else is grounded. Logic as theo-logic is that which grounds everything by causing it. It is the highest, and being the highest it cannot presuppose anything.[18] Hence, it not only causes everything but also causes that which grounds everything, namely, Being. When Being is considered as caused, it no longer is Being but a being. That which is the highest, the last (God), is the cause of that which is the first and the most universal (being). Hence, God as the highest and the last is prior to that which is the first and the most universal; God is *causa sui:* he is his own cause.

Such metaphysical thinking is thinking which omits the difference between Being and beings and which thus treats Being as a being. Being is the ground which grounds everything, but itself it is groundless (abyss) – it is not grounded. Everything which is grounded, including also that which is grounded by itself, is a being. It is not abyss, not Being. Hence, a metaphysically thought God as *causa sui* is a being. *Causa sui* is made possible by omitting the ontological difference be-tween Being (as the abyss) and a being (as that which is grounded). Being for metaphysics is a being which is the fundamental ground of everything and the fundamental cause of everything by being *causa sui.*

The metaphysical consideration of God means His consideration on a subject-object level, i.e. on a level which presupposes world, namely nature as *physis.* Thus metaphysics fails to consider God properly – as supernatural, in the sense of super-*physis,* reality. Therefore an affirmation of God as an absolute subject or an absolute value (subjects as well as objects and also values are intra-worldly, intra-*physis* reali-ties) is, according to Heidegger, a blasphemy.[19]

The theological understanding of God is founded on the forgottenness of the difference between Being and beings. Beings in metaphysics are founded in being, but being for metaphysics is most being being in the sense of most grounded being. The most grounded is the one which is grounded by itself. It is *causa sui* which in metaphysics is considered to be a proper name for God.[20]

Thinking which ceases to think metaphysically and aims to consider its grounds, is thinking which thinks the presuppositions of meta-physics. An inquiry into the presuppositions of metaphysics is an

---

[18] Martin Heidegger, *Identität und Differenz* (Pfullingen: Günther Neske, 1957), p. 69.
[19] Heidegger, *Holzwege,* p. 240.
[20] Heidegger, *Identität,* p. 70.

inquiry into the forgottenness of Being (which *eo ipsoi* s the forgottenness of the difference between Being and beings). By such an inquiry, this fundamental thinking ceases to think of God as *causa sui*, but merely thinks Being as not a being, a 'no-thingness,' i.e. it thinks Being as that which even though it grounds everything, remains ungrounded, is an abyss. Such a thinking has to proclaim *causa sui* as insufficiently fundamental and thus as that by which God, the superworldly reality, is demoted to an intra-worldly reality. An inquiry into the grounds of metaphysics has to proclaim the understanding of God as *causa sui* a blasphemy. For one who does not transcend metaphysical thinking, such Heideggerian thought may appear a godless thought. Disrespecting of God as *causa sui* is no atheism. To God as *causa sui* "man neither can pray nor can he offer sacrifices. Man can before *causa sui* neither fall on his knees timidly, nor can he play music or dance. Accordingly the godless thinking which must abandon the God of philosophy, the God of *causa sui*, is perhaps closer to the divine God." [21]

Heidegger does not lead human thought into the beyond-the-world realm. Ultimately his philosophy remains an attempt to carry natural thought to the utmost sources and grounds of reality without leaning on any prejudices whatsoever. It leads human thought up to the utmost peaks of man's walkable ground, to the poetical, divine heights without ever letting him lose the earth from beneath his feet. The Heideggerian man is a man who has stretched himself fully from being crumbled in the narrow worldless subjectivism and who has become open faced to the things in their true grounds, a man who walks on the earth in his full stature and talks the profound poetical language – a man who dwells on the earth under the norms of heaven.

Even though we may not accept all the shades of Heideggerian thought, nevertheless, his profound investigation of the grounds which ultimately support things and man, our dwelling and our thought, makes us unsure of many things of which we formerly might have been frivolously sure; and thus it stimulates or awakens us to our own thought. It leads us from the all-too-clear and the familiar into the open realm of the unknown. "It is more sound for a thought to wander in the strange than to settle into the familiar." [22]

Even though richly articulated, the thought of Heidegger is ultimately the same thought – the thought of Being, Being, world, *physis*,

---

[21] *Ibid.*, pp. 70–71.
[22] Heidegger, *Vorträge*, p. 226.

logos, *Dasein*, the interplay of foursome – all are ultimately the same, even though not identical in the sense of an identity of objects. Since philosophy is the human attempt to think *fundamental* reality, it has to remain the thinking of the same. The difference between philosophy and science is rooted in the thinking of the same since sciences progressively think something new.

> [In the sciences] lies the stimulation and attractiveness of the constantly new and the success; [in philosophy] lies the overwhelming of simply-the-same which does not permit any success, because nothing can succeed here, since thinking, insofar as it thinks Being, thinks it back down into the ground, i.e. into the essence of the truth of Being.[23]

No attempt has been made throughout the whole study to criticize Heidegger or to try to indicate any shortcomings in his thought. The aim of this study was not to criticize Heidegger but to introduce him. This study is meant to be a path leading the reader into the territory of Heidegger's thought – a path which helps the reader to penetrate and explore this territory, to get acquainted with and to feel at home in it. This does not mean that Heidegger's thought is beyond any criticism. If it were such, it would not be human. However, "who thinks in a grand manner, also errs in a grand manner." [24]

---

[23] Heidegger, *Satz*, p. 155.
[24] Heidegger, *Erfahrung*, p. 17.

BIBLIOGRAPHY

BACHOFEN, J. J., *Der Mythus von Orient und Occident*. München: C. H. Beck'sche Verlagsbuchhandlung, MCMLVI.

BIEMEL, WALTER, *Le Concept de Monde chez Heidegger*. Louvain: M. Nauwelaerts & Paris: J. Vrin, 1950.

BOLLNOW, OTTO FRIEDRICH, *Existenzphilosophie*. Stuttgart: W. Kohlhammer Verlag, (n. d.).

BURNET, JOHN, *Early Greek Philosophy*. London: A & C Black, Ltd., 1930.

Complete Greek Drama. New York: Random House, 1938.

FINK, EUGEN, *Vom Wesen des Enthusiasmus*. Freiburg i. Br.: Verlag Dr. Hans V. Chamier, 1947.

FREEMAN, KATHLEEN (ed), *Ancilla to the Pre-Socratic Philosophers*. Oxford: Basil Blackwell, 1952.

GRAY, J. GLENN, "Heidegger's Course: From Human Existence to Nature," *The Journal of Philosophy*, LIV, 8: 197–207, April 11, 1957.

GUTHRIE, W. K. C., *The Greeks and Their Gods*. Boston: Beacon Press, 1955.

HAMSUN, KNUT, *Growth of the Soil*. New York: Alfred A. Knopf, 1953.

HEIDEGGER, MARTIN, *Aus der Erfahrung des Denkens*. Pfullingen: Günther Neske, 1954.

HEIDEGGER, MARTIN, *Der Feldweg*. Frankfurt a. M.: Vittorio Klostermann, 1956.

HEIDEGGER, MARTIN, *Der Satz vom Grund*. Pfullingen: Günther Neske, 1957.

HEIDEGGER, MARTIN, *Einführung in die Metaphysik*. Tübingen: Max Niemeyer Verlag, 1953.

HEIDEGGER, MARTIN, *Erläuterungen zu Hölderlins Dichtung*. Frankfurt a. M.: Vittorio Klostermann, 1944.

HEIDEGGER, MARTIN, *Hebel – der Hausfreund*. Pfullingen: Günther Neske, 1957.

HEIDEGGER, MARTIN, *Holzwege*. Frankfurt a. M.: Vittorio Klostermann, 1950.

HEIDEGGER, MARTIN, *Identität und Differenz*. Pfullingen: Günther Neske, 1957.

HEIDEGGER, MARTIN, *Kant und das Problem der Metaphysik*. Frankfurt a. M.: Vittorio Klostermann, 1951.

HEIDEGGER, MARTIN, *Platons Lehre von der Wahrheit*. Bern: Francke Verlag, 1954.

HEIDEGGER, MARTIN, *Sein und Zeit*. Halle a. d. S.: Max Niemeyer Verlag, 1941.

HEIDEGGER, MARTIN, *Über den Humanismus*. Frankfurt a. M.: Vittorio Klostermann, 1949.

HEIDEGGER, MARTIN, *Vorträge und Aufsätze*. Pfullingen: Günther Neske, 1954.

HEIDEGGER, MARTIN, *Vom Wesen des Grundes*. Frankfurt a. M.: Vittorio Klostermann, 1949.

HEIDEGGER, MARTIN, *Vom Wesen der Wahrheit*. Frankfurt a. M.: Vittorio Klostermann, 1943.

HEIDEGGER, MARTIN, *Was Heisst Denken?* Tübingen: Max Niemeyer Verlag, 1954.

HEIDEGGER, MARTIN, *Was ist das – die Philosophie?* Pfullingen: Günther Neske, 1956.
HEIDEGGER, MARTIN, *Was Ist Metaphysik?* Frankfurt a. M.: Vittorio Klostermann, 1949.
HEIDEGGER, MARTIN, *Zur Seinsfrage.* Frankfurt a. M.: Vittorio Klostermann, 1956.
HEIDEGGER, MARTIN, *Hölderlins Hymne.* Halle a. d. S.: Max Niemeyer Verlag, (n. d.).
HESIOD, *The Poems and Fragments.* Oxford: Clarendon Press, 1908.
HESIOD, *Sämtliche Werke.* Wiesbaden: Dieterich'sche Verlagsbuchhandlung, 1947.
HÖLDERLIN, (*Feldauswahl*). Stuttgart: Cotta Verlag, 1943.
HOMER, *The Complete Works of Homer.* New York: The Modern Library, 1950.
HUSSERL, EDMUND, *Ideas.* London: George Allen & Unwin Ltd and New York: The Macmillan Co., 1952.
JAEGER, WERNER, *The Theology of the Early Greek Philosophy.* Oxford: The Clarendon Press, 1948.
JASPERS, KARL, *Tragedy Is Not Enough.* London: Victor Gollancz Ltd, 1953.
LEHMANN, KARL, *Der Tod bei Heidegger und Jaspers.* Heidelberg: Evangelische Verlag J. Comtesse, 1938.
LÖWITH, KARL, *Heidegger Denker in Dürftiger Zeit.* Frankfurt a. M.: S. Fischer Verlag, 1953.
MÜLLER, MAX, *Crise de la Métaphysique.* Paris: Desclee de Brouwer, 1953.
NIETZSCHE, *The Philosophy of Nietzsche.* New York: The Modern Library, 1927.
OTTO, F. WALTER, *Der Europäische Geist und die Weisheit des Ostens.* Frankfurt a. M.: Vittorio Klostermann, 1931.
OTTO, F. WALTER, *Die Gestalt und das Sein.* Düsseldorf-Köln: Eugen Diederichs Verlag, 1955.
OTTO, F. WALTER, *Die Götter Griechenlands.* Frankfurt a. M.: Verlag G. Schulte-Bulmke, 1947.
OTTO, F. WALTER, *Dionysus.* Frankfurt a. M.: Vittorio Klostermann, 1933.
PINDAR. *Odes.* Chicago: University of Chicago Press, 1947.
REINHARDT, KURT F., *The Existentialist Revolt.* Milwaukee: The Bruce Publishing Company, 1952.
STRASSER, STEPHAN, "The Concept of Dread in Heidegger," *Modern Schoolman,* XXXV, November 1957.
USSHER, ARLAND, *Journey Through Dread.* New York: The Devin-Adair Company, 1955.
VIETTA, EGON, *Die Seinsfrage bei Martin Heidegger.* Stuttgart: Curt E. Schwab, 1950.
WAHL, JEAN, *A Short History of Existentialism.* New York: Philosophical Library, 1949.
WAHL, JEAN, *La Pensée de Heidegger et la Poésie de Hölderlin.* Paris (Sorbonne): Tournier & Constans, 1952.
WELCH, E. PARL, *The Philosophy of Edmund Husserl.* New York: Columbia University Press, 1940.

INDEX

abyss 121, 126, 127, 128, 130, 132, 170, 202, 209, 210, 211, 230, 232, 282, 319, 320.
Achilles 179, 186, 191, 198, 218, 292.
Aeschylus 137, 181, 191, 218, 301, 303.
air 122, 123, 128.
Anacreon 198.
Anaximander 123, 124, 140, 146.
Anaximenes 122, 123.
Antigone 127, 208.
apeiron 123, 126, 128, 140, 141, 146.
Aphrodite 183, 184, 185, 188, 189, 219, 290, 314.
Apollo 177, 180, 181, 184, 189, 191, 196, 198, 199, 204, 205, 213, 218, 219, 286, 303, 304, 306, 310, 314.
appearance, appearing 102, 105, 111, 136, 138, 139, 140, 144, 145, 148, 157, 181, 187, 188, 193, 199, 201, 219, 220, 221, 235, 243, 248, 274, 283, 293, 296, 308.
arche 147, 148.
Aristotle, Aristotelian 6, 18, 19, 109, 116, 123, 147.
art, artwork 11, 12, 13, 14, 128, 129, 131, 152, 160, 161, 162, 163, 164, 165, 166, 167, 171, 235, 238, 239, 242, 243, 244, 245, 246, 247, 258, 259, 280, 281, 305.
Artemis 180, 181, 182, 183, 184, 188, 189, 219, 303, 314,
Athene 129, 176, 177, 178, 179, 180, 184, 189, 191, 196, 197, 213, 218, 219, 285, 304, 314.
Augustine, Saint 318.
Bachofen, Johann Jakob 136, 137, 167, 174, 190, 193, 196, 197, 198, 199, 202, 207, 261, 300, 304, 313.

Bäumler, Alfred 167, 190, 192, 286.
beauty 139, 160, 172, 178, 181, 182,

183, 196, 219, 274, 276, 291, 293.
becoming 105, 123, 141.
Biemel, Walter 116, 122.
Bollnow, Otto Friedrich 56, 60.
building 14, 15, 16, 236, 261, 262, 264, 266, 275, 277, 281, 287, 300, 311.
Burnet, John 209, 272.

care 2, 23, 54, 63, 64, 114.
care-taking 33, 35, 36, 37, 40, 41, 54, 62, 249, 265, 266.
category, categorical 27, 28, 45, 96.
cause 148, 235, 258, 318, 319, 320.
chaos 126, 127, 170, 175, 201, 203, 205, 206, 209, 210, 211, 215, 232.
child 214, 215, 222, 285.
Christianity 1, 143, 308, 313, 314, 315, 316, 317.
circumspection, circumspectly 35, 36, 37, 39, 119.
commerce 34, 36, 37, 39, 40, 118, 119, 121, 256.
common man (*das Man*) 10, 41, 42, 50, 52, 53, 56, 57, 58, 62, 106, 111, 113, 154, 263, 293, 300, 310.
concern 41, 54, 62.
conscience 58, 59, 61, 69.
Creuzer 190.
cult 201, 223, 233, 265, 287, 295, 296, 311.
cultivating 236, 275, 277, 281, 287, 300, 311.

death (includes mortality) 8, 15, 23, 54, 55, 56, 57, 61, 62, 69, 88, 103, 109, 199, 202, 206, 214, 215, 224, 225, 227, 228, 229, 230, 231, 246, 249, 254, 255, 263, 282, 284, 292, 293, 295, 300, 312.
decline 50, 52, 53, 54, 57, 59, 65.
Descartes 10, 96, 97, 98, 116, 117, 155, 318.

Printed in Great Britain
by Amazon